Religion and Society in
Twentieth-Century Britain

Religion, Politics and Society in Britain

Series editor: Keith Robbins

The Conversion of Britain: Religion, Politics and Society in Britain, 600–800
Barbara Yorke

The Post-Reformation: Religion, Politics and Society in Britain, 1603–1714
John Spurr

Religion and Society in Twentieth-Century Britain
Callum G. Brown

Religion and Society in Twentieth-Century Britain

Callum G. Brown

PEARSON
Longman

Harlow, England • London • New York • Boston • San Francisco • Toronto
Sydney • Tokyo • Singapore • Hong Kong • Seoul • Taipei • New Delhi
Cape Town • Madrid • Mexico City • Amsterdam • Munich • Paris • Milan

Pearson Education Limited
Edinburgh Gate
Harlow CM20 2JE
United Kingdom
Tel: +44 (0)1279 623623
Fax: +44 (0)1279 431059
Website: www.pearsoned.co.uk

First edition published in Great Britain in 2006

© Pearson Education Limited 2006

The right of Callum Brown to be identified as author
of this work has been asserted by him in accordance
with the Copyright, Designs and Patents Act 1988.

ISBN-13: 978-0-582-47289-1
ISBN-10: 0-582-47289-X

British Library Cataloguing in Publication Data
A CIP catalogue record for this book can be obtained from the British Library

Library of Congress Cataloging-in-Publication Data
Brown, Callum G., 1953-
    Religion and society in twentieth-century Britain / Callum G. Brown.– 1st ed.
      p. cm. – (Religion, politics, and society in Britain)
    Includes bibliographical references and index.
    ISBN-13: *978-0-582-47289-1 (pb)
    ISBN-10: 0-582-47289-X (pb)
      1. Great Britain–Church history–20th century. 2. Christianity and politics–Great
Bitain–20th century. 3. Christian sociology–Great Britain–History–20th century. I.
Title. II. Series.

BR759.B77 2006
200.91'0904–dc22
                                                                              2005057986

10 9 8 7 6 5 4 3 2 1
10 09 08 07 06

Set by 3
Printed and bound in Malaysia

The Publisher's policy is to use paper manufactured from sustainable forests.

For Jean Hendry (1955–2005)
and
Revd John Nicol
– united in devotion, bravery and a new humanity

Contents

List of figures, tables and analysis panels

Acknowledgements

Many of the ideas for this book have arisen from discussions and colli-
sions with audiences (both religious and secular, academic and lay) since
I published *The Death of Christian Britain* in 2001. I have benefited
greatly from reactions in Amsterdam, Birmingham, Cambridge, Dublin,
Dunblane, Edinburgh, Florence, Glasgow, Groningen, Lancaster,
London, Lund, Manchester, Paris, Rome and Swindon. In developing this
book, I have especially enjoyed the friendship and intense intellectual
engagement of four people. The first is Peter van Rooden of the Research
Center Religion and Society at the University of Amsterdam, who with
wife Jo Spaans has extended hospitality to me and my wife in discussions
about the similarities and contrasts between Dutch and British secularisation. The second is Gerald Parsons of the Department of Religious Studies
at the Open University who supplied splendid reportage on my work for
the new OU course, Religion in History. The third is Michael Snape from
the University of Birmingham, who has been extremely supportive of my
work, and generous in letting me read and exploit a pre-publication
version of his *God and the British Soldier*, which has contributed
immensely to Chapters 3 and 4. And the fourth is Hugh McLeod, also of
the University of Birmingham, who over nearly twenty-five years has
sought to instil wisdom and a sense of caution in me, and who generously
accommodated me at his Birmingham home during two research trips for
this book. I treasure the friendship of these four. In addition, I have had
extraordinarily useful correspondence with overseas scholars, notably
Nancy Christie and Michael Gavreau at the Canadian universities
of Trent and McMaster respectively, and Erik Sidenvall at Lund
University.

Many people, alive and dead, have helped with this volume. I am
grateful to Heather McCallum for commissioning the book. My editor,
Keith Robbins, helped shape the original idea and was extremely knowledgeable in his reading of a first draft, preventing me from committing

many errors. The book as a whole was read through for me by Lynn Abrams, David Bebbington and Michael Snape. Each of these took on this enormously onerous task with great selflessness, and each provided critical feedback on errors and advice for improvement. In addition, parts of the book were read by Angela Bartie, Paul Burton, John Harrison and John Regan, each of whom gave me specialist advice from within their own fields of expertise. Others guided me to, or provided me with, sources, for which I am very grateful: Edson Burton, Clive Dunn of BBC Norwich, Myrtle Hill, Gerald Parsons, Michael Snape, John Sawkins and my late partner Jayne Stephenson (who more than twenty years ago conducted unpublished research into working-class women's autobiographies that I draw upon here). To each of these I owe a great debt.

I have benefited since 1997 in having a group of very able and energetic doctoral and masters Cultural History students whose work nourishes mine in this book. Angela Bartie's research on moral battles in the 1950s and 1960s (including at the Edinburgh Festival), Paul Burton's work on Quakerism in Scotland and Annmarie Hughes' work on interwar feminism, together with Ian Hutchison's research on experience and depictions of disability, Paul Maloney's on the music hall, Nathalie Rosset's on cultural theory and popular culture, Sarah Smith's on children and cinema censorship and Hilary Young's on latter-day masculinity, have each informed the way I see culture and religion in this book. Undergraduate students on my Popular Culture class at Strathclyde University and my Sixties' class at Dundee University have also influenced parts of this book, notably through their reading of autobiographies. But I alone am responsible for errors of fact and interpretation.

I wish to express thanks to Stephen Parker for giving me advance permission to quote from his book, *Faith on the Home Front: Aspects of Church Life and Popular Religion in Birmingham, 1939–1945* (Bern, Peter Lang AG, 2006). Dr John Sawkins, School of Management and Languages, Heriot-Watt University, very kindly supplied me with post-1970 Methodist data in Table 1.2. I am grateful to the following for permission to quote from the oral history testimony in their respective collections: the Local History Curator of Birmingham Museum and Art Gallery, and the Head of Special Collections, Information Services, University of Birmingham for testimony in the Birmingham Black Oral History Project collection; to Arthur McIvor, University of Strathclyde, for testimony in the Scottish Oral History Centre Archive; to the ESDS Qualidata Archive, University of Essex, for testiminy in the Thompson and Lummis, *Family Life and Work Experience* Collection; and to

Dr Elizabeth Roberts, for testimony in the Elizabeth Roberts Archive, Centre for North West Regional Studies, Lancaster University.

My wife Lynn provided comfort and context throughout. This is more than words can say.

Callum Brown
Argaty, by Doune
February 2006

Publisher's acknowledgements

The publishers are grateful to the following for permission to reproduce copyright material:

Mary Evans Picture Library for Chapter 2: Respectable family at church; Pembrokeshire Record Office, part of Pembrokeshire County Council for Chapter 2: Evan Roberts (reference HDX/1609/1); Mary Evans Picture Library for Chapter 3: Christmas fraternisation, 1914; Topfoto/Topham/ Picturepoint for Chapter 4: Revd Harold Davidson, and *Daily Mirror* cover story; Mary Evans Picture Library for Chapter 4: Ham Yard Hospice: Soup Kitchen; Topfoto for Chapter 5: Church-going in Sunday best; Topfoto/Topham/AP for Chapter 5: Revd Billy Graham at Wembley Stadium; Topfoto for Chapter 5: Roy Rogers and Trigger, Harringay, 1954; Topfoto/Topham/AP for Chapter 6: Mary Whitehouse; Getty Images/Hulton Archive for Chapter 6: Maharishi Mahesh Yogi and The Beatles; Topfoto for Chapter 6: Hare Krishna band, Margate, 1972; Topfoto/Empics for Chapter 7: Revd Dr Ian Paisley; Corbis/Lewis Alan/Sygma for Chapter 7: Portadown Loyal Orange Lodge; Corbis/ Derek Hudson/Sygma for Chapter 7: *Satanic Verses* demonstrations, Bradford, 1989; Getty Images/AFP for Chapter 7: Crowded British mosque; Corbis/Gideon Mendel for Chapter 7: Findhorn Community; Her Majesty's Stationery Office for data used in Table 1.1, and Figures 1.1 and 1.3. Crown copyright material is reproduced with the permission of the Controller of HMSO.

In some instances we may have been unable to trace the owners of copyright material, and we would appreciate any information that would enable us to do so.

Series editor's preface

No understanding of British history is possible without grappling with the relationship between religion, politics and society. How that should be done, however, is another matter. Historians of religion, who have frequently thought of themselves as ecclesiastical historians, have had one set of preoccupations. Political historians have had another. They have acknowledged, however, that both religion and politics can only be understood, in any given period, in a social context. This series makes the interplay between religion, politics and society its preoccupation. Even so, it does not assume that what is entailed by religion and politics remains the same throughout, to be considered as a constant in separate volumes merely because of the passage of time.

In its completed form the series will have probed the nature of these links from *c.*600 to the present day and offered a perspective, over such a long period, that has not before been attempted in a systematic fashion. There is, however, no straitjacket that requires individual authors to adhere to a common understanding of what such an undertaking involves. Even if there could be a general agreement about concepts, that is to say about what religion is or how politics can be identified, the social context of such categorisations is not static. The spheres notionally allocated to the one or to the other alter with circumstances. Sometimes it might appear that they cannot be separated. Sometimes it might appear that they sharply conflict. Each period under review will have its defining characteristics in this regard.

It is the Christian religion, in its manifold institutional manifestations, with which authors are overwhelmingly concerned since it is with conversion that the series begins. It ends, however, with a volume in which Christianity exists alongside other world religions but in a society frequently perceived to be secular. Yet, what de-Christianisation is taken to be depends upon what Christianisation has been taken to be. There is, therefore, a relationship between topics that are tackled in the first volume, and those considered in the last, which might at first sight seem unlikely. In between, of course are the 'Christian Centuries' which, despite their label, are no less full of 'boundary disputes', both before and after the Reformation. The perspective of the series, additionally, is broadly pan-insular. The Britain of 600 is plainly not the Britain of the early twenty-first century. However, the current political structures of Britain-Ireland have arguably owed as much to religion as to politics. Christendom has been inherently ambiguous.

It would be surprising if readers, not to mention authors, understood the totality of the picture that is presented in the same way. What is common, however, is a realisation that the narrative of religion, politics and society in Britain is not a simple tale that points in a single direction but rather one of enduring and by no means exhausted complexity.

Keith Robbins, November 2005

Preface

Religion is back on the agenda. If the major events of the twentieth-century world were mostly about ideology, those of the twenty-first century seem so far to be mostly about religion. This dumbfounds many existing historical narratives and social-science presumptions about the decay of the religious world and the rise of materialist, social-science understanding. It was taken for granted for half a century that religion was sliding from cultural and political life in a calm, secularising reverie. We comprehended our world as a glide from religion to reason, from talking redemptive states to talking welfare states. But now Britons have been jolted awake by the 2001 terrorist attacks of 9/11 on New York and Washington, and subsequent attacks in places as diverse as Thailand, the Philippines, Bali, Madrid and London. The consequence is that we start to see the last fifty years in a different light. It is now becoming clear that the world has been experiencing three major religious trends. The first is secularisation, almost entirely de-Christianisation, which seems exclusively limited to greater Europe (that many assert encompasses European Russia, Canada and Australasia), in which religion occupies an ever-decreasing part of people's lives and identities. The second is the worldwide rise of religious militancy, most obviously taking the form of struggles between liberals and fundamentalists within religious traditions, and which with hindsight can be seen as mushrooming from the early 1970s. The third trend is the re-fashioning of religion as a spiritual experience devoid of central authority, formal teaching, membership and the need for any external god (or even, for some, any god at all) – what is referred to as the 'new age' or 'the spiritual revolution'.

In the vortex between these three profound cultural forces, the peoples of the world have been affected to varying degrees and in different mixtures, and few have been immune. Important shifts of alignment now become apparent. In the 1940s and 1950s, Britain seemed to share the post-war evangelical resurgence of the United States, and then, in the

1960s and 1970s, its secularising culture. But as Britain's 'swinging sixties' became a permanent slide from faith, it dawned on us in the 1980s and 1990s that the USA's hippy culture and campus revolt had not led to permanent secularising after all, but had given way instead to a reassertion of religious values that, to this day, propel its national culture on a redemption narrative that informs patriotism in ways now utterly alien to most Britons. In the process, Britain's religious culture became exposed as at root not American but European in character. Whilst the consequences of this for world politics remain far from clear, understanding how Britain got to this position demands our attention.

By studying secularisation, religious militancy and the spiritual revolution as interacting cultural developments, this book provides the first comprehensive narrative of religion in British society and culture throughout the twentieth century. It traces Victorian puritanism and social respectability as the dominant cultural force in the nation until the 1950s, framing the responses of the people to world wars, economic depressions, poverty and social protest. It shows the direct link from Evan Roberts' religious revival in Wales in 1904–5 to Billy Graham's crusades in London and Glasgow in 1954–5. Yet it also highlights the rise of ecclesiastical scandal, the loss of confidence in the churches and the mellowing in inter-war British Christianity. By the late 1950s, young people in Britain were starting to kick back against the hypocrisies and regimentation of Christian culture. By the 1960s, women were revolting against their assigned role of religious and moral guardians of the nation, rejecting church authority in favour of sexual liberalism and feminism. A peaceful secular revolt started – the product of indifference to conservative moral authorities, a rejection of ecclesiastical obsession with sex and a reduced space for religion in people's lives.

One religious response to unfolding secular morality and culture was militant liberal Christianity in the form of the gay Christian movement, the movement for women's ordination and the united attack on racism and apartheid. Late twentieth-century Britain was the world's paradigm of a new secular norm – a new moral order uncontrolled by religion, but embracing new quasi-religions and spiritual chic. But the progress of this moral order was to be shaken from 1989 by the rise of Islamic, Christian and Jewish fundamentalism. This book unravels the patterns of rapid religious change, and tries to provide the first coherent analytical framework for understanding Britain's extraordinary religious development from 1900 to 2000.

CHAPTER 1

Introduction

The secularising century

In 1900, most people presumed that Britain was a Christian nation. It appeared to be leading the world economically, morally and religiously, exporting Christianity through the Empire and church missionaries to those regarded as the 'heathen peoples' of Africa and Asia. In 2000, most people presumed that Britain was secular and had lost its Christian faith, practice and culture. Newspapers carried headlines of 'The Church in crisis', 'Elderly lose faith in religion' and 'Empty pews', backed up by opinion polls and social-science investigations.[1] But, at each end of the twentieth century, there were some commentators who found evidence for opposing propositions. In 1904, the *Daily Telegraph* newspaper asked, 'Do we believe?' In response, only 54 per cent of readers professed Christian 'faith', whilst a census in the same year by the *Daily News* showed that only 19 per cent of Londoners went to church, striking some commentators as evidence of a religious crisis at the heart of Empire.[2] By contrast, at the start of the twenty-first century, the *Sunday Telegraph* carried an optimistic banner headline, 'Revealed: Britain still believes in God', over a story that 62 per cent of people believed in the Almighty. One hundred years apart, the *Telegraph* newspapers were posing counter-intuitive propositions that seemed, from most evidence, to have got it the wrong way round: they should have been optimistic for Christian religion in 1900 and pessimistic in 2000.

This confusion illustrates how studying the history of religion in twentieth-century Britain can be especially difficult. In this book, we shall see how the nature of religion itself was constantly being questioned, and seemed to be changing, during those one hundred years. For one thing, this gave rise to a changing approach to religious certainty. In 1900, there was almost universal certainty in British government and the major institutions (including the churches) that Christianity was the only legitimate religion, that it was obviously superior to every other religion, and that without it social morality and civil order would collapse. By 2000, that universal certainty was gone (including from most churches). In its place had emerged two different dimensions on religion. The first dimension was that religious views were by then highly diverse, ranging across many traditions (like Islam, Judaism and the new age), and that together they underpinned the multi-cultural and multi-racial society of modern Britain. The second dimension was that, for most people in Britain in 2000, religion had diminished as an element in everyday identity and culture; religion occupied a smaller part of people's thoughts and behaviour than it did in 1900. Taken together, these two dimensions meant that religion no longer united the nation in the way it once had. And yet religion still mattered by 2000 – even for those for whom religion was personally unimportant, and who professed no beliefs. The rise of religious conflict in the 1990s and early 2000s was one factor, touching the lives or consciousness of most Britons. The world remained scarred by religious conflict between countries (between India and Pakistan, Israel and the Palestinians, and between Serbia, Croatia and Bosnia), by religious conflict within countries (in places like Sudan and Thailand) and by religiously-motivated international terrorism (notably by Islamic fundamentalist groups in very many countries, including in Britain). Conflict seemed to reaffirm awareness of religion around 2000.

It is a bit of a puzzle for a very secular people like the British in the twenty-first century to find religion so far up their political agenda. The weight of evidence, that we shall explore in this book, suggests that Britain at the start of the twentieth century was a strongly religious society, and that at the end of the century it was a weakly religious society. In between, the strength, significance and character of British religion changed more profoundly than in any other period of recorded history. The twentieth century was the first century in which weekly churchgoers fell below 10 per cent of the British population. It was the first century in which Christianity lost its dominance of public culture, private morality and the media of the day. It was the first century in which non-Christian religions became numerous, challenging the dominance that Christianity had held for a millennium, making Britain 'a multi-faith society'. It was the first century during which Christian behaviour became unenforceable by the state, with the repeal, liberalisation or effective collapse of traditional Christian-based laws on homosexuality, abortion, divorce, suicide, breach of promise (of marriage), censorship, blasphemy, and Sunday trading and entertainment. It was the century when two out of the three established or state churches of mainland Britain – the Church in Wales and the Church of Scotland – broke their effective dependence upon state patronage and legality, leaving only the Church of England as a somewhat fragile established church. It was the century when dissenting Protestant churches like the Methodists effectively lost much of their strength and place in British religious life. It was the first century in which women gained something like equal recognition, changing from the position in 1900 when they held few ecclesiastical offices in any church, to the position of 2000 when they were fully ordained as pastors in most Christian denominations (though not bishops in the Church of England) and when some churches had become dependent on women recruits. And between 1900 and 2000, the broader change of religious authority in British civil life was staggering. The churches and religious ideas lost influence in government, education and social welfare. The twentieth century was the century of Britain's greatest religious change.

One way of exploring how the degree of change was understood is to look at the shifting interpretation of the word 'secularisation'. In 1900, to many churchmen, 'secularisation' meant the state's takeover of church property and functions (specifically land and duties pertaining to the state or established churches of England, Wales and Scotland); these were functions like giving out relief to the poor, maintaining schools, influencing social policy in government and controlling charities. In 1900, 'secularisation' meant the policy of 'disestablishment', and implied an attack on the religious establishment which, its supporters argued, upheld the moral and religious fabric of the United Kingdom.[3] But by 2000, with loss of church property and functions in the state mostly accomplished, the meaning of secularisation had changed. It had come to mean the loss of popular Christian behaviour and faith – the decline of going to church and praying, the decline of marrying in church and baptising children, and the decline of believing in Jesus Christ as the Risen Lord. Religious activities declined as understanding of Christian belief lessened, and religion occupied a smaller and smaller space in people's lives, thoughts and understanding of their own identity. So, the meaning of secularisation shifted from a transfer of control from the religious to the secular, to a decline in the people's Christian faith.

It is the change in popular faith with which this book is most concerned. We start with a few statistics. During 1900–2000, there were dramatic falls in levels of churchgoing, church membership, religious marriage, baptism and Sunday-school attendance. Religious marriage fell between 1900 and 1997 from 85 to 39 per cent of all marriages in England and Wales, and from 94 to 55 per cent of all Scottish marriages.[4] The baptism rate fell in Britain's largest church, the Church of England, from 61 per cent of all births in 1900 to 19.8 per cent in 2000. This decline was then compounded by the collapse of recruitment of baptised babies into full church membership, which fell in the Church of England from 42 per cent in 1903 to 20 per cent in 1997, and in the Church of Scotland from 75 per cent in 1900 to 17 per cent in 1998.[5] Churchgoing, long regarded as the central test of a Christian's commitment, fell also. At the beginning of the century, national church attendance on a given Sunday in England was probably around 25–30 per cent of the population (with London, one of the lowest churchgoing places, showing a rate of between 19 and 26 per cent). In 1998, the national figure was 7.5 per cent, and local figures were often much worse.[6] The bulk of this collapse had been accomplished by the 1980s. In Aberdeen in the north-east of Scotland, church attendance fell from 26 per cent in 1891 to 9 per cent in 1984.[7]

A small core of committed churchgoers remained in 2000, but those disappearing from worship were often the churches' outer constituency – those who, in previous generations, had gone once a month or for special Christian festivals like Easter and Christmas. This extended and casual churchgoing constituency had largely disappeared during the century. This was very important because the numbers were large, making up perhaps one-third of the adult population even as late as 1950. But by 2000, the churchgoers were becoming less numerous and more cut off from the rest of the population. What was happening was the creation of a large cultural chasm between those who went to church intensely (usually weekly) and those who did not go at all.

This was reflected in another set of changes. In most homes between 1900 and 2000, there was a disappearance of saying grace before meals and prayers before bedtime; there was a declining observance of the Sabbath by not working or playing sport or games; and there was even a falling-off in the Christian family ritual of Sunday lunch. If truth be told, at the start of the twenty-first century, religion became a minor or even irrelevant 'thing' for most Britons. For the average young person, religion became something endured during religious education classes at school, or something confronted at a religious wedding or a funeral. But only a tiny minority of 16–25-year-olds in 2000 were attenders at church or Sunday school during their youth, or had read any holy scripture, and few of this age group attended a place of worship. The evidence shows that even their parents were unlikely to have attended religious rites during the last quarter of the twentieth century. It was the parents and in some cases the grandparents of the British children of 2000 who presided over the decay of Christian practice. Even surrogate symbols of Christian respectability and conformity had gone – the 'Sunday best' dress, the special Sunday roast lunch and the family promenade in the park that were commonplace between 1900 and 1960. Even the major religious festivals had declined in religious significance. By 2000, Christmas was marked with negligible *religious* observance in most households (as distinguished from the secular giving of presents and eating of large meals), whilst Easter, Lent and Whit were little more than names for public holidays. This all reflected the diminishing place of Christian culture in Britain. This had fallen by 2000 to possibly its lowest level ever, shaping few of the cultural forms with which most people came into contact.

Just as people's lives were secularised during the century, so too were the media that reflected and reinforced popular culture. Religious issues and motifs penetrated deep into the popular media of 1900 – notably in novels, magazines for the family, for women and for children, and in cinema films which developed during the next fifty years. But by 2000, Christian rhetoric was not only displaced from those media, but it had never developed to any significant extent in any of the new media thrown up by technological change: radio, television and the internet. In both its cultural environment and in the 'religious' or 'moral' conduct of its citizens, Britain had become by the end of the century a society largely shorn of its Christian heritage. Cultural activities during the week and the year became largely empty of religion. Sunday, the 'Christian day' set aside in the Bible as a day of rest in respect for God, is now devoid of widespread religious ciphers, with a tiny minority attending church.

Such change marks something more fundamental, possibly elemental, in the human condition. Religion in some form or other – from early ritual, to sophisticated beliefs in redemption and afterlife – is something that has probably been a constant in human history, something that has provided the major archaeological and architectural traces of the British peoples from pre-history to the Christian era of the second millennium. Religious structures – like churches with spires – stood proud of the landscape, whilst religious ritual punctuated the lives of virtually all of our forebears every week and every year. Christian culture interspersed the seasons and the week, in the form of rituals, clothes and ways of marking time. Even for the indifferent, the dissenting and the disbelieving, Christian religion provided a constant point of cultural referral against which to relate themselves. To be a rebel almost invariably meant rebelling against religion – whether by not attending the church building, ignoring church authorities over moral behaviour, or declaring oneself a secularist or atheist. Religion was also 'political' and 'constitutional', having important bearings on patterns of loyalty and disobedience, fealty or treason, and – come more democratic times – of how people voted. In England and Wales in 1900, to be a Tory or Conservative more often than not implied allegiance to the Church of England, whilst being a Liberal implied allegiance to Protestant Nonconformity. By 2000, such religious– political divisions had largely gone from mainland Britain. Only in Northern Ireland did religious adherence continue to strongly influence voting, with the bulk of Protestants voting for Unionist parties (that supported the maintenance of the Union with the rest of Britain) and the bulk of Roman Catholics for republican parties (that supported Northern Ireland leaving Britain and joining the Irish Republic).

But religion intruded into not only the way people spent their time, how their government operated and how they voted, it governed also how they felt about each other and about themselves. Personal identities were heavily constructed on religious frameworks. Daily consumption of cultural forms was influential in how each person constructed his or her notion of 'self', and offered a measure for self-esteem. In 1900, family magazines instructed women and girls how to be 'homely', virtuous, feminine and pious, giving them prayers to say and homilies to recite, establishing their femininity and womanly qualities in religious terms. They showed women how the right clothes and hairstyles could combine pious respectability with appearing feminine and cool. Men and boys in 1900 were told how to curb their 'baser' masculine instincts in speech and play, and how to achieve religious and moral respectability through avoidance of alcoholic drink, gambling and swearing. Everyday British culture was a moral maze, defined by a Christian core, which constantly berated the irreligious and praised the 'true Christian'.

Each of these levels contributed to British Christian culture in the early part of the twentieth century. Each level permitted people to shape their identities, activities, politics and moral sense. This culture was gone by 2000. It went during the twentieth century, and it was not replaced by any new religion. The dissolution of the religious in British culture represents one of the greatest cultural changes of all time. In no other century was religious change so rapid or so extensive. Never had something as close to a secular society existed before the late twentieth century.

Yet, it is important to realise an apparent contradiction. Most British people claimed in 2000 to 'belong' to a religion or religious community. In the government census of 2001, 77 per cent of people reported belonging to a religion, whilst only 15.4 per cent stated that they had no religion. The numbers having no religion were higher in Scotland (where the figure was 27.5 per cent) and in Wales (where the figure was 19 per cent), but lowest by a long way in Northern Ireland (where the figure was under 3 per cent). As Table 1.1 shows, the most popular religion was Christianity (71.6 per cent), with Islam the second most popular (2.7 per cent).

TABLE 1.1 *The religious affiliation of UK people, 2001*

Religion	Percentage
Christian	71.6
Muslim	2.7
Hindu	1.0
Sikh	0.6
Jewish	0.5
Buddhist	0.3
Other religions	0.3
No religion	15.4
Not stated	7.3

Source: Census 2001, National Statistics, website www.statistics.gov.uk. Crown copyright material is reproduced with the permission of the Controller of HMSO.

There was significant ethnic variation in the sense of religious belonging. In England, only 0.5 per cent of people identifying themselves as Pakistani declared themselves as of 'no religion' (with 92 per cent being Muslim). This compared with 11.23 per cent of Black Caribbean people, 15.3 per cent amongst white people, and a very high figure of 52.6 per cent of Chinese people. In Scotland, religious belonging was markedly lower for all groups: those claiming 'no religion' totalled 2.8 per cent of Pakistanis, 23.1 per cent of black people, 32 per cent of Caribbean people, and 63 per cent of Chinese people. Furthermore, white people who ident-ified themselves as 'Scottish' were more religious than those who didn't; 27 per cent of white Scots reported no religious belonging compared to 30.8 per cent of non-Scottish white people.[8] So, these figures tell us that religious belonging was still important to British people at the end of the twentieth century, and more so for those living in Northern Ireland and in England than those living in Scotland and Wales.

But claiming to belong to a religion and practising one are two different matters. A second survey, conducted in 2000, revealed more things about religious belonging. When asked, 'What religion are you?', 80 per cent claimed some Christian identity, a further 10 per cent claimed to belong to other religious traditions and only 10 per cent indicated being agnostic (unsure about the existence of God) or atheist (not believing in the existence of God). But when the same sample of people was asked, 'In your opinion, do you actively practise your religion, i.e. you attend regular church services?', only 31 per cent said 'yes' (only 23 per cent for Church of England claimants) and 69 per cent said 'no'.[9] This was a big disparity – 90 per cent claiming a religious belonging, but only 31 per cent claiming to practise it. In terms of actually going to church, the figures were even lower. With only 7.5 per cent of English people attending church weekly in 1998, it is striking how insignificant was religious observance amongst the bulk of the population.

Shortly, we shall explore how religious practice declined so much to this state in 2000 – when it occurred, where it occurred and what other demographic consequences there were. But before doing that, we need to explore the concepts that we bring to such a study. How do historians and other scholars look upon religious change, and how does Britain fit into international perspectives?

Theories of religious change

Religious change is one of the most complex of historical processes to explore. This is because religion is a very difficult topic for study, with various approaches brought to examination of the twentieth century.

What is religion? Public opinion as well as academic opinion is divided in how to define it. In 1947, an opinion poll asked people what 'religion is'. Thirty-six per cent of those asked felt it required 'a belief in God' or Christian doctrine, and 32 per cent that it required moral behaviour and religious observance; 14 per cent thought the church was unnecessary to religion, whilst 22 per cent didn't know what it was.[10] Academics are equally puzzled. Religion is difficult to study because it is a 'thing' that has to be studied in terms of its *consequences* (church buildings, the formation of church groups and the people's religious behaviour) and not the 'thing' itself. Going beyond this is a problem because religion is founded upon 'faith' – on *belief* – that is, by its very definition, *without proof* of its validity. Even if religionists argue that proof for faith may be found (by arguing that Christ or the Prophet Mohammed actually lived and did certain things), the foundations of the religion rest on the faith, not the proof. Faith is blind, as the saying goes. And people holding that faith are interesting, but difficult for exploration. There is no isolatable 'essence' of religion, only the reflection or shadow for us to study. We study it through what people do, what they say they do and what they say they believe, as well as through what religious ideas and administrative modes influence cultural media (like magazines or television), social organisations and government policy. It is the social and cultural significance of religion that we study.

Within this, historians, sociologists and religious studies scholars study religion using many methods – biblical scholarship, social science, intellectual history, social history, cultural history and others – so there is no central methodology. Some have claimed that science can understand religion. In psychology, a discipline located between science and social science, scientific paradigms and laws were brought to the understanding of the human mind and the self. In 1902, the early psychologist of religion William James created what he supposed was an 'empirical Science of Religion'. However, the value of this was greatly tempered by his explicit religious and moral judgements; he wrote that 'in our Father's house are many mansions, and each of us must discover for himself the kind of religion and the amount of saintship which best comports with what he believes to be his powers and feels to be his truest mission and vocation'.[11] If that claim to a scientific 'truth' might be criticised as spurious, gene scientist Richard Dawkins a hundred years later, in 2003, was openly hostile to religion, regarding scientific method as the only laudable approach to religion. He abhorred religious belief as a 'virus of the mind' with quasi-genetic characteristics of inheritance from parent to child.[12]

Such approaches are widely seen by most scholars of religion as equally problematic and unhelpful, and do not have a central role amongst specialists in the history of religion. Nevertheless, the underlying notion that rules or laws govern the place of religion in societies was widely held throughout both the nineteenth and the twentieth centuries. Church historians and church sociologists – most of whom, broadly, have a claim to a religious faith and an interest in the defence of religious interests – emanate from a tradition of study in the nineteenth century that has been extremely influential. From around 1800, a central idea developed amongst these students of religion that popular Christianity was withering in industrial and urban society through two processes. The first was a secularisation of the mind, produced by Enlightenment knowledge, in which people's growing understanding of science, the better appreciation of laws of physics, geology, astronomy and so on, created a strong 'this-worldly' mentality that over-rode the 'other-worldly' mentality of a religion that looked to heaven and to hell. The second process they identified was that a religion naturally survived best amongst a people when it was an uncontested single world view. This created a long-held view of sociologists and many historians that the type of society in which that occurred was rural and agricultural, and that from around 1780, with industrialisation and the growth of towns, a multiplicity of views of the world grew that undermined the social and religious bonds of rural society. In towns, according to this argument, people became alienated from church elites and social elites together, and became subject to a sense of alienation from control over their lives, resulting in a feeling of anomie or isolation. This interpretation originated mostly amongst clergymen, many of them British, who moved to the rapidly rising cities of the 1800s and 1810s and who struggled to maintain their hold over new urban dwellers. The people were apparently deserting the churches. With support later from thinkers like Karl Marx and Emile Durkheim, this interpretation had developed by the mid-twentieth century into 'secularisation theory' – a theory that with modernisation of societies came the decline of religion.

The idea of there being a link between Enlightenment knowledge, the modernisation of society and secularisation became ever more popular amongst scholars in the twentieth century. It was held by those with a religious faith and those without it, each equally using social-science method to exploit an understanding of the past to predict the future decline of religion. In religious sociology in the 1940s and 1950s, there was a belief in the continuing religious condition of British society, but there was some panic that it was under threat. Its leading empiricist at the time, John Highet, concluded that with 56.2 per cent of adult Scots being church members in 1947, no serious secularisation was then taking place.[13] In 1957, an industrial chaplain for the Church of England, E. R. Wickham, wrote an influential historical study of Sheffield to explain the origins of the religiously-alienated steel workers of the town. He wrote: 'From the emergence of the industrial towns in the eighteenth century, the working class, the labouring poor, the common people, as a class, substantially, as adults, have been outside the churches. The industrial working class culture pattern has evolved lacking a tradition of practice of religion.'[14] The working classes were 'blamed' for church decline – seen as products of a socially-divided urban and industrial Christianity that twentieth-century Britain inherited from the nineteenth century.[15] This theme became standard in works of church and social history for the next thirty years, creating for Christian workers a sense of pessimism about the eventual demise of their faith, and for secularists (especially Marxists) a confident prophecy of a world without religion. By the 1960s, the notion of Britain sharing with the United States an essential 'secular' nature came to dominate. In 1966, sociologist Bryan Wilson was able to proclaim the 'secular society of the present, in which religious thinking, practices and institutions have but a small part'.[16] Under Wilson's influence, a new orthodoxy emerged that secularisation was a linear and unstoppable characteristic of British society in the twentieth century – a position that is still alive amongst certain sociologists.[17]

Historians of the late twentieth century increasingly departed from this view, adopting new conceptual approaches. First, historians have challenged the theory of secularisation because of its illogicality in assuming secularisation as an inevitable consequence of modernisation; such a theory of inevitability is, many scholars argue, not plausible in history writing. Second, historians brought forward much evidence to challenge secularisation theory on empirical grounds. They pointed to how religion did not decline in urban and industrial Britain in the nineteenth century, how it grew and continued to grow and thrive in urban and industrial United States during the twentieth century, and how new forms of evidence (like autobiography and oral history) showed that the working classes were not as alienated from Christian religion as previous scholars argued. Third, most historians and many sociologists came to appreciate by 2000 that the centre of religious change in Britain was not in the nineteenth century (with its rise of Enlightenment knowledge and science, or its industrialisation and city growth) but in the twentieth century. And it was in the 1950s and 1960s that historians and sociologists came to identify the great religious crisis that instigated most of Britain's de-Christianisation. They looked to statistics of religious adherence and practice that showed that British people were highly religious in their practice from the 1840s to the 1950s, and only from the 1960s showed *serious* signs of decline. Fourth, those who formerly argued that the United States was leading Europe and then the rest of the world in secularisation were by the early 2000s being challenged to concede that the rest of the world was not following. On the contrary, it was Europe that was secularising almost alone in the world. With the exception of some countries (like Japan, Canada, Australia and New Zealand), the rest of the world was by the 2000s sustaining a very high level of popular religiosity and was showing no signs of significant secularisation.

In the USA, Latin America, Africa, the Middle East and South-east Asia, all main religious traditions were still strong in 2000 and showing no serious signs of decline: this applied to Christianity, Islam, Judaism and Hinduism. To add to this contrast, religious fundamentalism had been rising dramatically since the early 1970s within each of these religious traditions; the fundamentalists were reacting primarily against the *perception* of secular weakening within their tradition, and secondly within the world at large. By 2000, fundamentalism was a powerful political and social force in most parts of the world, but not in Europe. This included the United States, previously taken as the model secularising society, with its high consumerism, recreational culture and advanced modernistic society. During 1975–2000, Christian fundamentalism in the United States helped to sustain high levels of religious adherence and practice, and strong religious influence in political and moral behaviour that contributed strongly to the election of two presidents seen as sympathetic to that position: Ronald Reagan (1981–9) and George W. Bush (2001–). The result was that, despite its science and technology, and despite its modernity and consumerist values, the USA allowed religious ideas like creationism and 'intelligent design' (based on a literal interpretation of Genesis, the first book of the Bible) into the teaching of many children, leading to an adult population amongst whom over a quarter believed that God had created the world in six days.

So, Britain with Europe had emerged by 2000 as the exceptional continent. It seemed to be secularising when virtually nowhere else was. If true, this circumstance undermined secularisation theory, and made the twentieth century the most fascinating for study.

In response to this critique of secularisation theory, there have emerged a variety of new ideas about religious change. The first to note is the notion that the decline of Christianity in late twentieth-century Britain was part of a general decline in association – in joining trades unions, political parties, educational associations, voluntary bodies, even going to the cinema and football matches. In this view, society was seen to be changing in ways that had reduced communal activity and the sense of collective community, whilst on the increase were the sense of ethnic community, family activity and the isolation of the individual. The logical consequence of this line of thinking is that religious decline is not isolated, does not require a separate theory (like secularisation theory) and is part of a reorganisation of society that leaves religious sentiment strong. But this theory is seriously dubious, despite its popularity amongst some church leaders. The theory is weakened by the lack of evidence for this sentiment, clear evidence that associating has not declined overall (only certain forms), and by the evidence of declining belief and practice in the late twentieth century at a time when alternative forms of communality (such as particibant and spectator sport) seemed unaffected.[18]

The second area of response concerns new ideas from religious studies and cultural history. John Wolffe has argued that religion contributed between 1800 and 1940 to a tightly-disciplined sense of national identities – to Englishness, Scottishness and Welshness, as well as to British identity – which by the inter-war period gave way to a more diffuse and shifting kaleidoscope of beliefs in the wake of the Great War's brutality, but which by the 1940s was in decay. In this way, part of the cultural strength of the Christian religion in British culture was undermined by the mid-twentieth century.[19] Moving to later decades, an even more startling idea is the theory of 'the spiritual revolution', sometimes linked by scholars to a notion of the rise of postmodernity. Emanating from religious studies, sociology and psychology of religion, this theory argues that until the 1960s British people were dominated by a traditional conception of religion as a church with fixed doctrines and training in one religious 'truth', leading the individual to a sense of obedience to an external God. But from the 1960s, this theory suggests, the sense of God has been internalised (exemplified in the phrase 'the God within'), causing doctrinal training and a sense of one religious 'truth' to be undermined. This has left the individual to compose her/his own spiritual experience in a 'holistic milieu' of alternative spiritualities, therapies and medicines which mix care for the body with care for spiritual need. Pick 'n' mix spiritualities blend different means of transcendence: for instance, Eastern mysticism with Christian ideas, paganism with notions of the female goddess Wicca, and the arrival of personal development aids like yoga and Transcendental Meditation. This 'spiritual revolution' of the 1960–2000 period, it is proposed, disarmed ecclesiastical authority and public deference to clergy. The consequence, it is argued, was that de-Christianisation was not so much about secularisation as the formation of an entirely new notion of the religious and spiritual.

A third and slightly different approach for some historians is to look at the religious self as being fundamentally challenged since the 1960s by changes in the social construction of gender. The place of women and femininity in the idealisation of Christianity has received considerable attention. Since the eighteenth century, many scholars point to how the ideal of 'the angel in the house' was a daily issue to which women were asked to aspire and 'sinful' men were asked to submit. This linkage of

Christian piety with femininity was certainly extremely important in British culture from 1800 to 1960, and we shall explore some of it in later chapters. But in the 1960s and 1970s, some historians (including the present author) argue that this linkage was suddenly severed, leading to women rejecting Christian ideals that they should be morally accountable for their entire families, and rejecting the patriarchal Christian churches. With no role models or religious ideals, this hypothesis goes, the generations of the late twentieth century became suddenly secular, in a cultural revolution in which women reconstructed their identities as sexually active and secular beings. This impacted on the churches in the sudden breakthrough of women to be ordained clergy, in the rise of a gay liberation movement within the churches and in the mounting threat of schism over these issues towards the end of the twentieth century. But by far the much greater impact was the overall haemorrhage of the female young from the Christian faith.

This book steers between these different approaches. On the one side, the environmental circumstances of people's lives – their housing, economic prosperity and general physical wellbeing, together with their experience of war – clearly frame the progress of religion in society and culture. On the other side, historians now have a new sensitivity to cultural *experience* in understanding religious change, looking at the power exerted by the *representations* (sometimes known as 'discourses') of ideal Christian piety and how individuals navigated through them. These discourses have been circulated in society (in magazines, cinema, television and in everyday verbal exchange), and scholars are now drawn to examine how these had to be negotiated, absorbed or challenged by individuals in constructing their own identities. The result is that many scholars now spend less time asking how much environmental factors and events influenced people's religion (what was the impact of slum housing, poverty, prosperity, world war or 'class struggle' upon religious behaviour?) and instead spend more time thinking in terms of culture (what models of behaviour were being circulated in daily life and the media, and how far were they absorbed and modified by the people in their lives?). For these reasons, this book will do both things. It will locate religious change in the context of environment and materiality – wars, economic depressions, poor housing and high unemployment, in periods of prosperity and high consumerism, and in changes to relations between the middle and working classes. But it will also locate religious change in the context of culture and discourse – in ideals of masculinity and femininity, representations of perfect religiosity, expressions of individuals' sense of their religious self and their negotiation of heavy cultural demands upon their behaviour. Both the 'social' and the 'cultural' approaches will be examined, period by period, in the chapters that follow.

Introducing the faiths

Before doing this, it will be useful to introduce the British churches, their geographical distribution and their statistical characteristics.

Religious organisations in twentieth-century Britain came in a variety of forms. Christianity, the dominant native religious tradition, adhered to the Christian Bible as being or containing the Word of God, and proclaimed Jesus Christ in Palestine in the Middle East of two thousand years ago as the Son of God who died but rose again. The Christian tradition incorporates a prophecy of a second coming of Christ that would herald the rule of God on earth for one thousand years before Armageddon and the End of Time. This belief in the second coming was held to very weakly by the majority of British Christians, but very strongly by a minority of Christians (sometimes known as millenarians, from *mille*, one thousand), many of whom belonged to small religious churches and sects. In the twentieth century, Christianity was mostly organised in 'churches', which are often defined by scholars as either 'denominations' (meaning large churches which were usually open to new members and whose worship was welcoming to visitors) or 'sects' (meaning small churches, often inward looking and sometimes reclusive). So, larger churches tended to have a more varied and open aspect to society, whilst sects could be tightly controlled and cut off from many social activities. Most Christian churches appointed clergy (known as priests, pastors, ministers, vicars or rectors) to act as professional teachers of the faith and administrators of the Holy Communion (sometimes called mass), which celebrates Christ's first coming, death and resurrection. As organisations, churches could have either central or devolved management which could decide, amongst other things, who to admit to the church. Central management implied that funds were held centrally to pay clergy and maintain church buildings, whilst in devolved management, congregations themselves were the legal owners of property and employers of their own ministers. The system of administration varied between Christian churches, and so there was no single model for all churches.

English Christian religion was dominated by the Church of England, also called the Anglican Church, which accounted in the twentieth century for around 60–70 per cent of the faith community. It was the state or established church whose 'supreme governor' was the monarch. It was episcopal in style of government, meaning it was governed by a hierarchical system of bishops in which, in theory, power came downwards to the ordinary members, known as communicants (those admitted to the holy service of communion of taking bread and wine). The Anglican Church was divided into two provinces, those of Canterbury and York, each presided over by an archbishop. The Canterbury province covered all of the south of England and, until 1918, Wales, and its archbishop was also the head of the whole Church of England. Each archbishopric was divided into thirty or more bishoprics or dioceses, ruled by a bishop and divided into parishes, each with a parish church and clergyman (known often as the vicar or sometimes as the minister). There were in the region of 9,000 parishes, making the Church of England the most numerous, well resourced and geographically widespread denomination in England. In addition, the Church had overseas bishoprics and churches, many of which claimed an independent status during the century, but which stayed what was called 'in full communion' with it.

The status of being the state church meant a number of things to the Church of England. First, the monarch had the theoretical choice of who to appoint to be archbishop and bishops, though by the twentieth century it was customary for the king or queen to accept a nomination from the prime minister. Second, 26 of the bishops (about a third of them) had seats in the House of Lords. Third, the state gave sums of money to the Church for various purposes, though this financial burden was being increasingly reduced as the century progressed. Fourth, the parishes were not only ecclesiastical territories, but they were also civil ones created over hundreds of years in parallel to English civil government, imposing some restraint upon change. Fifth, the Church of England enjoyed an unparalleled position in both the formal and informal high society of the British state, being regarded as the Church of the aristocratic elites, and its courts and clergy being intimately intertwined with the monarchy, the agencies of government and national charities. This meant that the Church was the central institution in national ritual and pomp, providing the religious service for the monarch's coronation, and parish churches were often the location for displaying the flags of British army regiments. Many 'livings' or vicars' posts were held by government and monarchical figures; in 1957, for instance, the Crown could appoint clergy to 158 positions, the Lord Chancellor a further 558 and the Home Secretary 41.[20] Finally, sixth, the Church of England was the backbone of popular ritual, especially for the rites of passage – baptism, marriage and funerals.

English people of a Christian background, even when inactive in religion and without church connection, would tend to express an allegiance to the Church of England (when enrolling for the Army, for instance) and seek the Church's services for a wedding or a funeral celebrant. So, the Church of England was the default church of most English people, even when they were not active churchgoers.

If the majority of English religious adherence was to the Church of England, that Church was itself extremely varied in its religious culture. In religious policy, the Church was strongly split into large unofficial camps, usually referred to as the High Church and the Low Church, with a 'Broad Church' that encapsulated the centre ground and could claim to represent unity. The High Church was characterised by heavy decoration, ritual and use of candles, with an aesthetic sensibility that seemed to cocoon Christian faith in richness, grandeur and pomp. In many regards, it was close in doctrine to the Roman Catholic Church, and many of its clergy adopted the titles 'Father' and 'priest'. The Low Church tradition was less adorned, its church interiors more bare, its services simpler and closer in tradition to Protestant dissenters, and its clergy more usually titling themselves 'Revd Mr' and 'minister'. Much of the High Church described itself as Anglo-Catholic, whilst the liberal Broad Church and evangelical Low Church tended to describe themselves as 'Protestant'. On top of this, certain causes and outlooks united otherwise hostile groups; for example, most High Church ritualists and Low Church evangelicals tended to agree in opposing the ordination of women and the full acceptance of homosexuality. In this great diversity and confusion of alignments, the Church of England experienced constant tensions over doctrine and policy matters that were to bring it constantly close to schism.

A further 30 per cent of the faith community in twentieth-century England was also Christian. Around 10 per cent of people were Roman Catholic, a worldwide faith claiming a divine authority from God through Jesus Christ and his apostle St Peter, thence through the succession of elected popes during most of two thousand years, who became based in Rome at the Vatican. The Roman Catholic Church in England was almost wiped out at the Reformation of the sixteenth century, when Britain became overwhelmingly Protestant. But the Catholic community of the twentieth century derived from two sources: some faith communities that survived the Reformation (in parts of Lancashire and amongst some aristocratic families and their estate workers, for instance), and, more significantly, immigrants and their children, mostly of Irish origin, who migrated in the nineteenth and early twentieth centuries to Britain in search of work and new lives. But late in the century, the Catholic community became more diverse, with immigration from the Commonwealth and Europe. In 1900, the Catholic community was geographically concentrated in cities (especially London, Liverpool and Manchester) and in the north-west of England (notably in Lancashire), but, over the hundred years, rising prosperity led to migration of younger Catholics to other regions, towns and villages in England.

Of the remaining English Christians, nearly all were Protestant, derived from seventeenth- and eighteenth-century breakaways from the Church of England. They are usually collectively known as Nonconformist or free churches. Chief amongst these was Methodism, inspired from the late 1730s by John Wesley, and which had developed very strong support in the nineteenth century amongst working classes in three types of community: the industrial villages of the cotton and mining industries in the north, the Midlands and Cornwall; the fishing villages around the coast; and the agricultural villages in the south and east of England. But in time, for both social and doctrinal reasons, Methodism split into as many as nine churches, some with a strong middle-class aura in the industrial cities of the north and Midlands. But these were coming together again in the early twentieth century – including a major reunion in 1932. Secession, division and then twentieth-century reunion also affected other dissenting churches, especially those with an evangelical tinge like the Baptists and the Congregationalists. The Congregationalists, a Protestant group that left management largely at congregational level (thus the name), had developed by 1900 as a mainly middle-class denomination, but the Baptists (who placed emphasis on adult rather than infant baptism, once a Christian knew his or her faith, usually by complete immersion in water) were much more variegated and enjoyed considerable support in working-class, rural and island communities. The nineteenth century left a heritage of small Protestant denominations – like the Unitarians (who denied the Christian doctrine of the trinity of Father, Son and Holy Ghost) and the presbyterians (mostly drawn from Scottish immigrants). Most other dissenting churches were very small, such as the Society of Friends (the Quakers), which was distinctive in Christianity for being very liberal and even socialist in politics, strongly pacifist in its attitude to war and having what may seem to outsiders as an intellectual approach to faith and worship.

The Christian churches in Wales were a little different in their strength. The Church of England was until 1918 the official state church here, but though it was the largest single church, it was weaker than Anglicanism in

England, being outnumbered by Protestant dissent. Largely for this reason, it was disestablished (lost it state status) during 1914–20, and re-emerged as a new denomination known as the Church in Wales with its own archbishop. After this, the Church experienced modest growth, and made spectacular efforts to become more in tune with Welsh-speaking and working-class Wales. The dissenters, often known affectionately in Wales by the name of 'chapel', were led in strength by the Calvinist Methodists (the presbyterians), the Baptists, the Congregationalists and the Methodists, and there were significant numbers of Catholics in the major towns like Cardiff. Welsh religion had, as we shall see in Chapter 2, a very strong evangelical character, which led in the early part of the century to a distinctive experience of religious revival – in which Christian rebirth was often a passionate and cathartic event taking place in highly charged mass meetings. The Welsh were by no means alone in this, but were certainly strongly imbued with it.

Scotland was different from England and Wales for the strength of its presbyterian heritage. Presbyterians were Christians organised in churches with no head other than Christ. The Church of Scotland, which until the 1920s held the status of the established state church, was organised in parishes, with congregations electing lay elders and choosing a minister by congregational vote from approved lists. Each congregation sent its minister and an elder to sit on a district presbytery court, which in turn sent representatives to a regional synod court, and each presbytery and synod sent representatives to the national general assembly that met once a year in May in the capital, Edinburgh. This was favoured as a 'democratic' system, and the model applied in many other Scottish Protestant churches that were secessions from the Church of Scotland. This included the biggest, the United Free Church, which came into being in 1900 and which reunited with the Church of Scotland in 1929. It also applied to the much smaller Free Church and the Free Presbyterian Church that were concentrated in the Gaelic-speaking west Highlands and Hebridean islands, and that were fiercely strict in their faith and in religious rules (such as keeping the Sabbath free from work and play). Scottish churches had a reputation for being more strict in their faith, often associated with the sixteenth-century French theologian John Calvin, but as the century progressed this reputation became less deserved as Scottish society liberalised its religious attitudes very quickly. At the same time, Scotland had a large Roman Catholic community, some derived from pre-Reformation communities in isolated pockets and islands (such as the Isle of Barra in the extreme west), but mostly derived from nineteenth-century Irish immigration to Glasgow and the industrial communities of the Lowlands. With many small denominations (like Baptist, Congregationalist and a few Methodists), Scotland had a religious complexion which in terms of connections and development was to prove during the century very close to that of the rest of mainland Britain.

Ireland has had a very different religious complexion throughout the twentieth century. In the whole island in 1901, 74 per cent of the population was Roman Catholic, 13 per cent identified with the Protestant Church of Ireland (which was in communion with the Church of England) and 10 per cent was presbyterian (most in the north). The remaining 3 per cent (or 125,000) of the population was made up mostly of Methodists (62,000), Congregationalists (10,000) and smaller Protestant denominations.[21] Ireland until 1921 was part of the United Kingdom. In that year, the island was partitioned along a major religious divide. Religious adherents in Northern Ireland, which stayed in the UK, were three-quarters Protestant, composed mainly of members of the Church of Ireland, presbyterians and Methodists, who tended to be strongly Unionist (that is, favouring being united with Britain under the Crown). The remainder of its population was Catholic.

The division between Protestant and Catholic was fierce in Ulster, governing the religious, cultural and political life of the province. The Protestants included most of the elites, controlling the institutions of the state and the major employers, leading to widespread discrimination against Catholics. This religious division created two communities in almost constant friction with each other. They erupted into significant violence – in the 1910s, in the 1920s and again in the early 1930s, and in the so-called Troubles of 1969–98. As the century wore on in Northern Ireland, the ratio of Protestants to Catholics changed – from 35 per cent Catholic in 1901, falling to 31 per cent in 1971, but then rising sharply to 44 per cent by 2001.[22] The rest of Ireland gained its independence from Britain in 1921 as the Irish Free State, later known as the Republic of Ireland. It was strongly Roman Catholic, with a religious and cultural tradition linked to Gaelic language, and had fought a long and violent series of conflicts in politics and a civil war. However, it did have a significant Protestant minority, located especially around Dublin, including the episcopal Church of Ireland (which was in full communion within the Church of England), and some Methodists and presbyterians. But after the civil war, many Protestants migrated to the north, and Ireland became a separate state, with a civil state that was officially Roman Catholic in constitution and a people who by the 1960s were 93 per cent Catholic.

British religious faith diversified between 1900 and 2000. Judaism, the Jewish faith in a single God upon which Christianity built, had existed in medieval Britain, but it had been very small, and it suffered from persecution as in many parts of Europe. Jews migrated to Britain in larger numbers between 1870 and 1914 as a result of anti-Jewish pogroms in Russia, Poland and some other east-European states. Jews divided into major groups – notably the Orthodox and the Reformed Synagogues. By 1900 there were perhaps 250,000 Jews in Britain, rising to 300,000 in 1914; about half were in London with major communities in Manchester, Leeds, Glasgow and other cities, and these had grown in number to 267,000 by 2001.[23]

Meanwhile, new religions came to Britain from overseas. Some came from the United States, like the Church of Jesus Christ of Latter Day Saints (the Mormons) and the Jehovah's Witnesses, both of which recruited significantly after 1950, and increasingly from the middle classes. Some existing traditions were transformed by immigration. One such was Christianity in London, Birmingham and other cities where Afro-Caribbean and African Christians settled from the later 1940s, coming from the West Indies, Nigeria and other former British colonies. They strengthened and developed Britain's Pentecostalism as a version of Christian worship and faith that was rising in many parts of the world, making theirs one of the few elements in British Christianity to be growing vigorously after the 1960s.

Outside of Christianity and Judaism, Britain witnessed during the twentieth century the arrival of major religious traditions as migration from former colonies in the developing world rose, mostly after 1945. Unlike the Christian churches, these traditions are not usually thought of as 'churches' in the sense of denominations, because they lacked central administrative control and leaders. Islam was founded on belief in one God or Allah, based on the life and teachings of the Prophet Mohammed. The foundations of Hinduism rested on a multiplicity of gods, reincarnation, a diversity of routes to salvation and responsibility for one's own deeds (karma). Sikhism originated from Hinduism with some elements of Islam, with ten gurus or teachers who preached one God. Each of these three religions had no official system of central church authority. Followers and teachers in each tradition established religious centres which attracted the faithful, and they followed the migrations of their peoples from India, Pakistan, East Africa and elsewhere. Muslims were the most numerous, making up around 1,591,000 people in the UK in 2001. They were heavily concentrated in urban centres, with around 1 million in London (or about

14 per cent of the capital's population), 150,000 in Birmingham (15 per cent), 83,000 in Bradford (17 per cent), 25,000 in Oldham (11 per cent) and 12,000 in Leicester (12 per cent). There were very much smaller communities of 60,000 in Scotland (1.2 per cent) and 50,000 in Wales (1.7 per cent).[24] Adding the number of Muslims to numbers of Sikhs (numbering 336,000), Hindus (559,000) and Buddhists (152,000), these groups by 2001 made up 4.6 per cent of the UK population.

The faith communities were unevenly distributed across Britain. The religious geography of Britain took three main forms during the century – denominational division across the nation, between city and countryside, and within cities.

England inherited from the nineteenth century a firm pattern of Christian segregation, but it was not a system of religious ghettoisation.[25] The Church of England was most heavily concentrated amongst the people of London, the southern and south-eastern counties, the south-west, East Anglia and Lincolnshire. Nonconformity as a whole (including the Methodists) was comparatively weak in the capital, though there was some local strength (for example, of Baptists in Cambridgeshire, Suffolk and London), but they were strongest in the south-west, in the Midlands and north and north-west, and in Wales almost uniformly. The Roman Catholic Church was strongest in the north-west, closest to the ports of Irish disembarkation, and in London.

In Scotland, the Roman Catholic Church was again strongest in Glasgow and surrounding counties closest to immigration points from Ireland, but overall the tendency in the twentieth century was for Catholics to diffuse across Britain following new employment opportunities. In Scotland, the Church of Scotland and the short-lived United Free Church of 1900–29 were almost equally strong in all the Lowland counties, leaving the smaller and more traditionalist presbyterian churches like the Free Church of Scotland to be heavily concentrated in the Gaelic speaking counties of the Highlands and Hebrides. New churches were often very unevenly distributed. Mormons, for example, had heavy concentrations by the 1960s in Leeds, Manchester and Newcastle, though they became more dispersed as their numbers rose thereafter. In Northern Ireland, religious segregation increased during the century as transport and the Troubles allowed (or forced) people to group into defensible communities. By 2001, the west, south and north of Northern Ireland had the highest concentrations of Catholics (around 57–65 per cent of the people), whilst strongly Protestant were the populations of eastern Northern Ireland (62 per cent) and outer Belfast (74 per cent). In Belfast itself, the community was fairly evenly divided (47 per cent Catholic, 49 per cent Protestant), but this masked increasingly sharp ghettoisation into both large urban districts (such as predominantly Catholic West Belfast) and small areas (such as the predominantly Protestant Shankill Road area).[26]

Immigrant groups were almost always strongest in urban rather than rural areas. The natural inclination of those migrating is to stop close to ports of disembarkation, or to make for London or another major city where relatives or friends from their home community had travelled before, in a chain migration. This means that Islam, Hinduism and the Sikh religion have been strongest in urban Britain, including London, and in the Midlands and northern cities like Birmingham, Coventry, Bradford and Leeds. Within the Christian tradition, the Church of England has tended to be much stronger in rural rather than urban areas, with the notable exception of London where most Nonconformist churches have been historically relatively weak. In the rest of the country, Methodism has been strongest in the northern counties, in East Anglia and in Cornwall and Devon in the south-west, characteristically in mining, fishing and some agricultural communities. But most of the strength of Baptist, Congregationalist and other free churches in England has been in rural areas and market towns, with some strength in provincial cities like Birmingham, Manchester and Bristol. This association of Nonconformity with industrial zones and Anglicanism with agricultural zones was one inherited from the nineteenth century, but it should not be seen as completely uniform nor extreme. Many rural communities had considerable religious diversity within Christianity, but the greatest diversity almost always occurred in cities.

Religious segregation within cities was often very marked, though with the exception of Northern Ireland not on the same scale as that found in places like North American cities. To some extent, segregation was the product of churches having different social characteristics. In many cities, the Church of England tended to include disproportionately large numbers of the middle and upper middle classes, leading to heavier concentration in affluent districts. In London in 1904, the Church of England was most heavily concentrated in the West End of the city, whilst most Nonconformists (much less numerous than in northern towns) tended to be found in industrial suburbs and the East End. Jewish immigration produced heavy concentration in certain districts – notably in London's East End, centred on Bethnal Green. By the end of the century, segregation was still to be found, but had often changed. Jewish ghettoisation in the East End had almost disappeared by 2001, to be replaced by a heavy concentration in the north-west of London (Golders

Green, Finchley, Barnet, Camden, Brent and Harrow) and in the north-east (in Redbridge).

New immigrant groups introduced 'chains of migration' from overseas to certain city districts that created new heavy religious concentrations. Bethnal Green and the East End of London attracted large numbers of immigrants; from Jews early in the century to black Christians and Asian Muslims from the 1950s (especially as a result of the London Transport recruitment office being located in Bethnal Green from the late 1940s). Again, excluding Northern Ireland, the tendency to distinctive cultural and religious districts was always strongest in London. The 2001 census recorded heavy concentrations of Hindus in north-west and north-east London, Sikhs in west London (Southall, Hillingdon, Ealing and Hounslow) and in the east (around Woolwich), and other non-Christian religions in Brent, Harrow and Edgware. Indeed, the north-west of London became statistically the most religiously diverse place in Britain. One product of this concentration of new-migrant religions in the central, north-west and west parts of the metropolis was to make Christian London most heavily concentrated in the outer suburbs on the south and east, marking out a high degree of correlation between ethnic, religious and class segregation in the capital.[27]

Finally, we must note that one of the important trends of the second half of the century was the growth of less formal religions and quasi-religions. Many of these small groups or sects challenged the definition of what a religion or a church is – a topic to which we return in Chapter 7. They often mixed religious belief with physical exercises (such as yoga) and activities which aided bodily and mental health, or what is known as 'personal development'. Something like Transcendental Meditation (TM for short), which grew in popularity from the 1960s, was not a religion with a coherent set of doctrines, but one of many systems of thought, self-awareness and bodily conditioning that mixed with others to allow practitioners to cross the boundary between religious, cultural and health activities. So, faith itself became a more flexible concept, perhaps one without a clear definition. The very idea of 'religion' was re-emerging by 2000 as de-centred from an agreed core character, allowing a high degree of informal mixing of practices, flexible adoption of rites and perhaps a consumerist approach to faith. These challenged older notions that a would-be church adherent had to undergo religious education, training, testing and admission. Faith had become fluid for many, and those churches unwilling to adapt to public pressure for this seemed liable to experience resistance and rejection – especially from the young.

The statistical contours of religious change

Statistics are particularly useful in examining five aspects of religious change in twentieth-century Britain – church belonging, churchgoing, religious belief, gender and moral change. This section looks at each in turn.

There is little doubt that popular adherence to churches fell between 1900 and 2000. Table 1.2 shows the levels of church membership and adherence in four of the main Christian churches in mainland Britain. The measures vary between the churches, but they permit useful comparison; those for communicants and mass attendance are similar in that they are each a census taken once per year, whilst estimated Catholic population, which is based on baptised persons, is the least sensitive to church decline. What does the table show? Each of the four churches experienced significant growth until at least the later 1920s, and most experienced only temporary and minor decline until the later 1950s.

TABLE 1.2 *Christian church adherence, 1900–2000: selected churches*

	Church of England	Roman Catholic Church		Methodism	Church of Scotland
	Easter Day communicants	Great Britain, estimated Catholic population	England & Wales mass attendance	Members	Communicants
1900	1,902,000	2,016,000		770,406	1,154,593
1910	2,212,000	2,216,000		841,294	1,220,732
1920	2,171,000	2,501,937		801,721	1,268,931
1930	2,261,857*	2,781,000		841,462	1,287,672
1940	1,997,820*	3,023,000		792,192	1,301,871
1950	1,847,998*	3,499,374		744,815	1,295,803
1960	2,159,356	4,346,140	1,941,500	728,589	1,324,437
1970	1,631,506	4,828,710	1,934,853	617,018	1,171,459
1980	1,551,000	5,091,589†		487,972	965,684
1990	1,376,000	5,092,808	1,387,435	424,540	795,099
2000	1,163,000	4,773,019††	1,005,522	335,567	607,714

* I am adhering to these data given by Currie *et al.* from a 1962 Church of England source, but which differ from the figures of 2,285,000 (1930), 2,018,000 (1940) and 1,867,000 (1950) contained in Table 22 of [Anglican] *Church Statistics 2002* (online version, accessed March 2005). The two series agree on the figures for 1960 and 1970.
† The English and Wales constituent of this figure relates to 1981.
†† The Scottish constituent of this figure relates to 2002.

Sources: Figures are from or calculated from data in R. Currie, A. Gilbert and L. Horsley, *Churches and Churchgoers: Patterns of Church Growth in the British Isles since 1700* (Oxford, Clarendon Press, 1977), pp. 31, 128–9, 133–5, 153, 163–5; www.anglican.org.uk; *Church of England Yearbook*, 1979–2000; *Church of Scotland Yearbook*, 1971–99; Church of Scotland HQ press release, May 2005; www.catholic-ew.org.uk; www.scmo.org/bishops_conference; minutes of the Methodist Conference, (various), courtesy of John Sawkins.

The peak year for membership in each of the Protestant denominations was Church of England 1927, Methodism 1928 and the Church of Scotland 1956. Amongst these, only the Methodist Church experienced serious decline before 1950, indicating the declining fortunes of many English Protestant Nonconformist churches. (For other British churches, the peak years were Congregationalists 1906, Baptists 1906, Presbyterian Church of Wales 1926 and Church in Wales 1934.) However, there is greater evidence from Wales of serious decline in church adherence in the 1930s, from which there was to be no meaningful recovery; from a high-point of Christian communicants in 1926, most Welsh churches declined. On the one hand, this may be interpreted as evidence that Welsh Christianity entered a crisis earlier than elsewhere in Britain; on the other hand, it may be interpreted as part of the distinct early crisis afflicting most of British Nonconformity. Welsh Christianity, in other words, suffered between the wars from its Nonconformist leanings.[28]

By contrast, for the Church of England, the Church of Scotland, the Church in Wales and some others, there was significant recovery from wartime dislocation in the 1940s and 1950s, leading to an important peak of membership in 1955–9. Indeed, it can be safely said of British Christianity as a whole that there was a general equilibrium in formal church practice and adherence between 1900 and the late 1950s. But what is clear is that all the Protestant Christian churches experienced serious decline in membership from the early 1960s. Membership halved in Methodism, the Church of Scotland and the Church of England in the space of forty years, and other data show that most Protestant churches also experienced a sharp decline, though not as severe as that afflicting these three churches. Meanwhile, the Roman Catholic Church continued to experience growth in its estimated constituency due to a high birth rate and immigration of Catholics from Europe and Ireland, and a lower rate of youth disaffection in the 1960s. But, as the data for mass attendance indicate, when Catholic decline set in, it was the most severe of all – in the order of 30 per cent per decade in the 1970s, 1980s and 1990s.

So, taken overall, the level of church *belonging* measured by adherence in the population at large seems to have peaked in 1905 for England and Wales and 1906 for Scotland, followed by a relatively modest decline until the 1960s, when a catastrophic slide from church membership set in for Christian church membership. But church membership is a measure of a mostly passive religiosity. The most common measure of religious activity is that of church*going*. Was its pattern of change during the century different?

The evidence for churchgoing is more partial than that for church adherence, and inadequate for the purposes of constructing a century-long national table; moreover, it is far more difficult to interpret. In the 1880s and 1890s, local censuses around the country showed that church attendances as a proportion of population varied from about 18 to 33 per cent – though many of the higher figures were boosted because of counting individuals who went to church twice or even thrice on Sundays. By 1900–10, the figures fell more into the band of 18–30 per cent, with London at the lower extreme, and with rural and some northern, Welsh, Scottish and Northern Ireland towns at the upper extremes. In the middle of the twentieth century, it seems certain that the figures had dropped across the country, but not in a massive way – to perhaps 15–22 per cent. In Scotland, where the data are the best, the churchgoing rate for Glasgow in 1955 was calculated at 20 per cent, and was estimated for Scotland as a whole in 1959 at 17.7 per cent. It seems reasonable from qualitative evidence and contemporary comment to suppose that the figures for England and Wales in the 1950s would have been marginally lower than these. So, the first half of the century experienced a loss of something like a third of church attendances on a Sunday.[29]

Church attendance fell by about the same margin in the second half of the century. By the 1970s and 1980s, the figures for Sunday attendances as a proportion of population had fallen in almost every part of mainland Britain – to a range of between 9 and 20 per cent. In 1979–84, weekly churchgoing stood at 11 per cent in England, 13 per cent in Wales and 17.2 per cent in Scotland. However, some parts of Britain had higher figures in 1984 – notably the Hebrides and Lochalsh, where attendance was reputedly 54 per cent, and in Catholic urban areas such as Glasgow (19.5 per cent in 1984). Churchgoing continued to fall in the last two decades of the century. In England, the figure fell from 11 per cent in 1979 to 9.9 per cent in 1989, and to 7.5 per cent in 1998. In Scotland, churchgoing fell from 17.2 per cent in 1984 to 14 per cent in 1994, and to 11.2 per cent in 2002. By the last few years of the century, in most places, churchgoing had reached between 5 and 11 per cent of the population attending weekly. What was evident by then was that zones of previously high attendance were experiencing the sharpest decline. For example, the rate in the Hebrides and Lochalsh fell from 54 to 39 per cent between 1984 and 2002, and in Glasgow from 19.5 per cent to 14.2 per cent over the same period.[30] Only in Northern Ireland was churchgoing very high. In a 1993 survey, 15 per cent of mainland British people claimed to be 'frequent churchgoers', but in Northern Ireland the figure was 58 per cent.[31]

Taking the century as a whole, the practice of going to church for Sunday Christian worship slid continuously from public affection. However, the almost continuous nature of this slide conceals some important features. In the 1950s, for instance, there are data (examined in Chapter 5) that suggest that Sunday churchgoers were a mixed group of people – some of whom went to church infrequently, some monthly, some weekly and some more than once a week. Those who attended less than weekly were so large in number that the churchgoers of Britain may have made up as much as 30–40 per cent of the people. This meant, in mid-century, that Britain was a society with a profound Christian complexion. In the 1990s, on the other hand, the level of infrequent and monthly attendance had diminished much more than weekly attendance, representing how churchgoers had become a smaller and more committed group, but one which no longer interchanged with and recruited from others in society at large. This then helps to explain what we noted earlier – how church adherence collapsed in the last forty years of the century. The constituency of the more passive Christians only started to slide from church belonging and churchgoing after about 1960.

If measures of religious belonging and activity draw our attention to some dramatic change after the 1950s, data on religious beliefs show different chronologies of change. These data were only collected in the latter half of the century. Table 1.3 demonstrates that belief in 'a personal God' declined markedly only after about 1975, whilst belief in God responding to the barest of questions showed a marked decline only in the 1990s. By contrast, Table 1.4 shows that belief in something after death remained pretty constant, at around half the adult population, from 1940 to the 2000s. Meanwhile, the impact of education upon religious belief was highly variable. In 1947, 66 per cent of people with secondary education said they believed in life after death, but the figure fell to only 41 per cent for those with only primary education – which bucked the generally accepted notion of greater scepticism amongst the more highly educated.

TABLE 1.3 *Belief in God, 1940s–2000 (Percentage of respondents)*

Positive answers to:	1940s	1947	1968	1975	1981	1990	2000	2001
There is a personal God	43	45		41	32		26	
Do you believe in God?			77	76	73	72		61

Sources: S. Bruce, 'Praying alone? Church-going in Britain and the Putnam thesis', *Journal of Contemporary Religion* vol. 17 (2002), p. 327; P. Norris and R. Inglehart, *Sacred and Secular: Religion and Politics Worldwide* (Cambridge, Cambridge University Press, 2004), p. 90.

TABLE 1.4 *Belief in life after death, 1939–2003 (Percentage of respondents)*

		Yes	No	Uncertain/ no opinion
1939	Do you believe there is a life after death?	49	33	18
1948	Do you believe in life after death?	49	27	24
1951	Do you believe in an afterlife?	47	22	31
1957	Do you believe that there is or is not a life after death?	54	17	29
1961	Belief in life after death [no question cited]	56	18	26
1968	Do you believe in life after death?	38	n/k	n/k
1975	Do you believe in life after death?	43	n/k	n/k
1981	Do you believe in life after death?	46	n/k	n/k
1990	Do you believe in life after death?	44	n/k	n/k
2001	Do you believe in life after death?	45	n/k	n/k
2003	I don't believe death is the end	51	n/k	n/k

Sources: G. Gorer, *Exploring English Character*, pp. 274, 459; Mass-Observation, *Puzzled People: A study in popular attitudes to religion, ethics, progress and politics in a London Borough, prepared for the Ethical Union* (London, Victor Gollancz, 1947), p. 27; H.G. Erskine, 'The polls: personal religion', *Public Opinion Quarterly* (1965), pp. 145–57; P. Norris and R. Inglehart, *Sacred and Secular: Religion and Politics Worldwide* (Cambridge, Cambridge University Press, 2004), p. 91; ICM poll, broadcast on BBC2 TV, 26 February 2004.

However, the same survey found that there was virtually no difference in belief in God between social classes. The survey concluded: 'On most important points there are major differences between men and women, and between the generations; but class, however defined, appears to have little effect.'[32]

Social class, indeed, was something much explored in studies of religion by sociologists and historians. There seemed much evidence from the start of the century that working-class attendance and adherence was lower than that of the middle classes; this was especially the case drawn from Charles Booth's studies of London and Seebohm Rowntree's on York in the 1890s. In the 1960s, sociologists paid great attention to evidence of greater working-class alienation from the churches. But working-class religious activity was higher than commentators thought. Some studies found little variation in churchgoing by social class, whilst in some the upper working classes came out with the highest level of churchgoing – followed by the lower and upper middle classes, with the upper classes, the lower working classes and the poor with the lowest attendances. Looked at another way, social analysis of entire Christian congregations tended in nearly all cases to show the working classes in the majority, often making up between 50 and 65 per cent of worshippers (with higher figures in the Roman Catholic Church).[33]

Gender difference was often more striking than that of class. Throughout the twentieth century (as indeed the last five hundred years), there was a significantly higher level of religious practice and belief amongst women compared to men. This was not peculiar to Britain, but has been a widespread characteristic of Christianity over many centuries. In London in 1902–3, women made up well over half of all churchgoers – 68 per cent in the Church of England and 64 per cent in the Roman Catholic Church – and dominated the most popular evening services – 66 per cent of Baptists, 74 per cent of Primitive Methodists, 76 per cent at the Salvation Army and 87 per cent at Christian mission stations in working-class districts. Only in the Jewish faith was the gender balance seriously reversed, with just 22 per cent being female. Moreover, an analysis of churchgoing habits in London in those years shows that in districts where women were strong churchgoers, churchgoing by men and children increased. Where numbers of female domestic servants were high, all churchgoing increased, as they released the middle-class households to go to church. Women emerge as critical to patterns of overall churchgoing in the population at large, encouraging the rest of their families to go, and making most congregations highly feminised in composition.[34]

This trend of women outnumbering men was still strong until the 1970s. Women characteristically made up 63–75 per cent of most Christian congregations throughout the United Kingdom. The gender difference extended to belief, too. In a sample of Londoners in 1947, for instance, about two-thirds of men said they believed in God compared to about 80 per cent of women.[35] However, with religious decline from the later 1960s, it began to emerge that the gender imbalance eased as women started either to leave the church in greater numbers than men or, more probably, to become just as unlikely as men to be recruited in the first place. In Scotland, for instance, 37 per cent of churchgoers were male in 1984, compared with 39 per cent in 1994 and only 40 per cent in 2002. Two-thirds of those leaving between the last two dates were women, half of them aged between 20 and 44 years; amongst over 15-year-olds, 77 per cent of the net loss of churchgoers was female.[36] The Scottish case suggests that as Christian churches became smaller late in the century, men and women became more even in number.

Women's stronger attachment to church activity was a major factor underlying their generally higher level of religious identity during the century. Not only did women go to church more than men, but they were usually the critical figures in organising the rituals marking rites of passage – marriage and baptism. It is the female members of families who most often determine if they occur, when they occur and the manner in which they occur. But, in addition, women's sexual lives and control over their own fertility are important items of population history. The last theme of this section looks at how demographic behaviour changed very fundamentally in the century as a result of change in religious behaviour, influenced strongly by women.

Many population statistics measure moral change. This applies to statistics of illegitimacy, birth rate, age of marriage, number of marriages per head of population and proportion of marriages religiously solemnised – in each of which moral choices are either always or often involved. In all of these data, the twentieth century saw profound change, most of it in the last thirty years. These statistics tell us how the people organised their lives, and how that organisation changed from one period to the next. Over most of recorded human history, these data have moved only very slowly. Indeed, for most centuries, the movements have been marginal, and consequently such little change as did occur tended to be seen by demographers as economically induced – especially the impact of industrialisation and urbanisation in the eighteenth and nineteenth centuries. This was probably an accurate assessment. Minor changes in demographic data down to the 1950s were caused by economic fluctuations and social change. But the changes were *very* small. Little had changed in the construction of the family over the last five hundred years. And the reason the small changes were economically caused was because large changes only came with *religious* change. The big demographic changes came after the 1960s, when there was no sudden economic change, and they were governed overwhelmingly by moral, not material, considerations.

Most moral choices are based on religious precepts, and change to moral choice that may impact on the demography tends to be caused by decline of religious precepts. A classic statistical measure of the conjunction of moral and demographic change is the illegitimacy rate – the proportion of children born out of wedlock. Under Christendom for a thousand years, the church and the state enforced the notion of marriage as the morally correct unit for child-rearing. Figure 1.1 shows this measure for the countries of the UK (with England and Wales counted together) from 1900 to 2000. Two things are immediately striking. First, the level of illegitimacy was remarkably low for the first three-quarters of the twentieth century, being under 5 per cent in England and Wales and in Northern Ireland, and a little higher at nearly 7 per cent in Scotland for most of this period. There was little change to the course of these data series, except during and immediately after the two world wars. But then in the 1950s, there was a significant fall in illegitimacy, to be followed from the middle of the 1960s by the figures starting to rise. The rise was steady in the first half of the 1970s, then entered a period of steepening growth until the end of the century, when the rate in mainland countries was at or exceeding 40 per cent. A rise in the illegitimacy rate from 4 to 40 per cent in less than forty years signifies an extraordinary change to the British moral order. The second striking thing about the graph lines for each country is that they move almost in tandem, without any significant deviation. The moral order of the mainland in the UK showed little significant divergence.

Compare Figure 1.1 with Figure 1.2 – the numbers of infant baptisms in the Church of England, expressed as a percentage of all the live births in England. The striking feature is how as illegitimate births rose, church baptism of babies declined, suggesting an inverse connection between illegitimacy and baptism rates. This is confirmed by an examination of the statistical relationship between the two – what is called the correlation, which was −0.9136, indicating a very strong inverse statistical relationship.[37] This marks a fundamental change to the nature of the moral-demographic culture that determined illegitimacy. Most previous changes to illegitimacy measured by demographic historians from the

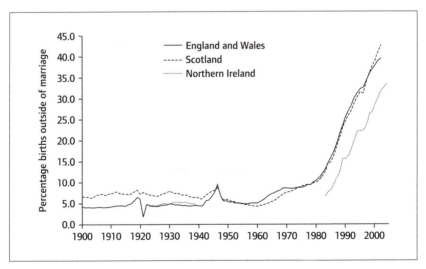

FIGURE 1.1 *Illegitimacy rates, UK countries 1900–2000*

Sources: Data are from or calculated from figures at www.gro-Scotland.gov.uk, www.gro.gov.uk, www.nisra.gov.uk, and *Annual Abstract of Statistics for Northern Ireland*, 1980–91. Crown copyright material is reproduced with the permission of the Controller of HMSO.

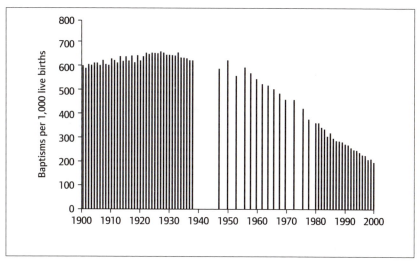

FIGURE 1.2 *Infant baptism, Church of England, 1900–2000*

Note: I have adhered to the data from *Church of England Yearbook* where they differ from data in *Church Statistics 2002*. The figures in the latter are higher for each year from 1900 to 1930 (e.g. 1900 – 650/609, 1920 – 678/630, 1930 – 699/654, 1950 – 672/632), but are the same from 1960. After 1980, the data may underscore marginally (I estimate at under 5 per cent) as they exclude baptisms at over 12 months.

Sources: *Church of England Yearbook*, 1984–2000; [Anglican] *Church Statistics 2002*, Table 17 (accessed online April 2005).

seventeenth century to the 1960s have almost universally been taken to represent couples 'straying' from the Christian rule of no sex (or at least no births) before marriage. Couples rarely broke this rule, and if a woman became pregnant, the couple usually got married before the birth. But from the 1960s onwards, the scale of the change indicates that something more fundamental than 'straying' from acceptable behaviour was happening. The rule was being widely ignored. It became acceptable not to marry before births, or not to marry at all, or even not to form a cohabiting couple. From that decade, late marriage, cohabitation and single parenthood each became acceptable and commonplace. Also marking changed attitudes was the dramatic fall in baptism of infant children. Together, these show that the moral (and thus the religious) rules underlying demographic behaviour had changed for the first time in Britain's Christian history.

A consequence of this was declining marriage, and the progressive de-Christianisation of those marriages that took place. The number of marriages in the United Kingdom fell by 35 per cent between 1970 and 2000, the result of later marriage and increasing bachelorhood, spinsterhood and single parenthood.[38] Figure 1.3 indicates clearly the steady fall

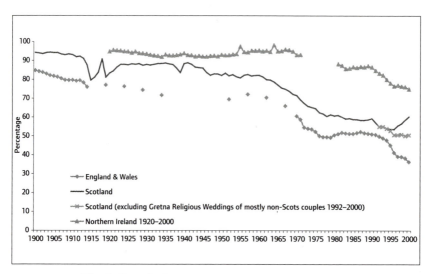

FIGURE 1.3 *The decline of religious marriage, UK countries, 1900–2000. The proportion of marriages religiously solemnised*

Sources: Data are from or calculated from figures in R. Currie, A. Gilbert and L. Horsley, *Churches and Churchgoers: Patterns of Church Growth in the British Isles since 1700* (Oxford, Clarendon Press, 1977), pp. 223–34; www.gro-Scotland; www.gro.gov.uk. Crown copyright material is reproduced with the permission of the Controller of HMSO.

in religious solemnisation of marriage in the middle decades of the century in most of the UK, together with the plunge from around 1963 in England and Wales and in Scotland, and its increasing steeper gradient in the 1980s and 1990s. Interestingly, Northern Ireland did not fit this pattern. It shows that religious marriage was higher than in the rest of the UK for the first half of the century, with it growing in the 1950s (from 93 per cent in 1951 to 95 per cent in 1961), and then holding fairly steady during the 1960s and 1970s (93 per cent in 1971 and 88 per cent in 1981). It suffered a short fall in the early 1980s, and only started a more substantial decline after 1990 (but still standing at 75 per cent in 2000). This reflects the general pattern of Northern Ireland's higher religiosity and limited de-Christianisation by the end of the century.

Change in moral behaviour can be explored further using advanced statistics (called correlations). (If you find this difficult, you may proceed to the summary of what they show in the next-but-one paragraph.) The statistics show that there were linkages between demographic and moral/religious activities, but that the nature of the linkages varied by decade. This is best seen in Scotland, where the statistics are very good. Testing the connection between church-growth rate, marriage rate and illegitimacy rate between 1900 and 1993 shows that only church growth and illegitimacy rates had a significant (inverse) connection (correlation of −0.6437) – showing that church growth tended to rise when illegitimacy went down. This seems to fit normal historical understandings about conservatism and moral behaviour. But when the century is broken down into shorter periods, the connections differ. Church-growth rate and illegitimacy had *positive* links during the First World War (0.2377) and the Second World War (0.8062), but no or weak connections in the post-war periods (0.0848 for 1920–38 and 0.0889 for 1946–62). However, there were significant or strong *inverse* links later in the century (a linkage of −0.8017 for 1963–84 and of −0.7273 for 1975–93). But comparing church growth and marriage rates, the results become even more interesting. These were significantly and *positively* linked in the 1975–93 period (0.7018), but strongly *inversely* linked in the 1963–74 period (−0.7862), with only weak or poor links for the rest of the century. This absence of constancy in correlation can be seen even more starkly between marriage and illegitimacy rates. These were positively linked in two periods, 1946–62 (0.6376) and 1963–74 (0.6018), but inversely linked in the First World War (−0.5409), the Second World War (−0.5248) and in the last quarter of the century (−0.8041).

What of economic determinants of decisions to marry and have children? Young couples would clearly have to think about sources of income to sustain a family. Another set of tests in Scotland on the years 1922–56 showed an inverse linkage (−0.5194) between unemployment rate and marriage rate, and a positive linkage between unemployment and illegitimacy (0.3431). This indicates that when the numbers of unemployed rose, the number of marriages went down, but the number of illegitimate births rose (though only slightly, suggesting breaches of the moral rules, not their abolition). Similarly, change in average wages and the marriage rate was positively linked between 1924 and 1936 (0.7114), showing that wage prosperity tended to go along with marriage.

What do these statistics show? From this exercise we may conclude that during the twentieth century, moral forces acting upon population behaviour changed direction and strength very sharply. This occurred *temporarily* in wartime, but *permanently* from the early 1960s. When the moral culture was conservative pre-1963, the marriage rate was high and the illegitimacy rate was very low. So steadfastly and unquestioningly conservative was the moral climate that, until the 1960s, it was broadly economic rather than moral variables that contributed to the minor fluctuations in the illegitimacy and marriage rates. Few people (especially women) dared buck the moral climate, leaving economics to be the big determinant of whether and when to marry or to have children – confirmed by the effect unemployment and wages had upon marriage rates and illegitimacy.

Consequently, these statistics tend to show that the economy influenced key demographic data in the first half of the century, but from about 1945 it was moral behaviour that was influential. But that is not the whole story. The period 1945–2000 broke down into two elements. In the first, during the conservative years of the later 1940s and 1950s, a *positive* correlation existed between church growth and demographic actions. But after 1963, this was then dramatically reversed into a *negative* correlation. Church growth and illegitimacy became cut adrift. Marriage rate and church growth became temporarily inversely linked in 1963–74 as secular marriages surged in popularity, but then permanently and positively linked as both secular and religious marriages declined together. What was happening was that, come the 1960s, the structuring of the family and the choice to have children became decisions largely divorced from economic determinants, and instead associated increasingly with moral ones. However, by then those moral decisions were part of a new secular and unchurched society in which marriage both declined and secularised. A new moral outlook had come into being.

In this way, the society we are examining in twentieth-century Britain altered its very rules of behaviour in the midst of our period of study. The position of religion and the morals it incurred changed, causing demographic social science to alter its very *modus operandi*. Thus in the 1980s, for instance, the Registrars General (who record population data for the government and influence social-science method) stopped labelling births outside of marriage as 'illegitimate', since the moral judgement was no longer widely acceptable. This makes the historian's lot a peculiarly difficult one. It means that we cannot accept ready-made formulae about morality, conservative religion and secular change. Nor can we accept statistics as being the only way, or always the best way, of assessing the changing nature of religion. Statistics can only measure change in a category, but if the category itself is fundamentally reconstituted (as with illegitimacy), then statistical method is not up to the task. Equally, the very category of 'being religious' may be changing at the same time. So, if the people stopped joining churches, but started spiritual quests without being 'counted', then we need to look beyond numbers. The religious change during the century was not merely of the incremental nature that social historians and sociologists are accustomed to measuring. It included change of a revolutionary nature with which the cultural historian may be better equipped to deal.

Notes

1 *The Guardian*, 22 April 2000; *The Observer*, 3 September 2000; *Scotland on Sunday*, 11 May 1997; *Sunday Telegraph*, 28 May 2000.

2 W.L. Courtney (ed.), *Do We Believe? A Record of a Great Correspondence in 'The Daily Telegraph'*, *October, November, December 1904* (London, Hodder & Stoughton, 1905); R. Mudie-Smith (ed.), *The Religious Life of London* (London, Hodder & Stoughton, 1904).

3 This meaning of 'secularisation' applies to each usage of it in *The Times* newspaper in the nineteenth century. The first and last usages were *The Times*, 10 May 1849, 17 May 1893.

4 C.G. Brown, *The Death of Christian Britain: Understanding Secularisation 1800–2000* (London, Routledge, 2001), pp. 167–8.

5 Ibid., p. 189.

6 Figures for London refer to *Daily News* census of 1902–3, analysed in ibid., p. 148; P. Brierley, *The Tide is Running Out* (London, Christian Research Association, 2000), p. 27.

7 Figures from C.G. Brown, *Religion and Society in Scotland since 1707* (Edinburgh, Edinburgh University Press, 1997), p. 59; and P. Brierley and F. Macdonald (eds), *Prospects for Scotland: From a Census of the Churches in 1984* (n.pl., Marc, 1985), p. 70.

8 Data from Census 2001, National Statistics, website www.statistics.gov.uk, and the Scottish Executive, website www.scottishexecutive.gov.uk.

9 *The Observer*, 18 March 2001, 'Britain Uncovered' supplement, pp. 10–11.

10 And 5 per cent offered other comments. Mass-Observation, *Puzzled People: A study in popular attitudes to religion ethics, progress and politics in a London Borough, prepared for the Ethical Union* (London, Victor Gollancz, 1947), p. 72.

11 W. James, *The Varieties of Religious Experience: a Study in Human Nature* (orig. 1902, London, Longmans, Green, 1928), pp. 368, 377.

12 R. Dawkins, *A Devil's Chaplain* (London, Phoenix, 2003), pp. 146, 162–77.

13 J. Highet, *The Churches in Scotland To-day* (Glasgow, Jackson, 1950), pp. 75, 79.

14 E.R. Wickham, *Church and People in an Industrial City* (London, Lutterworth, 1957), p. 14.

15 A. Gilbert, *The Making of Post-Christian Britain: A History of the Secularization of Modern Society* (London and New York, Longman, 1980); H. McLeod, *Class and Religion in the Late Victorian City* (London, Croom Helm, 1974).

16 B.R. Wilson, *Religion in Secular Society: A Sociological Comment* (Harmondsworth, Penguin, 1966), p. 262.

17 See, for instance, S. Bruce, *God is Dead: Secularization in the West* (Oxford, Blackwell, 2002).

18 See the discussion of this thesis in S. Bruce, 'Praying alone? Church-going in Britain and the Putnam thesis', *Journal of Contemporary Religion* vol. 17 (2002), pp. 317–28.

19 J. Wolffe, *God and the Greater Britain: Religion and National Life in Britain and Ireland 1843–1945* (London, Routledge, 1994), pp. 260–1.

20 G. Mayfield, *The Church of England: Its members and its business* (London, Oxford University Press, 1958), p. 44.

21 S. Connolly, *Religion and Society in Nineteenth-century Ireland* (n.p., Dundalgan Press, 1985), pp. 3–6.

22 R. Currie, A. Gilbert and L. Horsley, *Churches and Churchgoers* (Oxford, Clarendon, 1977), p. 222; National Statistics, website www.statistics.gov.uk, accessed 16 March 2005.

23 National Statistics, website, accessed 16 March 2005.

24 National Statistics, website, accessed 16 March 2005; H. Ansari, *'The Infidel Within': Muslims in Britain since 1800* (London, Hurst & Co., 2004), p. 173.

25 See for example C.G. Brown, 'Religion' in R. Pope (ed.), *Atlas of British Social and Economic History* (Routledge, London, 1989), pp. 211–23; and J.D. Gay, *The Geography of Religion in England* (London, Duckworth, 1971), esp. pp. 293, 273, 311, 315, 321.

26 National Statistics, website, accessed 16 March 2005.

27 This description of 2001 segregation in London is drawn from *The Guardian* supplement maps on religion and ethnicity, 21 January 2005.

28 D.D. Morgan, *The Span of the Cross: Christian Religion and Society in Wales 1914–2000* (Cardiff, University of Wales Press, 1999), pp. 162, 189; Currie et al., *Churches and Churchgoers*, p. 150.

29 Data for Scotland originally from Highet, *Scottish Churches*, p. 60; and J. Highet, 'The Churches', in J. Cunnison and J.B.S. Gilfillan (eds), *The Third Statistical Account of Scotland: Glasgow* (Glasgow, Collins, 1958), p. 956, as re-calibrated in C.G. Brown, 'Religion and secularisation', in A. Dickson and J.H. Treble (eds), *People and Society in Scotland vol. III 1914–1990* (Edinburgh, John Donald, 1992), p. 55. Other data from H. McLeod, *Religion and Society in England 1850–1914* (Basingstoke, Macmillan, 1996), p. 172; and Brown, *Death of Christian Britain*, p. 148.

30 P. Brierley (ed.), *Prospects for the Eighties* (London, Bible Society, 1980), pp. 26, 65; P. Brierley and B. Evans (eds), *Prospects for Wales* (London, Bible Society/Marc, 1982), p. 58. Brierley and Macdonald (eds), *Prospects for Scotland*, pp. 5, 12; P. Brierley and F. Macdonald (eds), *Prospects for Scotland 2000* (Edinburgh, NBSS/Christian Research, 1995), pp. 16; www.christian-research.org.uk; P. Brierley, *Turning the Tide* (London, Christian Research, 2003).

31 Northern Ireland Social Attitudes Survey 1992–1993, The Third Report, p.7, cited at http://cain.ulst.ac.uk/ni/religion.htm#3.

32 Mass-Observation, *Puzzled People*, pp. 21, 28, 80, 82.

33 H. McLeod, *Religion and Society in England, 1850–1914* (Basingstoke, Macmillan, 1996), pp. 62–6; Brown, *Death of Christian Britain*, pp. 154–5.

34 Ibid., pp. 156–61; McLeod, op. cit., p. 67.

35 Mass-Observation, *Puzzled People*, loc. cit.

36 Website www.christian-research.co.uk, accessed 16 March 2005.

37 A correlation measures the linkage between changes in one set of data with changes in another set of data, through indicating whether a linkage is positive or inverse, and the degree of linkage within a scale of 0 to 1 – with 0 indicating no linkage and 1 signalling a perfect linkage. The data used here were datasets of year-on-year figures, with 28 gaps (out of 101 datapoints) in the baptism data filled by linear extrapolation. This reduces the accuracy of the overall exercise, but the weakness is mitigated by the very high value of the correlation coefficient.

38 From 470,842 to 305,912 (using NI figure for 1971). Data calculated from figures on Scottish, NI and England and Wales websites of www.gro.gov.uk.

CHAPTER 2

The faith society, 1900–14

Christian clergy were generally cheerful in 1901. At a church conference in Edinburgh to mark the beginning of the new century, one commented: 'It is the remarkable feature of this present day that we can make an intelligent comprehensive survey of the countries and nations of the earth, and in doing so feel throb within us the love of man, the love of God, for the unity of humankind.'[1] To be alive in Britain in that year was to feel an intense heritage of religiosity in popular thought and people's activities. The British Empire was large and virtuous, bringing law and Christian education to the peoples of every colour and economic condition around the world. At home, the nation was characterised by a vigorous attendance at Sunday worship, the observance of religious rituals and widespread recognition of the religious foundation of moral worth. And though there were crises of self-confidence, especially in the performance of the churches, this buoyancy of Christian culture was to continue largely unabated until the outbreak of war in 1914.

The Victorian inheritance

Britain was a highly religious society in 1900. The Edwardian period (which properly refers to 1901–11, but is also commonly applied down to 1914) was in many ways indistinguishable in its religious culture from the longer Victorian period (1837–1901) that preceded it. Religiosity marked the social values of almost the entire society, and even in transgression from them, the sinful rarely felt free from a religious judgement.

What were the religious values of the time? There was a strong sense that Christian piety, churchgoing and religious decorum defined the respectable citizen. This applied in town as much as in the countryside. Flora Thompson, in one of the most famous autobiographies of the century, wrote of the religious life of Oxfordshire in the period leading up to 1900. She described the rural hamlet in which she grew up, Juniper Hill (which in her book she called Lark Rise):

If the Lark Rise people had been asked their religion, the answer of nine out of ten would have been 'Church of England', for practically all of them were christened, married, and buried as such, although, in adult life, few went to church between the baptisms of their offspring. The children were shepherded there after Sunday school and about a dozen of their elders attended regularly; the rest stayed at home: the women cooking and nursing, and the men, after an elaborate Sunday toilet, which included shaving and cutting each other's hair and puffing and splashing with buckets of water, but stopped short before lacing up boots or putting on a collar and tie, spent the rest of the day eating, sleeping, reading the newspaper, and strolling round to see how their neighbours' pigs and gardens were looking.

This sense of a rather mellow observance of Sunday as a holy day in rural society contrasted with Flora's experience of something rather more strict in the small towns of Banbury and Buckingham (which she amalgamated in her book to call Candleford). There, wrote Flora, the placidity of the Church of England folk was challenged by evangelicals – those with a more earnest approach to religion. One of these was the 'born-again' postman who alarmed people. Flora said that they 'almost ran in the opposite direction when they saw him coming, lest he should ask impertinent questions about their souls. "How is it with your soul?" he would unblushingly inquire of any chance-met acquaintance, or, more directly, "Have you found salvation?" and, in face of a question like that, what could a man or woman do but mumble and look silly?'[2] Even in small-town communities in which churchgoing was shunned by the majority, the born-again Christian could hold a powerful sway over everyday culture.

British people were accustomed to the intrusiveness of religion. Nearly every person would claim some attachment to a religion, most would be able to show an attachment to a church and very few of those with a faith were non-Christian. With around a quarter of a million Jews, those of other faiths numbered perhaps 50,000, and secularists a few thousand, the Christian religion had a dominant role in official and popular culture. It was the religion of state, school and local government, and was officially recognised by these in all sorts of ways. Town councils were

Analysis: The religious self in the early twentieth century

One way in which the importance of religion was expressed in the early decades of the twentieth century was in autobiography, biography and in obituary. In these, the life of a man or a woman was used as an example to others. It conveyed the high moral values expected in behaviour. But, in addition, it gave a sense of how the ideals of human life were represented in the form of progression and improvement – a 'redemption narrative' in which each person should strive to attain a moral and religious salvation.

The obituary was a highly prized device for celebrating the religious and moral life. Recognition of achievement in life's work was important as an example to others. The following death notice is for Mr William S. W. Limster, who died in 1904 at the age of 87 years. An apprentice ironmonger in Dundee in his teens, he opened his own business in 1845 in nearby Montrose. The *Methodist Recorder* said of him:

By his industry, foresight, and inflexible uprightness he built up one of the largest businesses in the district. His integrity and his successful career won him an eminent place in the esteem of his townfellows. He was a generous but discriminating supporter of philanthropic effort, but his private and personal benefactions were even more characteristic. The chief factor of his life was his religion. If he 'passed the time of his sojourning here in fear' it was the fear of Christian humility and not that of unchristian doubt. He governed himself with military vigour [his father had been a soldier], and disciplined himself sternly. But humour and playfulness had a place beneath a somewhat austere manner. At heart he was sympathetic and generous. His religion issued in well-regulated conduct rather than in conventional speech. But he gave indubitable evidence of his simple Christian faith. He was not exempt from life's frustrations and griefs, but his will was indomitable, and he sought and found grace whereby he was able to stand. ... For sixty years, amid all the vicissitudes of a small [Methodist branch] society, he was unmoveable in his attachment to the Wesleyan Methodist Church. His interest and generosity were unfailing to the end. He gave as God has prospered him, liberally and cheerfully, but always methodically and with deliberation.[3]

This obituary contains key evangelical words: 'industry' (indicating hard work and self-improvement); 'integrity' (meaning principled), 'generous but discriminating' (attesting to a charity-giver, but with the late-Victorian requirement for the recipient poor to demonstrate self-help); 'well-regulated conduct' (a religion shown in good manners rather than religious fervour); and giving 'liberally and cheerfully, but always methodically and with deliberation' (indicating strong 'liberality' – a favourite dissenters' word since they had to rely on members giving money – but balanced by Methodists' 'method' and 'deliberation'). These were the praise-words of the age.

Biography and autobiography were also popular genres, used to portray exemplary Christian and moral lives. Fictional and factual lives of great men and women, from *Pilgrim's Progress* and *Robinson Crusoe* to biographies of prominent clergymen and missionaries, became used almost indistinguishably to find moral examples. The Victorian best-seller *Self-Help*, which showed how Christian-based values and gritty determination created great men, was celebrated in the autobiography of George Gregory, born in 1888 to an illiterate Somerset miner. In recounting his own life, he wrote:

I took it home, read the stories of men who had helped themselves, struggled against enormous difficulties, suffered painful privations, became destitute, and overwhelmed by conditions. Many of them reached the lowest levels of depression, but went on to rise phoenix-like from the ruins of their plans and collapse of their expectations to find a way to success. Such information stirred dormant powers in me. I began to see myself as an individual, and how I may be able to make a break from the general situation of which I had regarded myself as an inseparable part.[4]

In a striking mimic of the narrative structure of *Self-Help* and numerous autobiographies of the time, Gregory recalled how the book inspired him to become an avid reader of science and to train as a mining surveyor, but how, driven by a social and religious calling, he decided rather to be an ordinary miner, a trades union organiser and a Congregationalist minister. This is one example of how the religious self was deep-rooted in British culture at the start of the century. The personal account was arranged in story form to show the life-course as composed initially of a descending trajectory (into despair, failure or sin), and then an upward trajectory to moral fulfilment and some form of redemption (whether received or achieved). The self-striving for salvation was to be widely portrayed until the mid-twentieth century in popular literature, films and magazine stories. And the influence of this 'conversion narrative' was reflected in people's accounts of themselves – including religious conversions which were commonly discussed in the religious press during evangelical crusades and 'revivals' in the 1940s and 1950s.[5]

opened with prayer, and in Scotland were 'kirked' in an annual church service; religious rules of behaviour and attitudes were engrossed in many criminal laws (on consumption of alcohol, illegitimate births, keeping the Sabbath); and community rules of behaviour intruded upon individuals' freedom of action. This was a society in which religion promulgated and justified moral rules, and everyone knew those rules. Those who didn't keep them were well aware of their transgressions, and were the object of scrutiny, derision, complaint and often prosecution. It is fair to describe Edwardian Britain as puritanical. This meant that strict religious rules were not merely enforced by magistrates and the police, but that individuals were expected to submit (by the sheer pressure of civic, community and family culture of the period) to enforce puritan behaviour upon themselves. The culture of Britain was thoroughly embedded in a stark choice that had been perfected for some five decades – the choice between rough and respectable. To be rough was to be 'common', immoral and to be given to drink, gambling and attendance at 'low theatres'. To be respectable was to be nice. The majority of people probably fell into neither camp, but the fear of appearing rough was very strong, and led to few who would openly oppose evangelical culture in public. It was this self-policing that gave both Victorian and Edwardian society a distinct religious climate, and one that was to be sustained, albeit with some liberalisation and a little challenge, for several decades into the 1950s and 1960s.

This matured Christian culture gave the churches assurance. Despite the sensationalism of some commentators, there was no sustained evidence of mass haemorrhage from the churches, and there was little to panic the clergy. In the Church of England, there was an assurance that the established state church had a settled place in national affection. Its clergy were generally regarded as, in the words of one commentator, 'a body of well-meaning, cultured gentlemen'. Though some might lack a high income, they were deemed as having very little to worry about and very easy jobs; the average country parson was reckoned to work 'perhaps three hours a day on weekdays and six on Sundays, the latter forming a demand on his powers for which the country parson generally feels the need of special rest and support'.[6]

Amidst such a sleepy existence, what really afflicted the Church of England was that its status as the state church made it the cultural property of competing groups. The contest between High and Low Church was rather fierce in the first few years of the century, with Protestants in the Church attacking the advance of what were seen as 'Catholic' prayers and rituals. Campaigners interrupted church services, with brawling and protest during prayers, resulting in arrests and convictions. In January 1900, the Revd R. C. Fillingham, the vicar of Hexton in Hertfordshire, was fined £1 for leading fifty supporters in a protest at Kettleboxton in Suffolk, when he stood up in the middle of prayer and shouted, 'Idolatry:

Protestants, leave this house of Baal'. Protesters were seemingly deliberately joining particular parishes to mount protests. At Carshalton, a
Church of England layman committed the same offence of shouting
'Idolatry' five times in the middle of prayer, but had the sympathy of the
magistrates who dismissed the charge when he claimed that he was merely
obeying the statute of Henry VI's reign that required all to attend church.[7]

The Church of England was regarded as common property, and this
made it the target for contest. Equally, though, as the cultural and constitutional heritage of the English people, it was endowed with unique
strength. One Army officer regarded the Anglican Church as due fealty as
much as the monarch, arguing that 'society supports Bishops, priests, ministers and pastors to teach the principles of the Christian religion, which
is the foundation of all civilized society, inculcating as it does obedience
to laws and to all constituted authorities'.[8] In this way, Anglicanism was
the religion of English good order, identity and patriotism – an undemanding religion, composed of doing good works and being mildly
submissive to rules of respectable behaviour. This made the Church
acceptable to the nation, and made the clergy reasonably optimistic about
their place in the national firmament.

Even more vigorous in terms of church growth in mainland Britain was
the Roman Catholic Church. After battling in the nineteenth century to
impose patterns of regular church attendance amongst immigrants from
Ireland, by 1900 Catholics in Britain had significantly higher levels of
church practice than Protestants – with between a third and two-thirds of
Catholics attending mass weekly.[9] Moreover, Catholic family size was
larger than that of Protestant families, and numbers were rising. Though
English Catholicism had retained a distinctive identity, much of the British
faith was by then strongly influenced by Irish tradition. This formed part
of the object of sustained anti-Catholic feeling amongst Protestants and
British civil institutions, and the Church constantly felt pilloried. In
response, what is often described as a 'fortress mentality' developed, in
which the Church fashioned the Catholic parish church into a centre not
just for religious worship, but, with the addition of schools and other
buildings, for education, recreation and welfare. This formed a 'cradle-to-
grave' environment to defend Catholicism from the dangers of a hostile
Protestant society. Thus, by 1900, the Catholic Church was in the midst
of rapid growth as an institution, with the construction of new churches,
the formation of urban parishes and the reinvigoration of church organisations. Of all the major denominations in Edwardian Britain, Catholics
achieved the most significant growth in numbers as a proportion of the

British people. As a result, its clergy, very large numbers of whom were Irish-born, were becoming more and more confident of their position.

Dissenters were also in bullish mood as the century started. The Wesleyan Methodist Church reported: 'The Church aggressive, as distinguished from the Church contemplative, is bracing itself for work at every point. She is waiting at the gates of a new century – waiting until new and enlarged resources shall enable her to do many things that she has long desired, but has not hitherto dared to attempt.' A Twentieth Century Fund was established to collect £1 million for home mission work and church extension, with a scheme of central city halls being erected in Birmingham, Liverpool, Manchester, Newcastle-upon-Tyne, Edinburgh, Portsmouth, Bermondsey and Deptford. The Methodist people, it was said, never before had 'so many good works on hand'. The type of church that greeted the twentieth century was one resonant of the nineteenth century, with money for church schemes galore – for 'Chapels, Schools, Mission Houses, Training Colleges', for the 'Home Missionary Committee, the Temperance, Children's Home, Local Preachers', Sunday School Union, Education, Middle Class Schools, and Chapel Committees'.[10] These names reverberated to the money-and-action rhythm of Victorian evangelicalism – a burning commitment to 'doing' good works and measuring the denominational strength through the money-giving of the members. The Methodists reflected much of what churches had become by 1900. The British Baptist Union also had a Twentieth Century Fund for church building – the title as much as the existence of the fund signifying an optimism for the churches in the coming century. Indeed, virtually every denomination planned a Twentieth Century Fund – though that intended by the episcopalian Church of Ireland was delayed due to the outbreak of the Boer War and was never set up.[11]

The evangelical obsession with schemes and money bred a measurement of success in statistics. And things were in many respects looking good. The 1890s and 1900s were the peak decades of most Christian voluntary organisations, with Sunday-school enrolments reaching their high point between 1895 and 1900, and many new organisations for young people being founded. Church membership reached its all-time peak of just over 50 per cent of the population in England and Wales in 1904 and in Scotland in 1905. And church religious organisations were being formed all the time. This extended beyond the parochial to the international. In 1898, the World Student Christian Federation was formed, which by 1919 had 190,000 members in 2,500 colleges in more than forty countries worldwide.[12]

Yet, church optimism was being tempered with doubts in some quarters in Edwardian Britain. After a century of unremitting growth, church decline started to become a prospect. There had been serious church concern for two decades with the religiosity of the London working classes, and censuses started to appear that cultivated a panic amongst some that the heart of the Empire, London, was turning into a 'heathen city'. To the evidence in 1904 that only 19 per cent of Londoners went to Sunday worship in 1904–5 was added the evidence of a new newspaper in that year, called *The Daily Paper*. In its launch edition, the newspaper carried the 'exclusive' statistics that in the London district of Paddington, out of a population of 143,690, Sunday church attendances accounted for only 22 per cent of them, whilst pub-goers represented 86 per cent. Whilst money flowed seemingly endlessly into evangelistic projects, many religious meetings were becoming poorly attended. This undermined confidence amongst many benefactors who gave money for religious projects: 'It would be a sorry day for Methodism if the British and Foreign Bible Society had to close its doors.'[13]

In the Church of Scotland, the new century was greeted with a conference on the state of parish work and of the home missions, of which it was said that: 'one hears from time to time about disappointments and failure here and there. This church is half empty; that one is doing next to nothing for any Christian cause; in another there is no proof of living interest in the Church's work, no healthy spirit of Churchmanship; its influence is scarcely, if at all, perceptible in the community.'[14] Sunday schools started to report problems of recruitment. In one twelve-month period in 1905–6, the United Free Church reported the loss of 300 teachers in Glasgow alone.

Signs of a tide turning increased with the books, pamphlets and tracts being printed to defend the faith from attacks in the 'atheistic press'. Secularist unbelief – that God did not exist – was perceived as a direct attack on Christianity, and a massive evangelical press advertised books with titles such as *Is Christianity True?*. Movements of the so-called freethinkers, of socialist secularists, and mounting public obsession with scientific discovery, unsettled the churches. In addition, many denominations were very publicly arguing over the literal truth of the Bible; questions of 'heresy' were being raised when liberal views on traditional beliefs were expressed.

At the same time, there was soul-searching amongst some churchmen that the remedy to religious doubt – mounting massive evangelistic church campaigns to win recruits – could in itself be harmful for church culture. One Methodist wrote: 'Some people suffering from chronic spiritual cramp cry out that the Church is cherishing the viper of pride. It is, they say, inflaming itself with a passion for multitudinous success and world-wide notoriety and bigness. We are not ignorant of the devil's devices in this direction. ... This has been a highly religious movement. Let us keep it so.' Yet, the temptation was great to be robust with ecclesiastical wealth: 'So long as the whole Church stays itself on God we have no fear for the quarter of a million [pounds]. The people have the money. ... Our Methodist people, being so largely of the trading and operative class, have reaped a full share of the prosperity. ... And the people are willing. Thousands are waiting to be asked.'[15] Here is a fear that the evangelical churches were measuring themselves against a capitalist growth culture. But a greater fear was that money spent was not saving souls. Many parts of Britain, cities as well as countryside, were by the 1900s 'over churched', with too many new large churches built in an excess of zeal in the 1880s and 1890s. In rural as well as urban areas, many congregations were thin-ning out. In such ways, evidence was there to be called to support a view that British popular religiosity was seemingly in grave doubt.

Another way in which doubt was raised concerned Britain's mission as a nation. What purpose did the country's Empire have if it were not clearly a Christian one? British churchmen were taken aback by the outbreak of an 'unlikely' war against the Boers of South Africa – a people that were not only Christian but strongly Reformed Protestant. Across the Christian spectrum, doubts were raised about the implications of this. An Anglican Church con-gress in Newcastle debated the implications of the war upon Christian faith and sense of nationhood, with open acknowledgement of the merit of those who regarded it as 'an unjustifiable war'.[16] Scottish presbyterians felt extreme unease in fighting a foe with close religious beliefs to themselves, and Scottish newspapers backed the war with some reluctance. A. H. Charteris, the most prominent minister of the time, reflected this schizo-phrenia when he spoke of 'the growing respect with which the enemy has been regarded, promising ultimate concord; [and] the religious emotions which have been awakened'. This was coded language for confusion over moral purpose and who had 'the right' in this war. Bolstered by the 'mud-dling' incompetence of British generals and the war office, and despite the patriotic support of our army, the Boers were somehow not a real enemy, but one that reminded Britons by example of their own failing Christianity.[17]

The Edwardian religious horizon was thus confused – outwardly opti-mistic, but inwardly clouded with doubts and confusions. For Anglicans, faith was part of a patriotic heritage, but one that had contested mean-ings. For many Nonconformists, the Victorian inheritance demanded a reverence for an evangelical-style, upbeat rhetoric. But amongst many immigrant groups such as Catholics and the Jews, the need for sustaining identity in a sometimes hostile society put emphasis upon faith as a community bond rather than as an individualistic piety. Religion became a focus, often internalised within homes, churches and synagogues, where it became intensely ritualised in family and community. Religious ritual and ideas remained important, making the people still receptive to religious culture. It infused much of their daily lives.

Religion in everyday life

Two different ethoses dominated British Christianity. The first was of a relaxed and undemanding religion that called for decency and good works, avoidance of excess and a certain level of obedience to ecclesiastical authority. This infused much of the Church of England and to a certain degree the Church of Scotland. These churches enjoyed popular acceptance in part because of their willingness to *be undemanding* of adherents – to accept mildness of manner, good behaviour and periodic outward devotion as sufficient evidence that a person was 'religious'. The second ethos was that of evangelicalism. This was favoured by most of the Protestant dissenting churches, as well as some in the Church of England and Church of Scotland. It was by its very nature louder and more intrusive. It offered a style of religion based on activity and commitment that was employed by many denominations. It demanded people strive much harder in their religious life, be attentive on churchgoing and church obligations, stricter in morals and behaviour, and to be seen to be so. Between these two ethoses, British religious culture in the first half of the twentieth century was to involve a constant negotiation.

The evangelical question, 'What is the state of your soul?' stood as the brutish, insolent interrogation that the British citizen faced and, for many, feared on a daily basis in the Edwardian period. It would be more rarely heard in polite society of the middle classes, but still even there, as amongst the working classes, it was a presence even when unspoken. There was an assumption of it in evangelical exchange, to which the majority felt that they had no satisfactory answer. The response, 'It's none of your business', was rarely invoked. Excluding the High and Catholic Church positions, this was a society in which Christian expectations were led by the purity of the evangelical; every other position was either a liberalisation and a watering down from purity, or worse, an abandonment of respectability altogether to secular socialism or

Analysis: Faith and new types of war, 1900 and 2001

Here is a newspaper writer reflecting on how Britain deserved to be defeated in war because of the greater religious faith of an enemy:

Under the apparent calmness there is a kind of panic. The trial is of quite a new kind. It was remarked some years ago that the Western world had ceased to fear the incidence of a sudden and vast calamity. Great earthquakes, desolating famines, outbreaks of disease fatal to huge populations, had scarcely happened within the memory of man. We found it difficult to understand the idea of Europe suspending marriage, lest the children produced should be too miserable, or the bursting under a great terror from all the restraints of religion and morality ... Especially in this country we had ceased to feel any real fear about war. We were strong, our Government was trusted, our generals and soldiers were thought capable of meeting the greatest antagonists. Worse than this, the idea of GOD had almost passed away from the general mind as expressed in the newspapers, or came only in a rare and fitful gleam. The GOD of the governing classes, if He existed at all, was thought of as a great and good-natured friend of Britain. Moral considerations had hardly any place for the time. ... Now things are changed. The customariness of our well-being has been broken. We have encountered serious checks in conflict with an army we despised, and have discovered that Boer farmers at the last outposts of civilisation were better equipped, more skilled in strategy than our own men, and quite as brave – they could not be braver. The result is seen in an exaggerated dismay. Our newspapers have been full of gloom, and it has been singular to observe the note of terror and suffering in such a newspaper as the Daily Mail, *which urged the war most vehemently, and was most contemptuous of the adversaries.*[18]

This newspaper column could almost have been written in 2001, for it reflects almost precisely the reactions of some commentators to the Al-Qaeda attack of 9/11 on the USA. But the article was actually written one hundred years earlier, in 1900.

The twentieth century began and ended with two wars against what were seen as highly religious foes. They were seen as new types of war, partly for that reason. The first was the war against the Boers in South Africa in 1899–1902, and the second was the 'war on terrorism', declared by the American, British and other governments after the attack by Al-Qaeda in 2001. Commentators saw this as contrasting with weakening British faith in both 1900 and 2001, and also as challenging a blinkered British vision of the benign nature of the world, life and progress. The Boers were Protestant Christians in South Africa being fought by British imperial armies. Boers placed Christian religion at the forefront of their racial identity, and the Reformed Protestantism to which they adhered was very similar to many branches of British Nonconformity, especially presbyterianism. As news of opening hostilities reached Britain in late 1899, a sense of moral unease developed. It created critical reflection on the calmness of late Victorian Britain, its moral sureness and the strength of the Christian and imperial mission that the country was engaged in on many continents. One writer said that the 'Boers are right, and that God is on their side'.[19] English and Scots Nonconformists, as well as Anglicans, were split by a war against the first Christian foe for nearly fifty years. Some commentators felt that the Boers were not right, but the strength of their Christian faith gave them a right to win their new form of war because that faith was lost to the British people.[20]

A very similar concern for religion promoting new forms of warfare, and an awakening from stupor, arose from the attacks on the USA on 11 September 2001. Islamic fundamentalist terrorists associated with the Al-Qaeda organisation launched suicide aeroplane attacks on the World Trade Center in New York and the Pentagon in Washington. The similarities in reaction across the century are striking. British commentators were again dazzled by the role of faith in new warfare: 'a brilliantly orchestrated feat of planning, coordination and execution backed by formidable religious convictions'.[21] In 1900, the apparently failing imperial nation was being defined by its failure to be fully Christian. In 2001, the apparently enfeebled West was being defined by its failure of Christian or any faith – essentially its secular condition. 'This week is one of the darkest in our history,' wrote a Brighton minister. 'It is to be feared that the present will be but a gloomy Christmastide for British people; the war obscures everything, and it is deemed unfitting to take part in the festivities.'[22] This was written at Christmas 1899, but could easily have been written in 2001.

bohemian disreputability. The deepest disparagement came in the elite term of ridicule 'heathens' – those who were characteristically poor, lower working class, inhabiting a world of slum and street life in which God was apparently absent, and about whom this term could connote an association with 'other' races overseas. Though biblical scholars challenged its use for being a mistranslation (of 'Gentile nations' rather than unbelievers),[23] churchmen still used it in the 1910s when dividing the people into 'the believers' and 'the heathens', thereby appealing to those middle classes who harboured a distaste for working-class character.

But Christianity was not uniform. The temper and style of Anglicanism in different parishes varied greatly – between extremes of the High and

Low Church camps. Whether a particular English village or town was High, Low or Broad Church depended on the history of the community and the inclinations of the local elites (usually the landowners). The vicar would be appointed by the bishop, often selected by the landowner, in the full knowledge of those inclinations. Yet, for many ordinary parishioners, unless they travelled to worship in other parishes or dioceses, awareness of the High–Low Church division was often limited, and discussion of it is rare in autobiographies or in oral testimony of the Anglican laity. Other divisions and changes were much more commented upon. One was the nature of the Church of England's establishment status and how this operated in popular culture. Flora Thompson relates how the death of one vicar in her Oxfordshire village brought a change in regime. The old vicar, Mr Coulsden, was seen as a 'gentleman', an imposing and aloof individual, clearly a social class removed from the ordinary parishioners, on a par with the major landowner. But the new vicar around 1900, Mr Delafield, was of 'the new order', more casual and was 'not proud and stuck up', greeting all with a 'Hail fellow, well met!' attitude that endeared him to some but annoyed others. Flora was sensitive to the fine judgements of the time, noting how Delafield dressed in 'well-worn flannels and a Norfolk jacket' that were 'very dark grey, of course; any light shade would have been too revolutionary'.[24]

The minister or priest, in Scotland as in England, was equally a figure of great local stature, marking the popular as well as religious culture of the community. This reflected how Christian religion was marbled through the everyday life, work and culture of the British people – no matter the dominant local form of religion. On the Catholic island of Eriskay in the Western Isles in the early years of the century, Father Allan assembled the entire fishing fleet in the harbour on the Feast of Our Lady in May and said Mass on board one of the boats. In many homes throughout Britain, children (especially of the working classes) were packed off to Sunday school to establish the family's place in the Christian community. Robert Roberts noted in Salford that Whitsuntide was preceded by a temporary influx of recruits to Sunday schools, 'all sent by their mothers to see their children walk in new clothes with the religious processions' – Protestants on Monday, and Roman Catholics on Friday. 'In one family we knew of,' he goes on, 'the desire to testify openly for the Lord was so strong that an elder son sneaked out at night and "did a job" to provide the wherewithal for his sisters' white dresses.'[25]

Christianity penetrated popular culture in many ways. In 1899, the Anglican newspaper the *Church Times* ridiculed what it jokingly called

The respectable family at church: dressed in 'Sunday best', this is how the ideal family wished to be observed in the Edwardian period. Note the strong expression of femininity in the young girl's dress. (Mary Evans Picture Library)

'the Undecimarian Heresy' – the notion held by narrow-minded clergy that the only lawful time to worship God was on Sundays at 11 am.[26] Clerical condemnation of non-attenders was ironic. Hundreds of thousands who didn't go to church were married women and female servants who stayed at home to prepare Sunday lunch – probably the most widespread Christian ritual in the British family in the first seventy years of the twentieth century. By 1900, it had developed into an occasion for affirming the family, and its Christian respectability. For the non-churchgoing family too, it was a vital occasion. Margaret Penn, brought up in a rural industrial village in south-east Lancashire, recalled in the household of her own adoptive parents:

Sunday dinner at the Winstanleys, as indeed in every other cottage, was the big event of the week, and Mrs Winstanley, aware of its importance, spared neither time nor trouble to make it enjoyable. It was the only dinner meal of the week at which they all sat down together, and it was

the only day on which they had a piece of hot roast butcher's meat. It
was pleasant walking home from Sunday school to anticipate the roast
beef and Yorkshire pudding, with a big rice pudding or apple pie to
follow, and a strong cup of sweet tea to wash it all down with before
setting out again for afternoon Sunday school.[27]

Food was important to the affirmation of religious identity and ritual. In Judaism, the making and eating of kosher food (especially the Friday night meal) was of increasing importance in the maintenance of Jewish identity amongst immigrants, as so much of the faith became asserted in the home rather than in the more open Jewish communities of Eastern Europe. With Christianity, especially in Nonconformist chapels in England, the chapel itself was an important venue for food. In Harrogate in the 1900s and 1910s, Robert Walker recalled the chapel anniversaries at which ladies dished out plates of boiled ham and tea from urns. He remembered also the temperance club tea parties for youngsters with more boiled ham and tea: 'boiled ham seemed to come very much into the picture, doesn't it. [Laughter] Tea parties of this sort and little lectures on the evils of drink.'[28] The ubiquity of the Sunday lunch was staggering. Robert Roberts recalled that: 'On the whole, it was a poor household indeed that did not try to get some kind of meat to make a Sunday dinner.'[29] Food was also used by the churches to attract children; Sunday-school treats of sweets, fruit and pies were commonplace.

The young, indeed, were the main object of interest to organised religion in the Edwardian period. The Sunday school had reached the height of its influence in the 1890s, attaining the status of the largest voluntary organisation in British history. In Margaret Penn's Methodist-dominated industrial village of Hollins Green in north-west England, all the children went to Sunday school: 'They all liked Sunday School, and only illness kept them away.' Pupils, especially girls, aspired to become Sunday school teachers: 'To be a Sunday School teacher was considered the greatest honour attainable in the chapel, and Hilda earnestly looked forward to the time when she too would sit on a Windsor chair with her scholars ranged cosily round three sides of her, expounding to them the teachings of the Gospel, and explaining the parables in plain, simple language.'[30]

The regime for children was impressive. Mr Wash from Halstead in Essex recalled that Sunday was strictly observed. He reported that 'we went to the Sunday school, and then from Sunday school into Chapel. Father went Sunday morning in the morning. Mother stopped at home to cook the meal. Sunday afternoon, back to Sunday school again. Then, we'd, you know, have a walk afterwards, not with the family, with the Sunday school sort of friends. And then Sunday tea, and then back to chapel in the evening ... including mother in the evening, you see, but not in the morning because Mother was cooking the meal. And that was the Sunday programme.'[31]

Not every day was like a Sunday, but weekday religious activities were also numerous. In the period 1890–1914, religious groups were being challenged by new 'secular' attractions – including cinema. In response, the nature of religious organisation changed to keep up with social taste. This was the height of what one historian has described as the 'associational ideal', with church and independent voluntary organisations providing a series of leisure activities dedicated to religious and moral objectives. Many were aimed at children – notably boys, the most troublesome for the churches. Congregations built church halls to provide venues on weekday evenings for new moral, militaristic and adventure organisations.

There were long-standing temperance and teetotal organisations: the Band of Hope for Protestant children, the League of the Cross for Roman Catholic adults and children, and the White Ribboners for women and children. But the growing fad was for the adventure of Empire, encouraged by boys' stories and novels of the period, leading to uniformed organisations with militaristic activities – including rifle drill and evening target practice on shooting ranges. There were the Boys' Brigades (often called the BBs, founded in 1883 with a Nonconformist leaning, and strong in Scotland and the provinces), the Church Lads' Brigade (founded in 1891 within the Anglican Church), the Boy Scouts (founded in 1907–8 as denominationally independent, but came to be often congregationally based), the Girl Guides (founded in 1910 as a partner to the Scouts) and various offshoots of these (such as bodies for younger children and for naval interests). The BBs mushroomed in the wake of the Boer War, recruiting 6,000 officers and boys. In 1902, almost 12,000 members of the BBs, the Church Lads' Brigade, the Catholics Boys' Brigade and the Jewish Lads' Brigade turned up for a Coronation Review for King Edward VII. By 1909, there were 63,000 BBs alone, but coming up rapidly in popularity was the mushrooming Scouting movement, and in 1911, after the next coronation (of King George V), 26,000 Scouts assembled for review at Windsor. Within seven years, there were to be 300,000 Scouts in Britain and around the world. The combination of religion with an imperial militarism was a recipe that attracted young boys, especially when they left Sunday school at the age of 9 or 10, and these organisations for both boys and girls were to be a staple of congregational activity in Britain for the next eighty years.[32] In this way, religiosity was combined with patriotism, adventure and recreational activities to become an important characteristic of twentieth-century Christian culture.

Yet, British religion did not become all play for children. There was a strength, even fierceness, to Christian culture, rooted in working-class life – whether for artisans or the extremely poor. Kate Taylor was born in 1891 in Pakenham in Suffolk, the fourteenth of fifteen children. Her father was an irregular rural labourer – a seasonal worker in farming, timber felling, bark-peeling, faggot-making, hurdle-making, sheep shearing and droving. The family lived in the 1900s in a row of four small cottages, sharing one washing copper and one oven, and so poor were they that the children paid for the grinding of the family corn by gathering acorns for the miller's pigs, and earned more by stone-picking, and by rook-scaring in newly-drilled fields from dawn to dusk on Sundays for twopence. In the midst of this struggle with poverty, religion was vital. Kate recalled in her autobiography (written around 1973) that her father had been brought up in the strict Plymouth Brethren, but by then was in the Salvation Army where he was a bandsman: 'I thought him very handsome in his uniform, but unfortunately often he would bring the bandsmen home with him to Sunday dinner. We were shut out in the backhouse whilst the bandsmen enjoyed the meal mother had prepared for us. The bandsmen would practise most of the afternoon in preparation for the evening service. After they had gone we would scavenge for any crumbs they had left from dinner. Father was foolish in his generosity, but his fellow bandsmen knew he had a family. They also knew our poverty-stricken condition. They were selfish and thoughtless in taking the dinner we needed.'[33]

In a similar way in the west of England, Fred Boughton was born in 1897 in the Forest of Dean in Gloucestershire, where his father was a traditional miner with an acre of land and sheep-grazing rights. His autobiography (written in 1974) locates religion in the everyday of family life, demonstrating the way in which he recalled in idyllic tones its suffusing of life:

The way the Foresters lived in those hard days would be impossible today. They never wanted anything they could do without, and their home life was wonderful. Our home life was typical and on a winter's night the fire would be burning bright, with a pot of stew on the hob and a tin of bacon roasting in the oven, the cat on the mat and, best of all, Mother would be sitting in her wicker armchair, knitting. Father would be mending boots, and each of us kids had a job, some knitting, some making rag mats, some cooking. Mother taught us to do every job in the house. I made myself a pair of knee breeches out of odd pieces of cord. Then when bedtime came we had a good hot supper. Then we all knelt round Mother's knee and said the Lord's Prayer and Father would say a few words about the goodness of God. Then we sang 'The day is past and over' and with humble thankful hearts ran off to bed. In the morning we sang 'We thank thee for another night of quiet sleep and rest.'[34]

Two important characteristics stand out from these memoirs – the recollection of a lost golden age, and the centrality of religion to that loss. Autobiographers of the Edwardian period (writing in the 1960s and 1970s) were remembering at a time when people were acutely aware of the decline of organised religion and of old-fashioned moral values. Both family and community of the 1900s were being recalled as defined by religious values.

Britain's Christian culture was strong, but with great variation. In a very poor part of Salford near Manchester, Robert Roberts recalled the dominance of religious identity but the lack of churchgoing: 'The great majority of Protestants, however, did not "practice" themselves, but saw to it, perhaps as a conscience salver, that their children went regularly to Sunday School.' He acknowledged that there was an underlying Christian core to the white racial identity of the slums, and racial or religious diversity was for most Britons barely discernible. 'Down Zinc Street,' he wrote of Salford before 1914, 'whatever one's social or economic position, everybody was "Christian"; therefore none of us liked the Jews. Not that we knew any: we detested them on principle.'[35] Racial tensions were often of this shadow variety, the product of a popular culture of stereotyping and caricature, not necessarily of familiarity. Victimhood was imagined by whites, not felt, but this fed bigotry just as satisfactorily. The first Sikh gurdwara in Britain opened in Putney, London, in 1911, and the first Islamic mosque opened in Woking in 1912 (following an 1891 Liverpool Muslim Institute founded by the white convert William H. Quilliam).[36] The numbers of black people were so small that racial tension was geographically limited, often to docks and ports.

Much more common was tension between traditions within Christianity. The most widespread was that between all Protestants on the one hand and Roman Catholics on the other. This was at its height in Ireland, especially in the north-east of the island in the six counties centred around Belfast and London/Derry, and troubles mounted in the early 1910s when a movement of Protestant para-militarisation rose under the leadership of Edward Carson to 'defend' Ireland from both Roman Catholicism and republicanism. The fight for Ireland was to consume the island in the 1910s, and to keep religious identity at the forefront of a society fractured into two major camps. By contrast, sectarian identity was less important but still strong on the British mainland. Catholic communities in Lancashire, Lanarkshire and in London had developed a strong association with the Catholic Church that acted as a point of identity, supported by an important cradle-to-grave social system for a community that was characterised by low-skilled jobs, poor housing and a great deal of poverty. In a similar way, the Jewish communities of London, Manchester, Glasgow and other smaller (often coastal) towns combined religion with language and cultural difference to sustain strong identities in poor working-class districts. In these ways, religion was tied to racial and political identities in everyday life.

Tensions were also strong between churches that were close together in faith terms. A heritage of ecclesiastical schism and social difference was remembered within families and streets. Margaret Penn described how in her Lancashire industrial village the dominant Methodism was split between the majority United Methodists, who were wealthy enough to have a proper red-brick and yellow-sandstone chapel and Sunday school, and the poor and smaller Primitive Methodists, who 'had a poor corrugated iron building with no separate Sunday School at all'. The split between them was 'over a grave question of policy, severing old friendships and causing life-long feuds even among close relations'. With time, the United's church had become shabbier whilst the Primitives had saved and saved and erected 'a magnificent new chapel of even redder brick and yellower stone'. Feelings hardened into a social distance, as Penn described in 1947 in the affectionate ironic tones of her older age:

... it was, generally speaking, firmly believed by the Uniteds that the Word, as preached in the showy new building of the Primitives, was not the true Word at all; and the faithful Uniteds looked down more than ever on the Primitives, regarding them as no more than heathens who had evolved some outlandish faith of their own ... a faith which, though it might sustain their stubborn pride adequately enough in this

world, was none the less a poor earthly thing that would never gain
them admittance through the shining pearly gates into the Life
Everlasting.[37]

Religious tensions and bigotry were part of the cultural formula that kept British streets the sites for competing religious preachers, tract distributors, temperance activists and philanthropists on the lookout for poor children to be salvaged from destitution. Religious conversion, argument and rescue were a daily diet in urban society. Everyday life buzzed with the competing demands of religious campaigners for one cause or other, with brass bands playing hymns or workers listening to a street preacher. Not all listened, though. Men went to public houses and licentious shows, they frequented prostitutes and boisterous sports events, and they gambled illegally, started fights and committed crimes. So, whilst many Christians merely acknowledged their religion in obeying the commands of convention in family prayer or Sunday quiet, others felt the call to attempt the redemption of people's immortal souls.

The culture of religious revival

Religious revivals were things much spoken of in British culture between the 1780s and the 1950s. A 'revival' occurred when Christians experienced a quickening of their sense of religious identity, often expressed as the influence of 'the Holy Ghost'. Men and women were invited to see themselves as 'sinners', and were encouraged to accept Jesus Christ as their saviour. This was to be their 'conversion', 'rebirth' or 'salvation'. Often it occurred in revivalist religious meetings, where a rousing preacher and a deeply affected audience could instigate scenes of fitful crying, agonies of self-recrimination, wailing and crying out, and (in extreme cases) of speaking in tongues (when a person spoke in a foreign language previously unknown to him or her). Scholars of many backgrounds – historians, theologians, psychologists and sociologists – sought throughout the twentieth century to understand revivals and the individual's conversion.

Revivals had been known throughout Christian history, but two American evangelists in 1873 and 1874, Dwight Moody (a preacher) and Ira Sankey (an harmonium player and singer), set a model for the techniques of subsequent religious revivals – ranging from small-scale community missions to the use of vast auditoriums in what might be called 'arena evangelism'. The model became for preachers and lay evangelicals to work continuously to encourage communities of people to create the conditions of revival, and to use Moody and Sankey's formula for revival services: moving hymns, a short sermon and the call to the anxious to come forward for guidance and counselling. Increasingly, this came to be backed up in the twentieth century with a public relations system that used posters, leaflets, press and (by the 1950s) radio coverage to bombard the public.

This style of mission work developed from the 1880s in working-class districts of cities, mining villages and coastal fishing communities. There were mobile campaigns in 'tent missions' creating summer circus-style visits to inner-city and industrial towns, street-corner preachers, tract distributors, door-to-door evangelists and workers targeting children. The new century was heralded with an example of this. In November and December 1899, there was an eight-week evangelistic campaign in Glasgow, with nightly religious meetings in most districts and adjacent industrial suburbs. In the lunch hours in central Glasgow, church meetings were packed – with the ground floor reserved for businessmen, whilst the gallery was reserved for shop girls from the large retail warehouses. In the evenings, Gaelic-speaking Highlanders went to meetings producing 600 to 1,000 'anxious inquirers' per night. The young were especially targeted. Over 9,000 boys and girls aged 10 to 20 years were 'personally dealt with as anxious inquirers'. The organiser said: 'God is saving the situation for the Church ten years hence, by converting the young people today.'[38]

This kind of continuous evangelism was accompanied by vigorous moral campaigning. Temperance promoters sought legal action to close public houses and reform men's behaviour. At the same time, middle-class churchgoers tended to find revivalism and evangelistic preaching as 'unfashionable' – what we might describe as 'uncool' and socially 'common'. Many clergy in the mainstream Protestant churches – even in the evangelical churches – were by 1900 really quite shy of encouraging 'unseemly' scenes of religious enthusiasm.

An American preacher, Reuben Archer Torrey (1856–1928), became heir to Moody's design of mass revival in organised events. Torrey wrote a handbook on revivalist methods and 'soul-winning'. One technique he advocated was the tent mission: 'The tent itself awakens curiosity. It looks like a circus.' It attracted those whom he targeted most – 'Roman Catholics ... thieves, murderers, drunkards and abandoned women'. To put on revival meetings day and night, week after week, would reach people who did not normally attend church. Torrey wrote in his handbook: 'The outside world's aroused to the fact that the church exists, and that there is such a thing as religion. They begin to think about God, Christ, the Bible, eternity, heaven and hell.'[39]

This was 'in-your-face' propagandisation of a kind that would later become better known in commercial advertising. Torrey and his student Charles M. Alexander put it into practice on a world revivalist tour, taking in Japan, China, Australia, New Zealand, India and, in 1903, Britain. They held revival missions in London, Edinburgh, Liverpool, Dublin and Birmingham, claiming 7,000 converts, 7,000 in Cardiff in September 1904, then more in a sustained campaign in Liverpool in which they used the 12,000-seater Tournament Hall to assemble the world's largest choir of 3,658. Then, Torrey and Alexander went to London, and in a mission from February to June 1905 centred on the Albert Hall, they held 202 meetings, attracted 1,114,650 attenders and brought over 17,000 to conversion. By the end of their world tour, they claimed 102,000 converts – 70,000 of them in Britain.[40] Their work helped to make revivalist culture commonplace in Britain in these years, and in Wales they helped to lay the basis for an extraordinary development.

On 27 September 1904 in Wales, a former collier and smithy worker, Evan Roberts, had an experience of the Holy Ghost, and felt he had seen a heavenly vision. A month later, on 30 October, he was preaching at Newcastle Emlyn, when he and others in the congregation felt something 'different'. Rachel Phillips recalled: 'There was some silent influence in the service touching the strings of the heart. I could not restrain from weeping through the service, and the people, especially the young, felt this influence. I could not see the face of Roberts; those who could see it told me that his face was shining, his countenance was changing, and appeared as if under a wonderful influence.'[41] Prayer meetings and moving religious worship followed in the next two weeks, in most of which young Evan Roberts played a key role. On 12 November 1904, the *Western Mail* newspaper based in Cardiff carried an account of a religious service at Loughor, west of Swansea:

The proceedings commenced at 7 o'clock and they lasted without a break until 4.30 o'clock on Friday morning. During the whole of this time the congregation were under the influence of deep religious fervour and exaltation. There were about 400 people present in the chapel when I took my seat at about nine o'clock. The majority of the congregation were females ranging from young misses of twelve to matrons with babies in their arms. Mr Roberts is a young man of rather striking appearance. He is tall and distinguished looking, with an intellectual air

*about his clean shaven face. . . . There is nothing theatrical about his
preaching. He does not seek to terrify his hearers, and eternal torment
finds no place in his theology. Rather does he reason with the people
and show them by persuasion a more excellent way. I had not been
many minutes in the building before I felt that this was no ordinary
gathering. Instead of the set order of proceedings to which we were
accustomed at the orthodox religious service, everything here was left to
the spontaneous impulse of the moment. The preacher too did not
remain in his usual seat. For the most part he walked up and down the
aisles, open Bible in hand, exhorting one, encouraging another, and
kneeling with a third to implore blessing from the throne of grace. A
young woman rose to give out a hymn which was sung with deep
earnestness. While it was being sung several people dropped down from
their seats as if they had been struck, and commenced crying for pardon.
Then from another part of the chapel would be heard the resonant voice
of a young man reading a portion of the scripture. While this was in
progress there came from the gallery an impassioned prayer from a
woman crying aloud that she had repented of her ways and was
determined to lead a better life henceforward. All this time Mr Roberts
went in and out among the congregation offering kindly words of advice
to kneeling penitents. He would ask them if they believed, the reply in
one instance being, 'No, I would like to believe but I can't. Pray for me'.
Then the preacher would ask the audience to join him in the following
prayer: 'Anfon yr Yspryd yn awr, er mwyn Iesu Grist, Amen' (Send the
Holy Spirit for Jesus Christ's sake, Amen). This prayer would be
repeated about a dozen times by all present, when the would be convert
would suddenly rise and declare with triumph, 'Thank God I have now
received salvation, never again will I walk in the way of sinners'.*[42]

Within two days, *The Times* in London had picked up the story, and
spoke of Wales 'being visited by a remarkable religious enthusiasm'. Its
reporter noted that Evan Roberts' ten-hour overnight services at Loughor
were 'marked by scenes of much religious excitement'. By 21 November,
the movement had spread to the mines of Glamorgan, and was entering
Bridgend, Cardiff and Monmouthshire.[43]

In 1904–5, Wales was in the grip of the most extraordinary religious
event of twentieth-century Britain. An apparently spontaneous revival of
religion, based on the evangelical conversion or rebirth, spread across the
whole of the province and into parts of England. Hundreds of thousands
were affected, and Welsh society was dramatically, if only temporarily,

transformed. Evan Roberts, its leading figure, toured the country preaching, and converts were made everywhere. Born near Loughor, the ninth of fourteen children, and leaving school at 12 to become a miner,[44] he belonged to the Calvinistic Methodists, and had begun in December 1903 a distinctive style of preaching, accompanied by singers (including his brother Dan), in which he recounted his personal spiritual experiences. In one, he recalled being depressed in mood about society's attitude to God, and took a night-time walk in his garden: 'About 4 o'clock in the morning, with remarkable suddenness, I saw a face in the hedge, full of scorn, hatred and derision, and heard a laugh as of defiance. It was the Prince of this world who exulted in my despondency. Then there appeared with equal suddenness another figure, gloriously arranged in white, bearing in his hand a flaming sword borne aloft. The sword fell athwart the first figure, and it instantly disappeared.' He interpreted this for his hearers as 'Satan is put to flight, Amen'. The congregation thereupon burst out with one accord, 'Hallelujah, hallelujah, praise the Lord!'[45]

Roberts was drawing on a tradition in Welsh culture of describing the conversion crisis – involving repentance, faith, assurance and forgiveness – in visual imaging using metaphors from the everyday and from the Bible. Visions of these were well known in Wales around 1900. One typical account comes from an old lady published ten months before the revival. She spoke of seeing two forms by her bed: 'I saw that the foremost had the most beautiful countenance I had ever seen; and I noticed his lovely fair hair was parted in the middle. Glancing at the other form, I saw he was black and ugly. "O, that is the devil," I said, and guessed the other was Jesus.' Such accounts were spread widely in Wales in the 1890s and 1900s in cheap religious books with colour prints depicting biblical scenes, and these may have given ideas for visions. And so Roberts and members of his congregations became prone to describing visions in highly emotional speeches, many published in the main Welsh newspapers, the *Western Mail* and *South Wales Daily News*, further cultivating this tradition. In one report, Roberts described 'a Roman in the act of nailing my Saviour to the Cross. I could see him kneeling on his arm; see the nails being driven in; see the hammer falling.'[46] Roberts was keen to interpret visions and these helped to spread awareness and heighten expectations.

Though women were reported as making up large proportions of many services, the impact on miners was astonishing. At the Curmaman Company coal pits, it was said at New Year 1905 that 'nearly all the ventilating doors underground have been covered with texts', biblical quotations chalked up by the miners.[47] And the results of the revival were 'measured' by how much manly vices were curtailed. Newspapers, politicians, chief constables and the clergy themselves reported on social improvement from the revival. The amount of alcohol consumed in Wales dropped dramatically, with reported emptying of public houses, a drop in drunkenness, and increased family expenditure on essentials such as food, heat and rent.[48] In Glamorganshire, lesser crimes had practically vanished in the last quarter of 1904, and the levels of major crimes also fell to the point of virtual extinction, with gaols lying empty, courts with no cases to try and police officers with nothing to do. Newspapers printed tables of the numbers of converts in each district. By March 1905, there were claims of 71,000 converts in South Wales and a further 10,000 in North Wales.

Meanwhile, the rest of the world sent invitations to Roberts to come and preach. In London, a mission run by Torrey at the Albert Hall felt the tide from Wales as crowds of men waited to go in: 'Numbers of them belonged to the collarless brigade; numbers to the class which usually frequents some cheap variety entertainment at this time.' An Anglican mission by the Bishop of London, interestingly, attracted large numbers of women.[49] In Scotland, there were hopes of getting Roberts to come to Glasgow to continue the work of revival that had been the object of persistent efforts over the previous five years. Roberts was the darling of British Protestantism, and the nation seemed to be opening the century with a religious event of a strength and intensity probably never before seen in an industrial society.

Yet, not everybody was pleased, and opposition to the revival was not hard to find. High Anglicans tended to denigrate it; one vicar said that: 'Most of them of the Church of England were shy – and even afraid – of revivals.' Some English correspondents dismissed the Welsh revival in a fog of racist commentary. One correspondent in *The Times* spoke of the Welsh Celt as being 'like the Jew, an invincible proof of the persistence of the race-type', comparing them to 'men sunk in ignorance and depravity' who, after a previous religious awakening in 1858, 'revealed a trail of immorality left by the revival, and showed how closely kin are sympathy and sensuality, emotion and lust', and condemning many Welsh people 'to end their days in rayless mania'. Other clergy complained of 'the unruliness of meetings' held by Roberts, their late hour, and the loss of respect for local pastors, whilst another called his movement 'a sham revival' led by someone who wished 'to be regarded as the fourth figure of the

Godhead'.[50] And many churchmen became highly suspicious over Roberts' antics in March 1905 when he locked himself away in a bedroom for six days, refusing to speak, and abandoning revival preaching amidst massive media attention. (See pages 66–8.)

It was not only jealous clergy who did not like Christian revivalism. Many in Edwardian Britain disliked being forced to accept it. Faith Dorothy Osgerby (1890–1976) was born at Beverley in East Yorkshire, the third in a family of seven children. Her father was a stonemason and cattle-dealer, and her mother was an imposing woman given to violence towards her children in the midst of a rather unhappy marriage. In her autobiography written in 1960, Faith gave vent at length to her feelings about religion:

Sundays were hateful days. My mother sent us to the Primitive Methodist Sunday School (much to the annoyance of Aunt Lizzie. She said all the family had always been Church [of England]). My mother sent us there because school began earlier and we had longer sessions and she wanted rid of us for as long as possible. What I learned there for my good I shall never know. The children behaved very badly (I suppose I did too). Teachers were a queer, mixed crowd who knew very little about what they were supposed to teach. They gave us to understand that we were all in danger of hell fire if we were not good. I knew there was no hope whatever for me.

Most of all I hated the time when an Evangelist came, because then I knew I should have to be 'saved' again. I shall never believe that it was right to teach little children religion in this frightening way. It made me unhappy for several days.

All those who wanted to be saved had to go forward near the pulpit and kneel on a cushion in front of everyone else. We went in groups. Some children absolutely refused to go and would have made a scene. If only I had dared! I remember on one occasion I made up my mind I wouldn't go, but unfortunately I happened to be sitting at the end of a row and the teacher (I remember her name was Miss Sissons) pushed me out into the gangway, so I was lost again. I remember we used to have to sing:

I'm H-A-P-P-Y
I'm H-A-P-P-Y
I know I am. I'm sure I am.
I'm H-A-P-P-Y

Because I'm S-A-V-E-D, etc
Through F-A-I-T-H, etc

Analysis: The silence of Evan Roberts, 1905

During the highly emotional Welsh revival of 1904–5, the missioner (lay leader) Evan Roberts claimed to be in verbal contact with the Holy Spirit. He maintained a punishing tour of the country, preaching to crowds everywhere. His movements and services were followed by the press in minute detail, as a celebrity religious figure.

In February 1905, Roberts failed to appear for a scheduled mission meeting at Briton Ferry. His secretary reported to the disappointed crowds that Roberts had said that 'the Spirit would not allow him to attend'. He then cancelled all engagements for several weeks, and holed up in the bedroom of a friend's house in Neath whilst all of Britain waited for news from him. He was due to expand his evangelistic tour to Liverpool (and there were invitations from the USA as well). He sent out written replies to written questions handed to him, and these were reported verbatim:

'I must remain silent for seven days. I must remain at Neath for this period. As for the reasons, I am not yet led to state them, but one issue of this silence is: If I am to prosper at Liverpool I must leave Wales without money – not even a penny in my purse. I can speak; I have the power; but I am forbidden to use it. It is not for me to question why, but to give obedience. I am sorry to cancel my engagements. It is the Divine Command. I am happy, and a Divine peace fills my soul.'[51]

Some evangelical papers were faintly hostile – mocking even – to Roberts' silence. *The Times* reported that Roberts had for seven days

Evan Roberts, the Welsh Evangelist. (Pembrokeshire Record Office, part of Pembrokeshire County Council. Reference HDX/1609/1)

'lived alone in a room at the house of his host, Mr. Rhys Jones', with no verbal communication with anyone. This aroused intense interest in the press, who camped outside the house in Neath, waiting on every sign and indication from the householder, Mr Jones, and submitting increasingly tense copy to the national and Welsh press. The public were held on tenterhooks. Newspaper reporting of Evan's silence veered from the reverential to the mocking. They were shocked that even his mother and his brother (who was also preaching in the revival) did not stop in Neath because Evan had said he would see nobody. Some papers mocked his claims to speaking with the Holy Spirit, whilst his silence was seen even by evangelical supporters as a 'breakdown'. Then, on the night of 2 March, he came out of his seclusion. The *British Weekly* reported:

On Thursday Mr. Roberts broke the silence he had so long maintained. In the morning his host, Mr Rhys Jones, of Godrecoed, Neath, heard footsteps on the stairs, and a moment later had the gratifying surprise of seeing Mr. Roberts standing before him, his face radiant with smiles. The revivalist told the assembled household that he had been in fierce conflict. He had had to contend with all the powers of earth and hell, but power had been given him and he had obtained victory. He looked rather pale and worn and delicate. He spent Friday quietly in the house and received a few visitors, including his brother, Mr. Dan Roberts ...

During his retirement, Mr. Roberts kept a diary. On the fifth day the entry in the diary contained the words:—

'I want to go to Palestine. I should like to go ere long, just to give my experiences afterwards to draw crowds to the foot of the Cross.' The entry on the sixth day contained a sequel to the Palestine wish:— 'You remember I said I would like to go to Palestine. Yes. Well, you know, I said I would have no money to go ... Well, a lady has written me to-day offering me £20 towards "one of the delightful trips to Palestine." Diolch (Praise).'[52]

The following day Roberts returned from Neath unexpectedly to his parents' home at Loughor. There he handed a prepared message to the press:

'Godrecoed, Neath, Saturday morning.— The principal object of the "silence" was not for the sake of my body, nor for my mind to have a rest, but to be a Sign. When I asked the Lord what was the object of the "Seven Days of Silence," He distinctly said — "As thy tongue was tied for seven days, so shall Satan be bound for seven times." Yours, under the guidance of the Spirit, Evan Roberts.'[53]

What happened in this silence was variously interpreted. *The Times* in London reported that the revival had lost some of its power because

Roberts was suffering from a nervous breakdown; he took only one service in the second week of March, and 'he was evidently far from well'.[54] Roberts maintained a longer silence after the revival subsided. For two decades he said virtually nothing about it, finally speaking in 1926, when he ascribed six causes to it: the regular work of the ministry; the unlimited resources of spiritual life in the churches; the wealth of biblical knowledge created by Sunday-school learning; Christian discipline; and the spirit of prayer at ordinary Welsh prayer meetings. The spirit of the revival, he added, came 'from the Great White Throne of God'.[55] Meanwhile, evangelicals were divided on how to report the silence; many histories of the movement failed to mention the events at Neath in February–March 1905.

... It was awful to think we had all to go to hell fire. Well, after a few days this awful burden seemed to grow lighter and I felt better again. Then I realized I was being punished because I had been naughty again. I was indeed a lost soul. My heart was black! There was no hope for me. Oh! Well! What's the use? If I am to go to hell, I might as well give up trying ...[56]

It was often the case that the culture of evangelical revival dominated the experience of children, whether they liked it or not. Flora Thompson's village of Candleford in Oxfordshire was mostly Church of England, and followed a relatively relaxed Christian culture in which the majority did not go to church on a Sunday. But yet the evangelical born-again Methodist had a powerful impact on everyday life, challenging the indolent with their lukewarm religion. Such intrusiveness was guiltily accepted, and rarely challenged. Only one young post worker stood up to the born-again postman in her village. When 'asked in an earnest tone, "Miss Lane, are you a Christian?" [she] replied haughtily, "I do not see that whether I am or not is any business of yours, but, if you particularly want to know, I am a Christian in the sense that I live in a Christian country and try to order my life according to Christian teaching." ' To which the postman 'only shook his head and said mournfully, "Ah, I see you've not found Christ yet." '[57] The rarity of riposte to evangelical interrogation speaks volumes about the acceptance of Christian culture in late Victorian and Edwardian society, and how its evangelical version was reluctantly accepted as its irresistible conscience.

Religion pervaded so much of life. It was to be found in labour and trades unionism, and in the battle for women's rights, signalled in prayers and religious hymns sung in defiance at strike meetings and suffragette meetings. In death and mourning, religion was ever present. Kathleen Woodward recalls how working-class women of Bermondsey, living hard lives in exploitation, swung between astrology and Christianity for comfort in death; she remembered one who 'had always felt that, as with a few prayers, a verse or two from the Bible "can't do no 'arm and might do some good" '.[58]

By the late spring and summer of 1905, the Welsh revival was quietening and life started to return to some form of normality. The lasting effects could be life-changing for some converts, but for others the impact was temporary. One of the most remarkable features of the Welsh revival was that it affected hundreds of thousands of miners so passionately when, within twenty years, men in the same occupation would become strongly radicalised by socialism and an atheistic communism.

Womanly virtues and manly vices

Christian culture of the early twentieth century inherited from the Victorians a highly gendered notion of religion and piety. Men and women were conceived in cultural terms as having different religious attributes. This cultural division affected how religion was discussed, portrayed and experienced by individuals.

Women were culturally portrayed as the epitome of piety. Piety was pure, undefiled, chaste, soft and homely, conceived as a feminine virtue characterised by a disciplined body and disciplined mind. Women's very movements in the Edwardian dresses of the period – slow, ponderous, appearing to glide effortlessly across the floor – symbolised the ideal. This put incredible pressure upon women to behave, dress and aspire in very strict ways. 'If a woman is good she is religious,' wrote the novelist J. M. Barrie, reflecting the cultural understanding of the period.[59] But it also meant for men a need to submit to womanly virtues in order to be more god-like. A man was expected in Edwardian culture to suppress innate masculine qualities – of temptations to drink, uncouth speech, physical brutishness and dissipation. But a man could never be wholly like a woman, and for him religious piety was represented as an unattainable goal. Women were the religious solution, men were the religious problem.

The Edwardian period introduced vigorous exploration in newspapers and magazines of how the female body should be nurtured as a symbol of Christian goodness. In the evangelical press, massive advertisements teased the woman reader over the location and nature of female virtue.

The following advert for corsets 'plays' with keywords in the lexicon of the Edwardian discourse on femininity:

There is no virtue in wearing uncomfortable garments and not necessarily any worldliness in dressing with good judgment and taste. Readers of this indispensable weekly are far more likely to develop an ideal life and demeanour if free from anxiety or irritation as to their garments, and if the 'Female form divine' has surroundings of comfort in daily life and activity. That at least is our standpoint in making known the merits and excellences of P & S Corsets [made from] Rustless Zairod. W. Pretty & Sons, Ipswich.[60]

The words here toy with femininity: 'worldliness' (which women must avoid, staying in their homely sphere), 'anxiety' (a symptom in the psychology of women's weaknesses that lead to fainting and hysteria) and 'activity' (suggestive of a greater liberation from the home and hearth). The advertising copy quoted here is an acknowledgement of how the Edwardian woman was (and should be) a worrier about her worry – how to worry was a necessary female activity, but how the worry itself could undermine physical and mental health. This reflected the growing popular knowledge at the time of Freudian psychology that linked women's religious tension with their supposed hysteria. The 'hysterical woman' had become a common image of both the scientific and popular imagination, and religion was perceived to be a major contributor to it. So, the advertisement teases women about their concerns with the quite rigid discourse on the virtuous women of home and hearth, and the fear of 'feminine complaints' deriving from distress induced by anxiety – mixed with the desire for just a little more freedom and worldly activity.

The same trend in magazine advertisements was apparent in the scores of medicinal compounds sold through religious newspaper columns, almost all targeted at the middle-class woman fearful of those anxieties. For instance, Iron-Ox Tiny Tonic Tablets claimed to help 'in strengthening and restoring weakened nerves, in producing quiet, natural sleep, in stimulating the appetite, in bringing worn and nervous women back to health'.[61] This proximity of advertising copy on the feminine body to articles aimed at the religious reader brought the gendered construction of Christianity into very sharp relief.

The effects of religious revival were gendered. Women and girls would faint as they came to Christ, whilst men tended to fall down weeping, struck weak in mental anguish. This division was widely represented in stories and newspaper articles, engendering a wider cultural knowledge of

how to behave in religious events. More often than not, the actual evince-
ment of conversion was something that was quintessentially about
empowering women and weakening men. The mission overseas was
expressed in the terms of exporting this virtuous form of manhood. A
Baptist minister, in celebrating in 1900 the twentieth anniversary of the
Baptist Missionary Society's Congo mission, referred to 'the marvellous
results in the establishment of churches, in the multiplication of converts,
in the creation of a new ideal of manhood'.[62] As the decade progressed,
books with titles like *Perfect Manhood* and *Perfect Womanhood* appeared
from the pens of Christian clergy, illustrating the intensifying examination
of how religious identity was deeply buried in separate conceptions of
male and female religious worth.

This made clothing a moral and religious issue. Fred Boughton from
the Forest of Dean, like so many autobiographers and oral-history interviewees, recollected the summer Sunday-school treat and procession early
in the century. Starting at the Methodist chapel, the children moved off
with a brass band in front, two pupils carrying the Sunday-school banner,
the classes marching in twos for four miles past crowds of people lining
the roadside, all trying to look their best. Fred recalled: 'Mother used to
make us sailors' blouses. The girls had blue skirts, and the boys had blue
knicks. The girls had two long plaits tied with ribbon and we all had coronation mugs hanging round our necks and tied with red, white and blue
ribbon.' James Brady in Rochdale in Lancashire also recalled of the 1900s:
'Even for the annual Whitsuntide processions when we all turned out in
our Sunday best, me in a neat sailor-boy suit with a wide collar and
Nelson-type straw boater. I always conspired to hold a blue riband
attached to one of those high blue and gold banners depicting Christ on
The Mount.'[63]

The sailors' suits and their even more grandiose alternative, the Eton
suits, are widely remembered in later twentieth-century recollections of
Sunday-best attire. Boys almost universally hated these clothes. Ronald
Walker from Harrogate recalled: 'I was dressed, Heaven help me, in
sailor suits, dark blue in winter, white on summer days in summer when
you haven't to sit down anywhere for fear you'd dirty your backside,
until I got – I don't know, 8 or 9, and then I was put into, of all things,
an Eton suit for Sundays. And these were very much your Sunday
clothes.'[64] Such garb created a tension, a deliberate tension, between the
respectable Sunday-best attire that boys uniformly had to wear to
church, Sunday school and special community or family occasions, and
the normal attire worn during the most enjoyable pursuits – games and

football. The invocation of a sense of deprivation of natural male desire was quite deliberate; 'natural' masculinity was being suppressed.

It was quite the opposite to the impact of female Sunday-best dresses, which most women recalled with deep affection. A woman born in Scotland in 1898 recalled Edwardian churchgoing: 'The parade to church in our button boots and our parasols … black button boots we had on, and eh a black dress. It was awfy fancy made with frills, puff sleeves and everything.' Another recalls being taken for a new Sunday-best outfit, but she made a scene in the draper's shop and was threatened with the punishment of *not* going to church:

And I remember this day; I always wanted green, I was terrible for green when I was young, and … I remember mother got the thing and the woman brought this brown – the coat and, you know, the wee muff for your hands and a hat and a wee muff with the white and black tails on the wee fur and your muff was the same. And eh, that's what I got for, for going to the Sunday school and the Church. … mother was fair taken on with this brown rig out, you know, and it was green I wanted and I kicked up terrible. Oh my mother was fair ashamed; I stamped my feet … 'I don't want that brown, I don't like it!' … I didn't win, mind you, … I had to take the brown … Oh my, the lecture I got when I got home (laugh). No church for me on Sunday, I wouldn't get it. But I got the church.

An Anglican woman from Deepdale in Preston born in 1900 said: 'I always remember we got white silk dresses on for Good Friday, they must have been lovely and they took us for a long walk and then in the evening the vicar gave a film show just standing still pictures we called them and he would be in the pulpit with a long stick, pointing, showing you the life of Christ, every year showing you the same one, and we were the second pew from front, my mother always went to the second pew, looking up at him, you know, oh dear bless us, same thing every Good Friday, bless us.'[65]

Nearly all women had fond recollections of Sunday-best clothes. One who didn't was Faith Osgerby, who remembered the Sunday-best clothes as signifiers of other religious abuse: 'Children were spiteful and jealous. Girls flaunted their new clothes, poking fun at others not so fortunate. Altogether a horrid lot. Teachers had favourites. I hated Sunday School. I didn't grow very fast and my Sunday clothes fitted me for 3 or 4 years. How I hated that red coat and that beastly horrid green felt hat I could have stamped on!'[66] Much rode on women's dress and deportment. It plugged into a series of moral signs, as historian Ellen Ross pointed out. Not just the woman's, but the whole family's reputation between the extreme poles of rough and respectable were invariably located by wives and mothers in dress, their sexual, drinking and socialising habit, and their housekeeping and supervision of children.[67] So, by the simple expedient of sanctifying a young girl's garb in a weekly church dress parade, Christian culture charmed her into an anticipation of her enormous moral role in adulthood.

The issue of gender in religious discourse reached a pinnacle between 1895 and 1910. Much religious literature for boys focused on the biblical story of Daniel (and the Lion) rather than on Christ, whilst men's relationship to the burgeoning sports of the Edwardian period attracted much evangelical worry. There was a new fear that the evangelical concentration on the female virtues as the centre of innate piety had 'softened men', had encouraged the Christianly man to be too meek and mild, and had thereby alienated great swathes of manhood and boyhood. Vigour and assertion became a new order of the day for some churches. In the Church of Scotland, the voice was heard for reasserting 'that manly individualism which did not shrink from asserting its right of private judgement'.[68] There was a consciousness by the 1910s that Christianity as 'a woman's religion' was alienating men, and perhaps was the cause of the slight fall in church membership and churchgoing that was noted during this period. But by 1914, a new and much greater test for men's religious attachment arrived – total war.

Intellectual change

The churches and popular media of Edwardian Britain were already familiar with intellectual challenges to religion. Some came from within the churches, fostering the danger of schisms, but some came from outwith them in the challenges of atheists and others.

Churchmen were divided by 'higher criticism'. This was a movement amongst theologians that challenged literal interpretation of the Bible through application of science-learned knowledge and tests of rationality. It had been around in church circles for almost half a century, and indeed had been the cause of much discussion in the middle decades of the nineteenth century. But it was really only in the 1890s and 1900s that the higher criticism entered into public debate in a major way across Britain. A massive literature of popular biblical criticism was available at bookstalls in cheap format, and newspapers and magazines carried articles and debates. The divisions cut across denominational lines, and indeed across traditions within churches.

Many churchmen welcomed the higher criticism for being a sign of the modernising of Christianity, for it being an attempt – an absolutely essential attempt – to keep pace with and not oppose the discoveries of science and evolution theory. Darwinism became popular amongst many churchmen who saw it as a commendable application of reason to the Christian Bible. Most churchmen, it must be understood, did not stand opposed to science. On the contrary, the modern church from the 1750s to the 1910s was fairly strongly behind the Enlightenment and its scientific precepts of inductive reasoning, and wished to project Christianity as also a centre of logic and reason. So powerful and unavoidable was the Enlightenment philosophy of rational knowledge, with its emphasis on truth, evidence and empirical facts, that the more biblical knowledge was scrutinised by the same criteria, and made to fit the extended logic and known world of Darwinist knowledge, the better it seemed to reflect on Christianity. This type of thinking made the higher critics much defended, even by evangelicals. One evangelical-leaning newspaper proudly noted that: 'In the face of many protests from friends, we have steadfastly maintained that the higher critics are doing a righteous, a necessary and a beneficent work, a work which must be taken account of and dealt with by the Christian Church, a work which will in the end build up the people of GOD in the most holy faith.'[69]

There were other dangers. In a more general sense, the retreat from a religious spirit in the daily lives of the people was something the churches constantly found it hard to combat. 'Not the least of the Church's dangers,' said a leading clergyman in the Church of Scotland in 1899, 'in the face of modern thought and life is the *secularisation*, the absorption in purely earthly aims to which the latter tends. We have seen how the various spheres of life become gradually emancipated from the Church's control.' The problem was not secularism, a decision to abandon religion, so much as an inchoate and disorganised drift from it. 'It is not necessarily that men undervalue religion and divine things, often they are simply thoughtless with regard to them.' The feeling was that modern thought was not so much anti-Christian as non-Christian, and that this was far more dangerous.[70] This was nowhere more apparent than in talk around 1901 amongst some Scottish university leaders of abolishing divinity faculties which taught trainee clergy.[71] In the Church of England, meanwhile, there was fear that the crisis over the growth of High Church ritual, associated especially with Anglo-Catholicism, would lead to schism.

Bishop Gore dismissed this as 'ridiculous', telling his congregation in Worcester Cathedral in 1904: 'No doubt infidelity prevailed, and there was intellectual unsettlement around. But the crisis was moral ... There was a very widespread defiance of law and restraint amongst young people, a very widespread laxity in domestic discipline.'[72]

Secularism had developed in England in the mid-Victorian period into a well-organised and militant atheism, campaigning against the 'lies' of religious leaders and fraudulent faiths. Britain's leading secularist campaigner, George Foote, scented victory over faith in 1912:

It is simple Christian impudence to call the inhabitants of England 'a Christian people'. Three-fourths of these alleged Christian people never darken church or chapel doors. They are not Freethinkers, of course, but they are not Christians. They are indifferentists. Talk about 'God' and 'Christ' and 'heaven' and 'hell' has ceased to interest them. They do not yearn for 'Salvation', which is the be-all and end-all of Christianity.[73]

But unlike in France and Germany, where secularism was a firm part of socialism and of constitutional affairs, unbelief never really took off in Britain. The heyday of secularist organisations was in the 1880s, and after 1893 their memberships were in decline. Secularism was widely viewed as extremist and crackpot, and the existence of God self-evident in reason and palpable in the existence of the British Empire. The state enforced the Christian religion with severity; small numbers of campaigning secularists were routinely tried and imprisoned for blasphemy – the last in 1922.[74] To disclaim God, even in a mild and intellectual manner, was to appear to fly in the face of sound commonsense – apparent in the compromises between science and religion. The major consequence of the rise of positivism, science and reason in the late eighteenth and nineteenth centuries had been to encourage a willing British Protestant clergy to transform Christianity into a 'rational religion', something that was as intellectually positivist, useful and clamouring for academic neutrality as any science. This heritage was very much alive and well at the beginning of the twentieth century. British theology had magnificently surfed the tide of Darwinism and evolution theory, with leading clergy joining in the modernisation of theology, whilst many of the most prestigious scientists and doctors were staunch Christians and churchgoers.[75] Science and Christian religion could still summon up close intellectual affinities. When, in 1904, Manchester University started divinity as a subject, it was regarded as an undogmatic 'scientific theology' – a type of phenomenology concerning 'facts not opinions'.[76]

The most potent spread of secularism was not in science, but within the Labour Movement. Whilst the majority of leaders of Labour organisations and trades unionists remained Christians and active churchgoers, atheistic ideas spread amongst Marxists and anarchists. The transition from a religious-based education (including in Sunday school) developed a thirst for intellectual independence – an evangelical individualism leading to secularist individualism, often with similar characteristics concerning the sense of destiny and redemption. Darwinism may have been absorbed by many theologians, but for some laity it was the trigger to atheism. Christian Watt, a poor fisherwoman and evangelical born-again Christian from the north of Scotland, wrote early in the century of her perplexity: 'My son believed in the Darwin theory and totally rejected his Christian upbringing. Strangely enough he did not smoke or drink, and kept on saying one can be as moral as an unbeliever. I told him he was a miserable sinner, he said I was being ridiculous.'[77] Like her, many were convinced that irreligion equated with immorality.

Religion and policy

The Edwardian period witnessed two opposing and apparently conflicting trends: the liberalisation of religious attitudes towards social reform and the advance of the restrictive Christian state. The truth is, both were happening simultaneously.

The churches were by 1900 past-masters in producing good spin on their own performance. There was underlying pessimism in many of the churches, not the least the Nonconformists in England and Wales and the presbyterians in Scotland. The statistics and censuses were already revealing that church growth had not just slowed but had, in many cases, reversed, and there was declining faith in the evangelical agenda of action that had for so long dominated the way in which the churches saw their mission in British society. On top of that was an emerging conundrum. The religious initiative was clearly passing from the hands of those who defended and promoted 'old-time' evangelical religion to those with a social-welfarist agenda – of public social reform in which the churches should participate. In essence, organised Christianity developed two different visions: that of man as a free moral agent, no matter his economic or social condition, who must choose to be moral to be prosperous; and that of man as a victim of his environment, his housing and economic conditions, who had to be assisted from immoral society to be made moral himself. This was a stark choice in a struggle over the free moral agent versus the environment – or individualism versus welfarism.

Individualism lay at the root of the advance of restrictive state action at both local and national level in 1900–14. The most obvious way in which religion intruded into life was in relation to keeping the Christian Sabbath holy. Sunday was a day that had developed legislative backing over many centuries, but this hardened in the late Victorian and Edwardian period. Well into the twentieth century, new ways of enforcing the Sabbath were developed. A great battle went on from 1896 to 1925 in Scotland over the Sunday opening of ice-cream and aerated water shops, mostly run by new Italian Catholic immigrants whose faith placed much less emphasis than Protestantism upon sabbatarianism. The opening of their shops made them magnets for rebellious young people, creating the embryonic secular youth culture that was to become such a concern to the churches during the rest of the century. A massive campaign by evangelicals developed, with religious meetings complete with mobile harmoniums on the back of lorries being conducted outside ice-cream shops. In Lerwick, the socialists sided with Mr Harry Corothie and ostentatiously parked themselves inside his ice-cream parlour on Sundays during demonstrations in 1905.[78]

Sabbatarianism was not merely a Scottish obsession. The *Daily Telegraph* and the *Daily Mail* ended publication of Sunday editions; Rhondda Council closed lecture halls and theatres on Sundays; and London's Metropolitan Police had by 1906 controlled the extent of costermongers' Sunday trading.[79] Sunday work was regarded as a sin, and was widely condemned by politicians, the churches and social reformers. Acts of necessity and mercy were permitted. But there was much hypocrisy. Lord Overton, a grandee of the evangelical Free Church in Scotland and the leading trustee of its successor, the United Free Church, owned a vast chrome works in Glasgow where he forced his men to work on Sundays. This became a *cause célèbre* when the Labour leader, Keir Hardie, publicised the poor health and working conditions at the factory.[80] For individual Christians of conscience, Sunday work by the Post Office was a moral problem. Flora Thompson recounts the story of Postman Brown who, though very fearful that dismissal would throw himself and his family into poverty, refused to work on a Sunday evening letter-box collection. He told his employer: 'My job on Sunday evenings, sir, is to worship my Creator, who Himself laid down the law, "Keep holy the Sabbath Day", and I can't go against that, sir.'[81]

The licensing laws were an area where evangelical Christians had been campaigning for half a century. Extreme opinion wanted the drinks trade banned, or possibly taken over by the state (so that alcoholic content of drink, ending of capitalist pressures to sell more and so on might be introduced). If total prohibition wasn't possible, some wanted local prohibition or reduction in the number of licensed premises. Evangelicals used local laws to harass the trade – obtaining bans on public houses close to schools, challenging publicans as to whether they were 'fit and proper persons', instigating challenges over the quality of toilet facilities, and so on. These campaigns for legal change operated in parallel with temperance marches to embarrass drinkers, operating pickets outside public houses and seeking to place teetotallers (notably from the Liberal Party) in Parliament, licensing courts and town councils. The opposition from the licensed trade, from the brewers and distilling companies, and from the Conservative Party (in which these trades were well represented), restricted success. Nonetheless, pub opening hours were heavily restricted across Britain – with short lunchtime opening, evening opening ending at between 9 pm and 10.30 pm, and Sunday opening banned in much of the country (except for hotels and restaurants). One major victory was the Temperance (Scotland) Act of 1913, which after a lapse of seven years enacted the introduction of local prohibition where a ward or parish could vote 55 per cent in favour of closing or reducing the number of public houses, whilst a similar measure permitting Sunday closing had already been introduced in Wales in 1881.

Individualism was challenged by welfarism, and notably through the rise of the Labour Movement. From the 1890s to the First World War, the churches were faced with two things: the dramatic spread of trades unionism from its traditional base amongst skilled workers to the unskilled and to women workers, and the rise of a kind of non-political Labour Movement that demanded ethical action on social issues. Churchmen and laity, especially of the intellectual middle classes, were by 1900 in the midst of a struggle to sustain the churches' influence amongst the working classes of Britain, who seemed to be turning from church to Labour for ways to improve wages, housing, opportunity and rights. Churchmen were divided in how to respond. Many traditional evangelicals regarded with horror the emergence of a challenge to the singularity of religious conversion as the route to social improvement. Others moved further from acquiescing in the evangelical interpretation of society to a Christian socialist one, in which there was overt recognition of the impact of environment upon the individual. What was widely termed 'the social question' – how to change society for the better – was moving inexorably out of evangelical precepts. Robert Flint, a leading Christian socialist in Scotland, said: 'The social problem *is* a religious one, but it is also an economic, political, moral, and educational one.'[82]

Christian socialism in the 1900s was an ethical movement rather than a political one. Women's exploitation in factory work was one area where many Christians found mutual concern with the Labour Movement. They gave support to efforts to unionise women, and lent their churches for meetings. As Londoner Kathleen Woodward observed, churches became sites of collision between socialists, suffragists and middle-class ladies 'of paler texture, more softly tongued, affecting less rough tweeds'. These were women 'of obvious gentility', with benevolent intentions and integrity, but who impressed working women 'chiefly with their futility, and dismayed us by their incurably spinster-like appearance'.[83] Middle-class Christian socialists could appear ridiculous, but they were trying to promote social improvement as the basis for an ethical economic system. It was they who challenged individualism and conversionist evangelicalism. One said of the working-class poor in 1904:

You must give them instead an environment that will check and neutralise heredity, and break the chain of evil habit. You must surround them with good influences, healthy, happy redeeming influences. ... You place the men and women you wish to rescue in a dwelling where the inmates form one family, where the sense of home, perhaps long lost, returns with its sweet, gracious benediction; where regular habits, fixed hours, and honest labour exert their steadying, restraining influence...You give the refining influences of pure literature, music, rational amusement, and recreation, and above all of religion.[84]

This Christian socialism was favoured by a relatively small but very influential group of leading clergy – perhaps a few thousand in total, most of whom were liberals in outlook – who were dotted across all the principal denominations: the Church of England, Congregationalists, Baptists and Unitarians, in the Church of Scotland and, though more hesitantly at first, in the Roman Catholic Church. The people's working and living environment became a cause for these clergy, and they were drawn to participate in various forms of social reform – the garden city movement, reform of the poor law system and the promotion of slum demolition and the erection of subsidised state (or council) housing. One supporter of the garden city movement, which sought to erect pleasant worker housing in satellite towns, described his vision in 1910 for the churches and society 'to be alit with civic ideals, to be alive with civic ardours, to be aglow with civic pride and patriotism'.[85] Whilst most churchmen regarded their move to this position as a matter of ethics, where to keep silent about social problems was a sin, some were drawn into the Labour Movement itself. The future Archbishop of Canterbury, William Temple, became convinced in the mid-1900s of the need for increased state intervention in social reform. This led him to join the Workers Educational Association in 1905 and become its president in 1908–24, and then to work with socialists in the Labour Movement and announce to the Lower House of Canterbury Convocation in 1915 that he had joined the Labour Party. But there was a more general failure of the churches, notably Nonconformity in Wales in 1910–11, to move from an ethical to a political socialism that backed Labour demands, and this was to prove within a decade and a half a challenge to their position in the affection of the British working classes.[86]

Such activities occurred against a background of rising unease at the relationship between church and state – which was always a muddle. At root, government was accepted as a religious state; one theologian said in 1904: 'The State is not a heathen, but a Christian institution "ordained of God for good".'[87] Yet, the state churches of England and Wales, and of Scotland, were facing various challenges to their status. Dissenting Protestant churches in all three countries urged politicians, and notably the Liberal Party, to end the link, to acknowledge religion as a matter for the individual and the churches as institutions that should survive by the liberal giving of their members not by church taxes. There was pressure too on moral grounds – that the link between the Church of England and the Church of Scotland to the drinks trade, for instance, was a moral block on the advance of a teetotal kingdom of God on earth. A second version of heaven on earth, that of one without poverty through ethical Christian socialism, created problems of neutrality for the church.

So, the relationship of Christianity to the state was an issue that popped up again and again during the twentieth century, perplexing lawyers and theologians. English Nonconformists fought one of their last great battles of honour in 1904 over the education rate (a local tax), with scores of ministers – Baptists, Methodists and others – going to gaol. The press closely followed what one paper called 'The Persecution'. The Revd Peter Miller, minister of York Road Baptist Chapel, Leeds, was arrested by a police inspector at his home for non-payment of 7s. 0½d (36 pence), the education element in the poor rate, and was placed in Armley Gaol for three nights. Crowds stood outside gaols welcoming the prosecuted in and out of prison.[88] Such issues of conscience illustrated the way in which English Nonconformity felt excluded from the machinery of state.

In Scotland during 1900–8, church–state relations were, if anything, a matter of even greater public participation. Scotland had three main Protestant churches – the Church of Scotland, the Free Church of Scotland (which had split from it in 1843) and the United Presbyterian Church (an amalgamation of eighteenth-century splits from the Church of Scotland). In 1900, the Free Church and the United Presbyterian Church united to form the United Free Church, which saw itself as a vigorous church, and was (by some measures) the largest church in Scotland. Formed amidst great celebration in Edinburgh, it seemed to augur a new era of ecumenic hope and reunification – being the first step to what one senior churchman called 'a United Church for Britain'.[89] But very quickly, this hope dissipated as a tiny fragment of the Free Church, most in the Gaelic-speaking Highlands and Hebrides of the north-west, refused to join, as they saw it to be liberal, sinful and contrary to the doctrines of original presbyterianism.

The remnant Free Church started a legal case claiming all the property of the massive United Free Church, and astonishingly won it. This was a devastating decision, ratified on appeal by the House of Lords in 1904, upheld on the grounds that the property of a church belongs to whichever party adheres closest to original principles (and not to the size of the church). Within days, the lawyers of the tiny Free Church claimed their prizes – starting symbolically by expelling the students and staff of the United Free Church College at the Mound in Edinburgh (in the building that was later, during 1997–2004, to be the Scottish Parliament). Congregations throughout the country organised a spectacular eviction from their church buildings in 1904, as they were taken over and, mostly, left empty by a tiny Free Church that had no use for them.

For more than half a decade, the Free Church case alarmed and exhilarated Scotland in almost equal measure. United Free Church critics lambasted the Free Church for being dyed-in-the-wool puritans of a sixteenth-century stamp, who closed their eyes to the modern world and theology. One critic said that the Free Church hopes 'it will be hermetically sealed against modern thought in all its forms, and particularly in the form of the higher criticism. We have previously argued that this is pure delusion, and that in any Church men will go on thinking, and that no compact and no terrors will avail to arrest the inevitable.'[90] The Free Church's ownership of the United Free Church's buildings was for its time a massive issue. The situation could not be allowed to prevail, and

Parliament, almost uniquely in modern church history, passed a special Act of Parliament in 1905 to transfer the churches back to the United Free Church.

Wales was wracked by a different type of church–state controversy in the 1910s – the question of disestablishment. The Anglican Church in Wales had long been a minority of the people, and the Church had always been associated in the nineteenth century with the interests of the landed and commercial classes. Nonconformity was the people's religion, Anglicanism was the religion of government. Disestablishment, as historian K. O. Morgan said, was in Wales 'a supreme national cause'. Another historian commented that church disestablishment was as to Wales what home rule was unto the Irish.[91]

As Wales developed its own national legislation from the 1880s, there was a perception that the aristocracy and squirearchy were losing control over local administration, Welsh education and the moral law. Prime minister William Gladstone included Welsh disestablishment in his 1891 manifesto, but two bills of 1894 and 1895 made little headway. Ten years later, another prime minister, Campbell Bannerman, set up a royal commission on the religious state of Wales, at the request of the Archbishop of Canterbury, Randall Davidson. But it moved very slowly, not reporting until 1911, and yet another bill floundered. The matter became a saga. In 1912, the House of Commons passed a disestablishment bill that was rejected by the Lords, but it was finally pushed through in 1914. After the war started, in the autumn of 1914, the Act was passed, but only with a proviso that it be delayed for twelve months, or until the end of the war. This caused great bitterness in the Church, and the Welsh churchmen were slow to accept the Act, believing it would be repealed, whilst some Anglican clergy campaigned against it.

The disendowment of the Church – the passing of its wealth to other quarters – caused great bitterness, with its annual income of £250,000 being slashed to £102,000. When the First World War ended, the Welsh Church Amending Act of 1919 restored all but £48,000, but the money was going to be tied up in a commission's funds for over twenty years. Nonetheless, this Act facilitated the disestablishment of 1922, which raised Wales to a separate province of the Anglican Church, divorced from Canterbury. One historian has described the outcome as 'freedom gained by surgery, a freedom imposed upon the Welsh Church by its enemies'.[92] Nonconformists had engineered the change, and the sense of triumph lasted long. But, this was how leading Anglicans in Wales realised that their Church could achieve integration in Welsh society. They had been perceived as an alien, non-Welsh church, the nearest thing to a colonial organisation in the midst of Welsh national consciousness. And for this reason, the Church in Wales (as it was henceforth to be called) set about a deliberate policy of Welshification, adopting the Welsh language amongst clergy – though ironically at the very time when it was in decline in secular society.

In these ecclesiastical disputes in England, Scotland and Wales, the people were much more involved than in similar disputes later in the twentieth century. They were issues followed in detail in the press, and the public were propagandised by hustings for the parties involved. Hundreds of thousands turned out for events instigated by big ecclesiastical controversies, and public passions were often inflamed. Riots occurred in some cases over disputed church properties, and police and even the military were called out on some occasions. In many ways, there was more popular delight in the sight of ecclesiastical disputation than in the prospect of personal salvation. Religion was a field of controversy in which the British public revelled. But from August 1914, their attitude to religion became fundamentally challenged by war.

Notes

1 Revd Dr C. Ruffelle Scott, quoted in *Church of Scotland, Second Church Congress, Aberdeen Oct 9th and 10th, 1901. Official Report of Proceedings* (Edinburgh, J. W. Blackwood, 1903), pp. 64–5.

2 F. Thompson, *Lark Rise to Candleford* (orig. 1939, Harmondsworth, Penguin, 1973), pp. 209, 407.

3 *Methodist Recorder*, 7 January 1904.

4 Quoted in J. Rose, *The Intellectual Life of the British Working Classes* (New Haven, Yale Nota Bene, 2002), pp. 69–70.

5 F. Colquhoun, *Haringay Story* (London, Hodder & Stoughton, 1955), pp. 205–30; *Lewis: Land of Revival: The story of the 1949–52 Lewis Revival as told by the islanders*, cassette tape (Belfast, Ambassador Productions, 1983).

6 *The Times*, 5 November 1900.

7 Ibid., 20 May 1901.

8 Ibid., 9 June 1900.

9 S. Gilley, 'The Roman Catholic Church in England, 1780–1940', in S. Gilley and W.J. Sheils (eds), *A History of Religion in Britain* (Oxford, Blackwell, 1994), p. 361.

10 *Methodist Recorder*, 29 March 1900.

11 C.A. Webster, 'The Church since Disestablishment', in W.A. Phillips (ed.), *History of the Church of Ireland vol. III The Modern Church* (London, Oxford University Press, 1933), p. 402.

12 *British Weekly*, 20 February 1919.

13 Census results cited in *Methodist Recorder*, 7 January 1904; ibid., 10 May 1900, 12 June 1900.

14 *Church of Scotland, First Church Congress, held by order of the General Assembly, Glasgow, October 25th to 27th 1899: Official Report of Proceedings* (Edinburgh, J. Gardner Hill, 1899), pp. 14–15.

15 *Methodist Recorder*, 7 January 1904, 29 March 1900.

16 The Revd J. Llewelyn Davies, quoted in *The Times*, 27 September 1900.

17 Quoted in *British Weekly*, 26 April 1900. See also J. Wolffe, *God and the Greater Britain: Religion and National Life in Britain and Ireland 1843–1945* (London, Routledge, 1994), p. 233.

18 *British Weekly*, 4 January 1900.

19 Ibid., 28 December 1899.

20 K. Robbins, 'Protestant Nonconformists and the peace question', in A.P.F. Sell and A.R. Cross (eds), *Protestant Nonconformity in the Twentieth Century* (Carlisle, Paternoster Press, 2003), pp. 221–2.

21 Malise Ruthven, in *The Guardian*, 10 October 2001.

22 R.J. Campbell, writing in *British Weekly*, 21 December 1899.

23 *Church of Scotland, Second Church Congress*, pp. 57–8.

24 Thompson, *Lark Rise*, pp. 523–5.

25 C. Hall, *Twice Around the Bay* (Edinburgh, Birlinn, 2001), p. 61; R. Roberts, *A Ragged Schooling: Growing up in the Classic Slum* (Glasgow, Fontana/Collins, 1978), pp. 94–5.

26 Cited in *Church of Scotland, First Church Congress*, p. 133.

27 M. Penn, *Manchester Fourteen Miles* (orig. 1947, London, Futura, 1982), pp. 174–5.

28 Testimony from Thompson, P. and Lummis, T., *Family Life and Work Experience Before 1918, 1870–1973* [computer file], 5th edition. Colchester, Essex: UK Data Archive [distributor], April 2005. SN: 2000. Interview 142, p. 21.

29 R. Roberts, *The Classic Slum* (Harmondsworth, Penguin, 1973), p. 90.

30 Penn, *Manchester*, p. 173.

31 Testimony from Thompson and Lummis, op. cit. Interview 143.

32 J. Springhall, B. Fraser and M. Hoare, *Sure & Stedfast: A History of the Boys Brigade 1883 to 1983* (London and Glasgow, Collins, 1983), pp. 94, 101, 103.

33 J. Burnett (ed.), *Destiny Obscure: Autobiographies of Childhood, Education and Family from the 1820s to the 1920s* (orig. 1982, London, Routledge, 1994), pp. 304–5.

34 Ibid., pp. 309–10.

35 Roberts, *A Ragged Schooling*, pp. 102, 93.

36 K. Knott, 'Other major religious traditions', in T. Thomas (ed.), *The British: their religious beliefs and practices 1800–1986* (London, Routledge, 1988), pp. 140, 143; H. Ansari, *'The Infidel Within': Muslims in Britain since 1800* (London, Hurst & Co., 2004), pp. 121–6.

37 Penn, *Manchester*, p. 174.

38 *British Weekly*, 14 and 21 December 1899.

39 R.A. Torrey, *How to Work for Christ: a Compendium of Effective Methods* (London, James Nisbet & Co., 1901), pp. 241, 281.

40 www.holytrinitynewrochelle.org/yourti17550.html, accessed on 17 January 2004.

41 Quoted in B.P. Jones, *Voices from the Welsh Revival 1904–5* (Bridgend, Evangelical Press of Wales, 1995), p. 20.

42 *Western Mail*, 12 November 1904, quoted at http://www.christian-bookshop.co.uk/free/biogs/roberts4.htm, accessed April 2005.

43 *The Times*, 14 and 21 November 1904.

44 D.B. Rees, 'Roberts, Evan John', *Oxford Dictionary of National Biography* (Oxford, Oxford University Press, 2004), accessed online.

45 *The Times*, 21 November 1904.

46 Quotations in J. Harvey, *Image of the Invisible: The Visualization of Religion in the Welsh Nonconformist Tradition* (Cardiff, University of Wales Press, 1999), pp. 64, 68.

47 *The Times*, 2 January 1905.

48 *The Times*, 8 May 1905.

49 *British Weekly*, 9 March 1905, 23 March 1905.

50 *The Times*, 24 June, 3 January and 2 February 1905.

51 *British Weekly*, 2 March 1905.

52 Ibid., 9 March 1905.

53 *The Times*, 3 March 1905.

54 Ibid., 20 March 1905.

55 *British Weekly*, 29 April 1926.

56 Faith Dorothy Osgerby, 'My memoirs', in Burnett (ed.), *Destiny Obscure*, pp. 83–4.

57 Thompson, *Lark Rise*, p. 407.

58 K. Woodward, *Jipping Street* (orig. 1928, London, Virago, 1983), p. 147.

59 Quoted in Wolffe, *God and the Greater Britain*, p. 7.

60 *British Weekly*, 19 April 1900.

61 Ibid., 13 October 1904.

62 Ibid., 26 April 1900.

63 Burnett (ed.), *Destiny Obscure*, pp. 311, 320.

64 Testimony from Thompson and Lummis, op. cit., interview 143.

65 Scottish Oral History Centre Archive, University of Strathclyde, SOHCA/006/Mrs E.2(1905), p. 5; SOHCA/006/Mrs U.1(b.1898), p. 8; The Elizabeth Roberts Archive, Centre for North West Regional Studies, Lancaster University, Mrs B.1.P, b. 1900, pp. 43–4.

66 Faith Dorothy Osgerby, 'My memoirs', in Burnett (ed.), *Destiny Obscure*, pp. 83–4.

67 E. Ross, 'Survival networks: women's neighbourhood sharing in London before World War I', *History Workshop* 15 (1983), pp. 4–5.

68 *Church of Scotland, First Church Congress*, p. 20.

69 *British Weekly*, 26 April 1900.

70 *Church of Scotland, First Church Congress*, pp. 57, 68.

71 *Church of Scotland, Second Church Congress*, p. 15.

72 *The Times*, 20 December 1904.

73 Quoted in E. Royle, *Radicals, Secularists and Republicans: Popular Freethought in Britain 1866–1915* (Manchester, Manchester University Press, 1980), pp. 38, 296.

74 D. Nash, *Blasphemy in Modern Britain 1789 to the Present* (Aldershot, Ashgate, 1999), pp. 167–92.

75 In the USA in 1914, a survey by Dr James Leuba showed that about 40 per cent of scientists expressed belief in a supreme being: www.aetheronline.com/mario/Eye-Openers/ science_&__religion_converging.htm, accessed 12 June 2005.

76 D. Bebbington, 'The secularization of British universities since the mid-nineteenth century', in G.M. Marsden and B.J. Longfield (eds), *The*

Secularization of the Academy (New York and Oxford, Oxford University Press, 1992), p. 267.

77 D. Fraser (ed.), *The Christian Watt Papers* (Edinburgh, Paul Harris, 1983), p. 128.

78 C.G. Brown, *Up-helly-aa: Custom, culture and community in Shetland* (Manchester, Mandolin, 1998), pp. 166–7.

79 Royle, *Radicals, Secularists and Republicans*, p. 297.

80 C.G. Brown, *Religion and Society in Scotland since 1707* (Edinburgh, Edinburgh University Press, 1997), p. 127.

81 Thompson, *Lark Rise*, pp. 408–9.

82 *Church of Scotland, First Church Congress*, p. 83.

83 K. Woodward, *Jipping Street* (orig. 1928, London, Virago, 1983 ed.), p. 119.

84 Revd David Watson, in *Church of Scotland, Third Church Congress, Edinburgh October 19th and 20th 1904* (Edinburgh, J. Gardner Hill, 1905), pp. 38–9.

85 A.S. Matheson, *The City of Man* (London, Unwin, 1910), pp. 143, 196, 199.

86 F.A. Iremonger, *William Temple, Archbishop of Canterbury. His Life and Letters* (London, Oxford University Press, 1948), pp. 330–2; R. Pope, *Building Jerusalem: Nonconformity, Labour and the Social Question in Wales 1906–1939* (Cardiff, University of Wales Press, 1998), pp. 123–64.

87 *Church of Scotland, Third Church Congress*, p. 12.

88 *British Weekly*, 13 October 1904.

89 *Church of Scotland, Second Church Congress*, p. 16.

90 *British Weekly*, 27 October 1904. The author was probably Sir William Robertson Nicoll, editor of the paper.

91 Quoted in D. Walker, 'Disestablishment and independence', in D. Walker (ed.), *A History of the Church in Wales* (Penarth, Glam., Church in Wales Publications, 1976), p. 164.

92 Ibid., p. 170.

CHAPTER 3

Trench religion, 1914–19

The Great War of 1914–1918 offered a great role for Christian religion in Britain. It was important to the times that God be on the side of Britain and her allies, and it was judged that victory would only be assured through the higher moral status of the British people. The honourable state that Britons had to attain in war was defined by Victorian and Edwardian religious sensibilities – of sexual virtue, abstinence from alcohol, curbing of pleasures and attendance on church ordinances. But as the war wore on, the confidence of the churches waned in the face of trench warfare at the front and social problems at home. 'The soldier has got religion,' concluded the compiler of an inter-church report on the war, 'I am not sure that he has got Christianity.'[1]

Organised religion and the war

The Christian faith was regarded as central to soldiering and to national leadership. In November 1912, twenty-two months before the outbreak of the war, George V's secretary wrote to the Naval and Military Bible Society, saying that the King instructed that it be confirmed to men in the Forces that 'it is quite true that he promised Queen Alexandra as long ago as 1881 that he would read a chapter of the Bible daily, and that he has ever since adhered to that promise'.[2] Copied and framed, this letter appeared in British military chapels. This act of the elite setting an example in religious devotions was part-and-parcel of British culture at the start of the war. The promising to a wife or mother was a characteristic genuflection to what was widely understood to be the superior piety of women. Soldiering was manly work, but it called for womanly religion to make it moral. This gave added impetus to the churches' participation in the war effort.

From the Army's point of view, religion was part of military patriotism and discipline. This reflected a wider view in the early twentieth century.

Varieties of British, Welsh, Scottish, English and Irish patriotism were viewed by intellectuals and artists, politicians and clergy, to conjoin moral worth with national cultural forms in art, architecture and myth.[3] For their part, most denominations craved that the government war machine recognise the churches and find a patriotic role for them. Most of the churches took upon themselves the role of patriotic flag-waver, and keeper of the nation's morale. In August 1914, there were bellicose sermons from clergy across Britain, and these continued for some time. One church leader said two years later that there was no alternative to 'the armed federation of the Allies', because: 'To make peace fundamental or final in our religion is not to follow the order either of Christ or His Apostles.'[4] This was a moral battle in which the most moral nation would win.

In the early months, the fervour of the recruits made the work of the churches seemingly easy. Young men and boys had been stirred by over a decade of patriotic warmongering, and there was general enthusiasm for volunteering. It was only in 1916 that conscription was really needed to maintain the flow of men. But in the last two years of the war, the churches' role became more and more difficult. The war had turned into a torrid affair, men dying in their thousands, sometimes on a single day, and national morale was faltering. The churches took it upon themselves to be part of the propaganda machine of the day, bolstering the recruitment posters, government newsreels and the calls to duty. One minister recalled: 'The Church, to an unfortunate degree, had become an instrument of the State and in too many pulpits the preacher had assumed to the role of a recruiting sergeant. Almost every place of worship the length and breadth of the land displayed the Union Jack, generally placed above the Holy Table, whilst some had great shields carrying the flags of all the allied nations.' Clergy were saying things they later regretted. The 'inflamed feelings of the times' led to one describing any person advocating talking of peace negotiations with Germany as 'a moral and spiritual leper and ought to be shunned and cut by every decent-minded and honest man' – what he later described as a 'monstrous and stupid utterance'.[5]

Very few churchmen opposed the war. The Society of Friends (the Quakers) was the most influential to become associated with pacifism by the 1910s, and conscientious objectors (those men who refused to fight on grounds of religious conscience) were vilified in public. A national conference of conscription opponents at a Quaker meeting hall in London was attacked by soldiers, and those suspected of being 'conchies' were subjected to public assault by other men, or handed white flowers or feathers by women, thus being branded as cowards.

In the war machine, the churches played an intimate role. Each regiment of the Army, and of the Royal Navy and Royal Flying Corps (later the Royal Air Force), had clergy known as chaplains, whose duty it was to sustain the religious needs and morale of the men during active service. The chaplains would follow the troops into the trenches, and significant numbers died in combat, but they did not carry arms and were not expected to fight. But the churches also gave other support during the war. They were strongly involved in the supply of clothes, Bibles, reading matter, tobacco and other articles of luxury. The provision of 'church huts' near troop concentrations and at transport hubs became the fad of all denominations – usually wooden or corrugated-iron huts, or merely commandeered premises, at which padres or chaplains along with women volunteers ministered to the needs of the soldiers. Those needs were often filling some of the gaps in the rest of the military system – the provision of food, drink and beds to sleep on for soldiers and sailors in transit. One of the largest organisations operating these was the Church of England's mission organisation, the Church Army, which by the summer of 1918 had over 700 recreation huts, tents and centres operating for British, American and colonial troops in Britain and war zones across Europe. In appealing for donations, the Church Army proudly stated that it maintained 150 huts within range of enemy fire in France.[6] The presence of the churches with the troops became seen as vital to morale.

The Army Chaplaincy service recruited clergy in roughly equal proportion to the religious affiliation of the men in uniform. For the Church of England, this bolstered their importance as the state church, which accounted for 70 per cent of men in the army – in part for being the 'default' church for those men otherwise claiming no affiliation. Each soldier had to have a religion, wearing an identity disc round the neck on which his name and number, and also his religion, were included. Enlisted men had to divulge their religion for this purpose, though officers were exempt. Bernard Martin was an officer embarking for France in 1916 when he spoke with a quartermaster:

'Why do you put a chap's religion on the disc, sergeant?'
He laughed. 'Precaution, sir, precaution. In war you never can tell.'
'Tell what?'
'Why, sir, if your number should happen to come up, you wouldn't want the chaplains to quarrel about who's to bury you.'
'I'm not really C of E,' I observed mildly.
The sergeant said in the tone of a wise man talking to an inexperienced

youth, 'You stick to C of E, sir. You wouldn't want to be buried by the Pope I'm sure.'
I laughed. 'I don't suppose it makes much difference.'
'Oh, it does make a difference, sir.' He spoke earnestly. 'It does. RCs go to Hell before they get to Heaven – that's official. RCs call it Purgatory. You're definitely better off as C of E, sir.'[7]

The level of official Army endorsement of religion was often nowhere near the high level of Christian culture within many regiments, which had a strong religious leaning, resulting from regional recruitment patterns. Regiments from Wales tended to be Nonconformist, Scottish regiments were often presbyterian, whilst other regiments were dominated by Irish Roman Catholics or Ulster Protestants. 'Pals' regiments (of men recruited together from a place, a factory or organisation) were sometimes strongly religiously bound; Welsh regiments were noted for strong chapel-going during training, whilst Orangemen from Glasgow opted to serve in an Ulster Protestant regiment. There was also a Jewish Pals regiment. Church organisations formed their own regiments – such as the 16th King's Royal Rifles (Church Lads' Brigade).[8] To these movements, the Army was entirely willing to oblige. Admittedly, religion was by no means the only definer of the groups of men who volunteered. William Murray from Fife recalled: 'The night war was declared in August 1914 we played the final o' a football tournament in Denbeath and we won the tournament. And the whole team joined the army the next day, the whole team. "Your King and Country Need You" and all this sort of stuff – patriotism, patriotism, it wisn't the sense o' excitement, it wis patriotism.'[9] With men joining with workmates as well, the Pals regiments had varied characters. But religious affiliation was seen as having a special quality that raised morale, bonded troops in training and increased the sense of common fight.

The British Army relied on volunteers from August 1914 until January 1916; thereafter, because of the decline in volunteering, conscription was introduced. It is clear that the religiosity of the volunteers before 1916 was higher than that of the conscripts after then. There was a higher degree of churchgoing amongst the units formed in the first eighteen months of the war than in the later two years.[10]

Churchmen used the pulpit for calls for recruits early in the war, and these seemed to have been highly effective. So strong was the religiosity of the volunteer regiments from August 1914 that the churches were given the impression that there was a religious revival in progress. One

Nonconformist wrote in 1915: 'Never before has such deep seriousness fallen upon our men, and in their quiet moments, and even amid the stress of battle, thoughts have turned to Christ and hearts have been surrendered to him.' In the same year, an Anglican bishop was struck by the piety he felt at a parade of the Third Battalion of the Coldstream Guards: 'I cannot remember a service for years where I felt the Real Presence and attended a heartier service. There must have been 800 present.'[11] This feeling was heightened as stories of men in battle filtered back to British culture. The Church of England organised a National Mission of Repentance and Hope in 1915–16, and the presbyterian churches in Scotland organised a similar event there. The Anglican mission was widely seen as Anglo-Catholic in construction, aimed at mobilising effort to recharge a high Anglicanism in liturgy and ritual, eliciting a reaction from Low Church and Nonconformist churchmen in the later stages of the war to refocus Christianity upon religious education and social justice. There was in this sense, as Michael Snape has put it, a hope amongst churchmen for a religious dividend from the war.

The sense of religious revival fostered in British Christian churches early in the war did not last. Most of the regiments with strong religious cultures were broken apart amid the high fatality campaigns, especially in 1916; with conscription from that year, religious culture was not re-created in the regiments of the later war years. At home, the hopes of missions turned to very little. The churches found that there was no mood for a religious revival in the midst of war, and the end of the war in 1918–19 brought a very different environment from that in which it had begun.

The experience of war

Some 22 per cent of British men, around 5.7 million of them, were in arms during the First World War. Of these, 705,000 were killed.[12] The First World War was an exceptionally tough war to fight, especially in the unremitting grime, discomfort, fear and high fatality of trench warfare. The artillery shell and the heavy machine gun created a fearful type of war, in which a single day could bring tremendous carnage. This was a profoundly challenging environment for religion.

There was no one religious reaction to the experience of war. Generals and the officer class in general tended to bring to the war the attitude that religion was part of social order and the hierarchy that they had learned in the Victorian and Edwardian middle and upper classes. Public school, university and the officer corps reinforced religion as part of the social fabric, the moral order and leadership. Sir Douglas Haig, General Officer commanding British forces on the western front, wrote to his wife on the eve of the Somme offensive that was to incur 140,000 British dead (21,000 on the first day): 'Now you must know that I *feel* that every step in my plan has been taken with the Divine help and I ask daily for aid, not merely in making the plan, but in carrying it out, and this I hope I shall continue to do until the end of all things which concern me on earth.'[13]

British Army chaplains came in for a brutal press from commentators after the war (including the poet Robert Graves, who accused Anglicans of cowardice, whilst Catholic priests came in for praise), and from some recent historians, for having 'reached an all-time low' and having 'sanctified the slaughter and surrendered themselves to the cult of arms'.[14] But a recent detailed reassessment by Michael Snape shows chaplains to have been critical to Army morale, being used from late 1915 in close harmony with Army Command objectives, and that this in itself demonstrated the strength of Christian culture and identity amongst British men who went to war. Nearly a hundred Anglican chaplains died in war, along with 68 of other churches, of whom 97 died in action or from wounds. The chaplains organised amongst the troops a 'scheme of reconstruction' that set out to provide soldiers with a forum to talk about what followed the war, and they came to be seen as offering a wide ethical and intellectual engagement between Army Command and the soldiers.[15]

By 1917, the churches themselves were deeply worried about the impact of war upon their membership. Many inquiries were instituted. One, *The Army and Religion*, brought to the churches the message of crisis, its organiser David Cairns writing: 'My feeling that what the Churches need is to have brought before them the real state of matters, viz. that they have lost, or are in danger of losing the faith of the nation, and that they have got to look deeply into the matter and set their hearts and minds to the problem of how the situation may, by God's grace, be retrieved before it is too late.'[16]

The churches analysed British religiosity in greater depth in 1917–19 than in possibly any other period of the century. One of the areas of 'blame' was religious education. Church of Scotland clergy reported that 'men who have been years in Sabbath schools have no real grasp of religion ... The percentage of men in the Army who are hostile to religion is small, but among them there is the most amazing ignorance of the fundamental ideas of our religion.'[17] Many clergymen took a highly official view of soldiers' religion. The religion of the trenches was seen as an 'emergency religion', one ill-founded on true Christian knowledge, and as something closer to superstition than a well-founded understanding of Christian teaching and the way to redemption through God's grace. There was disparagement and disdain from many war chaplains, some expressing contempt for soldiers' prayers for mere self-preservation. One chaplain said: 'Praying isn't like getting things out of a penny-in-the-slot machine: drop in a prayer and get a bit of chewing gum, or a blighty [a wound that compelled a soldier to return home], or the end of the war.'[18]

The intensity and disdain of some clergy for religious and spiritual feeling is remarkable. Maturer clergy were more mellow. David Cairns stated than even praying before going over the top, or for delivery after an attack, was 'a very elementary form of religion', yet very significant: 'It means that in presence of the most terrific display of material force that human history has ever seen men believe that there is an Unseen Power, inaccessible to the senses, which is yet mightier than high explosives, which knows all and hears prayer.'[19]

Whatever policy objectives the churches or the Army had for religion in war, the impact of combat upon the troops induced varied faith and spiritual responses. The dominance of artillery in warfare heightened the soldier's sense of fatalism; one Scottish presbyterian chaplain reported that: 'Almost every soldier in the line has become an Ultra-Calvinist – if not a man of faith, at least a man of fatalism.'[20] The bullet 'with your name on it' became a widespread philosophy in the trenches. Premonitions of death were widely reported, and for some Christians this could mean a special feeling to undertake church work after the war was over. This feeling could be especially strong amongst those who experienced near-death wounding.

Fear of death underlay what became known as 'trench religion'. Fatalism and the high casualty rate in the trenches contributed to a wide-scale use of amulets and charms amongst soldiers. It became common for a Bible to be carried in the tunic breast pocket in the hope of stopping a bullet. Clergy from the more reformed Christian churches, such as the Scots presbyterians, baulked at Protestant troops using crucifixes, Catholic rosaries and medals that soldiers were willing to take if handed out. In England, St Christopher's crosses seemed to have become widely worn as a result of the war. There was some spiritualist experience reported by men in combat. Much of this was based on visions – reports of ghosts and apparitions. Robert Graves, the war poet, reported seeing a ghost of an acquaintance, Private Challoner, walking past his billet a

Analysis: Combat and its effect on personal religion

Charles Warr, a young subaltern of 24 years in the 9th Battalion Argyll and Sutherland Highlanders, suffered close to fatal wounds at the second battle of Ypres in 1915. He lost his left elbow, his right arm was shattered, he had a bullet in his left leg, a shrapnel splinter in a finger of his right hand, and his scalp was slashed open. However, he was saved from a fatal head wound by the regimental badge on his Glengarry hat, which deflected a bullet. Dragged and carried by a sergeant under heavy fire to a field dressing station, he had crystal-clear experiences for some hours before descending into days of semi-consciousness:

I passed through a strange experience which completely altered my life and directed my feet upon another road. It was my own private and personal experience – the sort of thing one does not talk about – and so I don't propose to discuss it in any detail. All I need say is that it seemed as if, in the words of Rupert Brooke, I were enveloped in 'some white tremendous daybreak' and that I suddenly looked on life as I had never done before. There was born in me a purpose which, if I survived, I knew I must fulfil. A peace and spiritual serenity descended upon me that were deeper than the sea. I felt an inward cleansing that purged me of all worldly ambition and left me poised and sane and whole; and I knew that I had drawn very close to God. Like flashing light there came to me the certain knowledge that I was destined not to the things I had intended to do, but to give my life to help mankind in this tortured world and that, for me, the way to do it must be through the ministry of the Church. And that is all I want to say about it.[21]

Warr went on in 1918 to become a Church of Scotland minister, minister of St Giles' Cathedral in Edinburgh, a senior royal chaplain in Scotland, and, appropriately, the presiding minister at the opening of the Scottish National War Memorial in 1927.

month after he had been killed in action.[22] The appearance of angels in the midst of war was being circulated in fictional stories late in 1914, followed by further reports of sightings of the Virgin Mary, the crucifix in the sky and of Christ, and the story of 'the angel of Mons' was widely believed in high social circles.

These reports seemed to back up the popularity of Edwardian ghost stories and fairy stories in laying a popular culture receptive to stories of supernatural sightings and experiences. Whatever the roots, servicemen were not shy about religion. Praying before and during action was standard, the intensity of observance increasing with danger. Singing of hymns and psalms by troops was commonly reported, both in training and when 'in the line'. Even if praying in itself has been common in societies with weak religious cultures, the rest of this religious atmosphere would not have existed but for the strength of Christian knowledge, training and culture that the men brought from their daily lives. The generation who came of military age in the 1910s was raised in a highly religious atmosphere of the 1890s and 1900s, and this was expressed in war.

One consequence of this was the religious turmoil that the brutalities of war caused to men raised with high moral expectations of themselves and their comrades. Drinking, smoking and swearing were seen to rise amongst soldiers, including the religious fraternity, and for strict sabbatarians there was little place for the observance of Sundays in combat. Callousness with the enemy dead, the inability to sustain a sense of moral behaviour in the heat of battle, frightened many. One of the great effects of war was to induce a silence in the soldier on his return to civil life. It became a characteristic of the ex-soldier, commented upon by their children especially, that 'Daddy doesn't talk about the war'. Reticence became one of the ways in which men who had confronted brutality beyond description, fear beyond sanity and spiritual experiences of immense intensity or emptiness, dealt with the inconsequentiality of the organised church and the uncomprehending 'normal' society at home.

Manhood and womanhood in the war

Religion was conceived as lying at the very heart of the conduct of war. Truces between British and German troops at the front – to gather in and bury the dead, or to allow celebration of Christmas in the trenches – were seen as emanating from a common Christian culture shared by both sides in the First World War. (See pages 146–7.) When war could so easily turn to brutalism, the slaughter of the captured and the exploitation of over-run civilian populations, it was religion that was conceived as holding in check the baser instincts of the soldier. Indeed, the Great War seemed both then, and to an extent now, to have achieved a moral stature in the conduct of the ordinary soldier, in the restraint and essential goodness of the reluctant but patriotic killer. And it was Christianity that was conceived as lying at the heart of the moral decency of the soldier in the 1910s.

Behind this understanding of what faith 'was' in the 1910s, a view prevailed in wartime Britain that little had changed in how society understood the nature of religion. Men continued to be portrayed in the

The Christmas fraternisation between British and German troops, 1914.
(Mary Evans Picture Library)

media and in everyday discourse as the 'religious problem' whilst women
were 'the religious solution'. With victory being regarded as dependent on
a moral stature that had to exceed that of the enemy, there was pressure
not to disrupt the tried and tested formulae upon which religious identities were constructed. For instance, every week in the *Church Times*, the
newspaper of the Church of England's High Church wing, there were
pages and pages of small classified advertisements for women being
sought, or seeking, positions as companions, governesses, schoolteachers,
tutors and similar 'women's' positions in service. These advertisements
reflected society's idealisation of the female values expected by the upper
classes and the churchgoing women who served them:

Useful Companion – help wanted, middle-aged, to assist lady generally
with household duties, plain cooking, and little boy 4½. Must be
capable, conscientious worker. 3 in family. Help for rough. Mrs
Gibbens, The Surgery, East-st., Barking, Essex.

A Young Lady requires post as Kindergarten Mistress. Can teach usual
English subjects (junior), drilling, etc. – Apply Miss Keeley, Priory
House, Ramsgate. Excellent references.

Young Gentlewoman (not trained) desires POST middle January to help
trained Church Worker. Definite Teaching. Small Salary. Good
references.[23]

In these advertisements, keywords defined perfect Christian middle-class womanhood: companionate women, useful (not idle), conscientious, gentlewoman, above doing 'rough' work (such as cleaning, washing, coal-fire tending, which were reserved for general maids), ability to teach primary-school subjects to children of the upper middle classes or gentry (including drilling, still a fad despite the war), and the negotiating position taken by the young woman. The *Church Times*' classifieds was one location in which a very particular class of female service – not a 'servant' but a companion, governess or tutor – was dealt in, locating the servants and their employers by denomination and religious tradition. Conversely, the advertisements conferred certain moral and religious qualities upon the woman employees and upon the very particular relationship they had with their employers – a relationship of shared and mutually-respected personal Christian propriety, independence and status. In short stories of the time, there was discussion of women's infidelity in peacetime. In the Annie Swan story (see pages 100–1), the returning soldier speaks of how some soldiers 'got let down at home'. 'The women they cared about forgot, and – and filled the place – don't you know? It's as common as daylight in time of war. Don't blame some of them, of course.'[24] In this and other ways, Christian representation of the purity of women on the home front sustained a restrictive wartime culture of respectability.

Yet, the war challenged traditional gender roles. If men were still being asked to be masculine on the western front, women were drafted into war industries in large numbers to replace the lost male workers – in shipyards, mines, munitions factories, farms and all sorts of jobs, skilled and unskilled, where men were in short supply. Despite those new experiences for millions of women, there was a strong cultural impetus to reinforce traditional gender stereotypes. A woman's place was resolutely to be understood on a traditional formula of 'hearth and home' – that her innate goodness could only be cultivated and useful if it was located in attention to domestic duties, raising children and sustaining the home whilst a man was away at war. This natural goodness of women contrasted with men's innate religious disorder. Physical prowess and bravery in battle came at a cost – men were naturally impious, subject to weakness of character, and were tempted to drink, gambling and rough culture. In his New Year message at the beginning of 1918, the Archbishop of Canterbury said:

It is from sternly disciplined men, trench-trained and battle-hardened, that we are to draw and fashion for the coming years young clergy,

*young schoolmasters, young Parliament men. It is from the ranks of
women who have toiled unceasingly, uncomplainingly, in humblest
paths of common service, that our young wives and mothers will come.
In a different sense from that in which the words were first used, the
new world will come to redress the balance of the old.*[25]

The vision here is profoundly conservative and backward-looking.
Though he said that 'what lies ahead must needs be new', there is a certainty and desire for a return to old structures of gendered roles – of a
society that will have middle-class men toughened in war serving in leadership roles in a new and strengthened manner, and women returning
after war service to be wives and mothers. The sense of the 'new' here is
actually a chimera to us, locating religious and social newness within
unchanged structures of the status quo. In popular culture, too, traditional gendering of religion and morality was reinforced. Wartime
fiction, and stories at the end of the war, continued the Victorian and
Edwardian themes of men's innate weakness and women's inbuilt religious value. Adultery was an issue that was raised in popular culture
during the war; with so many men away, wives and 'sweethearts' at home
did not always stay faithful. Yet, stories tended to hinge their narrative
interest upon men's religious problems, not women's.

This continued focus upon men became emphasised within the
churches. The nature of the war was perceived as spiritually fundamentally different from the spiritual condition of peace or, indeed, of previous
wars. The trench conditions created what was felt to be an environment
of peculiar religious consequences. The first of these was the constant fear,
smell and experience of death and mutilation. Men experienced these
unremittingly for months on end, with little relief. The second was the
absence of women – the emblem of Christian piety – whose softness and
loving nature, combined in a silent and quiet female sensibility, had long
been understood to be essential to men's Christian condition. Cut adrift
from femininity and normal society, the churches were fearful that British
manhood was being permanently brutalised beyond the reach of religion.
A good example of the concern was expressed by an Anglican clergyman,
Canon James O. Hannay, who wrote of his experiences as a chaplain in
France. He delivered a public lecture in January 1918 in London entitled
'The Church and the Army'. He reflected:

*On the one hand, there were those who expect that the war would
produce a tremendous revival of religion, a revival both at home and
abroad, of the religious spirit latent in the nation; on the other, a smaller*

Analysis: Men, the religious problem, 1918

The following is an extract from a short story that appeared in the
British Weekly, an evangelical Protestant newspaper, a month after the
Armistice ending the Great War was signed in November 1918. It is a
characteristic moral tale of the 1880–1920 period, one in which the
author Annie S. Swan was well practised and very well known. It was by
then a long-established genre of melodramatic (and, for much modern
taste, intensely puerile) religious fiction that demanded that readers
confront their moral selves through a highly gendered notion of right and
wrong. Though it mentions female infidelity (in the typical oblique
innuendo of the time), its central message is that despite his brave
soldiering in the most bloody and demanding war, man is the moral
problem, woman is the solution.

'The Christmas Peace' by Annie S. Swan

[Dan is a soldier, returning after years of service in which he has seen
action at Gallipoli in 1916 and in Palestine. His wife Meg, with their son,
has not heard from him for many months. Dan is in some distress on
arrival home, doesn't embrace Meg, and she doesn't speak. Explaining
his failure to write, he says:]

*'I had some good pals out there, Meg, and some of them got let
down at home. The women they cared about forgot, and – and filled the
place – don't you know? It's as common as daylight in time of war.
Don't blame some of them, of course. I wouldn't have blamed you; and
now I see you, looking as you are, tell me is it all right?'*

*She found voice then – and dignity. 'I don't know what you're talking
about Dan . . .'*

*She smiled up into his face, and then, before she could keep him
back, he was kneeling at her feet – yes, kneeling with lips to the hem of
her gown.*

*'I said I'd do it – and I will!' he said with a catch in his voice. 'Out
there, as I said, I got face to face with myself, and I didn't like the
picture. How you stuck it for so long I don't know. I saw a selfish,
careless outsider taking all, giving nothing. I thought of your sweetness
and kindness and care for me, and marvelled how it was done. I didn't
know the preciousness of you, Meg, till I got away where – there were no
letters. . . . I want you to forgive me – to wipe the slate – to let me begin
again. . . . It's just all the small, mean, beastly pre-war days I want to
wipe out – the days when I strutted in and out of this house as if I were
God Almighty instead of the meanest worm He ever permitted to live. . . .
It was in Palestine I got the light. It's queer out there, Meg; it brings the
Bible all back, makes it real. I've seen chaps who never looked at it*

before devouring it as if it were the most entrancing novel. It was like that with me. What a Book it is! It can smite a man hip and thigh. Anyway, it got me. Will you forgive me, wife, and give me half a chance to show you that I've another side?'

She stooped down so that her cheek touched his hair ...

'I'm so happy, Dan, I can't say anything – everything's been said. I was afraid of to-night' – here she shivered in his arms – 'forgetting that God was remembering you and me as He remembers all that call upon Him.'[26]

class, who expected with equal confidence that it would finally chip away the veneer of religion that made the nation appear Christian. After more than three years of war we know that it has done neither. There has been nothing like a general revival of religion either at home or abroad, and certainly nothing like a wave of definite unbelief. What has happened is that it has changed the average man's attitude towards religion.

Before the war, men regarded the parson as an able man with little work to do, and looked upon the church as a whole with indifference:

There was little active hostility, though there was a suggestion of contempt. The ordinary man stood remote from the Church, neither blessing nor cursing; patient, tolerant, broadly indifferent. Now there is a change. Religion is still the parson's job, or the padre's, as the case may be. He is still paid for it; still has the church or hut; but no one expects any longer that it is all right; on the contrary there is a general feeling that the parsons have messed [up] their job. There is tendency to blame no particular individual or Church for the failure. The state of mind is just one of confused puzzledness; religion has failed us.[27]

Canon Hannay put his faith in High Church ritual as a means of bringing men to Christian belief and practice: 'The average Englishman, the man of the workshop of yesterday, of the trenches of to-day, wants religion ... [But] his religion is an imperfect thing – Christ and the Cross are not in it. In some degree then, the Church has succeeded. The souls of men are not asleep. That is something.'[28]

So shocked were some parsons that they felt that war was changing not just the *place* of religion in Britain, but the very *nature* of religion itself. This was not an entirely new phenomenon. In the nineteenth century, the science of phrenology (which argued for a connection between the shape of a person's head and their character) had been extremely popular, and given rise to a medicalisation of the body in the popular mind that carried this application from science to everyday culture. One element of its significance was to encourage the extension of the scientific treatment of religion, to justify the application of scientific and technical criteria to the world of other-worldly beliefs. It was in part an acknowledgement that religions were made by humankind. If that was the case, then, there was the possibility of introducing new religions, of inventing them or coming across them in the manner of scientific discovery. But equally, there was the development of a receptivity to movements or practices that transcended the religious and the scientific.

One minor but revealing evocation of this was a commercial product called Pelmanism. From 1915 to the mid-1930s, the British people – and especially the religious middle classes – became very familiar with advertisements in their newspapers and religious magazines for Pelmanism. The advertisements were characteristically full-page text adverts, with long descriptions and endorsements from generals, admirals, clergy, newspaper editors and Members of Parliament. Pelmanism enjoyed the most extraordinary range of endorsements from the good and the great of British life: Sir H. Rider Haggard, Sir Robert Baden-Powell, many MPs, 83 admirals and generals of the First World War, Sir Arthur Quiller-Couch, the editor of the *British Weekly*, and apparently six winners of the Military Cross. Reputedly, 100,000 servicemen of the British Army and Royal Navy were 'Pelmanists'.

The claimed scale of the uptake was truly astonishing, and explains the ability of its promoters to afford weekly full-page adverts in so many newspapers. But the advertisements did not actually spell out what was being offered. The reader was not told in the advert what the product was. There was no description to suggest it was a material product. Yet coyly, the advertisements said: 'Pelmanism is not a magical secret key to success; there is no "mystery" about it. It simply develops the faculties of the mind by regular and scientific exercise; just as the athlete develops muscles by exercise. But people do not always realise this.'[29] Despite its claims to the contrary, there *was* a mystery about it, deliberately cultivated in these massive and frequent advertisements. In the midst of war, the churchgoing middle classes were enticed by these oblique, mysterious advertisements to see in Pelmanism a new science-based discovery of something that would be of special interest to those interested in spiritual matters and was endorsed by some leading religious figures. What was being promoted seemed to be more than a product – a breakthrough in national skills resting on individual effort and application. Pelmanism was not a religion, nor an aid to spirituality, but there was more than a sly suggestion in the advert that it was one of these.

In reality, Pelmanism was something very simple. It was a system for improving memory using playing cards placed face down on a table and memorising their positions, and it is still used by some educationalists today. But the way it was branded and advertised during the Great War helps us to understand how religion rested in popular culture. Pelmanism was advertised primarily through religious newspapers, and claimed mostly men as its devotees. Its advantages were the acquisition of rapid promotion, bravery and honours. By implying some linkage to religion, it was acquiring a certain status with men, appealing to them as a religious 'thing' with scientific credentials. This alerts us to the increasingly popular notion in the 1910s that religion was being *understood* (not disproved) by science. Religions, including Christianity, were being understood increasingly in terms of links with science, with testing, with proof and with discovery. The advertising 'spin' on this memory game displays the conjunction that occurred in British culture between religion, spirituality and the world of science, and the appeal each had to make to men in terms of worldly attainment and strong masculinity. It suggested the birth of a new conception of how men and religion were linked.

Connections between religion and science emerged in a number of forms. One notable outcome was the Church of Christ, Scientist (or Christian Science) sect, formed in the United States by Mary Baker Eddy (1821–1910), who claimed a divine revelation to advocate that the Bible was an inspired guide to health and that Christian faith, through prayer, was a power in bodily healing. Christian Science grew rapidly in Britain during the 1910s, the number of its churches rising from 65 in 1911 to 169 in 1926, and its number of 'practitioners' (its term for clergy) from 219 to 585 over the same period.[30] Though always a very small church, Christian Science was one of the first of a number of later twentieth-century sects that combined divine revelation with a scientific understanding of bodily or mental health – what has been described as a modern form of magic that offered metaphysical change of scientific laws, in what were essentially 'secularised sects' which recommended religious means to secular goals.[31]

But the notion of religion being increasingly scientifically 'understood' was most apparent in the Great War in the craze for spiritualism. In this, attempts were made using various means (including mediums, séances and ouija boards) to make spiritual contact with the dead. The main appeal seemed to be to women wanting to make contact with sons or husbands killed in the war. Spiritualism had already been much discussed in both scientific and popular circles for twenty years, but the Great War increased interest dramatically. Celebrity spiritualists and books by prominent men – like Oliver Lodge's *Raymond* (1916) and Arthur Conan Doyle's *New Revelation* (1918) – proved immensely popular.

Most of the churches deprecated and condemned popular enthusiasm for spiritualism. But during the war, those who spoke out often tried to appeal to it by compromise. The Anglican archdeacon of Aston, George Gardner, said in early 1918: 'Spiritualism in certain quarters has become a regular cult – a form of, or substitute for, religion.' This was especially the case in large cities, he said, amongst those who have imbibed a smattering of what he called 'culture' – the lectures and promotional activities of spiritualists. His view was that spiritualism was attracting those who sought the novel and the sensational, whilst many actually now revelled in belonging to religious minorities as an act of defiance. And yet he acknowledged what many in his own church were feeling: 'Once more, in this time when death has claimed its victims from almost every household, many are being drawn by deeper reasons towards Spiritualism; because they crave with unspeakable longing for some definite sign that their departed friends are still alive.' In consequence, he urged the Church to admit that 'strange and inexplicable things do happen in connexion with the practices of Spiritualism'. He concluded: 'Those performances are not all humbug and trickery.'[32]

This message indicated significant support in the Anglo-Catholic wing of the Church of England. One Leicester vicar felt the Church was failing the people's needs for spiritualism, leaving it all to Sir Arthur Conan Doyle and Sir Oliver Lodge, who were seen as unnatural Protestant proponents of the movement: 'Has the Church no message?' he asked.[33] Catholic and Protestant were competing for a new spirituality of the people, even when criticising spiritualism, and were by the end of the war acknowledging an increased spiritualist perspective in their popular writings. For example, in *Reunion in Eternity* (1919), the author Sir William Robertson Nicoll, a Scottish Free Church minister, tried to reconnect with popular feeling through a restatement of a Christian sense of a life after death.[34]

Both Christian Science and spiritualism gave a fillip to the place of women in religious matters. Spiritualism was seen as overwhelmingly a woman's domain, and its rise contributed to the churches' acknowledgement by the end of the war that women's position in religion and society had altered. However, there was a sustained confusion about the nature of this change. For the conservatives in all Christian denominations, the message was one of women coming to the aid of specific religious traditions in rather conventional forms. Anglo-Catholics in the Church of England saw women as having a great role in fighting the threat of Protestantism in the Church; as one put it, women had a major task in the continuing counter-reformation: 'Women are on the threshold of great and magnificent opportunities.'[35] The same sentiment, even more vigorously put, came from the Congregationalist evangelical preacher Dr John Henry Jowett in a sermon preached at Westminster Chapel two weeks after the Armistice: 'They will bring to our national affairs a spirit that contends for the maintenance of the spiritual idea.' He continued:

The reforming fire needs to be fed by the breath of heaven. A woman's power of spiritual vision is her supreme endowment. She reaches spiritual realities, not by a tedious train of reasoning, but by intuitive discernment. We men say that woman is naturally religious. Her chief task in the next twenty years will be to keep alive in England the sense of God. . . . If our women abide by the Cross, they will save our Country.[36]

In a way resonant with Christianity in the mid-nineteenth century, women were loaded in British culture with the burden of its religion. This was even more acute for the role of women in sustaining rural Britain, attracting men back to the land, which led in the late 1910s to the foundation of the Christian-aligned Women's Institute in England and Wales, and the Scottish Women's Rural Institute. But renewed calls came for admission of women to the ministry and the priesthood in the Protestant churches. An Anglican, Maude Royden (1876–1956), perhaps came closest in the 1910s to being the first to preach the gospels, and be a priest, in the Church of England, having strong support from the Archbishop of Canterbury, and though she accepted a preaching post in the Congregational Church, strong opposition from high churchmen prevented success in the Anglican Church.[37] But the cause of women's suffrage, won in 1918, was enthusiastically supported by many – notably evangelicals, who associated it with continuing moral change. Its leading political supporter, Lloyd George, held it out as a prize for women during the war. He told a meeting of women on Procession Day 1915: 'You will get the vote but we must get you into the factories.' As a result, some 1 million women worked in factories, 300,000 in the Land Army, and 220,000 became auxiliaries in the Army and Navy.[38]

Yet, the war put into relief the chasm of thought between Christian feminism and what was perceived as an American, New York style libertine feminism. American feminists adopted the flamboyant and secular style 'New Woman' of the pre-war era, and their literature of free-thinking ideas was met with hostility by British churchwomen.[39] It was a more traditional vision of women's influence in society that attracted British churchwomen. Two weeks after the Armistice in 1918, Lloyd George calculated that female drunkenness had declined during the war by some 73 per cent as a result of 1.5 million new women in the industrial workforce and up to £200 million in extra female wages. And alcohol-related female deaths had fallen by half since 1914, with a 25 per cent drop in female suicide.[40] First-wave feminism was nearing its initial goal of women's suffrage, but the image of the woman who was gaining this was not a libertine, a rebel or a home-breaker. Rather, it was a woman of impeccable Victorian religious values. The franchise was this woman's prize for going back in 1918 to the home to become, once again, the angel in the house.

Reconstruction

The evangelical *British Weekly* newspaper greeted the Armistice with the headline, 'Beholding the fallen Satan'. This reflected a surge in the churches' sense of wellbeing that fostered immediate hope of religious renewal.[41] But the surge was short-lived, as the Great War ended amidst rapidly changing emotions for the churches. Many churchmen were in shock. 'Most of us who are living to-day,' wrote the general secretary of the Baptist Union in early 1918, 'have been born into one world and have come to live in another.' In a 'swift and even catastrophic' change, he went on, 'Landmarks and institutions are questioned or removed,' and 'The things which we have regarded as secure and stable have dissolved or vanished.'[42]

One manifestation of crisis came in January 1919, fourteen months after the Armistice, when a Church of England vicar wrote to the *Church Times* to explain his dismay:

Over 100 enlisted from my country parish. A good proportion of them were confirmed and had made their [first] communion; the majority had attended church fairly regularly, and many had been in the choir. When they joined up, most of them came to see me, and I gave them each a little pocket-money and a book or picture to remind them of their Church and duties. When first they came on home leave they called to see me; but subsequently none have come, and, worse still, very few have attended church. It has been very grievous. They went out spiritually equipped; now when they return they seem to have lost all their grip on religion. What can be the reason? [43]

This letter oozes with the sensibility of an old-time country parson, a state church clergyman who stood in the pulpit as much an agent of government as of God. He was a man who envisaged himself as a keystone in the fabric of rural English society, and one to whom all parishioners in a well-ordered community owed both a personal and institutional allegiance. For him, there was a close connection between enrolment to the Church and enrolment for the Army, two institutions of government, and both objects for the fealty of the common man. The men were seemingly loyal, and he had conferred upon them the honours and trinkets of belonging – a picture of the church, pocket-money or a book – as ritual aids to remembrance of duty (in a manner consonant with a Church of England ritualist). The vicar saw this as enough to make them religious – 'They went out spiritually equipped.' So their loss to him and their parish church is incomprehensible. He could not understand it. He was the vicar-who-stayed-at-home, who knew little perhaps of what these men had felt of war and of the changed relationship than now existed between the men, their church and parson.

The loss was not for the want of massive efforts to bring soldiers home to religion. The churches united with the government in 1918 and 1919 in an enormous administrative effort to capture the nation's military for the churches. The War Office passed to the churches on a daily basis the names of men being demobilised, with chaplains sitting in relay day and night in the discharging offices. The men were compelled to file before them, give their religion and the names of their own clergymen, with similar arrangements being put in place at discharging hospitals for wounded men. A notice was then sent to the minister in the home church to make arrangements to recruit each returning soldier. By mid-February 1919, the system was reported as not quite meeting its expectations. 'The ideal of sending direct from the [demobilisation] centre in order that the notice should reach a minister on the day a man returned home has not quite been reached, but rapidity of action and efficiency are alike impressing the men and their friends.' [44]

The evidence mounted in 1918 and 1919 that the working classes, and especially male soldiers, were turning against the churches of their youth. The Church of England National Mission of 1918 was a failure, and the archbishops of Canterbury and York appointed a commission, chaired by the Bishop of Winchester, to inquire into the work of the Church. The agenda they were working to was a class one. In his prefatory note to the inquiry report, the Archbishop of Canterbury wrote: 'An examination of the facts compels the conclusion that the existing industrial systems makes it exceedingly difficult to carry out the principles of Christianity... There is no moral justification for profits which exceed the amount needed to pay adequate salaries to the management and a fair rate of interest on the capital invested ...'[45] This attracted opposition from some in the Church, who protested against the leftward political stance being adopted and the critical position on capitalism.

Church social thought, certainly amongst many leaders in England, was towards a social gospel with the Church taking a leading social-service role in society.[46] But this was already under severe threat. Connections between the Labour Movement and the churches were weakened in the late 1910s by the 1917 Russian Revolution, the revolutions across Europe and the rise of worker radicalism at home. Yet, left-leaning clergy were determined that if the working people of Britain were to be sustained in their churches, then the churches had to take a critical stance on their working and living conditions. A Church of England report on Christianity and Industrial Problems in 1919 became the basis of the charter for the Industrial Christian Fellowship – an organisation that took over from the Navvy Mission Society. It continued to conduct missionary work in working-class areas, including open-air crusades. But it developed a strong political position, attracting the key participation of a prominent member of the Independent Labour Party, George Lansbury MP.[47]

The return to peace created a sense of polarisation within British society; demobilisation was a process, not an event, and with continued military action in Russia, British society at home retained a sense of division. In early 1919, it was reported that strikes were reducing church congregations in London – in part because public transport was closed, but also in part because of a growing division between Labour and the churches. 'There are abundant proofs that the economic order is changing, and that disastrous strikes will trouble the world till some adjustment is arrived at,' editorialised one evangelical. At the same time, however, it was reported that as many as a third of worshippers in some London central congregations were in uniform.[48] By the end of 1919, the nation was heading for economic boom and then bust – an economic collapse that was to prove divisive for the churches in ways that even the horrors of war had never been.

One of the forms this took was the apparent evidence of church decline. In a sense, the statistics on church decline had been showing evidence of a turning tide in membership since about 1908. But this was part of such a gradual change during the 1890s and 1900s – from growth to stasis to decline – that there had been a process of customisation to it. But in the context of war, the statistics looked daunting really for the first time, and started to be quoted in new tables designed to shock lethargic church administrations. The starkest falls were in the Baptist and Wesleyan Methodist churches, both in terms of adult membership and in terms of Sunday-school enrolments; the Methodists lost almost 15 per cent of their children between 1906 and 1916.[49] In point of fact, the situation was misread by the churches a great deal, because there was a significant fall in the birth rate at the time. Nevertheless, the trend was downwards, and it was the first ever in the history of the Sunday-school movement. The Nonconformists were the most affected, and seemed to resonate with a wider crisis of evangelical religion. Church attendance seemed also to be not just low, but declining.

A predictable response to this sense of crisis was to spend money on church organisation. The Church of England appointed Rogation Sunday in May 1919 for church members to donate extra money as a thank-offering for relatives safely returned from war to create a special church fund of £4 million for 'spiritual and social service' – everything from training of clergy and maintenance of the ministry to funds for widows and church extension.[50] Nonconformists judged that there was an unwelcoming climate for their Liberal-based evangelical social conscience, and they resented feeling bullied by a Church of England that sensed its time had come. Ecumenical negotiation by Protestant dissenters with the Anglican establishment was considered little short of treachery by some free churchmen; they argued that the Church of England contributed less than one-sixth of the £8.75 million spent in foreign missions *per* year, making it ill-committed to 'evangelising the heathen world' and, as a state church, not a true figurehead of 'democratic Christianity'. Many Nonconformists felt Anglican leaders were moral cowards – refusing, for example, to join Nonconformist church leaders in lobbying the prime minister for the release of imprisoned conscientious objectors (those who had refused to fight in combat). Anglicanism appeared morally populist but unprincipled.[51]

But despite this, one response to war and the sense of crisis that it induced was an impulse to church unity and union. With consensual change so much in the air in secular life (with a national government, the planning of international co-operation after the war and the trend towards social welfare), there was a feeling held by many that the dis-united churches represented something out of step with modern trends. There had been pre-war developments in inter-church discourse, especially at an Edinburgh Congress on Foreign Missions of 1910. But during the war, the churches of the British colonies and dominions felt iso-lated and independent of the mother churches, and they proceeded with extraordinary swiftness to conclude church unions. In Australia, Canada and South Africa, major unions across Protestant traditions occurred during the war years. This encouraged an enthusiastic ecumenical com-munity in Britain, where numbers from different churches started to meet across denominational lines. The Revd J. H. Shakespeare, general sec-retary of the Baptist Union, argued vigorously for union within Nonconformity and between it and the Anglican faith. He talked of 'the ugliness and the folly of our divisions', and stated that the decline of both churchgoing and church membership in the free churches 'is a very serious call to set our house in order, and to arrest a decline which otherwise implies that the denominations slowly bleed to death'.[52] But church union was vigorously opposed by many, especially a proposal that any act of reunion between the free churches and the Church of England would have to be a full one, and that in so doing there would have to be an accept-ance of 'the fact of episcopacy' – the system of election of bishops – in the Church of England, which free church adherents opposed.[53]

Churches emerged from the war with contradictory impulses – towards sectionalism, and towards ecumenical union. Scottish Protestants came out of the war feeling in various ways outmanoeuvred by the powers that be. The Education (Scotland) Act of 1918 was passed, giving the Catholic Church north of the border control over its own state-funded schools (a power Protestant churches didn't have, and which they fought for several decades to have repealed), whilst in England 'the unity project' had 'gone quite far enough' because – in a quite obvious dig about elites and the war – 'people were too preoccupied by the war to pay attention to private conclaves of ecclesiastics at Oxford'.[54] Meanwhile, the Anglo-Catholic wing of the Church of England feared it was being outmanoeuvred by the Protestant or Low Church wing during the war. High churchman Douglas Macleane prioritised union with the Roman Catholic and Orthodox Christian churches of Russia and Eastern Europe before any union with Nonconformists. The two extreme wings of the Anglican Church, the Catholic and the Low Church, essentially faced two ways. The pro-Catholic *Church Times* said: 'We must do nothing, then,

that will make reunion with the Eastern Churches more difficult.'[55] Such was the Anglo-Catholic fear of Protestant organisation that clerics from its stable eschewed the formation of Boy Scout troops (or groups) in their parishes, as the Scouting movement was seen as not only Protestant but rather too Nonconformist.[56]

So, the Church of England emerged from the war with a divisive frame of mind. Apart from the shock of war, and the apparent crisis of confidence in popular adherence to the church, there was a renewal and intensification of the struggle between Catholic and Protestant wings of the state church. In late 1917, there was intense criticism at the appointment of the Low Church theologian Dr Herbert Hensley Henson as Bishop of Hereford, regarded by one Anglican canon as an appointment that 'cannot but compromise the Church of England in the face of Christianity'.[57] Henson took a liberal view on the resurrection of Jesus Christ after the crucifixion, tending towards a metaphorical rather than literal interpretation of the Bible on this point. Calls for disestablishment rose with his appointment, whilst liberals saw the state connection as the bulwark of liberalism and religious liberty in the Anglican Church. (Ironically, Henson would some ten years later switch sides to become a fervent supporter of disestablishment.) From the ecumenical viewpoint, church reunion should lead to a new national church, to unite society in a liberal and broad Christianity by which the nation could be redefined – as the Anglican dean of Manchester called it, a church which should be 'as nearly as possible co-extensive with the nation'.[58]

A Life and Liberty Movement was initiated in the later stages of the war within the Church of England to secure a loosening of the state's control of the Church and its perceived interference in the struggles between the High and Low Church wings. With remarkable speed, it achieved one major success in the Enabling Act of 1919, which created in 1920 the Church Assembly, a body which could meet to represent the different views and regions of the Church.[59] Structural changes were in the air in Nonconformity too. In Scotland, the presbyterian churches quickly resumed planning for a reunion of the two great wings – the Church of Scotland and the United Free Church – whilst in England the Methodists were to consider reunion in the 1920s. With the formation of the Church in Wales at the same time, the war opened the valve to denominational change.

The Great War presents the social historian of religion with some contradiction. On the one side, as many traditional church historians have suggested, the First World War seemed a watershed because trench warfare

was a shock to men's faith, and because the strategies and systems at the dis-
posal of the churches to sustain popular religious activism – notably
confrontational evangelism – were gravely discredited in the context of rising
social-class antagonisms.[60] Other historians have located the war's impact in
the context of long-term secularisation, drawing on the view of contemporary
churchmen that British working-class men were in haemorrhage from organised Christianity in a combined rejection of deference to social elites and God.

Protestant evangelicals at the time bemoaned the decline of Sabbath
reverence after the war – the product, it was said, of men in the trenches
having to ignore such pleasantries. This pessimistic view was given new
weight recently by John Wolffe, who argued that the links between
Victorian religious culture and patriotism, discipline and tight social order
broke down in the stress of wartime – in the 20,000 British dead on the
first day of the battle of the Somme, and in the Easter Rising in Dublin in
1916.[61] On the other hand, there has been a recent development of a more
optimistic assessment that despite problems there was no sign of mass
defection from religion; many working people were deeply affected by
religious revivals in the years after the war, and, even if these were relatively few in number, British war experience cannot be characterised as a
general loss of religious faith.[62] What might have seemed like a crisis of
faith was actually a crisis of authority – or rather of popular deference to
establishment institutions like churches, and Christian endorsement of the
ideology of individualism. Much of what British churchmen at the time
characterised as loss of faith was actually loss of Edwardian reverence for
social authority – for obedience to the clergy. The class system was
changing, but popular Christian faith still retained resilience.

Notes

1 D.S. Cairns, *The Army and Religion* (London, Hodder & Stoughton, 1919)
   p. 156.

2 Framed copy of letter from King George V's secretary to the board of the
   Naval and Military Bible Society, dated 18 November 1912, on display in
   the chapel, Fort George Garrison, Inverness-shire, April 2005.

3 J. Wolffe, *God and the Greater Britain: Religion and National Life in Britain
   and Ireland 1843–1945* (London, Routledge, 1994), pp. 159–253.

4 Sir George Adam Smith, moderator of the United Free Church of Scotland,
   quoted in J.R. Fleming, *A History of the Church in Scotland 1875–1929*
   (Edinburgh, T&T Clark, 1933), p. 98.

5 C.L. Warr, *The Glimmering Landscape* (London, Hodder & Stoughton, 1960), pp. 118–19.

6 Advertisement in *Church Times*, 9 August 1918.

7 Bernard Martin, quoted in M.F. Snape, *God and the British Soldier: Religion and the British Army in the Era of the Two World Wars* (London, Routledge, 2005), pp. 144–5.

8 Ibid., pp. 160–3.

9 I. MacDougall (ed.), *Voices from War: Personal recollections of war in our century by Scottish men and women* (Edinburgh, Mercat Press, 1995), p. 91.

10 Snape, *God and the British Soldier*, p. 160.

11 W.E. Sellers and L.H. Gwynne, quoted in ibid., p. 166.

12 Quoted in ibid., p. 5.

13 Ibid., p. 65.

14 J. Bourke, *An Intimate History of Killing: Face-to-face Killing in Twentieth-century Warfare* (London, Granta, 1999), pp. 304–5.

15 Snape, *God and the British Soldier,* pp. 87–116.

16 Quoted in ibid., p. 2.

17 Cairns (ed.), *Army and Religion*, p. 121.

18 Studdert Kennedy, quoted in Snape, *God and the British Soldier*, p. 49.

19 Cairns (ed.), *Army and Religion*, pp. 7–8.

20 J. Black, quoted in Snape, *God and the British Soldier,* p. 28.

21 Warr, *The Glimmering Landscape*, p. 91.

22 Cited in Snape, *God and the British Soldier*, p. 39.

23 *Church Times*, 4 January 1918.

24 Annie S. Swan, 'The Christmas Peace', in *British Weekly*, 12 December 1918.

25 *Church Times*, 4 January 1918.

26 From *British Weekly*, 12 December 1918.

27 *Church Times*, 18 January 1918; M. R. Bellasis, 'Hannay, James Owen (1865–1950)', Revd Brian Taylor, *Oxford Dictionary of National Biography* (Oxford University Press, 2004): http://www.oxforddnb.com/view/article/33686, accessed 12 September 2005.

28 *Church Times*, 18 January 1918.

29 *British Weekly*, 4 April 1918, 7 November 1918.

30 R. Currie, A. Gilbert and L. Horsley, *Churches and Churchgoers: Patterns of*

Church Growth in the British Isles since 1700 (Oxford, Clarendon, 1977), pp. 218–9, 213.

31 B.R. Wilson, *Sects and Society: A Sociological Study of Three Religious Groups in Britain* (London, Heinemann, 1961); R. Wallis, *Salvation and Protest: Studies of Social and Religious Movements* (London, Frances Pinter, 1979), p. 312.

32 *Church Times*, 18 January 1918.

33 Cecil L Robinson, quoted in ibid., 15 November 1918.

34 W.R. Nicoll, *Reunion in Eternity* (London, Hodder & Stoughton, 1919).

35 *Church Times*, 20 December 1918.

36 Quoted in *British Weekly*, 28 November 1918.

37 S. Fletcher, 'Royden (Agnes) Maude (1876–1956)', *Oxford Dictionary of National Biography* (Oxford University Press, 2004): http://www.oxforddnb.com/view/article/35861, accessed 12 September 2005; *Church Times*, 20 December 1918.

38 *British Weekly*, 12 December 1918.

39 See book review of M.P. Daggett, *Women Wanted*, in *Church Times*, 15 November 1918.

40 Letter of 29 November 1918 to J.H. Shakespeare, quoted in *British Weekly*, 12 December 1918.

41 Ibid., 14 November 1918.

42 J.H. Shakespeare, *The Churches at the Cross-Roads: A Study in Church Unity* (London, Williams and Norgate, 1918), pp. 1–2.

43 *Church Times*, 3 January 1919.

44 *British Weekly*, 20 February 1919.

45 *Church Times*, 3 January 1919.

46 G.I.T. Machin, *Churches and Social Issues in Twentieth-century Britain* (Oxford, Clarendon Press, 1998), pp. 23–7.

47 K. Hylson-Smith, *The Churches in England from Elizabeth I to Elizabeth II vol. III: 1833-1998* (London, SCM Press, 1998), p. 177; *Church Times*, 30 May 1919.

48 *British Weekly*, 20 February 1919, 13 July 1919.

49 Figures calculated from data in Shakespeare, *Churches at the Cross-Roads*, p. 73.

50 *Church Times*, 16 May 1919.

51 *British Weekly*, 5 December 1918, 13 February 1919.

52 Shakespeare, *Churches at the Cross-Roads*, pp. 72, 145, 79–89, 87–8.

53 *British Weekly*, 5 December 1918; *Church Times*, 20 December 1918.

54 *British Weekly*, 5 December 1918.

55 *Church Times*, 16 August 1918, 3 January 1919.

56 Ibid., 25 October 1918.

57 Ibid., 4 January 1918; M. Grimley, 'Henson, Herbert Hensley (1863–1947)' *Oxford Dictionary of National Biography* (Oxford University Press, 2004): http://www.oxforddnb.com/view/article/33825, accessed 12 September 2005.

58 *Church Times*, 4 January 1918.

59 Hylson-Smith, *Churches in England*, p. 189.

60 D.L. Edwards, *Christian England vol. 3: From the eighteenth century to the First World War* (London, Collins, 1984), p. 358; Hylson-Smith, *Churches in England*, p. 154

61 Wolffe, *God and the Greater Britain*, p. 261.

62 Snape, *God and the British Soldier*; Machin, *Churches and Social Issues*, pp. 3–23.

CHAPTER 4

Christian culture in confusion, 1920–45

'To put it bluntly, religion attracts; the Church repels.' So said Cosmo Gordon Lang, the Church of England's Archbishop of York, in 1922, in analysing what many considered a religious crisis. The First World War, he felt, had shaken ideals as well as nerves, breaking confidence in ever-advancing social progress, with the result that 'post-war confusions had left a taste of moral failure'.[1] Optimism was gone, replaced by a confused prognosis of Christian Britain's condition. Did the future lie in ecumenical church union based on liberalism and compromise? Or was the way forward going to be in conservative retrenchment and religious puritanism?

Puritanism and the peace

The First World War had instigated an attack on pleasure, and this gave a fillip to the forces of puritanism. When religious crisis seemed to loom, the instinctive reaction was one of retrenchment not compromise, and a reversion to Edwardian Britain's presumptions about religion. At a church congress on the evangelisation of Britain in Sheffield in late 1922, it was alleged that under 3 per cent of young men regularly attended church (a figure that was probably a gross underestimate). The Anglican Bishop of London felt that an increasing number of people were going to football grounds on Saturday afternoons, and to golf links on Sundays, whilst churches are 'very empty'.[2] The religious problem was re-identified in the post-war period by evangelicals as essentially the same as before the war – men and their temptations and negligence.

To meet this, the early 1920s saw a resumption of evangelistic endeavour, both by churches and by the independent evangelical industry.

In 1921 and 1922, church evangelists targeted depressed communities suffering in the economic recession of the period. Hardship was severe in fishing communities (where fishing catches declined during the early 1920s), in coal-mining villages (because of declining wages and strike action), and in large industrial cities (as heavy manufacturing and the cotton industry declined sharply in adverse world trading). At Inverallochy on the Moray Firth coast, despair spread as fishing landings collapsed, and an evangelist called Jock Troup preached whilst children knelt in prayer in the road, bonfires were started of cigarettes, playing cards, snakes-and-ladders boards and dancing shoes, and fishermen 'knelt down together on the shore and engaged in silent prayer, wringing their hands and swaying their bodies to and fro'. In the coal-pit village of Plean in Stirlingshire, religious meetings became seen as a threat to public order and a police constable dispersed one Christian service. But these were sometimes short-term outbursts of religious despair. In a revival meeting of 2,400 people in Govan town hall in 1922, for instance, only 30 made public declarations of faith, and similar results were obtained from other denominations.[3] In Glasgow during the depression of 1921–2, a twelve-month 'New Life campaign' produced packed civic arenas, ending with the interdenominational Scottish Churches Missionary Congress and billboards around the city covered with large blue images showing Christ pointing with uplifted hand to the quotation, 'Go ye into the world and preach the Gospel.'[4] In Birmingham in late 1922, the Free Church Council organised a 'Personal Evangelism Campaign' which divided the city into 22 districts, each with a special missioner, and 230 congregations joined the campaign. In Portsmouth in 1925, a team of 50 evangelists reported 'good results' from a mission in rural districts. In 1923, the World Evangelical Alliance Congress at Westminster sought to further church co-operation, whilst 16,000 people attended the Anglo-Catholic Congress at St Paul's and the Albert Hall (bearing badges to be seen all over London), and 500 Baptists set off on a chartered ship from Grimsby to the Third Congress of the Baptist World Alliance in Stockholm.[5]

Whilst the mainstream churches organised ever-larger congresses and publicity campaigns on the streets, there was also a growth of smaller sects and groups – organisations which perceived the world to be hostile to true faith, and many of whom sought to withdraw from it. The sects were almost entirely evangelical, though in some regards this came to mean diverging things, with splits emerging between liberal innovative groups on the one hand and conservative traditionalists on the other. The conservatives formed the basis of what would later become known as

Christian 'fundamentalism', promoting a strictness founded on what they regarded as a close adherence to biblical injunction. More generally, a distinctive feature was the rising power of the concept of 'Christian fellowship', expressed in *the group*, over that of Christian denominationalism. The liberal evangelicals also favoured an innovative approach to the culture of the times, welcoming the infusion of art, music and literature in Christian life, with resort to the elegance and splendour in the religion's heritage: as historian David Bebbington has remarked of the 1920s, 'a Romantic gale was blowing across the Evangelical landscape'.[6] The conception of spirituality within British churches was changing, and in many ways it was in the sects that these views took shape in the 1920s and 1930s, before becoming more widespread within British Christianity from the 1950s and 1960s.

Within the innovators, there were varied beliefs – such as, that Anglo-Saxons were descended from the lost tribes of Israel, that evil in the world was rising prior to Christ's second return, and that a 'rapture' would save believers to be followed by a great tribulation leading to the end of the world. A growing and slightly ambiguous trend was that of the 'holiness movement' which emanated from a late nineteenth-century group that had put an emphasis on faith as a decisive experience after, or beyond, the evangelical conversion of the individual. The movement stressed a calm Christian outlook, with the individual coupled with his or her God, rather than engaged in struggle and effort as in a traditional evangelical outlook. This influence found favour amongst many in different denominations, including in the Church of England. Whilst 'holiness' could encourage a liberal outlook in some people, its overall impact was to strengthen puritanism. One of its early converts was Frank Buchman, who in the 1930s founded a movement dedicated to promoting conservative Christian morality, called the Oxford Group (later known as Moral Rearmament – see pages 198–201) that was to seek great impact on British public culture after 1945.

Amongst the flourishing groups were the Elim Foursquare Gospel Alliance and the Assemblies of God, which nurtured the growth of Pentecostalism before mid-century. Highly successful campaigns were held in Leeds and Sunderland in 1927, and at Crystal Palace in London in 1930, which gathered thousands for revival meetings that spread experiences like that of speaking in tongues (glossolalia, where a person speaks in a language unknown to them). In the midst of high unemployment and uncertainty over changing times, the effervescent religious culture within this Christian cluster attracted many working-class people, spilling out into public spaces. In 1930, a ticket collector aboard 'a Glory Train', going from Euston to Birmingham for a rally, moved through the carriages to find hundreds on their knees praying.[7]

It should be noted, though, that even when being innovative, evangelicals were usually being quite conservative in their general outlook on society, morality and behaviour. Take the Brethren, who, though thinly scattered, often had a proportionately strong presence in industrial towns and fishing villages. They found the 1920s fertile recruiting times for evangelising in working-class communities in a manner going out of fashion amongst many mainstream congregations.[8] In Lancashire by the end of the 1930s, it was noted that such sects had forms of worship and kinds of theology that were different and inviting. Groups with names like Hebron, Beulah, Mazdaznan (an American Zoroastrian sect that combined Christianity with Hinduism), Advent, Bethel, Evangelical, Holiness and Out and Out (a Methodist organisation) were small but moderately successful, and were described by one commentator as 'tremendously intense, utterly anti-pub, anti-alcohol'. The services allowed worshippers to participate more than in the mainstream churches; they were permitted 'to intervene, cry out, suddenly pray, become inspired by the spirit'. Communion wine was raspberry juice, and membership was denied to anyone who smoke, drank or went to the cinema. In a perceptive commentary, the anthropological organisation Mass-Observation noted the impact such sects had in Bolton in Lancashire, dubbed 'Worktown':

It is necessary to understanding the tremendous power of 'Nonconformity' in Worktown, for it influences the social life and success of the pub. This influence is not at all 'obvious'. It would be easy to spend a year in Worktown and, if you didn't go to church, think the Church was less important than the tram or the political party. But its leaders are also leaders of politics, police, magistrates' benches, local press, and business. And the strong Nonconformist tradition of a town once known as the Geneva of the North whose first two Mayors were Unitarians (in days when Unitarians were 'unbelievers') divides the place into Church and non-Church people.[9]

Religious militancy was mirrored across Britain. Within two weeks of peace in 1918, the temperance movement had an agreed agenda to move the country to prohibition.[10] Religious campaigners against alcohol as a social evil looked for inspiration to the United States, where in 1919 Congress voted to introduce prohibition banning all alcoholic drinks. Though some communities in Scotland voted in 1920 to create local prohibition, and others hoped to get similar measures elsewhere in Britain, not all Christians were approving of this. Many Catholics and Anglo-Catholics regarded temperance and prohibition as Nonconformist policies and opposed them, and by the late 1930s the bulk of the British public regarded the prohibition movement as out-dated and outmoded.[11]

Nevertheless, we should not underestimate how the aims and methods of the temperance movement were still very popular, especially amongst children, and caused division in communities and within families. Figures from central Scotland suggest that 45 per cent of young girls between 1890 and 1939 were in weekly-meeting temperance organisations (36 per cent in the Band of Hope and 9 per cent in the White Ribboners or the Good Templars). With 68 per cent of them attending Sunday school as well, this was a highly-religious and morally-strained upbringing for the young.[12] The Band of Hope's magic lantern stories of female victims of male drink are widely recalled in first-hand testimony:

> ... they had lantern slides and they were absolutely beautiful and it was usually always the ones that I can remember, with them being coloured – [they] remind me now of what I think of stained glass windows. You would see the mother would probably be in bed, and she'd either just had an addition to her family or she was ill with tuberculosis. And you usually saw the father who had been drunk, and it was always perhaps the eldest sister was looking after, you know, a big family. And this was brought home to you about, you know, drink, you know, how it was the downfall of your eh – So, with the result that when you would go to these things, you know, you'd sometimes come away with your face all tear-stained. ...[13]

Women were portrayed as the moral guardians of their families – of fathers, brothers, husbands and sons. The British Women's Temperance Association – known as the 'White Ribboners' because of their uniform – provided moral and spiritual protection for working-class women in vul-nerable occupations (notably mill-work) by confronting male drunkenness. Their main propaganda device was a community parade in which the daughter of a well-known drunken father would be dressed in white and placed at the head of the marching band. One woman to whom this happened in the early 1920s recalled: 'I went to the White Ribboners, and they had a parade. My father didn't know that I had been going to the White Ribboners. But he was standing at the corner when he saw us coming down with the white banners, and somebody said: "My Archie,

see who's leading it?" He says: "Aye, an' I'm going to the pub tonight." '[14]
Virtue and piety were on parade, and they were female.

Women were put under great moral and religious pressure – especially married women. The marriage bar operated by which single women lost their jobs or were expected to leave by employers, trades unions and the general community. When women workers got married in the 1920s at Cadbury's chocolate factory in Bournville, they were summoned to Dorothy Cadbury's office to be presented with a Bible, a carnation and the sack; men who got married merely received a Bible.[15] Religious leaders, especially women leaders, led the puritan assault on sexual 'impurity'. In the post-war years, there was a combined evangelical–medical rhetoric concerning the way in which immorality led to sexual disease and mental instability. This created fraught conceptions in young girls, with much pressure from mothers and the community. Winifred Foley, brought up in a mining community in the New Forest of south-west England in the 1910s and 1920s, recalled the 'care taken by the mothers of the village to instil virtue in their daughters'. When tempted at her first sexual encounter, she recited a popular ditty to herself:

There was a young lady so wild
She kept herself pure and undefiled
By thinking of Jesus
Venereal disease
And the dangers of having a child.[16]

The new fashions for women in the 1920s brought moral confrontation. In London, Rose Gamble's sister was regarded by her father as a 'guttersnipe' for wearing short hair, short skirts and make-up of the 'flapper fashion'.[17] Daisy Noakes trod a dangerous path when she became friendly with the village boys. She was told by her mother to by all means be sociable but above all else 'keep Pure'. Purity was crucial to the maintenance of the good woman, and if the churches did not explain what was meant, then family and community did. When Edith Hall impaled her genitals on a railing her virginity was considered ruined even though she had not had intercourse. Her mother was informed by an aunt: 'You must write a letter for her to give her husband when she grows up and marries explaining what has happened.'[18] Sex was a man's domain, and this was God's will. Dolly Scannell reflected her mother's attitudes when she recalled her own childhood ideas on sex: 'I felt that Father had some pleasure every time God decided to send another baby, but that mother didn't, and I felt too that a man *must have* this pleasure but a Mother *must not.*'[19] Women were often portrayed as not being right in having sexual desires. In the New Forest, rumours spread round Winifred Foley's village that a woman and her husband 'be so mad at it, they do get down in broad daylight, 'avin it on the mat in front o' the fire'.[20]

The inter-war years were ones of sustained sexual restraint, and in some cases intensifying self-discipline. Levels of illegitimacy, after rising during the First World War to 6.3 per cent of all births in 1918, fell dramatically in England and Wales in the early 1920s in the midst of the puritan austerity and religious revivals, reaching 4.1 per cent between 1923 and 1925, and hovering at around 4.2–4.3 per cent until 1940. Northern Ireland followed the same trend, having a low of 4.1 per cent in 1923 that was only seriously eroded around the early 1930s, whilst in Scotland levels of illegitimacy (though higher than in the rest of the UK) fell markedly between the wars (from 8.0 per cent in 1918 to 5.9 per cent in 1940).[21] These statistics show how the stigma of sexual misdemeanour was growing, not lessening. (See Figure 1.1, p. 32.)

But there were significant changes under way in the representation of ideal femininity during these decades. In fashion, the skinny look of the early 1920s was at first bohemian and shocking. However, by the late 1930s, women's fashions advertised in the religious press were emphasising women's utility around the home, not their curvy lines – the straight lines specifically aimed at those 'who like to look attractive while being busy about the house'.[22] By the late 1930s also, religious newspapers were unable to resist the pressures for advertisements which portrayed women in underwear and bikini swimwear.[23] Whether it was busy-ness or sexiness, the idealisation of the religious woman was of a different calibre from before the war.

This was also reflected in changes to women's leisure and activity. Before 1914, women were characteristically enveloped in church-based organisations, usually with overtly evangelistic or pietistic focus – Mothers' Prayer Groups, Sunday-school teachers, Women's Literary Clubs and so on. But there was a shift towards new organisations which emphasised the practical and the crafts in leisure – in England the Women's Institutes, and north of the border the Scottish Women's Rural Institute. Another element here was the shift from a middle-class world of servants; the Mothers' Union emphasised in 1926 that 'There is no "class element".'[24]

The modern woman was reinventing herself as domestic cheerleader and action woman, and moving away from having to live up to the status of moral angel. Yet, new ideas brought a moral maze for young women.

Margaret Penn found it hard to reconcile her rural religious outlook with the atmosphere of a Manchester factory. When she found that girls went to the theatre she was horrified; in her home community it was seen as depraved to attend such wicked follies. To her amazement, the girls were 'brought up just as respectably as herself – regular chapel-goers' who went to the theatre 'with their own mothers too!'.[25] But the respectable Christian self was not just about the mirror-image that society threw back at a woman. It was also about self-respect. May Hobbs was sent to prison and was conscious that she was regarded by church society as falling from grace. But she maintained her self-esteem: 'In spite of it all, I class myself as more of a Christian than all the frumps who go to church every Sunday. Half of them only go to ease their consciences.'[26]

On the face of it, men's position in the Christian culture of the inter-war years seemed to be little changed from Victorian representation. For puritans, men remained the problem, and their moral disciplining was depicted as depending on self-discipline and deprivation of 'natural' instinct. In David Thomson's Episcopal Church in Scotland, there existed some anticipation that a minister preparing a lad for confirmation would 'introduce his charge into knowledge of the physical transformation from boyhood into manhood'. This sex education was something his canon 'did clumsily', leaving to the last instruction session to tell him: 'The seed God gave you. ... Do you understand? ... You must not waste it. I hope, in God's name, that you never have wasted it and never will.'[27] But in the main, the articulation of moral disciplining for men was not about sex, but about games, gambling and drink.

Unusually, the Catholic Church often offered outlets for games withheld by most Protestant churches. In Liverpool, a great amateur billiards champion, Tom Fay, gave demonstrations to youngsters in the Catholic Young Men's Society Club in the Docklands area.[28] Bob Crampsey, brought up in a Catholic family in Glasgow, recalls how Sundays were days of Protestant subjugation, and how he and other lads were restrained from breaking taboos; he was banned from playing football by his mother because the neighbours would object, and the family had to 'go for a nice walk' instead.[29]

A leading figure in the Church of Scotland attacked the rich man who played golf or drove his motor car on Sundays: 'His soul is in darkness, selfish and arrogant and carrying of his heathendom on the wings of a prosperous independence.'[30] All across Britain, religious MPs resisted Sunday opening of cinemas for many years, including in Birmingham where there was a ferocious contest over the issue. Even when finally permitted in 1931, regional variation became stark: nearly all London cinemas opened on Sundays, three-quarters of English cinemas as a whole, but only 7 per cent of those in Scotland and Wales.[31] Cinema feature films came under increased scrutiny from religious and moral campaigners in the 1920s, especially in regard to children, instigating the film industry's escalation of self-censorship in the 1930s.[32] The Lord's Day Observance Society (LDOS) and the *British Weekly* newspaper fought against Sunday boxing contests – especially the 12,000 spectators who turned up to watch boxing in a former evangelical chapel in West Bromwich. The paper said that 'crowds of sportsmen (of a kind) gather Sunday by Sunday in order to satiate their basic instincts by gazing upon the brutalities of a Prize Fight' worth up to £400 to the winner, describing it as 'a blot on a Christian land'. In 1929, the LDOS successfully got boxing contests at Ilford, Gravesend and Stratford stopped, and sought Home Office legislation to stop them nationally. Similarly, church groups campaigned against work by builders on Sundays.[33] The pressure also came from the Catholic Church. In a Lancashire town, an observer for Mass-Observation noted a priest's service:

Make up your mind what you are going to do in Lent. I recommend you to keep the pledge. You may never fear that drink will get a hold over you if can do without it for the period of Lent. It is for seven weeks. Don't say it after me, but say it in your soul: 'In honour of the Sacred Thirst and in the Atonement of the intemperance of men I solemnly promise Almighty God and the Blessed Virgin Mary that I will abstain from all intoxicating drinks, and may Jesus Christ protect you.'[34]

Many churchmen were instinctively reacting to the sense of Christian crisis by drawing a line in the sand for men. By emphasising a puritan threshold between right and wrong, the crisis of masculine Christianity could be controlled and the faithful held in the churches' orbit.

In many ways the 1920s and 1930s saw a sharpening of edges to British Christian culture. Children were taught to understand the theological underpinnings of Christian division. Helen Forrester, brought up in Liverpool by a Nonconformist grandmother who told her of the 'horrors' of Catholicism, baulked at the prospect of being forced to attend confession at a High Anglican Sunday school, and told her elders: 'But we are Protestants. We say the General Confession during service. We make personal confessions only to God. I thought that was what being a Protestant was all about.'[35] Lines in the sand were being drawn with increasing intensity. In Lancashire, Mass-Observation noted how many worshippers, seeking clarity of religious view, found it in puritan sects: 'These churches, still with the touch of missionary-to-the-worker attitude, are not of course full just because of their attitudes to drink. But their attitude to drink is clear cut, and that apparently is what many people want from a Church.'[36] In Scotland in the 1920s, Libby Purves' father experienced 'a glum and joyless world of religious strictness' into which he had been born at Cupar in Fife. 'There was endless kirk on Sundays ... and threats of hellfire for the slightest blasphemy: and blasphemy could consist of even reading a secular book on the Sabbath, let alone running or playing.'[37]

Puritan innovation kept the Christian message in the public eye in the inter-war years. But it tended to destabilise ecclesiastical hierarchies, creating fellowships rather than church structures, thereby unsettling the appearance of unity in British Christian culture. The impression gained ground in many quarters by the 1930s that puritanism was failing in British society. A crisis seemed to be looming.

Religious identities in turmoil

In 1937, the Catholic Bishop of Salford said 'that it can no longer be taken for granted in England that one is talking to a Christian'. He expressed a feeling of many clergy that the people of the nation were starting to drift from a Christian identity. The chairman of the Congregational Union, Revd J. D. Jones, said in 1925: 'The situation is this: the great mass of our people seem to be drifting away from religion; the habit of worship is falling into disuse; the Sabbath is rapidly ceasing to be a day of rest; seventy-five per cent of the manhood of the country it has been estimated, are clean outside all the Churches.' Jones argued that his Church 'helped to create the middle class', but he suggested that 'the middle class is fast disappearing and the Church that caters for that class will soon have no constituency left'. Coupled with this, he felt, the problem was that 'the Church that has no message for the ordinary everyday man is no Church of Jesus Christ at all'.[38]

Part of the drift detected by the churches lay in the paradox of plebeian male religiosity in the inter-war years. On the one hand, masculinity was still widely portrayed as an innate problem for popular faith, and something that needed feminine attributes. Men were clearly alienated from church-going in very large numbers, making up no more than a third (and usually much less) of congregations. On the other hand, the inter-war decades witnessed perceptible innovations in working-class male spirituality.

The first of these in importance was the crisis of the masculine body created by the death and maiming of the First World War. This led to men adopting a comradeship based around war experience, one that simultaneously undermined myths of 'glorious war' and excluded non-combatants (which could take in both women and most of the British clergy). A remembrance culture[39] developed in the 1920s around rituals, and architecture and organisations of war-remembering – in the distinctive remembrance service on 11 November each year, at the war memorials and cenotaphs which mushroomed in every town and village of the country (as well as at national sites of remembrance at the Whitehall cenotaph and at Edinburgh Castle), and in the British Legion for ex-servicemen, which combined leisure and remembrance functions together. Signified in the annual red-poppy wreaths and lapel-badges sold in aid of the Haig Fund for war veterans' homes, this culture was partly independent from the official churches, yet exploited the connection. The British Legion recruited its own chaplains and conducted its own Festival of Remembrance that continued through the twentieth century, and the Legion came to form a separate part of British civic culture.

In a second innovation, the British Legion was joined by other organisations with some similarities, notably the Anglican Toc H association that started in 1920 from impromptu wartime centres for men near the western front. Based on principles of friendship, service, fair-mindedness and the kingdom of God, Toc H provided a distinctly male site for religion that tapped into the complex emotions that combat engendered (though it also went on to have a strong women's association); by the 1930s it had 1,000 branches, and was claimed as the largest voluntary organisation in the British Empire.[40] A third phenomenon exemplifies what was amounting to an increasing independence of spirit in male religiosity. It was in the 1920s and 1930s that religious themes started to penetrate sites of male culture. It became the tradition from 1927 for the English FA Cup Final to be started with mass singing, including most distinctively the hymn 'Abide With Me', whilst rugby matches, notably in Wales, were characterised by choral hymn-singing.

These trends hint at a new form of intermediate male relationship to organised Christianity – a series of cultural accommodations that, in part, provided an alternative non-church focus in which male faith might surface and be expressed. However, these trends also acknowledged the alienation many men felt from the churches, and the inability of the churches to meet their needs. Many men were giving up going to church on a Sunday in what seemed a permanent breach between much of British manhood and traditional Christianity. As historian Hugh McLeod has observed: 'For millions of working-class families it was a day for digging the garden, visiting relatives, or snoozing over the *News of the World*.'[41]

The churches, in their panic over popular faith, were no longer limited to pinpointing working-class masculinity. Sex was changing the churches' agenda. Despite concerns over class alienation from faith, churchmen started to allege that declining sexual morality was undermining the religious condition of the nation. Sex before marriage became the new critical indicator of de-Christianisation. The 1920s and 1930s saw the rise of birth control clinics, where couples could get advice about contraceptive methods, responding to the demand for condoms to limit family size and pregnancy outwith marriages. For practising Catholics, the widening use of artificial barrier methods of birth control (such as the condom) was taken by their Church, as it took the rise of easier civil divorce, as what the Bishop of Salford called 'examples of the breakdown of the moral life of the country'.[42] Protestant churches were divided on contraception and whether it made sex immoral (or 'unchaste' as it was put). The Church of England's Lambeth Conference of 1930 narrowly approved contraception, if used with 'moral obligation' and 'Christian principles', but conservative bishops were only assuaged by the Church calling for restriction on advertising and retailing of condoms – leading to condoms being sold until the 1970s mainly in men's barbers.

Meanwhile, King Edward VIII had an affair with an American divorcee, Mrs Simpson, and, amidst overwhelming public and political hullabaloo in 1936, he felt compelled to abdicate. Many churchmen condemned him. Archbishop Cosmo Lang of the Church of England said in a radio broadcast that Edward had 'sought his happiness in a manner inconsistent with the Christian principles of marriage, and within a social circle whose standards and ways of life are alien to all the best instincts and traditions of his people'. Those people, he went on, 'stand rebuked by the judgment of the nation'.[43] In truth, this was a misreading of public sentiment. The people were probably less rebuking of what was a genuine love-match, and more enthralled by the travails of celebrity. But for the time being, the people had little inclination to challenge the churches' reading of sexual morality.

Sex afflicted the churches in other ways. The British press was developing an insatiable appetite for scandal involving church clergy. The greatest of all the scandals was that of the Revd Harold Davidson from north Norfolk, who was defrocked in 1932 from the Church of England after being accused of purporting to rescue prostitutes by sharing their beds, and his ejection left a long-lasting scar. Scandal made the churches objects of derision, and exposed their vulnerability to the accusation of sheltering scoundrels and deviants. But Christian churches were also great objects for humour in popular culture. Jokes about parsons and churches were standard fare in the music hall in the inter-war period. Greed and hypocrisy were common themes of jokes: 'The bishop's going on holiday, so send in your missionary boxes quick.' In another joke, one comic mocked a hymn 'sung on Sunday by the Salvation Army. There was Beastly Bertie, the converted convict, two reformed sailors, two commercial travellers, me ... – so you can see what sort of people there were. There were 24 in the band – 4 playing and 20 going round with the hat.' Disdain for the converted Christian was reputedly rife in certain circles. A Lancashire barman spoke in the late 1930s about a man who belonged to the Salvation Army: 'Gets up and testifies on Sunday evenings. He got up and said "Before I joined the Army I had nowt, but look at me now, nice suit of clothes and watch and chain." Cries of Glory to God and Praise the Lord. This was at 8p.m. At 11p.m. same man was crawling upstairs at the S.A. hostel on his hands and knees, blind drunk. Two [S.A.] captains pitched him out.'[44] Such jokes about religion were not new, of course, and if nothing else they indicated the continuing place of the Christian churches in British culture. It was perhaps when the jokes *stopped* that the churches had most to worry about, and that was not quite yet.

Part of the religious crisis was to do with the British Empire and race. In a 1910 congress in Edinburgh, the churches of Britain and her colonies started to rethink the relationship between black and white Christian peoples, though it was some way from acknowledging a racial equality between them. There was still no withdrawal from mission enterprise. Even the Church of England, much criticised by Nonconformists for doing too little, produced in 1936 a large four-volume study of foreign missions to inaugurate a great drive to raise £250,000 per year to fund 500 new workers 'in aid of the needs of the heathen world'.[45] Such language of religious disparagement, racism and the imperial project was still endemic. In 1929, the Salvation Army announced that it was sending 300 boys to be trained in farming plus 200 domestic servants to Australia as 'Empire Builders', whilst others were being sent for service in India and Ceylon. The vocabulary of 'otherness' was still alive and well.

For many, British imperialism was still morally good. The presbyterian minister in Colombo, Ceylon, was concerned in 1925 with the British occupation of Mosul in Iraq because of the absence of any Christians there, and believed that it was being undertaken for commercial greed instead of for 'a higher notion – viz., the good of the people'. He went on: 'I am an Imperialist, not in the Jingo sense of that term, but in the sense that I believe God has so ordained that we as a nation should occupy certain parts of the world mainly for the better government and good, and I think it must be apparent to any thinking man that our occupation of so many places famous in Biblical history and dear to the Christian heart is nothing short of *providential*.'[46] But other missionaries worried more and more about military actions against overseas and colonial peoples. An incident in Shanghai in May 1925, in which British soldiers fired on a crowd, caused much debate. One Wesleyan minister in China defended British action on the grounds that 'the majority of the crowd was composed of labourers and rowdies of the worst type, who are far more dangerous in China than in England'.[47]

Meanwhile, South Africa was by the mid-1920s emerging as a special focus for British soul-searching on Christianity and race. What was called 'the Colour problem' was already being discussed, as missionaries reacted with distaste to the increasing segregation of society into black and white only zones. One writer challenged British churches: 'The country is no longer African, but has become European. It is the white man who runs the show, while the black man takes a back seat. In some places his presence is only tolerated because he cannot be got rid of.'[48] A Scottish minister from Natal defended degrees of segregation, saying that European and coloured children travelled to school in the same class of railway carriage, 'though rightly not in the same compartments'.[49] This reveals the distance to be travelled by European Christian thought towards a policy of racial and religious equality.

Various forms of racism and religious bigotry blighted Britain. Anti-Semitism developed in the inter-war years, reflecting the spread of eugenic and racist ideas across Europe. The Jewish community became well developed in the East End of London, in Manchester, in the Gorbals district of Glasgow, and was maturing in suburban areas and seaside towns as some Jewish families that had immigrated before 1914 started to prosper. Jewish identity was nurtured in different ways. As with many immigrant groups, one way was through Jewish women who, in the home, did much to sustain the religious identity of families through domestic rituals (of the Shabbat observance and eating kosher food).[50] Another was through distinctive economic activities – notably in tailoring, the furniture trades and jewellery. There remained in the 1920s and 1930s a profound working-class character to the Jewish faith, and communities were targeted by the

Analysis: The scandal of the Revd Harold Davidson

In March 1932, the Church of England put on trial one of its own parish clergy, the Revd Harold Davidson, aged 57, on a charge of immoral conduct with women over a ten-year period between 1921 and 1931. The twenty-five day trial was held in the full glare of the press in the Great Hall at Westminster before the Consistory Court of Norwich archdiocese (since Davidson's parish was at Stiffkey, pronounced 'Stookey', in north Norfolk). The trial and Davidson's subsequent behaviour and final destiny became the stuff of legend.

The trial heard evidence led by the Bishop of Norwich's prosecutor, Roland Oliver KC, that Davidson spent most of his time between Monday and Friday in London, only returning at weekends to conduct parish affairs in Norfolk. Whilst in London, he met and frequently dated with women, some of whom were alleged to be prostitutes, wining and dining them, and taking them to the theatre and cinema. Four women were cited, one being Miss Gwendoline Barbara Harris, who Davidson met when she was 16 years old. His chat-up line was, 'Excuse me but, are you Miss X the film actress?' He then came habitually to the girl's flat, starting 'on a course of seduction', taking her to his London flat in Shepherd's Bush where she spent one night in his bed. He then took her and another woman on a train to his home town of Wells in July 1929, where they became his domestic servants. Gwendoline told the court, 'He said he would marry me,' at which Davidson laughed in court. The prosecutor's questioning was as follows:

Did he, in your long association, talk about religion?
Once. He asked me to pray, but I did not, because he laughed at me.
Did he say anything about sin?
He said God did not mind sins of the body, but only sins of the soul.

Davidson was also alleged in 1931 to have gone to the flat of another woman, Betty Beach, an actress, who in his presence 'did a certain amount of gymnastics in her nightgown'. Davidson for several years chatted up other women 'of immoral character'. Miss Violet Low, a waitress at Yeg Wah Chinese restaurant in Bloomsbury, told the court that Davidson came three times a week with Barbara Harris, and would kiss her at the table. He followed Miss Dorothy Burns, formerly a waitress at Lyons Restaurant at Walbrook, about the shop in his clerical clothes, pretending to be chaplain to the Actors' Church Union. 'He kept on molesting me,' she said, and reported him to the chief inquiry office of Lyons who warned Davidson off. But he persistently tried to pick up 'trippies' – Lyons' trainee staff of 16–18 years of age before they became full waitresses. He acquired the nickname amongst them of 'the Mormon'. In addition, a photograph was produced in court showing him with a naked woman.

Revd Harold Davidson in a re-creation of the photograph that led to him being defrocked by the Church of England in 1932. The British public feasted on the scandal in press stories, and turned out in their thousands to see Davidson at Blackpool and Skegness. (Topfoto/Topham/Picturepoint)

In his defence, Davidson claimed to have helped 500 girls over a sixteen-year period. He claimed to have recruited some girls to appear in a film being made at Waterloo Underground station on rescue work amongst prostitutes. He said:

(Topfoto/Topham/Picturepoint)

I have been accused of misconduct with every one I have been associated with for years. I have been misunderstood. . . . I have been gossiped about by evil-minded people in connexion with every girl I have helped for years. I have been accused of being a white slave traffic agent and that I took girls to my rooms, and after prayer sold them to the Argentine.

He claimed the photo of him was a set-up by a woman who was paid £150 by a newspaper, and that his drape fell as a result of the flash bulb blinding him.

Davidson was found guilty on all counts – molesting, importuning, making improper suggestions to waitresses and immoral conduct with one woman. He then lost two appeals – one to the Privy Council, a second to the Archbishop of Canterbury – and was de-frocked on the grounds of 'grave scandal to the Church'.[51]

During his trial, Davidson became a celebrity. He was pursued and applauded by supporters (many from his parish in Norfolk) and by the press, and had a number of literary and bohemian supporters from London. After the trial was over, he capitalised on his fame. In early September 1932, he was arrested by police in Blackpool in Lancashire and charged with aiding and abetting Luke Gannon, described in court as an 'amusement caterer'. Gannon was summoned for causing a public nuisance by exhibiting Davidson in a wooden barrel on the footpath on Central Beach. A queue estimated by the Chief Constable at between 1,200 and 1,400 were waiting to pay to see Davidson in the barrel on the promenade, and approximately 16,000 had already successfully done so. This was an exhibition event in the form of popular shows, in a long line of side shows in British fetes, fairs and carnival, in which the tradition had developed of enhancing the sense of showmanship by making the display in containers, tanks or cages. Rarely if ever before had a Church of England rector been the willing exhibit, claiming that he had been the victim of a miscarriage by the bishops of the Church. Ever one to claim to be the wronged party, Davidson defended himself before Blackpool magistrates by saying it was not he in the barrel but an impersonator. The proceedings were dropped on an undertaking being given that it would not be repeated. However, Davidson left the court and did precisely that the very same day, in front of 3,000 customers, and was fined forty shillings (£2) before the same court four days later.[52]

Davidson was a showman through and through. Indeed, that had been his occupation before he became a clergyman, and he used his notoriety and fame to make a living in the years after being defrocked.[53] Three years later, during the height of the summer season at Blackpool, he was arrested again – this time not merely for an unlawful show on the promenade, but for an unlawful attempt at suicide (which was a criminal offence in Britain until the 1960s). He appeared on the seafront in his clerical dress in a wooden cabinet, with his daughter in another cabinet beside him, amidst posters which declared his intention to starve to death unless the Archbishop of Canterbury or his bishop restored him to his former position. At trial in Preston, he said: 'My life is finished. My life has been smashed. If the Archbishop would put it in writing that death would bring about reform, then I would cheerfully die.' Perhaps astonishingly, the jury found him not guilty.[54]

Indeed, it is one of the astounding features of the Davidson story that he attracted enormous popular sympathy. The British press loved him for the newspaper copy he provided, and the British people – especially the working classes – turned up in their thousands to see and cheer the showman-vicar who took on the hierarchy of the Church of England and the 'Establishment'. He had great success in the courts when juries sided with him. In November 1935, Davidson sued Blackpool Corporation for malicious prosecution over one of his arrests at the seaside resort. At the assizes in Manchester, Davidson sought damages of £254; the jury favoured him so much that it awarded him £382.[55]

But Davidson caused havoc in his wake. In addition to the young women whose lives he affected, Davidson left numerous victims. Major Philip Hammond, a magistrate from Holt in Norfolk, was fined twenty shillings (£1) plus costs for assault after telling Davidson, 'Get out, you —. I don't want to see you or any of your pimps,' and then kicking him.[56] In 1934, several newspapers got hold of a story that Davidson had regularly pimped for prostitutes, allegedly introducing Barbara Harris to a dentist from Euston Square in London, Mr Thomas C. Farmer. Farmer was then said to have regularly employed her. Farmer sued the *News Chronicle*, the *Daily News* and the *Daily Telegraph*, and denied that he was a friend of Davidson. The jury found for Farmer, but in a clear indication that the allegation might be more than an invention, it awarded him the minimum damages then possible – one farthing (a quarter of one penny).[57]

Davidson's fantastical story finally ended in tragedy, in the summer season of 1937, when he moved with a circus troupe to Skegness on the east coast. The story was perhaps fading a little by then, and his appearance in a barrel was tame. So, Davidson recited the story of the wrong-doing by the Anglican establishment against him from inside a lions' cage. At the town's Amusement Park, Davidson was inside the cage, with two lions – a lion called Freddy and a lioness. It was said that Davidson had protested at being 'shown' in the lions' enclosure, but he was evidently pressed by the show's organiser, and had been appearing for weeks under the watchful eye of a 16-year-old lion-tamer, Miss Renee Somer, who stayed outside the cage. But on 28 July, whilst talking to 200 people, Davidson tripped over the lioness, and was attacked by Freddy who dragged him by his neck to the other end of the cage. Miss Somer immediately leapt into the cage, struck the lion with a whip, and plunged an iron bar in its mouth, held it at bay, and then dragged Davidson to a corner of the cage from where he was rescued. When out of the cage, Miss Somer fainted. Two days later, Davidson died at the age of 62 in Skegness Cottage Hospital from the wounds, including a broken neck.[58]

Davidson's is an unusual case. He was the most notorious British clergyman of the twentieth century, and was clearly looked upon as a scandal by the hierarchy of the Church. The British press regarded him as a godsend, and the public held him in the highest regard. Interpreting that 'regard' is difficult. On the one hand, he was taking on the establishment, the small man who seemed to be the victim of over-zealous interpretation of his relationships with women. After all, no actual proof of adultery was brought forward. On the other hand, he appeared as a buffoon, a showman who sold himself as the victim of injustice, who would claim in courts that he was the victim of misidentification or that he did not actually write what was on the posters about his promenade show. And with wide reporting in the press, the British public could not resist paying to see a public appearance – be it in a barrel or a lions' cage. But it is also worth noting that Davidson was held in high regard by many of his loyal parishioners in Norfolk. He drew a large congregation to his church at Stiffkey, and he was buried in a prominent corner of the churchyard with an elaborate ornamental headstone that is still pointed out to visitors. Even now, it is said that there remains a strong sympathy in the parish for their former rector.[59]

anti-Semitic British fascists. On 4 October 1936, in the 'battle of Cable Street', some 3,000 British fascists were confronted by up to 200,000 communists, trades unionists and others, both Jewish and non-Jewish, in a violent episode that effectively faced down the fascist threat in Britain. Jewish identity was partly defined by ethnicity and partly by religion, and whilst the former remained robust, there were already hints in this period of the larger drift from the practising faith (by socialist Jews, for instance) that was to become more pronounced after 1950. Political and ecclesiastical acceptance of Jews developed reasonably strongly within British elite institutions, focused especially around a sharing of liberal and Labour Movement values. As a result, British Jewry was to some extent showing signs of starting to integrate through sharing with Christian culture the trends of prosperity and the revolt against deference, opening a route to secularisation.

Racism towards blacks and Asians was also cultivated in Britain in the 1920s and 1930s. The Catholic Archbishop of Westminster, Arthur Hinsley (1865–1943), lectured in 1937 on 'the backward races of Africa', in which he defined a backward race as 'one which has not had the opportunity, or perhaps the capacity, of reaching the level of civilization called generally European, distinguished in the main by its knowledge and practice of Christian principles'.[60]

Such articulations became significant in the context of rising Muslim immigration to Britain. This had developed very slowly in the late nineteenth century, and continued in the First World War. Arab and Somali seamen became very important to the British merchant marine during wartime, but most lost their jobs at the peace, causing widespread unemployment and poverty in the 1920s. Enforced repatriation developed – 500 Adenis were deported from Cardiff alone by September 1921. Significant communities of Muslims existed, the largest being at Cardiff, Newport, Barry, Liverpool, Tyneside, London and Glasgow. During the depression of the 1920s, pressure on government led to the 1925 Special Restrictions Order that tried to control the perceived 'flood' of Muslim immigration, leading to the use of aliens' certificates against Indian pedlars in Glasgow and Liverpool. The rise of council housing, built and rented out by local authorities to improve the housing of the working classes and the poor, became subject to deliberate racist management. Cardiff city council bowed to pressure from the white working class by amending by-laws to prevent Muslims from obtaining council-housing tenancies outside of a designated ghetto area of Bute Town, and something similar occurred in South Shields in the English north-east. British Islam started to get organised, notably with the foundation in 1936 of the Alawi order which established *zawiyas* (religious centres or lodges) in Cardiff, South Sheilds, Hull and Liverpool to encourage the revitalisation of the faith in a community predominantly composed of Yemeni and Somali seamen and their families.[61]

Within British Christian culture, Protestantism was dominant and asserted its supremacy. The state remained deeply anti-Catholic in its constitutional nature – a Catholic being forbidden from being head of state (or even married to one). The Catholic Church was constantly up in arms in the 1930s over what it considered unfair treatment by the BBC, formed in 1926 as a state corporation, which gave many radio broadcasts to other churches – a short-sighted favouritism, one observer felt, since Catholic services of Vespers and Compline 'would be infinitely more popular than some of those quasi-Protestant services which are neither flesh, fowl, nor good red herring'.[62]

Catholic–Protestant sectarianism remained endemic in many parts of Britain. Ireland split in 1921 with the formation of the Irish Free State (later the Republic of Ireland), becoming an overwhelmingly Catholic nation whose 1937 constitution linked it closely to the Catholic Church. Meanwhile, Northern Ireland remained inside the United Kingdom, and from the outset was Protestant dominated in numerical, political and institutional terms. Discrimination against Catholics pervaded Ulster society, and unstable and violent community relations were to scar the province for the remainder of the century. In 1922 alone, 232 people were killed in street battles as the province verged on the eruption of a religious civil war, and in 1932–5 more violence broke out during the high unemployment of the slump to create a decade of stormy relations.[63] Some institutions like the schools system became religiously segregated, whilst the police force became regarded as enforcing an essentially Protestant state. Protestant communities in the south after partititon, on the other hand, whilst they ultimately gave up their Unionist aims and often fell in number, nonetheless came to have less to concern them than many Catholics living north of the border.[64]

Across the water in Scotland, the inter-war period also witnessed acute anti-Catholicism, though without the levels of murderous violence as in Ulster. Protestant campaigns against Irish Catholic immigration arose, with the major cities of Glasgow and Edinburgh being scarred by the rise of sectarian politics and movements. These took the form of political campaigning at school-board elections against Catholic state schools created in 1918 – 'Rome on the rates' as it was dubbed – and grew in significance with extremist political parties contesting municipal elections, attaining significant representation and several councillors in the early 1930s. Two political parties emerged there in the 1920s to promote the ending of Irish immigration, whilst the two major churches, the Church of Scotland and the United Free Church, entered a period of the most infamous sectarian bigotry, blaming Irish Catholics for weakening the Scots race. A high-powered report by the Church of Scotland general assembly of 1923 stated of Irish Catholics: 'They cannot be assimilated and absorbed into the Scottish race. They remain a people by themselves, segregated by reason of their race, their customs, their traditions, and above all, by their loyalty to their Church, and gradually and inevitably dividing Scotland, racially, socially, and ecclesiastically.'[65] Penal laws against Catholics were still in existence, and were even used in the early 1920s to prevent Catholic priests in Scotland carrying the host (elements used in celebration of mass) in public, leading to their repeal by Parliament in 1926.

Lancashire was also scarred by Catholic–Protestant sectarianism, especially in the Victorian period. In the 1890s and 1900s, Liverpool witnessed intense economic and social conflict, including allegations against the police in the city, but in the inter-war period the sectarianism eased appreciably. Yet the culture of Ulster-led bigotry was sustained. In Protestant Everton Valley, Richard Passmore recalls that 'the high spot of the year, in many respects was July 12th'. He recalled that children knew it was the anniversary of the Battle of the Boyne, but few knew what the battle was about:

On that day every year an endless succession of marching bands – drum and fife, or concertina, or pipe, or occasionally a full brass band, processes along all the converging arteries to the city centre ... Each lodge featured a King Billy in seventeenth-century costume, full-bottomed wig down over his shoulders. This gentleman was sometimes astride a horse and was given, in any case, to waving a naked sword around his head. There would be a hefty male carrying a cushion on which reposed an open Bible. Around these two main characters would be the children, clad in white with orange sashes, the women in their very best, and the men, all in blue serge suits and inevitably wearing bowlers.[66]

Thousands of Orange Lodge members took to the streets with Catholics 'lurking in sidestreets' of the Pembroke Place areas of the city, and eventually a three-cornered battle broke out with police. A melee of 'rearing horses, truncheons and struggling men'. 'It was all great fun,' reports Richard Passmore, 'except, perhaps, to God, in whose Name all this was (in theory) happening. To us children, however, it was a free, colourful, dramatic and exciting spectacle.'

Yet, for all that Christian identities were confused and often conflicting, there were other optimistic signs for popular Christianity in Britain. For one thing, there was significant growth in the statistical indicators of religiosity. Church of England baptisms continued to grow per head of population until 1927, and thereafter the fall was only slight. Church membership showed slippage, but this was mainly small-scale and cyclical until 1939. From time to time, there could be great confidence within the churches. A Metropolitan Free Church Federation meeting of 600 ministers in 1926 was told by its leadership that 'the tide has turned' and that 'the religious outlook is very hopeful'.[67] In 1929, most of the Scottish presbyterian churches reunited in a massive explosion of ecumenical bonhomie, and the first moderator of the reunited Church of Scotland exclaimed to young people in a live radio broadcast from the reunion pavilion that 'half a century hence they may be telling children and grandchildren of the glories of this crowning day'.[68] Such euphoric optimism for the future was to prove misplaced, but for the time being there was no pressing decline of British Christian culture. Rather, the culture showed signs of becoming a comfortable and mellow ingredient in British life.

Mellow religion

Puritanism did not always fit well in the midst of people's severe economic hardships. This is best expressed by Robert Roberts' description of Salford when pawnbrokers stayed open late on Saturday nights so that it 'gave women waiting on drunken or late working husbands a few hours grace in which to redeem clothes and shoes before the Sabbath and so maintain their stake in English society'.[69] In this context, something else tended to prosper – the mellowing of religion.

In many respects, the inter-war years were when British Christianity became like an old sofa – relaxing, unpretentious and less demanding on the user. One form of this was the influence of the 'holiness' trend, which reached its greatest spectacle in High Church Anglo-Catholicism within the Church of England. The Anglo-Catholic lessening of evangelical influence in favour of ritual in liturgy and prayer had started as a sort of 'counter-culture' in evangelical Protestantism of Victorian England, but it had become by the 1920s and 1930s a burgeoning force. Its form of worship became almost more Catholic than the Roman Catholic Church, with many priests remaining unmarried in the Catholic tradition, holding a veneration for the Virgin Mary, and holding 'Mass' rather than the Protestant term of 'communion'. Reputedly 70,000 were attracted to a London congress in 1933, showing a vigour for the most part unmatched in the rest of the Church of England.[70]

With the Protestant churches, the presentation of evangelicalism underwent some compromising and mellowing of tradition. Take the chairman of the Congregationalist Union speaking in 1925: '[S]erious though the situation is, I am no pessimist. I do not believe that the Church is an effete institution. I do not believe that religion is on its dying bed. I do not betake myself to belief in a speedy Second Coming as a sort of refuge from despair ... The Lord will yet comfort Zion; he will redeem Jerusalem, and even already perhaps the time to favour her, yea, the set time, is come.'[71] This passage contains a complex set of allusions and signifiers which, together, seek to negotiate between the traditional and the modern. The allusion to the church as 'effete' is a reference to gender and class, a rebuttal to any notion that the church was either losing masculine vigour or being too bourgeois. The passage also shows a negotiation between the millenarian belief in Christ's second coming and the fact of it being unpalatable to many Christians – a negotiation achieved by seeing it as not 'speedy' but distant, beyond their lifetimes. This showed how, even in an evangelical church, the sense of imminence in Christ's second coming could be reduced, cultivating what might seem a less-demanding religious outlook than that of former decades.

The mellowing of Christian culture was evident also in the sense of a golden age of liberal familiarity and comfort. Don Haworth captured the mood when he described the place of Sunday in the community and family life of Bacup in Lancashire in the 1920s and 1930s. After attending Wesleyan Methodist chapel each Sunday morning, he recalled: 'We went for a walk and home for our Sunday dinner. It was a return to a warm and mellow world. Everybody was at home on Sundays. The doorsteps and window ledges had been freshly rubbing-stoned and smoke bellowed from the rows of house chimneys. People moved at leisure in their best clothes. ... It was familiar, welcoming and solid.'[72]

Sunday in industrial communities was invariably still a day marked out from the rest of the week, certainly in Protestant communities. Margaret Penn took a chapter in her autobiography of 1947 to describe the life of chapel and food in the Sunday routine of her family and the Methodist village in which she lived. With two sessions of Sunday school plus a chapel meal and worship, it was all religion. At the end of evening chapel, groups stood outside the chapel 'exchanging the week's news and waiting so that they could bid good-night to the Reverend Vane. They were all proud of their minister who, though little, was, they all stressed loudly, good.' Penn concluded: 'When he had bid the various groups a pleasant good-night, they broke up and went cheerfully home. Sunday, the happiest, pleasantest day of the week was over, and not one of them but looked forward to Sunday again; and so on from week to week.'[73]

Chapel life excluded few families in such villages; to belong meant sending children to Sunday school and adults attending chapel. But this was rarely recalled as an enforced religion. In Liverpool, Richard Passmore's mother in the 1920s watched him amusedly have 'brushes' with organised religion. His first came when a woman 'took to calling on Sunday afternoons and whisking me off to St. Mary's Sunday School'. The woman returned her flock back to his mother for whom 'it was simply one third of her brood off hands for an hour or more each Sunday afternoon'. For Richard, as for many children, the attraction was to qualify for the annual Treat or picnic.[74] Food indeed features a lot in memories of organised Christianity in the early part of the twentieth century. In Bolton in the 1920s, Alice Foley recalled that being a Roman Catholic involved special dietary celebrations: 'Easter Sunday stands out clear and joyous, not, I am afraid because it was the day of the Risen Lord but because we youngsters were allowed a whole egg to ourselves for breakfast.'[75] David Thomson, living on the Moray Firth coast, recalled that he was not allowed in his teens in the 1920s to eat or drink before taking communion, not even a cup of tea, to enhance 'the effect of the little sip of wine we had kneeling before the altar. I had never tasted alcohol before. I loved it. It gave me not only the only physical pleasure. It inspired me to think of Jesus Christ.'[76]

Observance of faith was linked to tasty breaks from usual dietary discipline. It was also linked to increasingly secular forms of leisure and recreation in church halls. So much so that in the new council-housing estates of the 1930s, halls were prioritised over churches. One critic remarked: 'Halls are being erected, not churches. The result is not congregations of worshippers, but congregations of whist players, dancers and people seeking social recreation.'[77] The church hall became seen by adventurous clergy as the site for experimentation and 'progressive' forms of religious outreach; one churchman remarked: 'There is a latitude allowed there which the strictest conservative in church matters would not tolerate in the House of God.'[78] And with church halls there grew a new sensibility to arts and to drama in church work, a development that was to grow in the 1940s and 1950s.

Even spiritualism came to enjoy a degree of normalisation in British religious cultural acceptance as it continued to grow in popularity in the inter-war period. Celebrity stories sustained newspaper interest. Its two most prominent exponents, Sir Oliver Lodge and Sir Arthur Conan Doyle, continued to attract attention. Doyle included a spiritualist episode in a 1926 short story in the popular weekend *Strand Magazine* which gave cause for admonitions on the 'possible dangers from the other side', with references to biblical warnings about 'a race of spiritual creatures, not made of flesh and blood, inhabiting the air around us and able injuriously to affect mankind'. By the mid-1930s, it was said that there were 40 spiritualist services in Greater London every Sunday night, and that the BBC was thinking of broadcasting them alongside conventional Christian worship. Some Catholics and Anglo-Catholics had considerable sympathy with spiritualism, but some Christian ritualists denigrated it: 'It represents the shallow but popular universalism of our day.'[79]

The Christian churches might complain about popular culture, but they kept responding to it. Another development was the Christian adoption of 'back-to-nature' ideas. The rise of rambling, camping, youth-hostelling and hill-climbing gave encouragement to the growth in the early 1920s of the Christian retreat – camps in large houses and abbeys in the countryside or isolated islands. The ordinary Christian laity as well as clergy could take a few days or weeks out of their ordinary lives and retreat to an isolated or spiritual place where soul and energy might be renewed and spiritual searching engaged. The most famous retreat was probably the Iona Community, which reinvested the island of Iona in the west Highlands of Scotland with a new spiritual function, combined with the meteoric rise of the myth of Celtic Christianity. From 1919, final year divinity students in the Church of Scotland went on retreat there, joined from 1926 by United Free Church students in advance of the union of the two churches. This combined with the development of the Spiritual Healing Movement in the mid-1920s which the Anglo-Catholics in the Church of England were seeking to adopt in whole or in part.

An associated development was the growing popularity of the Christian pilgrimage which brought both High Church Anglicans and Roman Catholics on pilgrimages to Walsingham in Norfolk, to Glastonbury, to Golant in Cornwall and to Haddington in East Lothian. The Glastonbury pilgrimage which started in 1923, aimed at the very High Church ritualists of both Roman and Anglo-Catholic traditions, had incense and 'full ritual', being held on a Saturday in midsummer to attract the greatest possible popularity. The Cornwall pilgrimage, organised by the diocesan authorities of the Church of England to Golant, did not attract the kind of numbers hoped for. But at Walsingham in north Norfolk, a wooden sculpture of Mary, Christ's mother, became the focus of an annual pilgrimage for devotional-group visits by train and bus by High Church Anglicans and Roman Catholics (notably from Lancashire), as well as some walking pilgrims from London, and also led the Pope to grant indulgences.[80] But only one pilgrimage attained genuinely mass appeal: the Catholic pilgrimage to Lourdes in southern France where, in the nineteenth century, a local girl had seen a vision of the Virgin Mary. Many were attracted to the shrine by the prospect of healing for illnesses from the water and the rock in the holy grotto where the vision occurred, with the sick and infirm being able to stay at specially equipped hospital-hotels. During the century, Lourdes developed a massive tourist industry, complete with avenues of hotels, restaurants and scores of shops selling religious trinkets. British Catholics became strongly attracted by Lourdes; as in France, ornate mini grotto-shrines were created as replicas of the Lourdes cave, illuminated with fairy lights, and displayed in churches or window displays. In the 1930s the Catholic Association organised fifteen-day tours from Britain to 'the Shrines of France', so that the faithful could make combined pilgrimages and holidays to Lourdes alone (at £11.50), or longer tours that took in Aix, Paris and Nevers (at £18.50).[81]

The mellowing of religion was detected in many ways. A complex study was undertaken by Mass-Observation in the late 1930s in Bolton in Lancashire to test the cultural influence of the Christian Sunday upon clothing habits. Hat-wearing was measured as very important to male churchgoers: 85 per cent wore a bowler to church, and even amongst those skiving church (in the streets) 26 per cent wore bowlers. Taking the wearing of a hat, and the type of hat, as signifying genuflection to religion, an investigation was made of pubs to see if men even dressed smarter there on Sundays. However, the results did not bear out this hypothesis. In the pubs, the wearing of hats stood at 69 per cent for caps, 5 per cent for trilbies and only 4 per cent for bowlers ('the hallmark of respectability'), with 22 per cent not wearing any hat. Only 35 per cent wore ties (compared with 62 per cent in a pub on a Saturday), and 26 per cent wore new suits (half the proportion of weekday drinkers). The study concluded that the findings 'contradict our idea that Sunday was the "classy" clothes day, the climax of respectability, setting the tone for its Saturday eve, and imposing a general pattern on long leisure periods'.[82] Yet, if people were less receptive to act upon the message of puritan Christianity, they still knew what they *ought* to be doing to observe Christian and community ritual. Rather than Britain secularising in these decades, people negotiated their way ever so slowly towards mild forms of forgetfulness or cocking a snook. Leaving a hat at home on Sundays was hardly the end of British Christian culture.

The growth of universities also shifted imperceptibly the place of religion in British life. Many new universities were failing to create, or delaying the creation of, professorial chairs in theology, whilst at Oxford and Cambridge philosophers like Bertrand Russell and A. J. Ayer openly attacked religion, and the Church of England in 1922 tried to ban modernist theological teaching.[83] Yet, the 'chapel culture' of Britain's older universities – where the college or university chapel was the centre of student social life in choirs, events and wearing of gowns – was still vigorous, given new life in the 1920s and 1930s by the admission of large numbers of women with high religiosity and the ability to attract young male students to chapel too. In the sexually segregated halls of residence, women students often found a matriarchal atmosphere in which saying grace at meals and attendance at chapel were expected parts of the life of the respectable female. This created new long-term pressures for the ordination of the educated woman: if women could now study divinity at university, why should they not become clergy?

In 1919, two women were appointed to the full Christian ministry in Congregationalist churches – with remarkably little fuss or noise from other Christian commentators. These were the first women clergy of mainstream churches in Britain, and even the Anglican Bishop of London accepted the likely increase of lay women in active church roles, though he studiously avoided the issue of ordination.[84] The issue came back repeatedly to haunt the Church of England. The Lambeth Conference of 1930 brought a restatement of bishops' opposition to the ordination of women, and offered Resolution 66 that instead insisted on 'the great importance of offering to women ... posts which provide full scope for their powers ... so that such women may find in the Church's service a sphere for the exercise of their capacity'.[85] Here again was a restatement of women's Christian subordination – to their 'sphere' and 'their capacity'. By the late 1930s, women could be licensed in the Church of England as Women Messengers, Catechists and as Parochial Women Workers, but a 1938 inquiry's recommendation to license women as lay readers was rejected by a large majority in one diocesan women's council. As the *Church Times* commented: 'It is perhaps significant that a gathering of women should reject the idea of the licensing of women lay readers.'[86]

In all sorts of ways, Christian culture was evolving into a more complex element of British culture. Christmas grew in importance as a seasonal ritual, marked in family and community life by increasing display of Christmas trees, decoration and the posting of cards. Perhaps most perceptibly, though, it became more child-centred, and thereby gave cause for a decay in the spiritual emphasis in public culture. Religious publications were feeling the wind of change too. A high proportion of the magazine and weekly press had been dominated since the late Victorian period by religious publishing houses, but secular competitors – especially for single women – appeared in the 1920s. Even religious magazines changed, with the *Girls' Own Weekly Paper* reducing its religious content – its moral tales of how the single girl should prepare for holy marriage, and its prayers and homilies for her to recite – in favour of features on ideal occupations for the newly educated woman and pictures of women in modish beachwear. The serious religious and church newspaper also came under threat. The *Church Times* reduced its news content in the 1930s, moving more to a magazine format with children's pages, whilst its book reviews shifted from the intellectual heavyweight tomes of theology to the more accessible, popular and emerging paperback religious market. This represented a change from being rather disdainful of popular culture to a more popular and magazine-style of journalism.[87]

The churches seemed to be responding to a sense that they were becoming just slightly more marginal to society. At the 1938 Empire Exhibition in Glasgow, the sight of the Anglican chapel as an exhibit (beside other stand-holders showing off new homes, machinery and the latest fads) was received with a bit of incredulity by passers-by. Relatively few visitors actually entered the chapel, causing the chapel organisers to sense an awkwardness – of the Christian church crossing some invisible threshold from cultural fixture to cultural curiosity.[88] In the mellowing of religion from puritan enforcer to liberal comfy sofa, it was becoming vulnerably exposed.

Church and state

In 1929, liberal evangelicals of the Church of England organised a Church and Civic Life Congress in Birmingham, led by Canon Guy Rogers, with Free Churchmen invited. It promoted public housing as an element in the development of what they called 'the City of God', with a Christian-socialist committee announcing the reconditioning of 180 slum houses in the city. But typically, the event was hijacked by rousing speeches from Conservatives denouncing 'the dole-fed, thriftless section' of the working class. One said: 'The pampering of the unfit will be our ruin if we are not careful. The defective children for whom we have to provide ought never to have been born.'[89]

This contest between Liberal and Conservative represented a great ideological battle between left and right in British Christianity in the inter-war period. From the mid-1880s to the outbreak of the First World War, many churchmen had responded positively in ethical and moral terms to the rise of the Labour Movement. Poverty, low wages and poor housing became seen as moral issues, and Christian silence on such matters as ethically unacceptable. But this all changed after 1914. The impact of war, the Russian Revolution of 1917 and the rise of Labour militancy in its wake all frightened the churches, as it did the British establishment in general. Many clergy became deeply opposed to Labour and the trades unions, and the gaps within Christian politics widened.

The issue for many left-wing churchmen was how to keep the British working classes within the churches. The rhetoric of clergy was highly varied. The moderate approach was represented by the Bishop of London, who said in 1922 that if employers thought of workers as individuals and

Analysis: The celebration of Christmas

The ways in which Christmas was celebrated developed into modern forms in the 1890s and 1900s. In those decades, the tradition of giving Christmas presents emerged strongly in the middle classes, with shops encouraging the practice for commercial reasons. Advertisements for special presents for adults developed in those decades. Christmas had become a public holiday in England and Wales only in 1876, but it remained in theory a normal working day in Scotland until 1958 (in large part as a deference to presbyterian hostility to the supposed 'popishness' of Christmas and as a snub to Scotland's Catholic community). For the bulk of working families, however, there was little prospect of receiving large Christmas presents, yet traditions of giving and of feasting were of long standing at Yule and were deeply embedded in European countries.

Christmas had a special place in the popular imagination. This was evident in December 1914 in the phenomenal scale of unofficial Christmas truces between British and German troops on the western front of the Great War. Later dismissed by many senior officers as 'fraternisation', and rather overlooked in the official record, personal testimony from troops on both sides showed how on Christmas Eve and Day there was a widespread cessation of hostilities between the armies. This led to meetings between opposing soldiers in 'no man's land', the exchange of food and gifts, singing of hymns and the playing of games of various kinds. It appears that thousands of troops were involved. Corporal John Ferguson of the Seaforth Highlanders recalled that after carol-singing between the trenches, soldiers edged towards each other:

Someone calling us from the enemy's trenches 'Komradd, Onglees Komradd', I answered him, 'Hello! Fritz' (we call them all Fritz). 'Do you want any tobacco?' he asks. 'Yes.' 'Come halfways'; we shouted back and forward until Old Fritz clambered out of the trench, and accompanied by three others of my section we went out to meet him. We were walking between the trenches. ... We shook hands, wished each other a Merry Xmas, and were soon conversing as if we had known each other for years. ... What a sight – little groups of Germans and British extending almost the length of our front! Out of the darkness we could hear laughter and see lighted matches, a German lighting a Scotchman's cigarette and vice versa, exchanging cigarettes and souvenirs. ... Here we were laughing and chatting to men whom only a few hours before we were trying to kill![90]

Attempts to repeat such meetings at Christmas 1915 were rebuffed by hostile fire ordered by senior army staff. But it demonstrated clearly the way in which a strong common Christian culture, and values emanating from it, enveloped the young men of Western Europe.

Christmas giving was a particular struggle for many families during the high unemployment, low wages and poverty of the inter-war period. It was common for children to receive an apple, an orange and nuts in a stocking at the foot of the bed on Christmas morning. Poor families sometimes got much-needed presents. Richard Passmore recalled of his childhood in Liverpool in the 1920s: 'At Christmas or on birthdays understanding friends would give us children clothing; I understood why, only too well, but yet I sometimes yearned for glamorous boxes, which rattled enticingly when shaken: a Meccano set, a model railway.'[91] Yet, the celebration had spread out along the calendar, though with diminishing religious content. One Catholic commentator wrote: 'Christmas-time is no longer the only dainty-time. Even its characteristic fare – turkey, plum pudding, mince pies – is no longer sacred to Christmas. It appears in restaurants weeks before Christmas Day. . . . But the religious anniversary of the Virgin Birth, of the Star of Bethlehem, of the Shepherd, of the Manger, remains unique in each year's calendar, never dragged forward, never postponed, never extended beyond its traditional spell.'[92] The last Christmas of peace in 1938 suggested that there was a modernity and liberalism to the church over this major religious festival. The use of cribs, Christmas trees and nativity plays for children had reached its maturity, and the central children's nature of the festival had come of age.[93]

After the Second World War, concern over commercialisation of Christmas grew. In 1954, the minister of Glasgow Cathedral thought it was turning into 'a cheerful carnival', whilst in 1962 one Christian sociologist remarked: 'It may well be (oddly at first glance but on reflection not so strange) the very intensity of the commercial build-up that sends so many "marginal" attenders to Church in a mood of reaction. And for regular attenders, the Christmas service may be an occasion for contrition over what they vaguely suspect to be (as it assuredly is) a highly un-Christian wallowing in the self-inflation induced both – though in different ways – by giving and by receiving. . . .[T]his Christian festival has been prostituted into a shot-in-the-arm for our mass consumption society.'[94] The trend towards commercialisation continued unabated for the rest of the century, with Christian clergy perennially complaining over the debasement of the religious festival into a carnival of selling and gluttony. By the 1970s, in offices and workplaces, Christmas lunches became occasions for parties stretching from early December. Christmas services remained the highest attended of all worship in the Christian calendar, but the proportion of the people going was diminishing.

'as brothers', and if workers 'considered it part of their religion to see that they gave a fair day's work for a fair day's wage', then this might lead to a trade boom and 'a Kingdom of God upon earth'.[95] But for right-wing churchpeople, notably for many evangelicals, the very term 'social reform' had reverted to a Victorian meaning – instead of meaning tackling poor housing and low wages, it meant combating drinking, gambling and sexual impurity.[96]

At the other end of the spectrum were real attempts to create a Christian contract with Labour. William Temple, a bishop and later arch-bishop in the Church of England, was a leading advocate of the social gospel, promoting the 1924 Conference on Christian Politics, Economics and Citizenship (COPEC) as the beginning of what he hoped would be a new era of co-operative Christian action on social problems and class healing. It promised much and many radical Christians invested in it. But the movement had by the end of the 1930s failed, being unable to agree on how to reconstruct society from first principles and failing to appeal to the British working classes.[97]

Temple and another archbishop, Cosmo Lang, argued for state inter-vention and for the church to support the people in economic distress, and many projects started. Slum housing was a rallying ground for radical clergy – even those who might be quite unradical on other matters. In Scotland, tenement housing of one-roomed and two-roomed homes created the worst overcrowding with, in 1931, 42 per cent of Glasgow people living more than two people per room, and suffering the most appalling diseases such as tuberculosis and scarlet fever. 'In the heart of conditions which are almost impossible to imagine,' wrote one man to challenge the 'indifference' of church people who opposed council-house building, 'there are to be found homes so obviously radiant with the spirit of Christ, where the souls of men and women have risen above the physical discomforts of their surroundings and have been able to cling to consolation which is divine.'[98] This encouraged many new church initia-tives, albeit on a smaller scale than the state could achieve. The fad in the 1890s and 1900s for the churches to become involved in model housing construction as charitable activity continued, albeit slowly, to grow in the inter-war period. At Flimwell on the Kent–Sussex border in 1938, a church housing organisation called the St Richard Housing Society built its first four model cottages for rural working people.[99] Such projects sus-tained church principles of charitable work, and signalled a move towards 'aid without evangelism', but they were of too small a scale to be critical in keeping the working classes within the Christian churches.

At the same time, the political establishment of Britain was becoming infuriated with the churches. Like the people, government was in a mood to liberalise society in the inter-war period, and opposed puritan evangelicals who were trumpeting on endlessly about prohibition, shutting down Sunday entertainments and controlling public culture. But the puritans did not give up easily, and British society continued to resonate to surveillance, suppression and guilt. With the temperance movement still active after the war, there were hopes of prohibition. But only in Scotland was there a chance, and that failed when, in 1920, evangelicals called plebiscites in over 500 local wards urging voters to close public houses, but only about 40 wards voted 'dry' (and most of them re-voted 'wet' a few years later).

If prohibition was a fading cause, anti-gambling grew as the nation was gripped by 'flutter-fever' in the 1920s and 1930s. The 1910s witnessed the rise of the football pools, which became effectively legalised in the 1920s, whilst from 1926 greyhound racing took off with the arrival from France of the totalisator betting system (which offered no fixed odds but rather divided a proportion of the totalised takings amongst the winners). These were followed in the 1930s by illegal betting houses (with telephone communications with race tracks), and an ever-growing system of illegal street bookmakers, runners and look-outs. Gambling was everywhere, and, except on licensed race tracks, it was all illegal. Richard Passmore worked at a petrol station and car showroom in central Liverpool where, directly under his desk in the basement, his mate Jim did painting and odd jobs. In reality, Jim ran a gambling and betting 'advising' enterprise with the connivance of the manager; Richard warned Jim of trouble via a remote electrical buzzer through the floor.[100]

Most churches and the press ranted against these activities, but the state liked the tax revenue from the pools and wanted to widen its income by legalising more. Winston Churchill suggested a tax in 1926 to which government agreed, and Prime Minister Stanley Baldwin was picked out for special fury for doing so whilst being 'in close touch with religious opinion'. British moral fibre was being threatened: 'Every village may before long have its ready-money betting office, where young people will be encouraged to squander their earnings on a form of hurtful excitement,' thundered the evangelical *British Weekly*.[101] In this atmosphere of religious frenzy, the state maintained gambling as a crime, and instructed the police to mount token raids and the courts to impose token fines.

This reflected both the powerful undercurrent of religious culture in many parts of Britain and the ability of the Christian churches to divert attention from their own divisions. The Church of England's splits between evangelicals, ritualists and liberals became quite severe in the inter-war period; one anti-ritualist said: 'The Church of England is weakened almost to ineffectiveness by partisanship.'[102] Attempts at ecumenical co-operation abounded in these decades, but in diverse and sometimes conflicting directions. Cosmo Lang, Archbishop of York, entered what he called 'a careful and thorough discussion' with the English free churches in the north of England, and Anglicans in Ireland conversed with presbyterians, whilst in the south of England the High Church Anglicans predominated as what one paper called 'the Catholic vote', opening 'conversations' with Roman Catholics during 1921–5 and with Eastern orthodox churches in the 1930s. Some Nonconformist observers at the 1930 Anglican Lambeth Conference said that they felt they were fighting to save the Church of England from union with Rome.[103]

The rancour of church division was hard to conceal from the English people. One technique was to unite the churches in public displays of unity against common enemies. The Communist Revolution in Russia in 1917 and the rise of the Communist Party and socialist ideology in Britain were portrayed to be secularist enemies that would overthrow not merely the Christian churches but also God himself. The Catholic Church took a particular hatred of communism, in large part because so many British communists were drawn from the Catholic communities of cities like London, Liverpool and Glasgow. The Catholic Archbishop of Liverpool in 1937 said, 'It is the Communists who are the enemies of the poor, for with false promises they rob the worker of his dignity and immortal hopes,' whilst leading Catholics in Scotland urged the Church there 'to restore Catholicism and stamp out communism'.[104] In 1938, secularists organised a 'Congress of the Godless' in London, attracting communist freethinkers and atheists from many groups, and thus the intense interest of the Home Office and MI5. Opposition was stormy, including an organisation of 'Militant Christian Patriots' whose meetings were dominated by Fascists – bringing them equally under police surveillance.[105] The Christian churches were brought together in their own, more 'religious' opposition, in a conference at Westminster Abbey on the 'Anti-God Menace' organised by the Christian Evidence Society, attracting 2,000 representatives from the Roman and Greek Orthodox churches, Syrian and Armenian churches, the English free churches, the Church of Scotland and others. For them, the two greatest godless enemies were German Nazism and science. The rallying cry was joined: 'We have no cause whatever to be afraid of the anti-God battalions. Christianity flourishes in the face of opposition.'[106]

Meanwhile, important changes were made to church–state relations in Wales and Scotland in the inter-war period. The disestablishment of the Church of England in Wales, creating the Church in Wales in 1920, brought a new sense of confidence, and with a revitalised constitution in 1922 it was described as 'a catholic and a national Church'.[107] By 1938, it was regarded by all as a boon, bringing clergy and laity together in a new united democratic control of the Church in Wales, in which bishops were elected by an Electoral College.[108] In Scotland, plans for reunion between the established Church of Scotland with the equally large United Free Church of Scotland, under way from around 1904, were finally accomplished in 1929 with a church format that severed most of the kirk's links with the state – ending church taxes, state financial support and the power of most church courts, and passing church-controlled properties (like graveyards) to local authorities.[109] The settlement was a compromise and obfuscated the damage to the traditional church–state connection: principally, the monarch's representative (called the Lord High Commissioner) still sat at the General Assembly of the kirk every year. But the architect of the settlement described it, in the true language of bureau-cratic spin: 'It was an emblem, and could impart nothing which did not belong to the reality.'[110] Though the rhetoric of its being a 'national church' was loud and persistent for decades, the reality was that the Church of Scotland was no longer a church of the state.

Despite inter-church initiatives galore, there was a mood of depression amongst many in the churches – a kind of shambolic aimlessness as Victorianism and puritanism competed with economic depression, pol-itical radicalism and liberalism. Lorna Sage's grandfather, a vicar in the Church in Wales in the Rhondda valley, was evidently depressed beyond measure. After twelve years in the same parish, he wrote in his diary in April 1933: 'Here we are at the end of winter time, and I am still at St. Cynon's. O God give me the chance now at last. Thy will be done.' Seeking another parish, he learned he had failed: 'They have really cast me aside in favour of a young fellow who has only been ordained since 1924. Well this is the limit. What on earth am I to do now? No hope and no chance.'[111] The depression amongst many ministers and parsons provoked concern with the entire future of popular faith in Britain. For some, the lurking crisis in international affairs in Europe seemed to cast a light upon the religious condition of Britain. After the Munich Crisis in October 1938, Father Rosenthal, vicar of St Agatha's Anglo-Catholic parish at Sparkbrook, near the city centre of Birmingham, wrote in his parish mag-azine that 'the troubles of the world are the result of forgetfulness of God'.

'The process goes on without violence,' he continued, 'continuously, steadily, as a kind of impersonal motion of secular change. It marks the passing of our English civilization away from the Faith in which it is founded, and out of which it has been fashioned. The great sin of our country is forgetfulness of God.'[112]

For many in the churches, the sense of a changing, hostile and secularising world was overpowering, and there were frantic efforts to keep up. One of the new developments of the 1920s and 1930s was the sudden spread of the radio. The BBC's managing director, a stern Scottish presbyterian John Reith, ensured that his stations played a part in traditional Christian dissemination when, in September and October 1925, he introduced a weekly Sunday night religious Christian service on his London Station, 2LO, broadcast live from St Martin-in-the-Fields Church located beside the BBC headquarters. But for some this was not enough. In May 1926, a 64-year-old woman from Hertfordshire, Miss Kate M. Cordeaux, published a letter in the *Radio Times* requesting 'hearing something daily of God' in a Christian radio service. Despite lukewarm support from the churches (and the refusal of Archbishop Cosmo Lang to back her), she attracted 600 letters of support in 48 hours and 7,000 in two months, mostly from women. For a year and a half, Reith put her off, but under the pressure of Cordeaux's campaigning, he finally relented, and from 2 January 1928 a daily service was instituted that continued until the end of the century (and is still going today on Radio 4).[113] This service inspired British religious broadcasting to be overwhelmingly conservative, unevangelising and, for many, High Church and pro-establishment in tone.

For some churches, there was just not enough religious content to programmes. Roman Catholic intellectuals lambasted the BBC in the mid-1930s for 'pampering of the class that wants jazz and crooning [male love singers]' for being a defeatist 'estimate of our people's cultural state'.[114] But the churches feared each other more than they feared jazz. They became hyper-sensitive to the balance between Anglican and free church, High and Low Church, but Reith argued that he was seeking 'the best preachers' irrespective of denomination. To please the religious lobby, Reith in January 1930 moved the time of the Sunday evening religious programmes lest they turned people from going to church.[115] In the long term, British religious broadcasting had created a distinctive blandness and staidness that would prove hard to shed in the religious crisis later in the century. But in the short term, religion seemed in some ways to be adapting rather well to the new technology. On King George VI's coronation day in 1937, transmitted to millions by radio, it was said that 'a sense of the holiness of the day' was conveyed to listeners; one asked whether it was permissible to eat during 'a sacred broadcast'.[116]

The state had to cope with churches that constantly called upon it to act in the name of Christian culture, and to favour one denomination or tradition over another. The state for its part was wishing to find excuses to disengage from religious politics. In Wales and in Scotland, it became possible to see how the disestablishment of the state church could be effectively implemented with no clear damage to the Christian state or to the people's religious condition. The disestablishment of the Church of England seemed to some to be next on the cards. Where once the Church was seen as a bulwark to the good order of the state, by the 1930s the state was increasingly finding that it was the irritating problem rather than the solution.

Depression and faith

The inter-war period was characterised by unremitting high levels of unemployment, child poverty and the collapse of entire communities due to structural decay in staple industries. Coal-mining, shipbuilding, the iron and steel industries and the textile industries suffered especially badly, creating intense regional economic crises accentuated by the Wall Street Crash of 1929. In general, Wales, Scotland, the north and the Midlands fared worse than London and the south, where in the 1930s new consumer industries fostered by suburban growth and the rise of the car-driven middle-class family led a shift in the economic centre of the nation towards the south. How was faith affected by depression? Did it make the churches more class-divided?

There was a very real economic struggle for Christianity in the 1920s and 1930s. With depression setting in, emigration of artisans booming and poverty growing, the people were driven apart between labour and capital. One Church of Scotland minister in the industrial town of Greenock recalled: 'The unity of the nation, which had been cemented during the war, broke up. Class divisions had never been more bitter. The world of industry was seething with unrest. Crisis followed crisis. Labour and capital were continually at loggerheads, my congregation, of course, being entirely in the capitalist camp.'[117]

The economic rationale for religion gained strength in many working-class families. Grace Foakes recalled of the 1920s: 'At a certain East London church if you went to the Sunday school you were invited to stay for tea so that you were there for evening service. I was often sent there when I didn't want to go but I was told that I wouldn't get the left-overs which fed us on a Monday night.'[118] Economic depression intensified the sense of social class, division and class struggle in community and church. Looking back, May Hobbs commented: 'It seems a bit late in the day for the churches to begin worrying about their social image. They had their chance and spent hundreds of years upholding the powers that be while making sure the ordinary people knuckled under to their masters.'[119] Alice Foley recalled with distaste one hymn she used to sing in church in Bolton:

The rich man in his castle
The poor man at his gate
He made them high or lowly
And ordered their estate.[120]

In most parts of Britain, there persisted some sense of one church being for the elites and others for the people. In the Rhondda, it was noted: 'You could do nearly nothing in the Church of Wales and get away with it, no one took official notice, a vicar was a gentleman after all. Chapel would have been different, much more a matter of openly devout busybody closeness with the congregation.'[121] The sense of social division in religion was heightened in the Labour Movement by organisations like the Socialist Sunday schools that were dotted around northern England and central Scotland. These promoted a humanist ideology of universal brotherhood as an alternative paradigm to that of belief in God of the churches, and in 1926 produced their own 'Hymn Book' and activities that exactly mirrored and competed with Sunday-school activities. But despite this, the vast majority of trades unionists remained Christians, many of them churchgoers and chapel-goers, who did not adopt atheist or secularist views. 'By today's standards,' wrote Grace Foakes in the 1970s, 'I suppose one would have said we had religion rammed down our throats.' She recalled being taken as a child on a sunshine holiday with some middle-class socialists who took her to a Socialist Sunday school. She was placed on the platform to sing, but was hastily removed when she burst into 'Gentle Jesus'.[122]

Tensions between Christian churches and Labour reached a high point in May 1926 with the General Strike, when a call went out for all trades unionists to back striking coal-miners involved in a long-running dispute in their industry. Industrial relations were deteriorating in Britain for many months beforehand in the midst of high unemployment, falling wages and increasing working-class misery, and the whole of the Labour Movement came to see that the miners were ill dealt with by both mine owners and the government. The Coal Commission was due to report its findings in May of 1926, and in late 1925, the archbishops of Canterbury and York designated Sunday 25 April of the following year to observe 'Industrial Sunday' on which trades unions and employers would be encouraged to promote improved harmony in industry. But even by December 1925, the left-leaning Industrial Christian Fellowship of the Church of England was infuriated that many elements of the Church had decided not to observe the Sunday.[123] This remained a source of annoyance to Christian socialists in the churches.

From being the very epitome of the spiritualised Christian occupation, miners changed in official public rhetoric to demonic pagans. In 1904–5, the miners of Wales had been swept along by Evan Roberts' evangelical revival; twenty years later, they seemed swept into atheistic communism as they went on strike and became the warriors of class struggle. This was an extraordinary transformation. Caricatures of grimy miners, living below ground in darkened places, abounded in the 1920s, and the religious press was no exception. Patronising and brutal, one article on 'The Miner and His Folk' described the typical miner as 'simple, sincere, kind, homely, loveable', but noted: 'There are thousands who are wayward and evil. Even the terrors of the mine cast no fear.'[124] Some Christian clergy opted to confront the challenge of the deeply radicalised 'little Moscows' of south Wales and central Scotland, where the Communist Party and radical socialism were very strong. One Methodist minister, Reginald Barker, combined opposition to unbridled capitalism with an attempt to keep the miners and the unemployed of the Rhondda for Christ. He organised a Christian trades union, set up an unemployed work scheme making toys and engaged communist orators in debate. In his view, God alone could prevent revolution through personal redemption and amelioration of capitalist individualism: 'We who stood with Christ in the Rhondda believe that in the Christian Gospel we have the transforming power, that character is bound up with conduct; but we also believe that Christianity is incompatible with the present system.'[125]

Most British churchmen were not so compromising, and, indeed, most Christian churches were extremely hostile to the General Strike. The Anglican Bishop of Ripon considered it a threat to Christianity, and urged church unity. The minister of St Giles in Edinburgh told his congregation that 'from the Volga to the Atlantic democracy is battling for its life', and considered that 'the social and political fabric of this country was in imminent danger of irretrievable catastrophe'.[126] Religious newspapers were directly affected by the strike, putting out emergency editions and taking pride that churchpeople were out organising strike breakers by running trams and other essential services during the six days of the event. The evangelical *British Weekly* told readers 'to give to those who are about us an example of firm, calm, friendly patient behaviour',[127] and its editor urged obedience to the government. But there was genuine concern that the moral conscience of the Christian nation may have been lost as 'the great masses pass by' the churches; wealthy Christian people had made a 'too sudden return to the old pre-war carelessness and gaiety and extravagance', and had failed to revere their 'own kindred which had nobly laid down their lives'.[128]

The Catholic Church was hostile to the strike; though not all his bishops agreed, Cardinal Francis Bourne argued that to break an agreement to work was a sin. In a similar vein, the High Church *Church Times* said that it had long argued that 'loyalty to the Catholic faith compels keen and active sympathy with the present claims of labour', but concluded that 'the general strike is for the Christian a sin'. 'The nation is faced with the deliberate attempt by men more or less affected by the political and economic theories of Moscow to establish what would be not the dictatorship of the proletariat but the dictatorship of half a dozen determined Trades Union officials.'[129]

The Archbishop of Canterbury, Randall Davidson, sought to negotiate in the strike, and many thought that he had succeeded when, on the Wednesday afternoon before it began, he appeared to have secured the withdrawal of the Strike Notices. He tried to broadcast an appeal for industrial peace on the BBC, but was refused permission.[130] In the event, the strike went ahead, dividing the country sharply between those sympathising and those breaking the strike. When it was over, some churches like the Church of England sought to avoid triumphalism, and encouraged settlement in the more intractable coal strike. This attracted great criticism. William Temple, Christian socialist and future archbishop, replied to it in *The Times*: 'As Christians, and most of us as Christians charged with official responsibility, we saw two parties doing great injury to the community by a continued conflict which was bound to be ended by negotiation sooner or later; our religion and our office required of us that we should do anything which lay in our power to bring, in the literal sense, to reason.'[131] A leading Congregationalist minister from London urged 'thanksgiving to GOD for the return to us of a new beginning of our social peace', whilst the Baptist Union president called for the miners' case to be 'fairly and dispassionately examined'.[132] The BBC broadcast a religious service of reconciliation, conducted by one of the ministers who broadcast news of the 1904 Welsh revival, who pleaded for 'the restoration of a just peace', accompanied by a scripture reading chosen by the Archbishop of Canterbury.[133] But most churchmen were plain hostile, agreeing with the Revd James Harvey, moderator of the general assembly of the United Free Church, that the defeat of the strikers was 'a victory for God'.[134]

The General Strike of 1926 left a bitter taste in the mouth. Many in working-class communities, especially the 1 million miners of the nation, ever after regarded the mainstream Christian churches as agents of capital. This in part fed the inter-war growth of minority Protestant churches and sects, some of whom, like most Brethren miners in Scotland, joined the strike, contributing to significant growth that led to the Brethren reaching their all-time peak of membership in around 1930.[135] By contrast, the mainstream churches developed a near contempt for miners in the inter-war period, making them the prime object for evangelisation efforts in the later 1920s and 1930s. In Scotland, this involved young theology students being 'sent into' many villages to convert miners and their families, but the results were disastrous with (as one leading Church of Scotland figure commented) 'striplings of twenty odd years daring to reason with hard-bitten communists out of the pits'.[136] The failure of the Welsh churches to make a stand with the miners and their families in 1926 was widely attributed with instigating an alienation from the churches that may have been much sharper in inter-war Wales than in any other part of Britain.[137]

For all that the working classes were looked upon as 'godless communists' by so many of the powerful people in inter-war Britain, the religiosity of working-class communities was extremely strong. The miners in particular were an occupation in which religiosity veined through not just family and community, but the very sense of life itself. Jim Bullock recalled in a Yorkshire mining village the importance of Sunday Methodist chapel: 'This was the moment they had been waiting for all week, when they could tell God publicly about the injustices that they had suffered at work, sometimes through the hands of the people who had been praying just before themselves. To them God was no longer an unseen being in heaven, he was here in the chapel by their side; he could hear them, and most important of all he could understand them.'[138] Church was a central part of working-class life, especially for the young. A Glasgow girl recalled: 'The paradin' up and down Vicky Road on a Saturday, arm-in-arm wi' your chum, lookin' for a fella ... and them lookin' for us ... was a reg'lar in its way as goin' to the kirk the next morning.'[139] The church and romance were by no means separate. Molly Weir, also from Glasgow, recalled: 'All our romantic attachments were formed with those boys whom we met through the church. Our religious observance, which played so large a part in our lives, became more thrilling and exciting when we could peep across at the lads under cover of our hymn-singing, and later we joined up with them for a few delicious moments on our demure walks over Crowhill Road after evening service.'[140]

Economic recession had varied consequences upon the churches. Some of the churches continued to evangelise amongst the British working classes in a way seemingly little changed from the Victorian and Edwardian period. The Rhondda Crusade of the Anglican Church in Wales in the summer of 1938 was partly resonant with an old-time religion: open-air religious meetings and prayer circles combined with discussion groups on the social implications of the gospel. The last was a clear necessity to a crusade operating in a community with 24 per cent unemployment (compared to a national English average of 12 per cent).[141] But elsewhere, there was a clear decision by the 1930s to abandon much of the structure of evangelistic revivalism. That strategy was seen in the midst of depression, in the wake of industrial unrest and the rise of militant labour, to have failed.

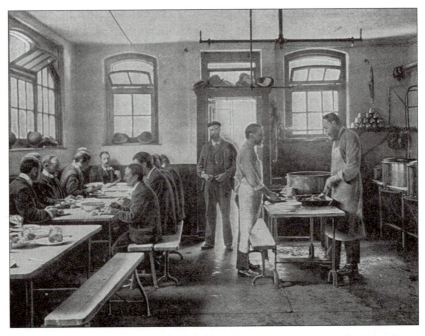

British churches were accustomed to laying on soup kitchens to feed the poor, the unemployed and homeless during times of distress. (Mary Evans Picture Library)

The commencement of massive slum clearance and re-housing in council-housing estates created a new dynamic which many in the churches thought required new methods. For a hundred years, evangelisation in many British cities had proceeded on the basis of rich congregations, as 'an outlet for their superfluous energies', founding and financing mission stations in working-class areas. The Church of Scotland came round to a view that 'this has merely aggravated the evils. It has meant the weakening of existing congregations in the districts by setting up a rival congregation too lavishly endowed alongside them'. Moreover, the missions did not close because 'the self-righteousness and vanity of their promoters will not allow them to withdraw'.[142] Yet, there were many communities in which the churches were the bulwarks of the unemployed during recession, strike and hardship. In Edinburgh in the early 1930s, economic conditions were described by the minister of St Giles' Cathedral as 'grim and menacing'. 'We did what we could in the way of relief among our parishioners and members who were most badly hit.' The parish committee in those 'dark years' distributed bread, meat and coal, and were 'like ministering angels in houses which were depressed and dreary with men, once first-class artisans and craftsmen, now dull and listless with the soul-destroying tedium of unemployment and queuing up for the "dole", and the women at their wits' end to keep their homes together on a weekly income which hardly be described as even on a mere subsistence level'.[143]

Depression also fostered sectarian identity. The Ancient Order of Hibernians was an organisation that presented in social halls and parades a sense of identity in an environment where Orange parades fostered Protestant identity. In the depths of depression, the numbers marching seemed to have increased – marches of 30,000 to 40,000 being reported in central Scotland towns between 1929 and 1932, in what has been seen as a deliberate policy of mimicking Orangemen.[144]

Many clergy reported the non-attendance of those who could not afford clothes and (where it still persisted) the pew rent for a seat in church in Sunday. Depression could strike at the confidence of the faithful. 'By 1931,' noted Don Haworth of Bacup in Lancashire, 'Methodists had virtually abandoned theology for politics.'[145] For Richard Passmore in Liverpool, faith was a dark and muddled thing in the midst of childhood poverty, as his mother coped with three children single-handedly. 'I had unconsciously absorbed some of my mother's suspicion that somewhere Out There was a malevolent fate, determined to thwart all our strivings, finding a perverted satisfaction in our suffering. At the same time I was, of course, a Christian: if you ask how I could reconcile these two opposing conceptions of the human condition I cannot explain.'[146]

And yet there is little evidence that the depression caused a significant membership crisis for Christianity. An analysis shows that there was absolutely no statistical relationship between variations in the levels of unemployment and presbyterian membership in Scotland between 1922 and 1956.[147] The churches continued to enjoy massive support from the nation's children. Sunday schools and Bible classes only suffered marginal decline, and all the evidence points to a very vital role for religion in the life of children in working-class areas. Organisations like the Boys' Brigade were also important in areas of declining staple industries. Church brigades emerged in the 1920s and 1930s as amongst the most conservative organisations of organised religion, being deeply committed to the vision of the 'tempted boy', and opposing liberal leisure. The BBs opposed increased cinema attendance, gambling, drinking, greyhound racing and juvenile smoking, and recommended the pledge of total abstinence as a condition of membership, as well as forbidding smoking in uniform. The aim was to create 'Boys of grit ... who will be profoundly disgusted if the Boys' Brigade becomes "soft".' If the BBs became conservative and hierarchical in the inter-war period, it retained popular support. The Jubilee Conventicle at Hampden Park football stadium in 1933 attracted 130,000 inside the ground, with a further 100,000 locked out, unable to get in, leading to claims that it was the largest open-air service in Britain.[148]

So, for all the commotion raised by churchmen about puritanism giving way to a mellowing sense of religion, little changed in most people's religious practice. When older people were asked in the 1980s and 1990s how they had spent their time as youngsters in the 1910s, 1920s and 1930s, they provided a powerful sense of a nation still pulsating to the throb of Christian culture. Something like 60 per cent of children were enrolled in Sunday schools, and attending religious services of one kind or another twice or three times on Sundays was extremely common. One Catholic recalled being a teenager in Stirling in the 1920s: 'Well, you went to mass in the morning. You had dinner, and when it was a good day you went for a walk. And you finished up in church at night again – Benediction, what we call Benediction at night ... Oh I remember that the Sunday best was special dresses with velvet.'[149] It was the same for most Protestant children, including this woman, also from Stirling:

We went to an awful lot of religious meetings in those days. Not I think for any religious feeling, but the fact – material gain, you know. We got

*a wee bag with maybe different things in it – cookies and things in it,
and that was a sort of draw. Not that we were hungry; we werenae as
bad as all that, but just it was something different – of getting something
for maybe a penny or something. There was a wee Railway Mission at
the end of the street Millar's Garage is now – a lovely wee Mission hall.
. . . And then y'see when we went to the different Sunday schools – I
went to the South Church Sunday school because my parents were away
in St. Ninian's church, y'see. I chummed with the same wee girl going
up to school. . . . And then I was in the Salvation Army again. My friend
joined the Salvation Army. I didn't, but I was a Sunbeam for a day or
two. [Laugh] I used to belt out: 'A sunbeam, a sunbeam, Jesus wants me
for a sunbeam.' . . . I must have been 10 or 11 or something by that
time. O yes, it was all religion. And another thing. Another friend,
another pal of mines, her father was a caretaker of the Baptist church.
Now we went to Baptist Church meetings. I don't know why we didnae
sprout wings! [Laughing]*[150]

The motives were mixed, but the enthusiasm was clear.

The Second World War

War with Germany broke out on 3 September 1939. Seven months later,
before the war had made a significant impact upon Britain in terms of casu-
alties, the *Sunday Dispatch* newspaper conducted a competition to
consider the best feature film fade-outs. Readers voted on the best ways in
which films ended. An analysis of the 577 entries showed that 25 per cent
of *Dispatch* readers selected fade-outs featuring death, 20 per cent featuring the supernatural, 12 per cent featuring comedy and 9 per cent
tackling hope. The films that they voted for were mostly several years old,
with *Three Comrades* of 1938 topping the poll, which had shown two dead
comrades beckoning a third to join them, marching arm in arm through the
skies. The authors of the study concluded that though many people did not
accept the idea of the afterlife (49 per cent according to opinion polls), this
did not mean that they were content to reject it. Hollywood's depictions, it
concluded, filled a gap between belief and unbelief.[151] Faith was expressed
by popular culture in a fitting balance of uncertainty.

This is an instructive motto for appreciating the sometimes contradictory understandings of the Second World War. Religion was certainly still
a major element in military life. For some, a strong faith made them stand
out. Richard Passmore from Liverpool joined up in the RAF to make a

career in the late 1930s, and found that he was regarded by a fellow airman as 'having religious mania' because he attended evensong in the local town. Religion in the armed forces was, for many, something they were forced to do at parade on a Sunday morning. A young Scottish soldier, who had never gone to church and didn't want to, said he 'used to try and dodge church parade on a Sunday until I found out that if you dodged church parade you got stuck cleanin' boilers, or loadin' coal, or workin' in the cookhouse peelin' spuds. So I then became Church of England ... the one that had the shortest service.'[152] Historian Michael Snape has revealed the official significance attached to organised Christianity within military service in the Second World War. Montgomery's North Africa campaign in 1942–3 with the Eighth Army involved his use of the chaplaincy service to embolden and stiffen spiritual and moral feeling, greatly assisting morale, and contributing to success. Montgomery's shake-up of the training and personnel of the Eighth Army involved the chaplains. He attributed the victory at El Alamein to include the chaplains; at the victory service in Cairo, he said that: 'I would as soon think of going into battle without my artillery as without my Chaplains.'[153] This approach was carried forward by Montgomery into the role of the chaplaincy service in the later stages of the war, in what Snape describes as 'the notion of the consecration of British arms to a higher purpose'.[154]

One development was a noticeable fall-off in chaplains' disdain for working-class religion. The more relaxed character of much inter-war religion was allowed to flourish in the chaplaincy service – despite some criticism from clergy early in the war about working-class recruits. One Anglo-Catholic Army chaplain said of early conscripts: 'One has had to face the hard fact that the vast majority of nominally "C. of E." men do not attempt to practise the Christian religion.' For them, he said, 'Christianity means merely their acceptance as ideals of a code of morals described by respectability. They have no realisation of all that is implied by their duty to God, and no consciousness of their need for grace. We are dealing with a pagan generation.'[155] But this was a decaying view of working-class religiosity, both amongst combatants and on the home front. Moreover, the pessimistic view of the people's faith was being contradicted by Mass-Observation. It came to the conclusion that only between 1 and 4 per cent of people claimed to have actually lost their religious faith; the overall effect was judged to be that those with faith had it confirmed in war, those without had their lack of faith confirmed, and those with weak faith had it weakened still further.[156] And yet, religious ritual was clearly an important facet of many people's routines. One housewife reported: 'I do not pray, not since I was a child, but at night I say to myself, "Please God keep my Dad and Mum safe" (they are dead), and when sirens have sounded I find myself saying "Oh, God, stop this awful war before there's more damage and lives lost".' Just after the Second World War, even one in four self-confessed atheists reported that they prayed to God in times of physical or mental stress.[157]

Asking older people of their memories of religion in wartime indicates on the face of it a strengthening position of religion. One study of Birmingham concluded that 'spirituality operated to strengthen the resolve of the people in their daily war effort. Wartime Britain, in many ways, was tangibly and self-consciously religious, and generally assumed itself to be Christian.'[158] In Birmingham, the war invigorated the sense of Christian devotion after perceptible decline of church attendance during the inter-war years in many parishes – in some cases with a halving of Easter Day communicants. Certainly, there was no slowness to appreciate religious symbols in the war. The declaration of war of Sunday 3 September 1939 was heard in churches and Sunday schools. Clergy who had been despondent over popular faith in the 1930s, and had suffered falling church attendances, argued for crisis prayers to carry people in to the realm of the spirit. Alban Tilt, vicar of Sparkbrook, said: 'At such times as these [people] will turn to God with wild cries for mercy and help and preservation, but will find little help or peace or comfort or assurance from doing so.'[159]

There was a change in clerical attitudes to war in 1939–45 compared to 1914–18. It was more sombre, calm, resolute, and much less gung-ho and naive; above all, there was less expectation of religious deference to the parish priest. There was a more developed notion of the war as a fight for a Christian civilisation based on common sense, decency and social justice. Evil became something viewed as increasingly material and external (the Nazi enemy), not internal to the individual. Interestingly, there was no real or substantive church expectation of religious revival amongst the people as a result of the war, as happened during and immediately after the Great War.[160]

This helps to account for the blandness with which Britons later tended to remember their experience of religion during the 1940s. Religion represented a routine of churchgoing, a duty to be endured, or an affectionate hallmark of community and family ritual. True, for a few, the war reinvigorated Christian culture. But whilst the majority of oral-history respondents recalled going to church in the inter-war and war periods, few recalled in any detail what went on. Only the strange was recalled. Victoria Massey was evacuated during the war from London to a Welsh valley where religion was taken very seriously. She remembered how those in the front row of the pews had to recite a verse, and how she couldn't speak Welsh: 'The minister would dance up and down in his high pulpit, waving his arms and roaring like a bull, then his voice rising up into a seagull crescendo, his hand thumping on the Bible before him, he screamed at the congregation in guttural Welsh.'[161]

Some forms of official religion were still enforced by the state, however. Government tribunals refused to recognise conscientious objectors for non-combat duties if they claimed to object on merely moral or political grounds – they had to have *religious* grounds, and were then organised for war-work in Christian Pacifist Units.[162] More broadly, the government recruited religion to the war effort as an aid to morale. There was a Religions Division of the Ministry of Information (MOI) that produced its own tracts, made two films and published a wartime weekly propaganda paper, *Spiritual Issues of the War*, that churned out stories on the state of European churches and the war.[163] Following long-standing practice, the government called a National Day of Prayer in May 1940 after the evacuation of the British Expeditionary Force from Dunkirk, and another was held on 3 September 1943, which packed out many churches. Many reported that hymns and communal singing were important during the war. A popular ditty and Sunday school song appeared on the walls of many public air-raid shelters:

God is our refuge, be not afraid,
He will take care of you all through the raid.
When bombs are dropping and danger is near,
He will be with you, until the all clear.[164]

In this way, there was an overt effort by the state to sustain the place of religion in national life.

But it was the subtle rather than the blatant propaganda that was more telling. The infusion of religious themes into wartime propaganda in the Second World War reached heights of refinement probably never seen before or since. Films of unique and astounding quality, even to the modern eye, were made in the war. Three stand out – *A Canterbury Tale* (Archers Film Productions, 1944), *Went the Day Well?* (Ealing Studios, 1942) and *Mrs Miniver* (MGM, 1943), in each of which a national Christian religion was depicted as underlying British society and as holding the nation together. These films resonated with a sense that

British character and the nation's identity were underscored by a religion made placid yet sturdy by long familiarity. Whereas First World War culture in books and magazines depicted national victory as the product of evangelical conversion and hard-line moral conviction of sin, Second World War films touched a national sensibility of a more mild-mannered religion in which talk of church doctrine and even of God took a back seat. The religion depicted in these films was constructed around a sense of a sublime transcendence rooted in folk Christianity and national heritage.

Yet, some things seemed little changed since 1918. Issues to do with the supernatural remained at the top of many people's minds. A survey by Mass-Observation in 1941 reported 86 per cent of women and 50 per cent of men admitting to some form of superstitious belief or practice.[165] There was evidence of a spiritualist craze during the war — the 'Cross of Light' campaign – in which a crucifix was believed to form a protective spiritual force across the country, and this evolved into a Poster of Light that was put up around the country.[166] As in the First World War, people reputedly marvelled at the survival of crucifixes, statues and St Paul's during bombing in London. Women rather more than men were said to be 'susceptible to visions'. In 1941, at the start of the German bombing blitz on British cities, around 40–50 per cent of people reported some belief in astrology; but this figure declined rapidly to around 30–35 per cent in early 1942, under 30 per cent later that year, and a steady level of under 10 per cent from 1943 to 1947.[167] Yet, on the other hand, a study of young people during the Blitz in London found little religious *activity*: only 1 per cent participated in religious activities compared to 34 per cent who went to the cinema.[168]

For all the variety of reactions to war, there is clear evidence that Christian culture remained at the forefront of the national reaction to wartime emergencies. War Office statistics showed that in 1942 of the 2,476,956 men and women in the Army, only 1,486 – 0.06 per cent – professed to be atheists.[169] Religious ideas and ideals were circulating strongly in popular culture, and the agencies of the state saw clearly the benefits to the war effort of employing religious-based concepts in the maintenance of morale. The war demonstrated that the power of religious culture – however much resisted by individuals and rebels, and scoffed at by the mocking – remained at the forefront of the media which it consumed. This applied to servicemen and women too. As Michael Snape has recently observed: 'The continuing existence of the Chaplaincy service was not simply a historic hangover or a function of the foibles of pietistic

commanders, but it was fundamentally indicative of the abiding importance of religion in contemporary British society and of the military value
of religious belief in modern conflicts of unparalleled magnitude.'[170]
Moreover, there was a general sense in which government regarded
religion as a bolster to both morale and to the very purpose of war. A War
Office report, reviewing the state of morale in the war, stated that: 'There
is no doubt that religious faith will increase the powers of endurance and
self-sacrifice of soldiers who possess it.'[171]

But there was less evidence of religious revival in the Second World
War than there had been in the early years of the First World War. The
strong religious culture of regiments was largely absent by 1939, in part
because the heady mix of patriotism and religious bonding was no longer
as apparent. Indeed, conscription did not really permit the religious
culture of regiments in 1914–15 to be recreated. However, there were
some instances of revival – especially in the early stages of captivity of
British prisoners of war in the European theatre, and even more strongly
and for longer periods amongst POWs in the Japanese theatre. There,
Christianity itself became a form of resistance to the very bad treatment
experienced. In the Japanese camps in Singapore, Java, on the
Burma–Thailand railway and in Hong Kong, religious culture was created
with the construction and consecration of churches, the organisation of
Christian discussion groups and the promotion of a Christian-centred
moral resistance within captivity. An Australian prisoner facing execution
for trying to escape from Singapore told a British chaplain: 'I have my
New Testament here, sir, and I am going to read it while they shoot
me.'[172]

With less concern for revival, a liberal social-reform agenda was dominant in most British churches, notably led by the Archbishop of
Canterbury, William Temple. In a well-selling Penguin book, *Christianity
and Social Order* (1942), he supported the state's Beveridge Report of the
same year, which planned the introduction of the welfare state (National
Health Service, full employment programme, council-house construction,
comprehensive state education for all and a social-security system). The
Education Act 1944, and its Scottish equivalent of 1945, were seen by the
churches as beneficial for introducing compulsory religious education in
British schools – an avenue into the re-education of the British young in
Christianity – whilst wider state educational functions in promoting community and sports facilities were welcomed as means of social
improvement. More generally, the coming welfare state was viewed sympathetically by many in the churches, including evangelicals, as the

government enveloping material systems for sustaining moral conservatism. This would impose tighter controls on individual behaviour in a programme of reclaiming the wayward boy and girl in a moral climate fostered by a new economic wellbeing. A new, more highly regulated society, in which want was to be banished and morality would rise accordingly, was envisaged.

However, not all clergy were optimistic for religion as a result of the war. In Birmingham, the Anglican Bishop Barnes, though in many respects a modernist, said in 1941 that '... the government has allowed the traditional Sunday to be destroyed. It is to become the continental pleasure-Sunday. Cinemas, theatres, music-halls, are to be open: Monday is to be a day of rest for the artistes. The new change will finish the destruction of our Sunday schools. We shall get a truly pagan England.'[173] The war seemed to some commentators to herald the end of the deferential society. A report by Mass-Observation concluded that 'people are losing faith in the goodwill and potentialities of authorities', and that 'all the great hierarchies of organisation by which their lives are increasingly ordered aren't really *concerned* with them and their wants and needs'. This it was felt applied to the churches as to political parties. 'Goodwill and hope centre increasingly on the individual, the person and not the programme, the actions and not the ideals.' The report quoted a woman ex-member of the Salvation Army:

The one predominating effect war has had is this – I scoff at organised religion. Once a uniformed member of the Salvation Army – but now I see how wrong they are! Uniform still appeals to me very much – but only saints should wear uniforms. Religion is what we make it – either a club or a deep personal experience. War has pointed this out to me because war has dragged me out of it all. Where I used to be in it all day, now I've had to stand aside and so get a new view. In future, I'm a free-thinker, interested in everyone's religion, but belonging to none in particular. War has also given me a new self-confidence and a hard-boiled outlook on anything and everything. I've come to the conclusion that everyone is extremely selfish and cruel, and even when peace does come they'd celebrate it on Monday and cut each other's throats on Tues ...[174]

For others, the war radicalised them. John Craig had completed the first year of a History and Economics degree at Glasgow University when conscripted during the war – not to the armed forces, but as one of 48,000 young men (known as the Bevan Boys) selected from December 1943 by ballot to work in the coal mines. At Polkemmet colliery in West Lothian he was introduced to the unique comradeship induced by the appalling and dangerous conditions of underground working. Fellow miners regarded him as from another world: 'Of course, they soon discovered I'd been to university. They immediately assumed that because you were attending university you'd come from the upper classes and went home at the weekend to a girlfriend dripping with fur coats.' The experience radicalised him, and after the war he returned to university to study theology: 'I had a vision of a better world, a better society. We know from history that Labour came in with a great surge after the war. The politics of the miners was part and parcel of the political awareness which was new to me in my intensity.'[175] A brave new world of the social state seemed to beckon after war. For some this implied an end to traditional religion; for others it meant that the Kingdom of God was about to materialise.

Notes

1 *The Times*, 11 October 1922.

2 *British Weekly*, 19 October 1922; *The Times*, 17 April 1922.

3 P. Thompson *et al.*, *Living the Fishing* (London, RKP, 1983), p. 205; J.A. Stewart, *Our Beloved Jock: Revival Days in Scotland and England* (Asheville, N.C., 1964), pp. 8–17; *Stirling Observer*, 12 January 1922; *British Weekly*, 19 October 1922, 28 January 1926 and 12 October 1922.

4 *British Weekly*, 19 October 1922.

5 Ibid., 7 June, 12 and 19 July, 30 August 1923.

6 D. Bebbington, *Evangelicalism in Modern Britain: A History from the 1730s to the 1980s* (London, Unwin Hyman, 1989), pp. 181–228 at p. 183.

7 I.M. Randall, *Evangelical Experiences: A study in the spirituality of English Evangelicalism 1918–1939* (Carlisle, Paternoster, 1999), pp. 211–2.

8 N.T.R. Dickson, *Brethren in Scotland 1838–2000: A Social Study of an Evangelical Movement* (Carlisle, Paternoster Press, 2002), p. 191.

9 Mass-Observation, *The Pub and the People: A Worktown Study* (London, Victor Gollancz, 1943), pp. 162–3.

10 *British Weekly*, 5 December 1918.

11 See the anti-prohibition leaning of the *Church Times*, 21 May 1926, 30 December 1938.

12 C.G. Brown and J.D. Stephenson, '"Sprouting Wings?": women and religion in Scotland c.1890–1950', in E. Breitenbach and E. Gordon (eds), *Out of Bounds: Women in Scottish Society 1800–1945* (Edinburgh, Edinburgh University Press, 1992), p. 100.

13 SOHCA/006/Mrs X.2 (1920), p. 11.

14 Brown and Stephenson, '"Sprouting wings"?' pp. 105–6, 115–6.

15 Memoirs of two listeners featured on Radio 2, *Terry Wogan Show*, 22 March 2005.

16 W. Foley, *A Child in the Forest* (London, Futura, 1978), pp. 114, 253.

17 R. Gamble, *Chelsea Girl* (London, Ariel, 1982), pp. 33, 184.

18 D. Noakes, *The Town Beehive: A Young Girl's Lot: Brighton 1910–34* (Brighton, Queenpark, 1980), p. 65; E. Hall, *Canary Girls and Stockpots* (Luton, WEA, 1977), p. 17.

19 D. Scannell, *Mother Knew Best: An East End Childhood* (London, Macmillan, 1974), p. 11.

20 W. Foley, *Child in the Forest*, p. 119.

21 Data from Registrars General figures, obtained from online tables at GRO and GRO-Scotland.

22 Advertisement for women's clothes, *British Weekly*, 24 October 1929.

23 *The Tablet*, 12 June 1937.

24 *Church Times*, 2 July 1926.

25 M. Penn, *Manchester Fourteen Miles* (London and Sydney, Futura, 1982), p. 214.

26 M. Hobbs, *Born to Struggle* (London, Quartet, 1974), p. 18.

27 D. Thomson, *Nairn in Darkness and Light* (London, Arena, 1987), pp. 203–4.

28 P. Ayers, *The Liverpool Docklands: Life and Work in Athol Street* (Liverpool, University of Liverpool, c.1984), p. 50.

29 B. Crampsey, *The Young Civilian* (London, Headline, 1988), p. 175.

30 A.H. Dunnett, *The Church in Changing Scotland* (London, James Clarke, 1933), p. 63.

31 G.I.T. Machin, *Churches and Social Issues in Twentieth-century Britain* (Oxford, Clarendon Press, 1998), pp. 56–7.

32 S.J. Smith, *Children, Cinema and Censorship: From Dracula to the Dead End Kids* (London, I.B. Taurus, 2005).

33 *British Weekly*, 7 November 1929, 20 February 1930.

34 Quoted in Mass-Observation, *The Pub and the People*, p. 156.

35 H. Forrester, *By the Waters of Liverpool* (London and Glasgow, Collins, 1983), p. 15.

36 Mass-Observation, *The Pub and the People,* p. 164.

37 L. Purves, *Holy Smoke: Religion and Roots: A personal memoir* (London, Hodder & Stoughton, 1998), p. 9.

38 *The Tablet*, 20 February 1937; *British Weekly*, 15 October 1925.

39 I am grateful to Mike Snape for allowing me to use his term here. This paragraph owes everything to conversations with him about masculinity and religion.

40 C. S. Nicholls, 'Clayton, Philip Thomas Byard (1885–1972)', rev., *Oxford Dictionary of National Biography* (Oxford University Press): 2004 www.oxforddnb.com, accessed 1 September 2005; www.toch.org.uk.

41 H. McLeod, *Religion and the Working Class in Nineteenth-century Britain* (Basingstoke, Macmillan, 1984), p. 66.

42 *The Tablet*, 20 February 1937.

43 Machin, *Churches and Social Issues*, pp. 87–97,102–3; J.G. Lockhart, *Cosmo Gordon Lang* (London, Hodder & Stoughton, 1949), p. 405.

44 Mass-Observation, *The Pub and the People*, pp. 160, 327.

45 *British Weekly*, 28 January 1926.

46 Revd W.C. Fleming, in ibid., 28 January 1926.

47 C. Stanley, in ibid., 28 January 1926.

48 Ibid., 18 March 1926.

49 Revd James Scott, in ibid., 20 May 1926.

50 R. Burman, 'The Jewish woman as breadwinner: the changing value of women's work in a Manchester immigrant community', *Oral History* vol. 10 (1982); idem., 'Jewish women and the household economy in Manchester, *c.* 1890–1920', in D. Cesarani (ed.) *The Making of Modern Anglo-Jewry* (Oxford: Basil Blackwell, 1990); H. Srebnrnik, 'Class, gender and ethnicity intertwined: Jewish women and the East London rent strikes 1935–40', *Women's History Review* vol. 4 (1995), pp. 283–99.

51 *The Times*, 30 March, 2, 4, 5 and 7 April, 21, 24–27 and 28 May, 9 and 30 July, 11 August, 22 October and 10 December 1932.

52 Ibid., 8 and 12 September 1932.

53 Ibid., 31 July 1937.

54 Ibid., 6, 10 and 22 August 1935.

55 Ibid., 28 and 29 November 1935.

56 Ibid., 15 October 1932.

57 Ibid., 16 and 18 May 1935. A year later, the dentist again took action against the *Morning Post* newspaper over the same alleged libel; ibid., 28 August 1936.

58 Ibid., 29–31 July, 2 August 1937.

59 J. Penny, 'Time to forgive the Stiffkey 1', *The Guardian*, 24 November 2001.

60 *The Tablet*, 23 December 1937; M. Gaine, 'Hinsley, Arthur (1865–1943)', *Oxford Dictionary of National Biography* (Oxford University Press, 2004).

61 H. Ansari, *'The Infidel Within': Muslims in Britain since 1800* (London, Hurst & Co., 2004), pp. 40–4, 107, 118, 130.

62 *The Tablet*, 21 December 1935.

63 J. Hickey, *Religion and the Northern Ireland Problem* (Dublin, Gill and Macmillan, 1984), p. 23.

64 T. Dooley, *The Plight of Monaghan Protestants 1912–1926* (Dublin, Irish Academic Press, 2000), p. 59.

65 *Reports on the Schemes of the Church of Scotland, 1923*, pp. 750–61.

66 R. Passmore, *Thursday is Missing* (London, Thomas Harmsworth Publishing, 1984), pp. 56–8.

67 *British Weekly*, 28 January 1926.

68 Revd John White, ibid., 17 October 1929.

69 R. Roberts, *The Classic Slum* (Harmondsworth, Penguin, 1973), p. 11.

70 W.S.F. Pickering, *Anglo-Catholicism: A Study in Religious Ambiguity* (London, Routledge, 1989).

71 Revd J.D. Jones DD, quoted in *British Weekly*, 15 October 1925.

72 D. Haworth, *Figures in a Byegone Landscape* (London, Methuen, 1987), p. 123.

73 Penn, *Manchester*, p. 177.

74 Passmore, *Thursday*, p. 31.

75 A. Foley, *A Bolton Childhood* (Manchester, Manchester University/WEA, 1973), p. 26.

76 Thomson, *Nairn*, p. 233.

77 Quoted in A. Muir, *John White C.H., D.D., LL.D.* (London, Hodder & Stoughton, 1958), p. 326.

78 Dunnett, *Church in Changing Scotland*, p. 112.

79 *British Weekly*, 25 March 1926; *The Tablet*, 25 November 1935; *Church Times*, 30 April 1926.

80 *Church Times*, 1 January 1926, 30 April 1926, 2 July 1926; *British Weekly*, 22 April 1926; *The Tablet*, 21 December 1935. An indulgence in the Catholic Church is a remission for the sins of a penitent believer.

81 Ibid., 5 June 1937; Ayers, *Liverpool Docklands*, p. 57.

82 Mass-Observation, *The Pub and the People,* pp. 157–8.

83 D. Bebbington, 'The secularization of British universities since the mid-nineteenth century', in G.M. Marsden and B.J. Longfield (eds.), *The Secularization of the Academy* (New York and Oxford, Oxford University Press, 1992), pp. 270–3; *The Times*, 3 May 1922.

84 *British Weekly*, 27 February 1919.

85 Ibid., 21 August 1930.

86 *Church Times*, 25 November 1938.

87 See, for instance, ibid., 8 December 1938.

88 See the report in ibid., 29 July 1938.

89 Professor E.W. McBride, quoted with a cynical enthusiasm by *British Weekly*, 5 December 1929.

90 Quoted in M. Brown and S. Seaton, *Christmas Truce: The Western Front December 1914* (London, Pan Books, 2001), pp. 61–2.

91 Passmore, *Thursday*, p. 61.

92 *The Tablet*, 21 December 1935.

93 Reports of how churches celebrated Christmas are in *Church Times*, 30 December 1938.

94 Revd Neville Davidson, quoted in *The Herald*, 27 December 2004; Dr John Highet writing in *British Weekly*, 1 November 1962.

95 *The Times*, 17 April 1922.

96 See an article on The Temperance Council of the Christian Churches, *British Weekly*, 15 October 1925.

97 Machin, *Churches and Social Issues*, pp. 32–6; J. Kent, *William Temple* (Cambridge, Cambridge U.P., 1992), pp. 115–34.

98 Dunnett, *Church in Changing Scotland*, p. 92.

99 *Church Times*, 25 November 1938.

100 Passmore, *Thursday*, p. 134.

101 *British Weekly*, 22 April 1926.

102 *The Times*, 11 February 1922.

103 Ibid., 16 February 1922, 9 March 1922; *British Weekly*, 4 September 1930, 8 October 1925. A. Dyson, 'The Christian religion', in T. Thomas (ed.), *The British: Their religious beliefs and practices 1800–1986* (London, Routledge, 1988), p. 109.

104 *The Tablet*, 20 February and 12 June 1937.

105 D. Nash, *Blasphemy in Modern Britain 1789 to the Present* (Aldershot, Ashgate, 1999), pp. 218–36.

106 Dr Kempthorne, former Bishop of Lichfield, quoted in the *Church Times*, 16 September 1938.

107 Mr Justice Sankey, the constitution's author, *The Times*, 21 April 1922.

108 *Church Times*, 5 August 1938.

109 For a discussion of the issues, see C.G. Brown, 'The myth of the established Church of Scotland', in J. Kirk (ed.), *The Scottish Churches and the Union Parliament 1707–1999* (Edinburgh, Scottish Church History Society, 2001).

110 The Revd John White, quoted in *British Weekly*, 22 April 1926.

111 Quoted in Lorna Sage, *Bad Blood* (London, Fourth Estate, 2001), p. 47.

112 The parish magazine of St Agatha's Church of England, Sparkbrook, Birmingham, vol. xiii (October 1938), quoted in S.G. Parker, *Faith on the Home Front: Aspects of Church Life and Popular Religion in Birmingham, 1939–1945* (Bern, Peter Lang AG, 2006), p. 55.

113 *British Weekly*, 8 October 1925; 'The Lady Behind the Daily Service', BBC World Service programme, broadcast 6 July 2005.

114 *The Tablet*, 25 November 1935.

115 *British Weekly*, 9 January 1930.

116 H. Jennings and C. Madge (eds), *May The Twelfth: Mass Observation Day Surveys 1937* (London, Faber & Faber, 1937), pp. 270, 327.

117 C.L. Warr, *The Glimmering Landscape* (London, Hodder & Stoughton, 1960), p. 119.

118 G. Foakes, *My Part of the River* (London, Futura, 1976), p. 35.

119 M. Hobbs, *Born to Struggle*, p. 18.

120 A. Foley, *A Bolton Childhood*, p. 52.

121 Sage, *Bad Blood*, pp. 47–8.

122 Foakes, *My Part*, pp. 31, 81.

123 *Church Times*, 1 January 1926.

124 Ramsay Guthre, writing in *British Weekly*, 20 May 1926.

125 R.J. Barker, *Christ in the Valley of Unemployment* (London, Hodder & Stoughton, 1936), p. 79.

126 C.L. Warr, *Scottish Sermons and Addresses* (London, Hodder & Stoughton, 1930), pp. 49–50.

127 *British Weekly*, 6 May 1926.

128 Revd John A. Hutton, in ibid., 13 May 1926.

129 *Church Times*, 14 May 1926; see also K. Aspden, *Fortress Church: The English Roman Catholic Bishops and Politics, 1903–63* (Leominster, Gracewing, 2002), pp. 162–73.

130 Machin, *Churches and Social Issues*, pp. 38–9.

131 *Church Times*, 14 May and 21 May 1926. Temple quoted in F.A. Iremonger, *William Temple, Archbishop of Canterbury. His Life and Letters* (London, Oxford University Press, 1948), p. 343.

132 *British Weekly*, 20 May 1926.

133 Ibid.

134 Quoted in S.J. Brown, 'The social vision of the Scottish presbyterianism and the union of 1929', *Records of the Scottish Church History Society* vol. 24 (1990), p. 91.

135 Dickson, *Brethren*, pp. 196, 325.

136 Dunnett, *Church in Changing Scotland*, p. 124.

137 D.D. Morgan, *The Span of the Cross: Christian Religion and Society in Wales 1914–2000* (Cardiff, University of Wales Press, 1999), pp. 154–5; R. Pope, *Building Jerusalem: Nonconformity, Labour and the Social Question in Wales 1906–1939* (Cardiff, University of Wales Press, 1998), pp. 167–249.

138 J. Bullock, *Bower's Row* (London, EP Publishing, 1976), p. 123.

139 A. Blair, *Tea at Miss Cranston's* (London, Shepeard-Walwyn, 1991), p. 75.

140 Molly Weir, *Best Foot Forward* (London, Collins, 1994), p. 285.

141 *Church Times*, 5 August 1938.

142 Dunnett, *Church in Changing Scotland*, p. 52.

143 Warr, *Glimmering Landscape*, p. 143.

144 J. Bradley, 'Weaving the Green: a history of nationalist demonstrations among the diaspora in Scotland', in T.G. Fraser (ed.), *The Irish Parading Tradition: Following the Drum* (Basingstoke, Macmillan, 2000), pp. 111–25.

145 Haworth, *Figures*, p. 125.

146 Passmore, *Thursday*, p. 118.

147 The coefficient of determination was −0.03. The data used were the annual growth rates of Church of Scotland plus United Free Church communicants 1922–56, regressed against numbers of British unemployed for the same years.

148 J. Springhall, B. Fraser and M. Hoare, *Sure & Stedfast: A History of the Boys Brigade 1883 to 1983* (London and Glasgow, Collins, 1983), pp. 129–130, 132–3.

149 SOHCA, Mrs B.1 (b. 1907).

150 SOHCA, Mrs W.1 (b. 1913).

151 Mass-Observation, *Puzzled People: A study in popular attitudes to religion ethics, progress and politics in a London Borough, prepared for the Ethical Union* (London, Victor Gollancz, 1947), pp. 35–41.

152 Passmore, *Thursday*, pp. 151, 156; Eddie Mathieson quoted in I. MacDougall (ed.), *Voices from War: Personal recollections of war in our century by Scottish men and women* (Edinburgh, Mercat Press, 1995), p. 211.

153 Quoted in M.F. Snape, *God and the British Soldier: Religion and the British Army in the era of the two World Wars* (London, Routledge, 2005), p. 125.

154 Ibid., p. 127.

155 P. Mayhew, quoted in ibid., pp. 26–7.

156 Mass-Observation, *Puzzled People*, p. 23.

157 Ibid., p. 55.

158 Parker, *Faith on the Home Front*, p. 60.

159 Parish magazine of St Agatha's, Sparkbrook, 11 November 1940, quoted in ibid., p. 81.

160 Ibid., pp. 174–5.

161 V. Massey, *One Child's War* (London, BBC Books, 1978), p. 62.

162 Special arrangements were made for non-religious objectors. MacDougall (ed.), *Voices,* pp. 265–7, 283.

163 Parker, *Faith on the Home Front*, pp. 126–7, 183.

164 Mass-Observation, *Puzzled People*, p. 59. My thanks to Stephen Parker for first drawing my attention to this poem.

165 Parker, *Faith on the Home Front*, p. 87.

166 Ibid., pp. 88–9.

167 Mass-Observation, *Puzzled People*, p. 60.

168 T. Harrison, *Living through the Blitz* (London, Collins, 1976), p. 310.

169 Snape, *God and the British Soldier*, p. 146.

170 Ibid., p. 138.

171 PRO WE227/6, J.H.A. Sparrow, *The Second World War 1939–45. Army Morale.* (1949) I am grateful to Michael Snape for this reference.

172 J.N. Lewis Bryan, *The Churches of the Captivity in Malaya* (London SPCK, 1946), p. 10. I am grateful to Michael Snape for this reference.

173 Parker, *Faith on the Home Front*, p. 112.

174 Mass-Observation, *Puzzled People*, pp. 153–4.

175 Quoted in *The Herald Magazine*, 12 February 2005.

CHAPTER 5

Faith in austerity, 1945–59

The late 1940s and the 1950s were afterwards recalled by Lorna Sage, a feminist academic, as the period of 'post-war moral rearmament, with everyone conscripted to normality and standing to attention'.[1] This was a widespread sentiment. These years constituted one of the high points of British Christian culture, surpassed only by that of the Edwardian period at the beginning of the century. But the 1950s were remarkable in one respect. Whilst the 1900s witnessed some liberalisation of Victorian religious puritanism, the 1950s experienced the *intensification* of moral conservatism over and above that of the 1930s and the war years. There was an increasing expectation that the citizen would act in Christian ways. Through looking at themes of moral austerity, evangelism, women and the emerging issues of class, race and youth, this chapter explores the perplexing period between the end of the war and the dawn of the revolutionary sixties.

Austerity amidst plenty

The late forties and the fifties saw much that was new. To counter the economic shortages of the depressed 1930s and the ravages of war, the welfare state was formed and educational opportunities expanded, whilst council-house building provided hundreds of thousands of new homes. With full employment, bellies were full, and welfarism spread the fruits of labour more widely than ever before. There was new technology – the spread of television, nuclear power stations and (from 1957) space exploration. But in the midst of the new, there resonated the revitalisation of

By the 1950s, Sunday-best dress for going to church had become markedly more utilitarian and drab during the austerity of the post-war years. (Topfoto)

older values. There was an austerity in the air that seemed to belie the spread of plenty and innovative consumer goods.

The British people in the later stages of the Second World War started to show signs of responsiveness to a renewed conservatism in morality. The war undoubtedly put pressure on sexual purity, strained abstemiousness from alcohol and undermined some of the values of the Christian society of early twentieth-century Britain. This resulted in some moral panic at home, much as happened during the First World War. Women became the target for both community and state pressure to restrain sexual infidelity when husbands were away at war. Religious marriage dropped as a proportion of total weddings in the war years, as young people married quickly. But pressures for a return to conformist ideals started to surface – perhaps in 1943 when it was clear that the tide of war was turning in the favour of Britain and its allies. The arrival of American troops in Britain in 1943–4 put puritanism on the agenda. There was widespread concern with American servicemen proving sexually attractive to British women: the Americans were relatively rich, had a more liberated and articulate culture of hedonism, and brought a popular culture in their wake of dance, music and consumer goods (such as women's stockings) which proved a heady brew in liaisons with British women. American servicemen were described in a popular slogan as 'over-paid, over-sexed and over here', and in this atmosphere there was a resumption once again in British popular culture of close scrutiny of women's moral behaviour.

So, a surge for moral purity – for a moral austerity – became evident in both popular and official culture. This chimed with the material circumstances of the time. Austerity was the watchword of the age, defining a period when in the economy, in leisure, in family and personal life, people's behaviour was characterised by restraint and duty. The nation in the late 1940s entered a difficult climate in which moral and religious issues intertwined in ironic ways with economic and political affairs. Politically, Britain seemed to swing to the left, electing a Labour government in 1945 that promised 'never again' to allow the unemployment and deprivation of the 1930s, and promising to institute full employment and the welfare state of National Health Service, council housing and state education. The result was a regime of deficit-spending, where government borrowed heavily (mostly from the USA) to rebuild the war-shattered economy and to protect the British people from economic problems. Yet, in contradiction of these seemingly left-wing-led ideas, Britain joined the anti-communist crusade of the United States. The Cold War started that pitted the USA and Western Europe (including Britain) in the NATO military pact in opposition to the Soviet Union under Stalin and its East European allies. This placed Britain in a position of supporting an American anti-left-wing agenda. In this atmosphere, religion mattered. For, under American leadership, the anti-communist agenda adopted the character of a right-wing Christian evangelicalism. Britain elected a

Labour government from 1945 to 1951 at the very time that a moral conservative agenda was spawning growth in Christian fundamentalism.

In this way, austerity came to characterise the religious as well as the material climate, defining individuals and their identities. The novelist John Carey was later to remark: 'I admire austerity because I grew up in the war. Austerity gets into your bones.'[2] Government rationed nearly all the materials of daily life, from meat to thread. It continued to ration furniture (until 1948), clothes (until 1949), petrol (until 1950, reintroduced 1956) and food (until 1954), with rationing of building supplies continuing well into the 1950s. Rationing defined a wider sense of shortage. Towns heavily bombed by German wartime raids left an air of disorder and ruin. This applied to the churches too. In some urban centres, such as London, Hull, Coventry and Clydebank, there were whole areas in which churches as well as houses had been completely obliterated. The Churches Main Commission negotiated compensation terms with the government, getting a total of £40.5 million for churches struck by bombs.[3] But payments were not completed until the early 1960s, and this left many congregations with roofless churches and no sites for rebuilding, and jeopardised Christian family connection.

A worsening problem in the 1940s and 1950s was the uneven distribution of the clergy. In the Church of England, too many clergy held comfortable rural deaneries, too few worked in urban areas, and too many were sited in the south of England (the archbishopric of Canterbury) compared to the north (the archbishopric of York). For example, in the late 1940s the rural bishopric of Bath and Wells had one clergyman to every 920 people, compared to one to every 3,000 people in northern bishoprics. Programmes of parish amalgamation in both the Church of England and the Church of Scotland, euphemistically called 'readjustment', failed to keep pace with demographic need. But there was a cost to tampering with long-standing family tradition. A woman from Stirling observed that when her own church closed and she transferred to a neighbouring congregation, she felt awkward and few spoke to her, and she said that 'sometimes you thought you were taking somebody's seat'. As a result, like many more people were to do in the 1960s and 1970s, she stopped attending church.[4]

Irrespective of these problems, little changed during the 1950s in the status of the mainstream churches. There remained a strong sense of continuity, especially for the Church of England. As the established or state church, the Anglican communion held a special place in the social landscape. As one handbook of 1957 said, the parson was 'given unusual opportunities through the establishment of the Church of England, for establishment inevitably suggests to civic and secular bodies that when they desire the recognition of Christianity for their activities, they should turn to the Church of England'. Many organisations and people held a sense that they 'need the Church'.[5] The sense of a solid and immoveable British 'establishment' reached the peak of its social currency in these years – the sense that the nation was safely in the hands of an informal network of political grandees, judiciary, senior police and military officers, senior civil servants, heads of public schools and universities, and church leaders. The establishment was at its most self-satisfied, with the church safely ensconced within it, upholding national values and morality. If the 1930s and wartime had created some uncertainty amidst the mellowing of values, the 1950s witnessed retrenchment.

Moral austerity was marked by increasing state control of new media. In 1955, the Children and Young Persons (Harmful Publications) Act permitted printers, publishers and sellers of horror comics for children to be fined and imprisoned for breaches of moral codes, and, despite attempts at liberalisation, laws on censorship of theatre, adult publications and films remained pretty firmly in place.[6] Churchmen took a lead role in claiming art and arts festivals for Christian moral purpose in the 1950s. This applied especially to the Edinburgh Festival, started in 1947 as an element in post-war moral revitalisation, which led the Church of Scotland to purchase a theatre as a vehicle for moral enhancement. Yet even by the later 1950s, at the Edinburgh Festival as in the arts more generally, a host of challenging dramatists, artists, humorists and writers were promoting disregard for convention, religion and the establishment.[7]

But the artistic underground had little penetration into the dominant media of the day – radio and television. Television became an accessible popular service in 1952–3, and quickly emerged as the object of dispute concerning its religious and moral function. When commercial television (ITV) started in 1954, Labour MPs took the Tory government to task for permitting commercials on Holy Days and Sundays.[8] The BBC felt bound by its charter to uphold a fairly restricted sense of popular culture and national values. Its director-general said in 1948: 'There are many demands of impartiality upon the Corporation but this is not one of them. We are citizens of a Christian country, and the BBC – an institution set up by the state – bases its policy upon a positive attitude towards the Christian values. It seeks to safeguard those values and to foster acceptance of them. The whole preponderant weight of its programmes is directed to this end.' Religious broadcasting, he went on, was openly considered as having 'an inherent duty to make people join the Christian faith'. Whilst the Christian churches readily accepted this policy (though the Catholic Church felt under-served), smaller churches and atheist bodies like the Rationalist Press Association and the National Secular Society did not. A Parliamentary Committee on broadcasting stated in 1949 that 'the object of religious broadcasting should be conceived, not as that of seeking converts to one particular church but as that of maintaining the common element in all religious bodies as against those who deny spiritual values'. However, it did agree in relation to religious questions that 'the BBC's highest duty is the search for truth'.[9]

Under this rubric, Christian campaigns to evangelise enjoyed extraordinary access to public service radio from 1945 to 1955. The broadcasting of special services and sermons introduced religious events to a wider audience, and this airtime promoted the sense of celebrity surrounding preachers and evangelists. Broadcasting of religious issues was deferential to Christian culture and to church leaders, conforming with parliamentary policy of regarding the UK as 'formally' a Christian country, though in the later 1950s the pro-Christian role was ostensibly weakened; by 1960, there were 8 hours per week of religious broadcasting on BBC radio, but only 1.5 hours on BBC TV and a further 2.5 on ITV. Ironically, the result of this restricted output was to exclude virtually all non-Christian religious broadcasting, but at the same time ended the BBC's role as a vehicle for conversion. Instead, both BBC and ITV aimed 'to reflect the worship, thought, and action of those churches which represent the main stream of the Christian tradition in the country'. The Roman Catholic Church objected, arguing that presenting the commonality in the Christian tradition eroded distinctive denominational approaches to 'religious truth', whilst the Church of Scotland successfully argued for distinctive Scottish religious television programmes. But pressure was starting to build on the broadcasters to reflect the religious diversity of the nation.[10]

How did the British people reflect the culture of religious austerity? The evidence is confused. On the one hand, if asked, Britons rated religiosity pretty low in their priorities. One opinion poll in the mid-1940s asked people what they thought was the most important thing in life, and faith came eleventh and last (after happiness, health, family, money, love, work and most other aspects of life).[11] In another poll in 1948, the British Institute of Public Opinion asked a sample of British people, 'What did you do last Sunday?' Only 15 per cent claimed to have gone to church – 18 per cent of women, 12 per cent of men, 11 per cent of Church of England members, 25 per cent of free church people, 27 per cent of Roman

Catholics and 18 per cent of the others. There were also enormous regional variations to religious affiliation and practice. Throughout the century, the highest attendances were recorded in Northern Ireland, Scotland, Wales and the north, east and south-west of England (in that descending order). Londoners and those living in the south-east recorded the lowest level of religious belief and activity, but the variation from higher zones was not that great in the 1950s. London and Scotland were cast as the extreme cases – as the most secular place and the most highly religious zone of mainland Britain. Yet, some figures show London and Scotland as very far from being at opposite extremes. In 1947, an opinion poll in a London suburb showed 39 per cent of people recording that they were church attenders, of which 28 per cent had been in the last six months. Of these about 10 per cent said they attended in the previous week.[12] For comparison, adult weekly church attendances in Scotland in 1954 were 14.2 per cent of population.[13]

On the face of it, this seems like a country in which Christian activity was low, and not far removed from the character of Britain in the 1990s. However, the evidence of religious 'coolness' is deceptive. In another survey in 1947, only 11 per cent of men and 18 per cent of women claimed to go to church weekly, almost exactly mirroring the responses to the first survey. But a further 18 per cent of men and 26 per cent of women claimed to go between once every three weeks and once every two months, and another 15 per cent of men and 12 per cent of women claimed to attend church less frequently. Thus a total of 44 per cent of men and 56 per cent of women claimed to be churchgoers, far exceeding figures later in the century. The Catholics were the most frequent church-goers – 79 per cent of them claiming to be churchgoers and 52 per cent claiming weekly attendance. Anglicans were the least observant, with only 48 per cent claiming to be churchgoers and only 8 per cent claiming to go weekly. What makes such figures interesting is that though only 15 per cent of the population claimed to go to church weekly, 50 per cent of the adult population claimed to be churchgoers in a vast outer constituency of church membership. This gave British Christian culture its massive base of support.[14]

This gave Britons their common religious tradition. In 1951, a major survey by the *People* newspaper amongst a demographically balanced panel of 5,000 respondents found that 75 per cent of English people described themselves as 'being of a religion or denomination'.[15] The figure reached its highest in the south-west of England (81 per cent), in small towns and villages (78 per cent), amongst 15–34-years-olds (76–77 per cent), women (79 per cent), the middle middle class and lower working class (79–80 per cent), and those on the lowest wages. At the other extreme, it reached its lowest in London and the south-east, north and north-east of England (73 per cent), in the largest cities of London, Birmingham, Manchester and Liverpool (69 per cent), men (72 per cent), in the over 65 age group (70 per cent), the divorced and separated (65 per cent), those on the highest wages, and those who were either unable to describe their social class (68–71 per cent) or who declared themselves lower-middle, upper-working and middle-working class (73–4 per cent).

Many of these answers and differences were not surprising. The stronger sense of religious belonging amongst women rather than men, in married and single people rather than the divorced and in smaller towns rather than large cities fits most profiles of popular religiosity from the 1900s to the 1990s. But a number of points are distinctive and note-worthy. First, the degree of variation in the 1950s between highest and lowest by geography, social class, age and so on is remarkably small. The widest variation (known as the range) between highest and lowest response rates is no more than 10 per cent, and most are in the region of 1–4 percentage points of divergence, suggesting a remarkable degree of homogeneity across British society as a whole. Second, the sense of working-class religiosity by these measures was very strong, and much stronger than in the middle and upper classes as a whole. This contrasts with most presumptions both then and since amongst sociologists and church leaders as to the middle-class character of British churchgoing. The data reveal the upper-working class with the highest levels of weekly or more frequent attendance; also, there was no significant statistical relationship (correlation) between variations in churchgoing by social class and variations in claimed religious belonging by social class.[16] In other words, just because a social group *claimed* to associate with religion did not make them strong churchgoers. Finally, what leaps out from these figures as really quite surprising is that it was the oldest in society who considered themselves as the least religious belonging, and the youngest – those in their late teens and twenties – who evinced strongly religious views. The level of religious activity in the under-18s was extraordinary: 11 per cent attended church more than once a week, with a further 18 per cent weekly and 13 per cent monthly. It was also high in the 18–24 age group, with figures of 8, 10 and 11 per cent respectively. Such levels col-lapsed in middle age, to rise a little in the 45–64 age group and a little further in the over-65s.

In another survey in the 1940s, just under a quarter of young people claimed to have gone to church in the last six months, but the proportion of those who went weekly and monthly were found to be identical as among the elderly.[17] By contrast, virtually every similar survey from the 1960s to 2000 shows the over-65s to be the highest religious group and the young to be the most indifferent and alienated from religion and the churches. In this context, the self-proclaimed religiosity of the young and of the lower working class is of some note in early 1950s' England.

So many people claimed in 1950 to be churchgoers at some point in the year that what is revealed is a highly religious society underpinned by a widespread Christian culture, sustained by the churchgoing activity of young people who grew up during the war years. Nor was the religiosity of the people purely to be measured in terms of churchgoing. Amongst parents, 58 per cent claimed to teach their children to say prayers. Some 44 per cent of respondents claimed to make private prayers daily or more than once a day (58 per cent of women, 31 per cent of men, 65 per cent of the poorest economic groups and 71 per cent of over-65s), but only 49 per cent of the under-18s and 37 per cent of the 18–24-year-olds. Strong on *social* religious practice, the young were not so strong on admitting to *private* religious practice. At the other end of the age scale, the elderly were split starkly between those with high religious activity and those with low activity.

What of religious belief? Amongst the 5,000 respondents in the 1951 survey, 20 per cent claimed to 'believe in the Devil', 18 per cent in Hell and 47 per cent in an afterlife (with the highest scores for each amongst the upper-middle class, the under-18s and over-65s). The belief being expressed was a remarkably materialist one. Written answers revealed literalness and a preoccupation with the here-and-now, all spliced by a sense of humour. The nature of the afterlife was described by a 41-year-old woman from West Bromwich: 'It will be a wonderful place with everything just right and there will be plenty of lovely food without rationing I hope.' A middle-class married woman from Berkhamsted wrote of the afterlife: 'More peaceful than the present, with no cold, war, or washing up. I hope there will be animals, music and no towns; a kind of ideal earth in heaven.' A younger woman from Bishop's Stortford wrote: 'I believe it will be a very happy place, with no colour bars, no "class" distinction, no intonation of speech, a place where everyone will have a job to do, no matter whether he was a king or peasant in this world, a place where there will be a common language. Jesus Christ and his twelve disciples will be a form of government, there will be no opposition, for there will be nothing to oppose.'[18]

This deeply informed sense of Christianity contrasted with that of many in the 1950s amongst whom overt religiosity was about keeping up appearances. Women were notably compelled to conform to 'respectability' through the everyday use of religious platitudes and homilies that 'controlled' behaviour in the community; rebuke was levelled by loud remarks about 'respectable folk' and their place in the natural order of things.[19] The sense of shame was great for a woman. Women were the guardians of moral strictness, and they tended to feel that women should be sexually inexperienced at marriage. Within marriage, the guilt continued; given a choice of more than ten things that a wife might do if her husband had an affair, 2,000 women placed 'talking with spouse' first and 'make self more attractive' second (whilst men said they would respond to a wife's infidelity by placing separation and divorce pretty high up the list).[20]

Moral change in Britain was nowhere more explicitly demanded than in personal sexual behaviour. In the whole of the modern era, sexual activity outside of marriage appears to have reached its low point in the 1950s in England and Wales, and to have dipped dramatically in Scotland after a high point in the inter-war years. (See Figure 1.1, p. 32.) Across the whole of the UK in the late 1940s and 1950s, the low figures for illegitimacy confirmed the austerity of the moral and religious climate. They reflected a high degree of sexual abstinence before marriage and of marriage following immediately upon discovery of pregnancy. Virginity dominated amongst both men and women into their twenties. Moreover, the culture of virgins was widely acknowledged. Men undergoing their two years' National Service in the armed forces, which they continued to do until 1963, later became the butt of British humour for their sexual inexperience – being portrayed as 'the virgin soldiers' and as 'the innocent'. Ian McEwan wrote of a young man undergoing National Service as more morally naive, unadventurous and abstemious than older men and women who served in the war: 'It was not so extraordinary a thing in nineteen fifty-five for a man of Leonard's background and temperament to have had no sexual experience by the end of his twenty-fifth year.' As the poet Philip Larkin noted, sexual intercourse was not invented until 1963, 'which was rather late for me'.[21]

Cultural conservatism in the 1950s was best exemplified in island, Highland and isolated coastal zones, notably in Scotland. In South Uist, Christina Hall recalls as a teacher that October was the month of the Rosary, and the little local authority school 'became a chapel as the villagers congregated to say the rosary and sing hymns to Our Lady', in which she had to lead the prayers and the school children led the singing. Moral behaviour was strict, when 'cohabiting was unheard of and gays stayed well hidden in the closet'.[22] Catholic identity was fiercely enforced by the cascade of experiences of a faith that was strongly working class. As one Catholic historian has written: 'The common experience of poverty, the hardship of World Wars, the Great Depression and, for most males, of National Service in Britain until 1961, helped to reinforce Catholic cohesion. Opportunities for diversity, dissent or differentiation were limited. Few had the leisure, income, qualifications or desire to break with local ethnic, family or ecclesiastical loyalties.' The post-war period fostered 'a massive religious resurgence' in which 'Catholic solidarity, Marian devotion, revivalism and anti-Communism merged'.[23] This was characterised by the arrival in Britain in 1952 of the US-based Blue Army of Our Lady of Fatima, an organisation promoting the centrality of the Virgin Mary to faith, and the fight against communism in Russia and at home (notably amongst Catholic trades unionists and left-wing activists).

This intensification of Catholic identity included some of the fiercest imposition of Christian moral codes created by priests and secular orders of nuns upon children. In the years since the 1950s, accounts have emerged across Britain, Ireland, North America and Australia of the rigid and even cruel regimes in some Catholic children's homes, though homes of other denominations were not immune from such faults. For some of the young, the religion experienced in the 1950s was uncompromisingly repressive and guilt-inducing. Betsy White recalled how a priest kept calling on her and her very young sister in the fifties, upbraiding them for being 'wild' and not being at Catholic chapel, and terrifying them into tears with tales of Purgatory; the unrepentant priest said: 'It is only right that we should fear God.'[24]

The British people at mid-century present a conundrum. They come across as infused with religious ideas and critical self-awareness. They seemed unhappy and oppressed by guilt, teaching their young to be good, to say prayers and to go to Sunday school. For the elderly, there was a schism between those still strong in church connection and those, a sizeable proportion, who were deeply alienated from the churches. The young, in turn, were profoundly active in social religiosity, but less contemplative in prayer than their elders. Religion was a social thing, the church a location of associational activity perhaps unsatisfied by other social institutions. And it was some of the young who were the most affected by the resurgence of Christian evangelism.

The crusade decade

The puritan climate of the late 1940s and 1950s benefited the churches. Conservative evangelicals felt empowered by the mood of the times to urge their denominations towards an evangelistic spirituality and lead society back to traditional moral sensibilities. Even in the midst of the new – the rise of the welfare state through radical action on housing, health and education – there was a return to old-time religion. Even one of the great advocates of social action, William Temple, the Archbishop of Canterbury, nonetheless commissioned a report that was published in July 1943, 'Towards the Conversion of England', which signalled that after the war the way forward for British Christian society was through evangelising work. Welfarism and conversionism became bedfellows in a joint crusade to refashion the British nation.

From 1945 to 1956, Britain experienced one of the most concerted periods of church growth since the middle of the nineteenth century. Anglo-Catholicism was in relative decline, foundering in the midst of Protestant resurgence on one side and moves to modernisation within the Roman Catholic Church on the other.[25] But Protestant evangelism was seen to be prospering, bringing new converts from the war generation and their children. The 1949 Mission to London was promoted by the High Church Bishop of London, William Wand – with the motto 'Recovery Starts Within'. Some 8,000 helpers were trained and committed to the work, and took their mission to many different venues and parts of London.[26] Radio missions became the technological fashion of the mid-1950s; one in Essex in September 1954 consisted of a fortnight of broadcasts on different radio channels of religious services, talks and sermons, with 120 of the 200 Protestant churches in metropolitan Essex participating, using house-to-house visitation with pairs of Anglican and free church home visitors.[27] In Scotland, a variety of initiatives in evangelistic mission work developed from the late 1940s, including the Christian Commandos, the Edinburgh Churches Campaign, the Stornoway Convention, the Iona Community Parish Mission and the Radio Mission on the BBC in Scotland. In an act of consolidation, the Tell Scotland Movement was promoting from late 1953 what was described as 'a consistent rather than a periodic mission'.[28]

By far the most noteworthy religious events of the decade were the 'crusades' of the Revd Dr Billy Graham. He was a Southern US Baptist preacher, brought up in a wealthy American middle-class family, who came to England first in the spring and again in the autumn of 1946, speaking in 27 cities and to 360 meetings over a period of five months.[29] In early 1954, he achieved further fame by having a small starring role in a Hollywood evangelical feature film, *Oil Town, USA*, which featured Graham as the vehicle for the religious conversion of a father and daughter. Graham's fame in 1954–5 was a puzzle to many. Initially, some evangelicals opposed him, telling him explicitly in 1952 not to come to Britain on the grounds that his approach was culturally adrift from the British people: 'Billy Graham's campaign would set back the work of evangelism for another 25 years.' To religious critics, he seemed to be famous for being famous. British radical clergy were concerned with Graham's right-wing conservative evangelicalism and how it ignored the social Christianity in British church tradition, and his anti-socialist rhetoric ruffled many feathers in the British Labour Party.[30] All in all, Graham was not someone to whom British clergy gave a unanimous welcome.

So, there was some perplexity when, on Graham's arrival in 1954, he was mobbed by 3,000 people at London's Waterloo station. Graham was already well known, having for six winters held mission events at the Royal Albert Hall.[31] Prior to his arrival for the 1954 crusade, huge posters went up all across London with his image, proclaiming 'Hear Billy Graham' and 'Thrill to the Music of Tedd Edwards'. One critic from Dorking noted the absence of reference to God or the gospel: 'But to the irreligious multitudes who and what is Billy Graham, and what kind of thrill is this that might be expected at Harringay Arena? Let the Campaign organizers think again. Do they really and seriously imagine that the people of London will be beguiled into attendance at Harringay by this kind of advertisement?'[32]

One key to Graham's success was funding. The London crusade of 1954 cost more than £171,357, with about £40,000 donated by Billy Graham's own organisation in America, with further unidentifiable funds from American evangelical or business organisations. But hopes were dashed that British business would donate handsomely to the crusade. A letter was sent out to Federation of British Industry members, appealing to business fears – especially of 'the growth of Communism which is seeking to infiltrate the whole of our national life'. 'The only answer to this,' the letter continued, 'is militant Christianity. Dr. Billy Graham brings such a message to the British people, and the coming Crusade is the result of his desire to present to our people the message which has had such a marked effect upon the American way of life.' The response to this letter was disappointing, with only £1,236 identifiably coming from business, most made of £25 donations or less. The Cold War rhetoric worked less well

Analysis: Religious films

The new media technologies of the twentieth century provided religion with both challenges and opportunities. People's habits were changing, and many religious organisations saw the need to keep up with trends in popular culture and taste. But not only was the medium changing, but the message too. Film, radio and television changed the way in which people absorbed, ordered and understood the world, and the churches had a challenge to keep pace.

The rise of the cinema initially offered a challenge to the churches, as working-class people especially found a cheap and enchanting escapism from hard-working lives in the flea pits and nickelodeons in the two decades after the invention of moving film in 1896. The churches' first response was to use 'secular' film (showing scenes of empire and landscapes) as part of the diet of entertainment in existing religious voluntary organisations. By the early 1900s, the film was seen as a medium that could put across the Christian message, and the Salvation Army pioneered films to be shown in its halls around the country.[33] But during the First World War, the arrival of American films raised a moral panic that films were the route to the Americanisation of Britain through display of a morally degenerate culture (of dance crazes, jazz musicians and flapper girls in skimpy dresses with short hair). This made the churches vacillate over the moral integrity of the medium, and various inquiries were instituted by moral guardians.

However, despite the problems, attempts were made to convey the Christian message via film. In 1922, the Church of England praised a film of Christ's life, *From the Manger to the Cross*, made in the Holy Land at a cost of £20,000.[34] But such films caused problems as most churchpeople came resolutely to oppose any actor playing either Christ or God on film, as they considered this a modern blasphemy. This clearly restricted the use of film and divided Christian opinion. For example, the film *Green Pastures* about religion and American blacks depicted God as an old black pastor, arousing church dispute; some clergy described it as 'sheer blasphemy', but others thought it 'fundamentally reverent'.[35] If the clear dramatic potential of depicting God or Christ was denied, then Christian films tended to become either boring or ridiculously unsophisticated. One called *Cross Beams* was made by the RAF in 1938 for its own personnel, but was criticised by churchpeople as naive and too metaphorical – by being about a pilot lost on the moors who was found by 'the Shepherd'. There were other grounds for dispute; some churches opposed even showing the sacred sacraments (holy bread and wine). It was not yet clear what was acceptable to be shown on screen, and sensitivities prevented a meaningful genre of Christian film developing in this country.[36]

But in the 1950s and 1960s, the mood changed again. Films became better censored with the foundation in the later 1930s of a system of film classification in Britain, and film studios became scrupulous in following ever-tighter moral guidelines. This enabled the wider screening of overtly Christian films. In the vanguard was the American evangelist Billy Graham, who used film as an aid to his 'crusades'. He released a feature film called *Oil Town, USA* prior to his 1954 Harringay crusade in London. In this story, a rich Texas oilman, Lance Manning, gave up his religious faith and became an aggressive, cruel and vindictive employer of whom it was said, 'his God is gold'. But his cruel behaviour led his 20-year-old daughter Chris to find Christ – her perfect female piety represented in her dress of Easter bonnet and white gloves. After confrontations with his daughter, Manning considers suicide, but is brought to a sense of his own sin through watching Billy Graham preach on television. Though a mawkishly sentimental film, and rooted in a white American evangelicalism of the Deep South quite alien to British culture and experience, the very alien-ness of American culture was, however, part of the attraction of this Hollywood-style film.

Graham went on to make two British-based feature films – *Souls in Conflict* (1954), set in England, and *Fire in the Heather* (1955), set in Scotland. The first of these told the stories of four different characters from different walks of London life, each troubled with their moral lives. One of these is Ann, an actress (an occupation long portrayed as ethically suspect in evangelical Christian rhetoric). She is shown in religious turmoil because of an immoral actor fiancé, but is 'saved' on hearing Billy Graham at Harringay Arena. Here, Graham gives his characteristic 'sinner-centred' sermon: 'Sin is a moral disease: I am a sinner, you are a sinner, we're all sinners.' This is a film where the homely American Christian culture worked with a British audience because of its familiarity with the underlying religious rhetoric: acknowledge sin, act moral, save yourself and society, beware tempted men, and women should keep pure. The film presented Graham as the successor to a very long line of Christian heroes to save Britain from moral collapse. 'In every century,' one character says of Graham, 'God seems to send a spiritual awakening just in time, doesn't he?'

This kind of sentiment had some acceptance in the 1950s, but by the 1960s it was becoming treated by many as ridiculous. The notion of sin was being widely rejected, and indeed was dropped from most British-made religious films of the decade. Films tried to tell old stories but reduced the sense of gloom. The Methodist Church film *Adventurous Journey* (1963) showed a young woman not as sinful but as vain, powdering her nose instead of joining the family at the breakfast table, and as attracted to church neither by tradition nor evangelical preaching, but by a trendy vicar (who wears no dog collar) and a 'swinging' church youth club with its own pop group (a clone of Cliff Richard's backing band The Shadows).

Some Christian films were liberalising the view of faith. In *School for Sinners* (1964), Anglican chaplains take on trendy roles themselves – one who is a biker joining 'the ton-up-kids', prison chaplains and industrial missions in Sheffield, exploring the way in which clergy had to move into the heart of the culture and workplace of the people and, in so doing, see the sites of sin as merely liberal culture. But others tried to shock. In the late 1960s, the Mothers Union produced an extraordinary film, *Who Is My Neighbour?*, that opened with a very violent and terrifying rape scene, and hit home its message in a traditional commentary: 'Life is hard for young people today. They have everything and nothing ... The permissive society gives them no help. Promiscuity before marriage is not a sound training for fidelity after marriage. Girls are very important people. They will be the wives of our sons, the mothers of the next generation.' These stereotypes of moral danger still underlay the main Christian message of the 1960s. Men were portrayed as drinkers, gamblers, profligate and sexual predators – as in a Church of England film *Focus on Commitment* (1971), which showed a caricature of a drunken, middle-aged, wealthy businessman who preyed on women. Unfortunately for the genre, neither the caricature nor the message was being perceived by target audiences as much of a moral danger any more. Some commercial musicals and films with religious themes worked better through adaptation to pop music and a 'hippy-style' of religious praise; these included *Joseph and The Amazing Technicolor Dream Coat* (1968, revised 1972) and *Hair* (1968). But many traditional churches regarded these productions as part of the 1960s' problem, not part of the solution.

A greater issue was the rise of anti-religious mockery in film and television. Feature films like *The Wicker Man* (1973) portrayed religion as weird, telling a story of a highly Calvinist island off Scotland which had been turned by a perverse landowner, played by Christopher Lee, to human sacrifice and group sex, ending in the burning alive of a local policeman.[37] Satirical films, such as *Monty Python and the Holy Grail* (1975), deliberately challenged the pomposities of religious stories. On television, documentaries in the late 1960s and 1970s told the stories of religious groups of all sorts (both Christian and New Age) in which there was bizarre behaviour, sexual lewdness, use of drugs and brainwashing of converts; one such group was the Jesus Army that was sensationally portrayed in a TV documentary in 1971.[38] No longer was religion accepted at face value as a zone of correctness and respectability.

By the mid-1970s, the Christian churches were making less use of films. Church organisations could not match the production values of Hollywood, and this made their films look amateurish and unappealing. The moral message about 'sinning', and the redemption narrative that men were the problem and women the religious solution, had lost resonance in British culture. Not until portrayal of Christ became more acceptable at the turn of the century – notably in the film *The Passion of the Christ* (2004) – was a new narrative form found that had a powerful impact upon part of the potential audience for the Christian message.

with business in Britain than in the USA, and most of the £100,000 of British donations came in small contributions by individual, not corporate, Christians.[39] The money gave the crusade its buzz of Hollywood and its razzamatazz. Graham reported that $50,000 was spent on publicity alone – an unheard of sum for that era. Billy Graham's backers organised advertisements for him around London, a daily column 'My Answer' in the *Daily Sketch*, wall-to-wall coverage in daily and regional newspapers, and exposure on the nightly *Epilogue* on BBC television.[40]

Feted by celebrities, politicians and a press hungry for excitement in the midst of austerity, Graham's operation was backed up by nearly 3,000 counsellors trained by his American staff, and a headquarters located in Holborn in central London. Business methods were used in the conversion of souls, with a 'decision card' drawn up that started a paper trail for each would-be convert and encouraged church attendance.[41] Children were particularly targeted by Graham and his crusades. A famous Hollywood film star, the cowboy Roy Rogers and his horse Trigger, then enormously famous for their western movies for children, made appearances across Britain. On a Saturday morning in late March 1954, reputedly 35,000 children turned up to see Rogers and the horse. Rogers explained that, 'Billy is one of the greatest men raised in America,' and felt that it was his mission to bring the Word to children.[42] The following year on a Scottish crusade, Graham preached to a packed indoor arena at Kelvin Hall of over 10,000 children bussed in by the local authority in Glasgow from their schools.[43]

What was it like to attend a Graham crusade assembly? The meetings were conducted in large arenas or football stadia, bedecked in flowers and ribbons, with a stage, microphones and film cameras in operation. The sense of Hollywood and celebrity was immediately unusual to British churchgoers more accustomed to the cold, dark pews of the British church. The services were also very different from the norm. They were introduced by gospel-style hymn-singing by mass choirs of up to 3,000 men and women, bedecked in white dresses and black suits, making a

Revd Dr Billy Graham preaches to over 100,000 people at Wembley Stadium, 1954. (Topfoto/Topham/AP)

stark moral backdrop. Singing was led by Graham's assistant, and by a soloist whose voice alone, it was said, was enough to raise the spiritual temperature. Billy Graham came on to deliver a stark, short, didactic sermon. Always clutching the Bible in his hand, with a finger marking a page and occasionally bringing it up to eye level as if consulting it for authority, Graham looked straight at his audience. In his films, he talks to camera straight, with no autocue or dummy boards, in an impressive command of speaking skills. He speaks firmly, verging on loudly, and calls his listeners to account. He speaks in the words of a nineteenth-century evangelical tract, calling everyone a sinner: 'You are a great sinner. You were born a sinner. Every day you have been thinking sin, speaking sin, doing sin. Have you not?' He barracked and challenged his audience repeatedly on their transgressions, using the words 'sin' and 'sinner' over and over. In the context of the 1950s, he reflected the great concerns of moral rectitude that characterised the decade. He cited the command-ments: 'Thou shall not commit immorality. You can commit immorality by a thought, by a look, or by an act. Thousands of you are guilty of immorality. God calls it sin.'[44]

This was a confrontational and unequivocal form of religion. By calling each listener a 'sinner', there was no latitude or uncertainty in the importance Graham attached to moral failings. He plugged into and helped breed the sense of guilt in fifties' Britain. He was especially concerned with the 'secularism' of the metropolis. He told his first congregation at Harringay: 'Would it not be great to see everybody in the City of London discussing Christ? To see hundreds of people praying across London? Would it not be wonderful to see secularism and materialism hurled back? Would it not be grand to see our trains and coaches filled with people singing Christian hymns as they did in the days of Wesley?'[45] And there is no denying Graham's success in 1954 and on a second visit in 1955. Though many heard Graham live more than once, over the twelve-week crusade there were a total of 1.75 million attendances, rising to 1.9 million when numbers at relay services were included. The closing day's events attracted 65,000 people to an afternoon service at White City greyhound stadium, and a further 120,000 to an evening service at Wembley football stadium. In Scotland the following year, a further 1.2 million attended events at a Glasgow-based crusade, which included another mass service to 120,000 people on Easter Sunday at Hampden Park football stadium. This ability to fill the national football stadia of England and Scotland was symbolic of Christianity's outreach in the 1950s. The stadia, as homes to the leading working-class sport, also symbolised the democratic nature of Christian culture, and Graham preached deliberately to all social groups – from the staff and students of the Royal College of Science and Technology in Glasgow, to thousands of shipyard workers at Clydebank.

Yet, the success in numbers attending did not translate into significant church growth. The numbers in his audiences making 'decisions for Christ' (by coming forward for spiritual counselling) in 1954 and 1955 were minute: only 36,431 (2.1 per cent) in London and 26,457 (2.2 per cent) in Scotland, and they were mostly the young in their teens. Of those who 'came forward' in London in 1954, 65 per cent were women and over 50 per cent were under 19 years of age; in Scotland the following year, 71 per cent were women, 73 per cent were under the age of 30 years and 11 per cent were under 12 years.[46] Yet, British church membership figures peaked in 1956 and then fell. Despite the millions attending, Graham's work did nothing to arrest the imminent commencement of rapid secularisation. The real success was in its role as spectacle. Reared on a diet of Hollywood films, Britons responded to the showbiz razzamatazz. One academic in 1954 gave his judgement on Graham's apparent success:

> *In drab, welfare-state, metropolitan London, youth dreams of escape*
> *and the chief stimulus to escape from the restrictions of this life is*
> *offered by the picture-theatres. Now Billy Graham looks like a film-star,*
> *speaks with the accents of a film-star, has a wife as pretty as a film-star,*
> *and draws great crowds of children to his rallies by means of Roy*
> *Rogers and his wonder horse, Trigger. The place and the atmosphere*
> *where his 'conversions' are won are not the chilly, respectable,*
> *conventional churches – but a Sports Stadium of vast proportions where*
> *literally thousands of others have come for the same reasons. The*
> *brightly decorated awnings, the vast choir singing 'snappier' tunes than*
> *the churches use for their hymns (here is a parallel with Moody and*
> *Sankey), and the quiet, intimate, compère, use of the microphone, are*
> *the channels to get him to modern youth.*[47]

The British had become accustomed to American evangelicalism through novels and films.[48] And British churchmen were won over to the role of novelty and experimentation; one said: 'This is a phenomenon with no parallel in Christian history, and the devil must have many sores to lick.'[49] Graham's parting shot to London was that Britain was 'on the verge of its greatest spiritual awakening'.[50]

Crusade Christianity was an element of something greater in post-war Europe. It was part of a much wider attempt by American organisations and churches to re-convert Britain and her continental neighbours to Christianity, and so resist socialism, atheism and communism in the midst of the Cold War with the Soviet Union. Organisations from the United States were from 1946 sending money, religious campaigners and expertise to promote the 'conversion' of Britain. Leading American politicians supported the enterprise. On the platform at Billy Graham's first meeting in Britain were two US senators – one Democrat, one Republican. Graham made his political position clear in an American publication in which he attacked Britain for letting in socialism and emptying the churches during and after the Blitz; for this, he was attacked in the Labour *Daily Herald* (under the headline 'Apologize, Billy – or Stay Away!'), whilst his remarks were described by British Christian socialists as 'either unpardonable ignorance or malicious libel'.[51]

Billy Graham and his crusades fitted into other wider movements. He attracted the support of those influenced by the inter-war growth of 'fellowship Christianity', including sects like the Brethren; indeed, at least 28 per cent of Graham's British spiritual counsellors were members of the tiny group

Thousands flocked to Harringay in March 1954 to attend film star Roy Rogers children's rally, and others to hear Billy Graham. Roy Rogers, his wife Dale Evans and his famous horse Trigger were top of the bill. (Topfoto)

of Brethren.[52] In a different vein, the crusades overlapped with the work of a well known but slightly shadowy Christian organisation called Moral Rearmament. Originating as the Oxford Group in the 1920s, it too brought American evangelical influence to Britain after 1946, seeking to inculcate strong 'family values', to fight 'immorality' and to assist in the struggle with 'ungodly' communism. In its work, it represented what many commentators regarded as a significant characteristic of post-war evangelical religion – relegating God and Christ to the background, and bringing moral rectitude to the foreground. It presented Christian faith as a moral development that helped the nation, rather than moral development as an aid to Christian faith. Operating through highly-placed individuals in government, business, trades unions and public life, it mobilised conservative campaigning in European nations, attracting businessmen of the sort who assisted Graham.[53] Its impact is difficult to gauge, especially since the conservatism of the 1950s was to be quickly followed by the liberalism of the 1960s in which Moral Rearmament fought a losing battle. But it represented one of the greatest attempts to mould British public life to the agenda of American evangelicals.

Analysis: Moral Rearmament

The Moral Rearmament (MRA) movement was a Christian pressure group, founded in east London in 1938 that campaigned vigorously in the 1940s and 1950s (and with less success in following decades) in Britain and Europe, promoting evangelical values, fighting immorality and opposing communism. It was formed from a group at Oxford University in the 1920s and 1930s under the leadership of Frank Buchman (1878–1961), a Lutheran who in 1908 underwent a conversion experience at Keswick in the Lake District, and who became convinced of the use of Christianity to form a moral society devoid of strife. He toured American and British elite universities recruiting students and graduates to the work of moral campaigning. These recruits included the British Wimbledon tennis singles finalist of 1932 and 1938, Henry 'Bunny' Austen (1906–2000). A Moral Rearmament movement (also known as 'The Oxford Group' and the Caux Foundation) emerged in the United States in 1940, and during the 1940s it became more oriented as an anti-communist organisation, opposing the class struggle and promoting liberal market values, Christian individualism and high moral standards. Over some decades, it was to form a significant strain of influence within British Christianity.

In its internal workings, MRA emphasised group solidarity and fellowship, attracting especially the independent young woman looking for excitement which she could not find in conventional churches or politics. In the 1930s, one woman noted how it appealed to 'a post-War generation, lonely in the midst of crowds, hungry in the midst of plenty, with neither standards nor stable background'.[54] It fostered what critics saw as a sect-like loyalty to an organisation that was half-hidden from society, yet sought to conquer its moral order. It claimed a direct route to holy revelation that bypassed the emphasis upon church, doctrine and theology of traditional Christianity, and fostered a heavy focus on morality as the ultimate outcome of its work. It mirrored many of the characteristics of what was later to be represented as the 'looniness' of new age sects: emotional self-expression, secretiveness and group loyalty, and the power of charismatic leadership.[55] Its greatest impact was not, however, through recruitment or conversion – it was through campaigning against the agents of immorality, godlessness and communism.

In Britain by 1946, MRA had some 100 moral rearmament workers, half of them ex-serviceman from the United States. Its leadership included Buchman's successor, Peter Howard, a former England rugby captain who had worked with the British Fascist Oswald Mosley in the early 1930s.[56] The organisation's right-wing agenda was especially noticeable in the intensely Cold War atmosphere of the 1950s. It espoused an almost apocalyptic outlook on world politics, social relations and immorality. Buchman told a conference in the Ruhr in 1950 that class struggle was being superseded: 'The one hope of the world was unity. Moral Rearmament offered the world the last chance for every nation to change and survive, to unite and live.'[57] MRA propagandised amongst leading labour relations groups, claiming that through its methods: 'Homes will be re-united, class war will be superseded; production will increase; wealth will be more justly distributed; nations will find security; East and West will reach a common understanding; youth will find a constructive purpose; crime and corruption will decrease; inflation will be checked; government will cost less; taxes will fall; the danger of war will be averted.'[58] Buchman was a fantastic self-publicist. He was nominated by his own body for the Nobel Prize for Peace in 1951, and, like Billy Graham, he succeeded by hitching a born-again Christian moral message to the mast of the anti-communist witch-hunt and hysteria of the 1950s.

In practice, what MRA did was challenge at every turn evidence of moral decay. In the 1930s, it had done much to foster revival-style meetings and even, in some places, entire parishes in which sympathetic vicars had nurtured enthusiasm for moral renewal.[59] But Buchman became uneasy with traditional revivalism, and from the 1940s steered his organisation to foster renewal of society by other means. Using American evangelical expertise, propagandists and money, it used letter-writing campaigns, theatre plays (it owned the Westminster Theatre in London from 1946 to 1998) and insider influence, and held training courses and issued pamphlets.[60] In its work it tended to call upon Christian faith to bolster personal morality rather than the other way around. To accomplish this, it would come to urge four moral absolutes: Absolute Honesty, Absolute Purity, Absolute Unselfishness and Absolute Love.[61] In 1946, MRA published a pamphlet 'Battle Together For Britain', which spoke of God as an aid to moral improvement. The nation was to be raised by its call to 'Clean up the nation from bottom to top/Start with yourself in the home and the shop'.

Moral Rearmament presented itself, and Christianity, as a philosophy rather than a theology (as with Pelmanism, that we looked at earlier, the relationship between a thinking course and religion). One 1947 commentator noted of MRA that it was 'religion with God relegated to the background, the stress on everyday action, general principles of behaviour, belief in standards of behaviour acquired through personal experiences of the need for standards; a philosophy rather than a theology, a coherent way of life rather than a faith'.[62] It was a movement founded on the sense of purpose conferred by 'groupism', and upon a tight-knit fellowship and confidence this erected, resulting in an implicit opposition to traditional ecclesiastical structures and the conferring of great power to its own leadership.[63]

▶

MRA supporters wrote letters and articles for newspapers, and also sent complaints to promoters and local authorities responsible for theatres or other venues where 'immoral' shows were being performed. They badgered British officials about the impact of immoral behaviour upon tourism and inward investment. The Edinburgh Festival, founded in 1947 and by the late 1950s the world's largest arts festival, became a particular target of MRA interest during its annual three-week run in August and September, and letters to the local press and to the city corporation were common.[64] In industry, many British Christian businessmen were drawn to MRA, including Gerald Steel, general managing director of the United Steel Company from 1950 to 1957. Steel was an influential lay figure in the Church of England and its industrial mission work who hoped for moral transformation of his industry through MRA, and defended it from attacks in his own church.[65] Another businessman, W. F. Vickers, from Leeds, explained that MRA 'has drawn a new battle line in both management and labour; what is right, not who is right. It has challenged men to apply the standards of absolute honesty, purity, unselfishness and love in personal, family and social life. Its aim is to make the guidance of God the final authority in every decision.'[66]

MRA claimed some notable converts amongst British trades unionists and Labour MPs – including Alice Cullen, MP for Glasgow Gorbals – as well as a variety of leaders from around the world (including the Prime Minister of East Nigeria).[67] But from the early 1950s, opposition to MRA became more noticeable. This had simmered since 1928, when a young socialist, Tom Driberg (1905–76), had made an exposé in the *Daily Express* of Buchman's aims, methods and effects on young Oxford students, and from then until the 1960s he waged an unrelenting propaganda war against MRA. By the early 1950s, Driberg was an MP, and the Labour Party was divided over his attempts to block Moral Rearmament, but many on the left shared Driberg's derision and suspicion.[68] Churchmen too were uneasy. In 1953–5, the Social and Industrial Council of the Church of England undertook an inquiry into MRA, and its critical report was hotly debated by the Church Assembly. The report criticised the way in which MRA seemed to bypass the incarnational role of Jesus Christ by suggesting direct revelation from God to MRA workers in a process known as 'the dictatorship of the Holy Spirit', and for developing in its followers psychological problems of 'a repressed and unreleased inferiority'.[69] Described as 'utopian and escapist' 'and 'psychologically dangerous and gravely defective in its social thinking',[70] Anglican critics thought MRA would 'harden into a sect'.[71] But after more than a day's deliberations, evangelicals in the Church of England managed to stop the Assembly from reaching a decision to condemn it.

MRA's fortunes started to falter after 1960. Its apocalyptic messages, in full-page newspaper advertisements (like 'The Hour Is Late. For God's Sake, Wake Up', proclaiming the dangers of communism[72]), attracted concern from conservative and radical Britain alike, and by the early 1960s there was a groundswell of hostility to its conspiratorial methods and alien moral agenda. A Conservative MP, Patrick Wolrige-Gordon, MP for East Aberdeenshire, was threatened in April 1962 with de-selection by his constituency party after announcing his engagement to the daughter of Buchman's successor, Peter Howard.[73] Its work, in a sense, continued under a different banner. Mary Whitehouse was a member of MRA, and her National Viewers' and Listeners' Association continued the pursuit of the same moral agenda. (For Mary Whitehouse, see pages 250–1.) With 4,000 staff in 1966 (a quarter in the USA),[74] MRA was able over many decades to claim on an international stage some notable supporters highly placed in government and non-governmental organisations (NGOs), and changed its name in 2001 to Initiatives of Change International.[75] It was influential in introducing evangelical methods into many areas of life – including Alcoholics Anonymous (AA), an organisation whose two 1930s founders had been Oxford Group members in the United States.[76] But a more general return to puritan values in the 1940s was the basis of its apparent influence. Fostered in an atmosphere of moral austerity, MRA flourished. When that atmosphere dissolved, its fortunes dwindled. However, its style of fellowship, close-knit groups and emphasis on Christian action rather than doctrine made it a contributing influence in the rise from the 1960s of the movement for charismatic renewal.[77]

So, the legacy of crusade Christianity upon Britain is complex. On the one hand, the events were enormously popular and culturally penetrative, giving the impression in the mid-1950s that Britain was on a path to Christian growth. One religious columnist wrote of the missions and crusades: 'So many and so varied have been such enterprises since the end of the war that it is obvious now as never in the life-time of most of us, that the missionary imperative is taking a grip of the whole Christian community in such a way that will not let go.'[78] On the other hand, the effectiveness of conversion Christianity had little impact either on numbers coming forward or on long-term church growth. British religious culture proved, in the end, resistant to Americanisation, and confidence in this brand of evangelism rather quickly evaporated. The president of the Methodist Conference, once a supporter of Billy Graham, Moral

Rearmament and the fight against communism, was by July 1955 a pessimist, reporting poor church attendances a year after Graham left; the result, he said, was too many churches with 'all the depression for all concerned of a few people in a large building'.[79] Graham's crusades had also instigated a theological controversy in the Church of England that raged in his wake, both over his methods and over the fundamentalist nature of his theology, with the Archbishop of York issuing a warning: 'We must not allow ourselves to be stampeded into these great campaigns.'[80] Henceforth, enthusiasm was for evangelistic events that were 'occasional', 'expressive' and localised, and based on the work of the parish and on teaching, rather than on spectacle and bright lights.[81] Though Graham was to return again and again to Britain, the widespread enthusiasm of British churchmen evaporated as few new converts came to church and, moreover, as de-Christianisation started to set in.

Women's liberation deferred

During the years 1945–60, women more than men felt the force of moral and economic austerity. The Canadian novelist Angela Carter recalled: 'I grew up in the 50s – that is, I was twenty in 1960, and by God, I *deserved* what happened later on. It was tough in the fifties. Girls wore white gloves.'[82] In peacetime, concerns over Americanisation of British culture and liberal sexual values became translated into a wider puritan agenda fostered by demographic concerns about British womanhood. Women who took over men's jobs at the start of the war were pressed to surrender them at the end of the war and return to 'normal' – to the home and raising a family. The nation was short of labour, and there was a 'pro-natalist' government policy – campaigns and advertisements to encourage women to return to child-rearing to raise the birth rate. Conveniently underpinning the justification for demographic policy was puritan religion: a women's moral place was in the home looking after her husband. In this way, the British state was not averse to religious conservatism bolstering government policy.

Moral conservatism was so intensely imposed upon teenage girls that some were planning sexual revolt during puberty. Lorna Sage recalled of herself and her best friend in the mid-1950s: 'Gail and I were determined never to marry or have children, thanks to our parents' example. Love and marriage went together like a horse and carriage. Dad was told by Mother, you can't have the one without the o-o-ther. We knew better and decreed them absolutely separate in our imaginations.'[83] The fifties sought to recreate in the young the values of early-century evangelical culture, circulated in the popular songs – values that had wavered in the 1930s and perhaps even more so in the war years. But the 1950s did more than send women back to the home. 'I see now,' wrote historian and biographer Carolyn Steedman three decades later, 'the relentless laying down of guilt.'[84]

The decade recreated the values of older generations and forced them upon the young – 'a point between two worlds' where the child 'was 'a repository for other people's history'.[85] And if the girl transgressed the rules, the consequences were dire. Lorna Sage became pregnant in the late 1950s at the age of 17. Her parents planned to send her to a Church of England Home for Unmarried Mothers 'where you repented on your knees (scrubbed floors, said prayers), had your baby (which was promptly adopted by a proper married people) and returned home humble and hollow-eyed'.[86] But Lorna was self-educated in readings of feminist Simone de Beauvoir and existentialist philosopher Jean-Paul Sartre, and she and her boyfriend were determined to navigate their way to an alternative future: 'As the dank, disgraced autumn of 1959 turned to winter we reinvented marriage, for better and for worse. If we got married we would no longer be legally in the guardianship of our parents ... They didn't think we should marry at all – we were far too young and too irresponsible. It was an insult to matrimony. It was also shaming, it would make us look lumpen, real white trash, common as muck. On the other hand if we were bold enough to go to a magistrate for permission we'd probably get it, because I was pregnant and we weren't – they weren't – respectable or well-off enough for their objection to count. And the case would be in the *Whitchurch Herald*.' Here, Sage encapsulates a mindset that gripped so much of Britain in the fifties.[87]

British women expected in the 1940s and 1950s to carry the burden for the religious respectability of their husbands and children. Indeed, it became apparent to sociologists in this decade that women were the primary preservers of religion between the generations, passing religious tradition from mother to daughter. This was sustained in a secret world of folk customs that were perceived by practitioners as linked to Christianity, including the wearing of amulets and the keeping of lucky charms around the house. It was also apparent in the practice of 'churching' a woman after childbirth – a rite that most British Christian churches had officially observed in the seventeenth century but which, though it was still conducted by some Anglican and Catholic priests, had fallen from official favour. In this tradition, the priority to tender 'thanks to God that you're safe' prevented a woman from going out of the house after childbirth without 'cleansing' herself with a special church service. One woman in Bethnal Green told a sociologist in the 1950s: 'It's a very old-fashioned custom. It's superstition really. It's supposed to be unlucky if you go out before you're churched.' Another reported: 'My mother believes it. She's superstitious like that. I don't believe it really but I did stay in for three or four days after I got back and before I got churched.' Women's religion represented a family tradition that lay at the heart of customary family networks, binding married women to their mothers and being part of the impulse in inner-city areas of living close to their mother's home. With rehousing to large council-housing estates and new towns in the 1950s and 1960s, usually far distant, young wives were allowing the affirmation of religious identity through family tradition to break down.[88]

This was a period of transition for some women in families, but the general cultural environment seemed to be tightening in the 1950s. Christina Hall recalled of her Catholic island of South Uist in the Western Isles in the 1950s and early 1960s that, whilst 'attitudes towards people of different colour were relaxed', being a single mother bore 'a dreadful stigma'. Clergy used the state apparatus to enforce single-religion facilities. In that community the priest kept Protestant children out of the Catholic youth club. Marrying out of your religion, or mixed marriages as they were usually called, was thus an enormous stigma. Christina recalled: 'If you hit the jackpot and married someone of another religion while in the early stages of pregnancy, it could change your life forever. A father could meet the ferry at Lochboisdale pier and tell his pregnant daughter and her new husband to get back where they came from and stay there. It happened; I knew the girl.'[89] All this made it extremely hard for a woman to be relaxed about religious identity. The social tensions were strong within communities, families and institutions like schools and churches. Opportunities for leisure were still markedly divided between the rough and the respectable, and within the respectable a considerable portion of what was available as routine recreation on a week-by-week basis was in the hands of the churches and religious voluntary organisations. Sunday schools, Bible classes, youth fellowships and similar organisations still dominated the life of young people; many congregations ran coffee bars and youth clubs, and this remained the basis of a great deal of recreational activity. Moreover, popular culture continued to look upon religion as a woman's domain. When asked his view of religion, one young man from London told an opinion pollster in the 1940s: 'Doesn't touch me much –

it's all right for women, especially when they're getting on a bit – but I don't think I need it just yet, thanks.'[90]

For women in their twenties, there was still heavy pressure to seek and find a husband, and to want to be a mother. Ironically, with the arrival and expansion in this decade of things like radio, television and new kitchen appliances, it was thought that technology was making a woman's domestic confinement more bearable. After the Second World War brought women new jobs and training opportunities, the peace back-tracked on such advances, encouraging many women to return to home, marriage and child-rearing, and to put off education and careers. Women's liberation was deferred in the late 1940s and 1950s, and the deferment required the re-circulation of a traditional discourse on 'domestic ideology'. The film *Brief Encounter* (1945) transformed the mellow, unpuritan religion of wartime films into an intense peacetime exploration of moral worth. By signalling the unbearable shame for a woman if she sexually strayed, the film located her guilt in an unconsum-mated love affair, tortuous self-recrimination, and her eventual return to husband and children.[91] This message came to be reinforced ad nauseam in women's magazines of the decade. Conservatism based on motherhood, cookery and gardening returned to dominate women's popular reading. As late as 1961, *Woman's Own* advised: 'You can't have deep and safe happiness in marriage and the exciting independence of a career as well ... It isn't fair on your husband. I believe [any man] would tell you that he would rather his wife stayed at home and looked after his children, and was waiting for him with a decent meal and a sympathetic ear when he got home from work.'[92]

It was in this conservative family context that women's piety was re-affirmed between the end of the war and 1960. Even as women's economic and educational opportunities started to widen, and the old-fashioned marriage bar to wives working eroded rapidly in the 1950s, the moral clo-sures upon younger women became, if anything, fiercer. Women students felt the force of the fifties' moral contradictions. On the one hand, the numbers of women going to university and college increased. Yet, the effect was to reinforce the difficult moral conditions the single woman was expected to negotiate. Universities were essentially secular bodies by the middle of the twentieth century, with little control exerted in any formal sense by churches. This concerned some university leaders. Sir Walter Moberly, chairman of the government's University Grants Committee in 1949, reported regretfully that 'the universities of to-day are, implicitly, if unintentionally, hostile to the Christian faith'.[93] One consequence of these widely held views was that undergraduates became targets of evangelism. Week-long joint missions were held in Oxford and Cambridge universities in consecutive years in 1953 and 1954 by Anglican, Roman Catholic and free church clergy, led by Michael Ramsay, later to be Archbishop of Canterbury, attracting nightly audiences of reputedly 1,500 students.[94] The arrival of increased numbers of women students intensified 'chapel culture', in which activities conducted in the name of religion lubricated student social life. Female students' lives were often centred on single-sex halls of residence, chapel worship, and scrutinised dating. Christianity remained the amber of life in which many single women moved during university expansion.

Yet, this apparent devotion to religion may not have been all that it seemed. During 1955–8, Pat Fraser and Elizabeth McCudden studied pharmacy at the overwhelmingly male Royal College of Science and Technology of Glasgow. Pat recalled that 'the war was over ten years, and really the war didn't hit us. It was before the '60s, and, you know how, the days of individuality, hedonism you could say, feminism and all that kind of thing. We were terribly conservative.' Pat and Elizabeth were not especially religiously active, nor was their college a major religious centre. Yet, in their first year, Billy Graham was invited to preach in the college's assembly hall during his Glasgow crusade. He brought his counsellors for 'after meetings', and the packed hall of students and staff was about 70 per cent female – described by the *Daily Express* as 'girls in sweaters and drainpipe trousers, youths in duffle jackets and beards'. Pat and Elizabeth recalled how they joined the Student Christian Society for the social life: 'We did it to look the guys up and down.' But they joined the mountaineering society for the same reason.

Their behaviour conformed to a widespread female code of the decade. When they went on dates with men, they, like many women students, did not drink alcohol. Elizabeth said: 'I was too afraid to drink because I wanted to be whiter than white.' One fellow woman student appeared 'mature' because she had boyfriends, went out on dates, dressed smart, but she 'ended up having to get married' and dropping out of college: 'We would have thought of her as very risqué.' But their friend's fashionable clothes signalled moral ambiguity, whilst Pat and Elizabeth felt the moral controls heavily self-imposed upon their bodies. Pat recalled: 'You didn't wear trousers, trousers were out of the question ... you wouldn't wear trousers as a student. Everybody had dark skirts and I suppose a sweater.' Elizabeth chipped in: 'A blouse and a cardigan. We dressed like our mothers.' In this atmosphere, as women students they did not feel theirs was a feminist challenge. 'We were very accepting. We were there to be prepared for the world of work. It would never have entered our head to kick up and want to be with the boys.'[95]

In an atmosphere of moral retrenchment and re-statement of 'traditional' gender roles, the movement for the admission of women to clerical roles seemed unlikely to make headway in the 1940s and 1950s. In the Church of England, the Lambeth Conference of 1948 heard and rejected a proposal from the diocese of South China for the ordination of women to the priesthood for an experimental period of twenty years.[96] The Anglican Group for the Ordination of Women was founded in the early 1930s, but had really not achieved much by 1960. The incremental approach – of extending women's role little by little – was the strategy adopted from the mid-1950s, but even then little was achieved. After another rejection in 1956, the group's secretary said that 'the present position concerning women's work in the Church of England is causing frustration and anxiety'.[97] The same position appeared in other denominations. In 1960, Scotland's main church, the presbyterian Church of Scotland, could not agree on the issue: its district presbyteries voted 18 for and 21 against admission of women as ministers, though 27 to 19 for women elders (senior lay figures in each congregation who help rule the church).[98] The churches reflected the civil society of the 1950s. Women's position was held in check by the conservative economic and cultural climate imposed after the end of the Second World War. This thwarted ambition, especially strong amongst middle-class women; the Archbishop of York noted 'the bitterness and frustration' of women in the church.[99] The danger was that when the deferment was cancelled and women's frustration burst triumphantly upon society, it would do so catastrophically upon the churches.

Harbingers of change: class, race and youth

The late 1950s and early 1960s witnessed the rise of a number of issues which the churches slowly began to perceive as major problems for British Christianity. The country's moral culture started to change perceptibly in the 1950s, and some churchmen were in the vanguard of this. Changes like those regarding racial equality and nuclear disarmament would become defining for the post-1960 moral revolution, when they would set in train a more liberal agenda regarding society's view of the equality of all people. What was under way would undermine the legitimacy of former officially accepted 'us-and-them' divisions of society based on

'essentialist' (meaning inherited and bodily) characteristics of people –
barriers based on class, racism, sexism and homophobia. At the same
time, age barriers started to be questioned. Old hierarchies and deference
were being chipped away.

The political arena was one in which there was an increasing role for
radical clergy in the 1950s. Before the full significance of the anti-
apartheid movement became apparent, the major issue of the 1950s was
that of the atomic and hydrogen bombs, and the formation of the
Campaign for Nuclear Disarmament. One of the leading religious figures
in this movement was the Methodist Conference leader Donald O. Soper,
who campaigned openly and extensively across the UK against first
America's then Britain's own development of the hydrogen bomb. Such
activities split the Christian community between conservative and radical.
The Protestant churches of Northern Ireland tended to be less liberal than
elsewhere. When Soper campaigned in Belfast in 1954, he was heckled by
the Revd Ian Paisley of the newly formed Free Presbyterian Church, who
held up a banner – 'Dr. Soper denies the virgin birth of Christ'.[100] (See
'The troubles in Northern Ireland and the Revd Ian Paisley, 1969–98,
pages 284–7) In this way, the issues that separated radical and conservative clergy were extensive, and used interchangeably in the mounting
inter-clerical dog fighting of the second half of the twentieth century. In
Scotland, the leading campaigner on such issues was the pacifist Revd
George Macleod, founder in 1938 of the Iona Community, which united
political and spiritual renewal. In 1954, he moved a resolution in the
general assembly of the Church of Scotland against 'weapons of mass
destruction'.[101]

A more significant issue in the long term was that of race. Immigration
of black and Asian peoples to Britain in the late 1940s and 1950s only
dawned slowly upon the consciousness of government and Christian
churches as being a significant issue in terms of social policy. Racism was
apparent from the start. In May 1948, 200 white men stoned a house in
Birmingham where newly-arrived Indians were staying, and by the mid-
1950s the level of immigration was high enough for Oswald Mosley,
British Fascist leader in the 1930s, to be again campaigning in the city on
anti-immigration issues. Opposing this in the mid-1950s, a strongly anti-
racist Anglican Church leadership pushed Birmingham Corporation to act
over race issues in employment and housing, urging the appointment of a
committee on overseas nationals, and pressing in 1954 for the creation of
a welfare office and social centre. But in 1955, the Bishop of Birmingham
was forced to back down when he tried to assign a black Jamaican priest

as chaplain to the 'coloured' community, and when an appointment was finally made in 1959, it was of a white clergyman.[102] By the end of the decade, British society was starting to appear deeply divided after a race riot in London's Notting Hill by white working-class youths chasing 'niggers' over five days of the August bank holiday in 1958.[103]

Western Christian churches turned a corner on the issue of race in September 1954 when, at a meeting of the World Council of Churches in Evanston, USA, they condemned as contrary to the gospels 'any form of segregation based on race, colour or ethnic origin'. They called upon member churches and bodies to 'renounce all forms of segregation or discrimination and to work for their abolition within their life and society'.[104] This statement redefined Western Christian approaches to the race issue for the postcolonial world. However, numerous problems remained. The decay of the British Empire was a severe test for the mainstream British Christian churches. They had been accustomed since the 1790s to promoting the gospel across the globe side by side with the English language, law, education, customs and sense of moral being. Now, with the withdrawal from Empire and black immigration to Britain, the morale of the Christian mission faltered. In 1954, branches of the London Missionary Society were reporting that 'there are no new supporters', leading to a dramatic fall in income and the need for retrenchment in their activities: 'The old appeals are faded and gone. We must not appeal – we must challenge people to their duty.'[105]

At the same time, the Christian churches of the former colonies were throwing off the shackles of colonial oversight and influence from the former 'mother country'. The formation in 1947 of the Church of South India (CSI), based on a union of the Reformed, Anglican, Congregationalist and Methodist traditions, marked one important beginning to the fracturing of the perceived one-way relationship between coloniser and colonised, but it also marked the beginnings of Christian ecumenicalism. In 1954, the CSI, with 1 million members, elected as Moderator Bishop its first non-white 'national' leader, the Most Revd Hospet Simitra, who declared his Church's independence from British churches and their money: 'Indian Christians should dare to be poor, dare to be unsupported from outside, and dare to go forward in their own strength.' He galvanised the Church into being conscious 'of meeting at an epochal moment in the life of the nation and the Church'.[106]

Colony after colony was in crisis, and offered troubling thoughts for the Christian churches at home. Also in 1954 came reports from Bombay of a 'Quit India' movement amongst orthodox Hindus using passive resistance to British Christian missionaries.[107] In Kenya, the Mau Mau rebellion against British rule in the early 1950s left the churches puzzled as to what Christians should do after military suppression there.[108] The community of missionaries and their supporters and families, who made up a sizeable and distinct bloc of the British Christian tradition, started to reconsider some of their experiences over preceding decades in the light of the growing native hostility to missions. There was talk of a 'missionary failure', in coming to recognise that there had been an imperialistic impulse in missions, and that the resistance to missions (notably in China in 1925–7 and in the 1940s) was the reaction to imperialism.[109] The issue of South Africa and the construction of racial apartheid started to be felt in the British churches. Prominent people like Alan Paton, author of *Cry the Beloved Country* (1948), a novel that tackled the role of the Christian in the midst of apartheid, urged British Christians to be aware of racial tension in the Christian church, advising them to ecumenical reunion in a 'visible' organisational way as well as in the 'spiritual unity' that was at the forefront of church politics at the time.[110]

Events in the former Empire framed Christian church problems at home. Initially, Christian commentators put the blame for the race issue on 'the coloureds'. Afro-Caribbean immigrants of a strong Christian background found little welcome in British churches, and were stunned to find how insincere British religion was. A Caribbean immigrant said that 'when you get to [Britain] you find that Christianity is just a veneer'. British evangelicals rejected this, blaming coloureds and 'bad negroes' for not making the effort to join churches on arrival, and American service-men in Britain for creating the strongest colour bar.[111] But in the mid-1950s, the churches began to develop concern about what it was like 'being black in Britain'. 'There is no colour bar in Britain,' said the *British Weekly*, 'but doors are shut in his face; rooms vacant when telephone arrangements are made, miraculously fill up when a black face appears at the door.'[112]

Britain's immigrant population in the early 1950s was nearly all Christian by background. There were about 30,000 Muslims, mostly Pakistani: of these, 2,000 to 3,000 were in east London and less than 1,000 in Birmingham, and, because of the lack of mosques, most religious observance was conducted in the home; only for the large Eid festival was a hall hired so everybody could pray together.[113] By contrast, the black immigrants were overwhelmingly from the Caribbean, and nearly all were Christian. Since many initially viewed their move as temporary, there was a strong expectation of joining Christian worship with British people in their own congregations. Black migrants had been raised in a strictly religious society in which virtues of British Christian denominational traditions had been transposed to the colonial setting. Black Christians were familiar with gendered Christian identities; female piety was extolled very strongly, and paraded in women's Sunday-best attire of cotton dresses, hat-covered heads and white gloves, whilst men were often made to feel their piety was a problem.

Yet, even for those who questioned and 'tested' religion, there was a strong familiarity with its tenets. Ryland Campbell recalls in Jamaica in the 1930s and 1940s that 'when I was growing up like a boy, I went to every church right, I went to Catholic church, I went to Presbyterian church, I went to Salvation Army, shake tambourine thing, see they are still saying one God'.[114] Esme Lancaster, born in Jamaica in 1917, recalled that early in the century the Anglican and Roman Catholic churches were joined by new ones: the 'Presbyterian and the Pentecostal church, started to flourish quite a lot in my teen, when I became teenager, those churches, ahm, began to flourish'.[115] And though she was Anglican, she was rejected in her application to join her local congregation in Birmingham by a racist Church of England vicar, and joined the Pentecostal church instead. 'They refused us going, coming into the churches. Then, as I knew that time, I must serve God, there were other avenues open. Pentecostal people were coming here and ... forming their own churches – binding themselves – and so I joined them.'[116] For Christian and non-Christian alike, evidence was emerging that religion was failing to overcome the divisions of a multi-racial society.

For most churchmen, race was perceived as less of a problem in the 1950s than that of social class. Amongst mainstream church leaders and intellectuals, there emerged a widespread acceptance that the working people of Britain had become alienated from the churches at the time of the Industrial Revolution and urban growth in the late eighteenth and early nineteenth centuries. Canon E. R.Wickham, an Anglican industrial chaplain in Sheffield, wrote a path-breaking book on *Church and People in an Industrial City* in 1957, in which his own despair over the failure of industrial chaplaincies developed into a sophisticated thesis of irredeemable plebeian alienation from the churches in industrial towns. This philosophy that the churches had 'lost' the people a long time before argued that what was left by the 1950s was a church of the middle classes. Industrial chaplaincies actually were sustained in Britain, despite the failure of the French worker-priest version. At Luton in 1955, an experiment was developed in industrial chaplaincy dedicated to 'aggressive

Analysis: The immigrant's story

Esme Lancaster was born in 1917 in Wilmington, Jamaica, and was raised in the Church of England. She came to England in 1950, and in the early 1990s, when she was interviewed, she reported: 'I am a Pentecostal; and I'm very glad I am.' She went on to explain why. [117]

In Jamaica, Esme had been a very loyal and devoted Anglican. She had sung in the church choir, had been a member of the Daughters of the King (a local voluntary organisation for young Jamaican women), and had then joined the Mothers' Union. She was a Guide mistress, and had been the Akela (or leader) of the Anglican Brownie group.

She recalled:

You see, one thing about it is that over the Caribbean, people are very Christian-minded – Christian more Christian then. And the thing is that surprise me is that we looked in England when we were children to be for Christianity, the root of Christianity as such, the missionaries were all white, coming to our country telling us about God, telling us about this and the other, you know. And we saw so many things, you know, and believe them that this country was all for Christianity. And when you come you'd be accepted as a Christian you know. And when we came here the difference is that it is not so. When you talk about God, you know, they ask you, they called, some of them call him the bloke upstairs, you know. And once I had a little badge and it [was] marked 'Jesus saves'. And I went into the post office to buy some stamps and this girl looked up and say 'Jesus saves. What does he save, Green Shield stamps?' I said, 'Yes, I am one of the Green Shield stamps that he saved.' I said, 'Fancy that,' I say, 'you were the people who are trying to civilise people, coming round and telling us there's a God, and now you come here you telling that I says "yes I am one of the Green Shield stamps that he saved". And I said one thing about it, if you were fooling us when you were telling us about Christ, about God and what God did, I said you made a big mistake. I said, because this thing it – we've found happiness in Him. So if you were only doing us to cover yourself, to show that we can – give you confidence – I said well, you're wrong. Because we now know the confidence is in Him, not in you.

Esme's story is one in which the Anglican Church's Christianity that nurtured her in Jamaica turned out in the land of its origin to be not just hollow but racist.

Esme had become a teacher in Jamaica, and then came to England in the early 1950s to train as a social worker:

The conditions of living when we first came here make me cry for months and months and months – till we began to find improvement in our living standard. 'Cause we're never used to living in such a – in such large family: people around us, especially strangers– people who you don't really, never used to before – this had happened. And I think also that it helps to build the community spirit with each other, when people sat together in the living-room or the dining-room and begin to talk about home; and ... you get to understand quite a lot of it that you didn't know when you were even in your own country.

Q Were you very homesick?

A I was, most of the time I was.

Q How did that make you feel?

A Oh well, I want to cling to the church more than anything else when I found out, 'cause there was where you find you can have fellowship. We have social gathering and, to me, I find the church brought me the most of the kind of life that I used to live at home. I've never gone to any dance-hall, any – I've come here [social centre], never gone, went to a bingo hall, I've never gone into a pub. 'Cause we did not go there when ere in Jamaica. Those were places that we thought – well, it wasn't very good for women, especially.

Religion made her homesick – the religion she was missing rather than the religion she found in England. Esme told the interviewer the following account of her first encounter with English Christianity, telling the story twice, the same almost word for word – indicating how important it was to her:

I was a member of the Anglican Church in Jamaica, and from a child sang on the children's choir, grew up as a DOK which means a Daughter of [the] King, and from there into Mother's Union which is the adult member of the church, women. I sang in the cathedral Choir in Spanish Town where we met the Queen when she came on 1952. 'Cause that was a time I went back to Jamaica ... Then, after that, I came back [to Birmingham] and now, when I came to this Church [St Michael's, Handsworth] I came with my transfer [certificate] and that is supposed to be [for] the nearest Anglican Church. And then I went there and had taken my transfer cards and my Mother's Union card and whatever. I was told by the vicar that should come back. And each time I go back, 'he's busy', I should come back. And then one Sunday that was St George's Day, and he went in the pulpit preaching, and he was saying: 'I don't know why for the life of me you people are leaving this country, going away, and others are coming and enjoying it and you are leaving.' And he went on and then at the end of the service he came to the door, shook hands, and then said to me – he didn't shook my hand anyway – he said to me: 'I'm asking if you could find another church to worship because I don't want to lose my parishioners.' And he told me of Hockley Brook, a church in Hockley Brook, that would take me.

Forty years later, in the 1990s, the congregation that she was asked to leave, St Michael's in Handsworth, was inviting black people in: 'I'll go there if it's a funeral or a wedding and I'm invited there but my worship could not be there because that's where I came and was turned back.' The effect on Esme was more of sadness than anger:

It makes me feel very discouraged because in Jamaica we were worshipping with black with white with everybody. All nations that were there, there's no discrimination, nothing to say well you can't live here, you can't there, there's no special seat in our churches down in Jamaica for white, black or whatever, we all sit together anyway where one finds a seat they sat.

Esme had a distinguished career as a social worker, and after retiring and spending over five years in South America, came back to England in 1984 to set up pre-school playgroups and the Young Mothers' Relief Association. She was awarded the MBE in 2000 for services to the community in Handsworth.

evangelisation in industry and the world of the non-churchgoer', and industrial chaplaincy was sustained in the British churches during the rest of the century.[118]

But the concept of working-class haemorrhage from religion became an *idée fixe* of British church and academic thinking. And it seems with hindsight to have been entirely misplaced. For one thing, the investigations of the 1950s and early 1960s that reported working-class loss to religion were followed by new ones of the 1970s and 1980s that were to argue the opposite.[119] For another thing, many churchmen were convinced of the success of crusade evangelism in the mushrooming new council-housing estates being erected on the peripheries of Britain's large cities, and in the 30 new towns designated in Britain between 1945 and 1970. At the time, austerity imposed severe restrictions on building new churches, resulting in dislocation in serving the religious needs of people being cleared from city-centre slum housing. In the large Ruchazie housing scheme in the east of Glasgow in 1954, the Church of Scotland was only permitted to erect a hall for 100 people; its opening service attracted 240 before any parish work had properly started.[120] But working-class faith was not destroyed. A series of surveys in the Pollok housing estate to the south-west of Glasgow, which contained at its completion 20,000 people, showed that when it began in 1950, 30 per cent of households admitted to no church connection; but this fell five years later to only 18.4 per cent, as churches and pastors were put in place.[121] Signs of vibrancy in working-class Christianity were strong in the later 1950s. In South Uist, the local priest led the small community to the erection of a thirty-foot-high statue of Our Lady of the Isles to celebrate the Marian year – a statue that dominated the skyline, and overlooked a new British Army missile testing range that the priest had opposed for fear it would unsettle the fragility of the community and its faith.[122]

But problems were brewing. In 1956, the year after Billy Graham's two crusades in London and Glasgow, virtually all the statistics of British Christian adherence started to fall. From that year, there was a steady tumble of denominational adherence, religious adherence and baptism rates in the Church of England, and the figures for the other major Protestant churches had also started to fall by the later 1950s or were flattening out. The falls were slow in the late 1950s, but even by 1963 they were showing the steepest peacetime decline of the century. In industrial south Wales, even in a well-ministered and outwardly flourishing Nonconformist parish, a survey of church members in 1955 showed that 44 per cent had not attended worship for more than a year, and that 30 per cent of those who *did attend* went purely 'through force of habit' or 'for the sake of the children'.[123] Church membership appeared to some clergy to have become a sham.

A widely-heard analysis inside the churches (less so in academic circles) was that the young, not the working class, were the front edge of secularism. Perceptive church clergy noted the restlessness of young people. The young still attended Sunday schools in large numbers, and had turned out to hear Billy Graham. But by the mid-1950s, both girls and boys were restless with the Christian yoke of social respectability upon them. Lorna Sage from small-town Shropshire noted: 'The magic of the Church no longer impressed us. Our own bodies were more mysterious than the wine and wafers, and the whimsical notion put about by the Mothers' Union that the spell of the marriage service changed a couple's every atom in order that they could make babies had never seemed very convincing in Hanmer, where so many brides went bulging to the altar.'[124] The problem of youth was one that the 1940s and 1950s developed into a moral panic. In the wake of the war and rationing, there was some sense that moral values were disturbed, making pilfering, the black market and the street-corner 'spiv' acceptable and even romantic. 'There ought to be more religion in the younger generation,' one Londoner told a pollster towards the end of the war. 'They're like a lot of heathens, stealing things from the bombed houses.'[125]

Concerted academic, popular and government concern with juvenile delinquency emerged. This was ably popularised by the 1947 film version of Graham Greene's earlier novel *Brighton Rock* (1938), which depicted in graphic and tense scenes the rise of a gang culture in a coastal community – a criminal delinquency founded not on industrial decline nor depression, but on a popular culture infused with boredom and uncontrolled machismo. Studies of young people in gangs mushroomed in the 1950s, reflecting and nurturing both official and popular 'moral panic' with 'the juvenile delinquent', the 'ned' and the Teddy Boys (young men who dressed in Edwardian-style suits). One of the causes identified was the loss of religion amongst the young. This crisis was particularly felt in the Boys' Brigade, an organisation founded on what was once a heady brew of religion and discipline. But its military image became in the later 1950s very suddenly offputting to a youth keen to avoid National Service (which was abolished in 1960). Matters came to a head during 1954–65, when the Brigade Secretary, Major-general D. J. Wilson-Haffenden, became a fan and official for Billy Graham's London crusades (of 1954 and 1966), and openly attempted (in his own words) to use the BBs 'to definitely go for an ardent evangelical thrust, to win boys for Christ'.[126] This campaign alienated many people (including some non-evangelical churchmen in Scotland), and almost certainly helped to instigate in 1961 the beginning of BB membership decline.

Much of what was troubling British Christian culture by 1960 had to do with young people. But the issues were wider. There was an exhaustion in the traditional churches in Britain. The austere moral world they had nurtured in the 1950s – that of puritan law and regulation, strictness of behaviour, silence about sex and an overbearing *niceness* – was being challenged from within as well as from without. A new breed of clergy, including adventurous theologians and chaplains at colleges and universities, were turning against the morality that had defined religion in British society. Liberal theology was suddenly travelling in the direction of a liberalising people, and indeed seemed to reduce the sense of there being a popular assault upon the churches.

Hostility to religion, to the churches and to Christianity was small scale, muted and unmilitant. Unlike in France, secularism as a campaigning and anti-religious movement was extremely weak, and it certainly did not enjoy a mass appeal. Instead, Britons were languid about their religion, even when not in favour of it. Apathy rather than hostility was the watchword in this country, best expressed in 1947 by Mass-Observation in concluding their religious survey of the 'puzzled' British people: 'Much of the existing goodwill towards religion among the non-religious is based on the idea that religion is harmless, and has little practical bearing on anything except the internal peace of mind of the religious. Positive goodwill borders on negative tolerance, and tolerance borders on apathy. But the goodwill element must not be minimised.' Religion was acceptable for its discipline, conservatism and structures. The non-churchgoing could say: 'Oh, yes, I think it's nice for children to be taught to believe in Christ. I *do* think it's nice.'[127] So, what was to unfold in the 1960s was not really an eruption of anti-religious sentiment and intellectualism. Rather, liberal theologians were already revealing their absence of certainty that moral conservatism could be justified as the basis of religion and society. And this chimed with a revolt against restraint and authority amongst young people and amongst women. Rather than religion, it was conservatism, deference, gendered tradition and authority that were to be the object of social assault. But Christian culture was about to be the victim of the fallout.

Notes

1 L. Sage, *Bad Blood* (London, Fourth Estate, 2001), p. 89.

2 Quoted in *The Observer Magazine* 19 June 2005, p. 11.

3 S. Parker, *Faith on the Home Front: Aspects of Church Life and Popular Religion in Birmingham, 1939–1945* (Bern, Peter Lang, 2006), p. 210.

4 G. Mayfield, *The Church of England: Its members and its business* (London, Oxford University Press, 1958), pp. 21, 24–5; Scottish Oral History Centre Archive, SOHCA/006/Mrs. C.1, pp. 10–11.

5 Mayfield, *Church of England,* p. 50.

6 *The Herald* 12 February 2005.

7 I am grateful for discussions with my postgraduate student, Angela Bartie, on this subject.

8 *The Times*, 1 June 1954.

9 Sir William Haley, quoted in HMSO 1951 Cmnd. 8116, Report of the Broadcasting Committee, 1949, pp. 63–7.

10 HMSO, 1962 Cmnd. 1753, Report of the Committee on Broadcasting, 1960, pp. 87–92.

11 Mass-Observation, *Puzzled People: A study in popular attitudes to religion ethics, progress and politics in a London Borough, prepared for the Ethical Union* (London, Victor Gollancz, 1947), p. 105.

12 Ibid., pp. 50–1.

13 Data based on Highet census, recalibrated in C.G. Brown, 'Religion and secularisation', in A. Dickson and J.H. Treble (eds), *People and Society in Scotland vol. III 1914–1990* (Edinburgh, John Donald, 1992), p. 55.

14 Data in or calculated from figures in G. Gorer, *Exploring English Character* (London, Cresset Press, 1955), pp. 270–1. I am very grateful to Dr Michael Snape for pointing me to the existence of this book.

15 Ibid., p. 459.

16 Ibid., pp. 449, 451. The correlation coefficient between religious belonging by social class and church attendance once per week or above by social class was 0.165.

17 *Puzzled People*, pp. 51–2.

18 Gorer, p. 257.

19 J. Seabrook, *The Unprivileged* (Harmondsworth, Penguin, 1973), p. 72.

20 Gorer, p. 418.

21 L. Thomas, *The Virgin Soldiers* (London, Constable, 1966), turned into a film in 1969; I. McEwan, *The Innocent* (London, Picador, 1990), p. 57; P. Larkin, 'Annus Mirabilis' (1967).

22 C. Hall, *Twice Around the Bay* (Edinburgh, Birlinn, 2001), pp. 75, 84–5.

23 B. Aspinwall, *The Catholic Experience in North Ayrshire* (Irvine, John Geddes printers, 2002), pp. 30, 59.

24 B. White, *Red Rowans and Wild Honey* (orig. 1990, Edinburgh, Birlinn, 2000), pp. 18–19.

25 W.S.F. Pickering, *Anglo-Catholicism: A Study in Religious Ambiguity* (London, Routledge, 1989).

26 K. Hylson-Smith, *The Churches in England from Elizabeth I to Elizabeth II vol. III: 1833–1998* (London, SCM Press, 1998), pp. 226–7.

27 *British Weekly*, 9 September 1954.

28 Ibid., 4 February 1954, 4 March 1954.

29 Hylson-Smith, *Churches in England*, pp. 218–19.

30 *British Weekly*, 17 June 1954; *The Times*, 30 March 1954.

31 *British Weekly*, 18 February 1954, 25 March 1954, 1 July 1954.

32 Ibid., 11 February 1954.

33 D. Rapp, 'The British Salvation Army, the early film industry and working class adolescents 1897–1918,' *Twentieth Century British History* vol. 7 (1996), pp. 157–88.

34 *The Times*, 17 April 1922.

35 G.I.T. Machin, *Churches and Social Issues in Twentieth-century Britain* (Oxford, Clarendon Press, 1998), p. 77.

36 *Church Times*, 8 December 1938.

37 S. Sutcliffe, 'Religion in The Wicker Man: context and representation', in S. Harper *et al.* (eds), *The Wicker Man: Film and Cultural Studies Perspectives* (Dumfries, University of Glasgow Crichton Publications, 2005).

38 *The Lord Took Hold of Bugbrooke*, a Granada TV documentary of 1971.

39 D.J. Jeremy, *Capitalists and Christians: Business Leaders and the Churches in Britain, 1900–1960* (Oxford, Clarendon Press, 1990), pp. 397–410.

40 *British Weekly* 17 June 1954; Graham quoted at his own Billy Graham Center website at http://www.wheaton.edu/bgc/archives/bulletin/bu0403.htm, accessed 19 June 2005.

41 This is explained in *British Weekly*, 22 April 1954.

42 Ibid., 1 April 1954; F. Colquhoun, *Harringay Story: A detailed account of The Greater London Crusade 1954* (London, Hodder & Stoughton, 1955), p. 110.

43 T. Allan (ed.), *Crusade in Scotland* (London, Pickering & Inglis, 1955), p. 19.

44 This description is derived from watching Graham's films *Oil Town, USA* (1954) and *Fire in the Heather* (1955).

45 *The Times*, 2 March 1954.

46 Colquhoun, *Harringay Story*, pp. 232–3; Allan (ed), *Crusade in Scotland*, pp. 8, 108.

47 *British Weekly*, 17 June 1954.

48 *The Times*, 2 March 1954.

49 W.G. Scroggie, *British Weekly*, 1 July 1954.

50 *The Times*, 19 May 1954.

51 *British Weekly*, 4 March 1954; Colquhoun, *Harringay Story*, pp. 73–5.

52 I.M. Randall, *Evangelical Experiences: A study in the spirituality of English Evangelicalism 1918–1939* (Carlisle, Paternoster, 1999), p. 277.

53 Jeremy, *Capitalists and Christians*, p. 405.

54 Margaret Harrison, quoted in Randall, *Evangelical Experiences*, p. 244.

55 D. Bebbington, *Evangelicalism in Modern Britain: A History from the 1730s to the 1980s* (London, Unwin Hyman, 1989), pp. 235–40.

56 *The Times*, 5 November 1968.

57 Quoted in ibid., 29 May 1950.

58 Quoted in Church of England, *Moral Re-armament: A Study of the Movement prepared by the social and industrial council of the Church Assembly* (London, Church Information Board, 1955), p. 36.

59 Randall, *Evangelical Experiences*, pp. 238–68.

60 *The Times*, 11 November 1948, 26 October 1961.

61 T. Driberg, *The Mystery of Moral Re-Armament: A Study of Frank Buchman and his Movement* (London, Secker & Warburg, 1964), p. 12.

62 Mass-Observation, *Puzzled People*, pp. 146–8.

63 Bebbington, *Evangelicalism*, pp. 235–40.

64 I am grateful to my postgraduate student, Angela Bartie, for this information from her study of the Edinburgh Arts Festival and the Festival Fringe.

65 Steel dissented in 1955 from the Church Assembly Report that criticised MRA. Church of England, *Moral Re-armament*, p. 47. See also Jeremy, *Capitalists and Christians*, pp. 218–19.

66 Article in *British Weekly*, 8 April 1954.

67 *The Times*, 26 October 1953, 18 July 1956.

68 Ibid., 16 and 22 September 1953; F. Wheen, *The Soul of Indiscretion: Tom Driberg: Poet, Philanderer, Legislator and Outlaw* (London, Fourth Estate, 1990), pp. 67–9, 225–6.

69 Church of England, *Moral Re-armament*, p. 23.

70 *The Times*, 29 January 1955.

71 Church of England, *Moral Re-armament*, p. 29.

72 *The Times*, 9 June 1960, 31 January and 10 May 1961.

73 Ibid., 14 October 1961, 14 April 1962.

74 Information from Religious Movements Homepage Project website at the University of Virginia http://religiousmovements.lib.virginia.edu/nrms/moralrearm.html, accessed 15 January 2005. More information at http://www.uk.initiativesofchange.org/.

75 IoC website, http://www.caux.ch/en/, accessed 13 January 2005.

76 See http://religiousmovements.lib.virginia.edu/nrms/moralrearm.html.

77 Bebbington, *Evangelicalism*, p. 238.

78 William Smellie, *British Weekly*, 4 March 1954.

79 Dr Leslie Weatherhead, *The Times*, 5 July 1955.

80 Ibid., 22, 25, 26 and 27 August, and 13 October 1955.

81 Committee of the House of Clergy of the Church Assembly, ibid., 11 June 1956.

82 Quoted in S. Rowbotham, *A Century of Women: The History of Women in Britain and the United States* (London, Viking, 1997), p. 338.

83 Sage, *Bad Blood*, p. 201.

84 C. Steedman, 'Landscape for a Good Woman', in L. Heron (ed.), *Truth, Dare or Promise: Girls growing up in the fifties* (London, Virago, 1985), p. 117.

85 Ibid., p. 105.

86 Sage, *Bad Blood*, p. 237.

87 Ibid., p. 244.

88 M. Young and P. Wilmott, *Family and Kinship in East London* (orig. 1957, Harmondsworth, Penguin, 1962), p. 57. See also S.C. Williams, *Religious Belief and Popular Culture in Southwark c.1880–1939* (Oxford, Oxford University Press, 1999), pp. 88–9, 96–7.

89 Hall, *Twice Around the Bay*, pp. 75–6, 116.

90 *Puzzled People*, p. 83.

91 *Brief Encounter*, starring Celia Johnson and Trevor Howard (Dir. David Lean, Pinewood Films 1945).

92 Monica Dickens in *Women's Own*, 28 January 1961, quoted in C.L. White, *The Women's Periodical Press in Britain 1946–1976* (London, HMSO, 1977), p. 11.

93 Quoted in D. Bebbington, 'The secularization of British universities since the mid-nineteenth century', in G.M. Marsden and B.J. Longfield (eds), *The Secularization of the Academy* (New York and Oxford, Oxford University Press, 1992), p. 273.

94 *British Weekly*, 18 February 1954.

95 Allan (ed.), *Crusade in Scotland*, p. 96; testimony quoted in C.G. Brown, A. McIvor and N. Rafeek, *The University Experience: An Oral History of the University of Strathclyde 1945–1975* (Edinburgh, Edinburgh University Press, 2004), pp. 88, 100, 103, 105–6.

96 *The Times*, 18 August 1948. In 1959, the Episcopal Church of Sweden decided to accept women as ordinands; ibid., 20 April 1959.

97 Ibid., 3 January 1957.

98 Ibid., 12 May 1960.

99 Ibid., 8 November 1962.

100 *British Weekly*, 22 April 1954.

101 Ibid., 24 June 1954.

102 A. Sutcliffe and R. Smith, *History of Birmingham volume III 1939–1970* (London, Oxford University Press, 1974), pp. 364–8; J.L. Wilkinson, *Church in Black and White: Black Christian Tradition in 'Mainstream' Churches in England: A White Response and Testimony* (Edinburgh, Saint Andrew Press, 1993), p. 33. I am grateful to Edson Burton for drawing my attention to the last reference.

103 *The Guardian*, 24 August 2002.

104 *British Weekly*, 16 September 1954.

105 The Glasgow LMS branch, quoted in ibid., 4 February 1954.

106 Quoted in ibid., 11 February 1954.

107 Ibid., 10 June 1954.

108 Ibid., 11 March 1954.

109 Victor Hayward, writing in ibid. 3 November 1955.

110 Ibid., 1 April 1954.

111 Ibid., 25 March 1954.

112 Ibid., 3 June 1954.

113 H. Ansari, *'The Infidel Within': Muslims in Britain since 1800* (London, Hurst & Co., 2004), p. 50.

114 Testimony of Ryland A. Campbell, Birmingham Black Oral History Project, Birmingham City Archive and Special Collections, Information Services, University of Birmingham (hereafter BBOHP), PT6, p. 21.

115 Testimony of Esme Lancaster, BBOHP PT12, p. 11.

116 Testimony of Esme Lancaster, ibid., p. 12.

117 The testimony comes from the Birmingham Black Oral History Project, Birmingham City Archive and Special Collections, Information Services, University of Birmingham, Transcripts, BBOHP PT12, pp. 11–25; PT13, pp. 14–16, 27, PT 15, pp. 2–6, 14–15. The interviewer was Doreen Price. Additional information on Esme's life comes from D. Price and R. Thiara (eds), *The Land of Money? Personal Accounts by Post-war Black Migrants to Birmingham* (Birmingham, Birmingham Black Oral History Project, 1992), p. 29; and from www.birminghamblackhistory.com/esme, accessed on 31 January 2005.

118 *British Weekly*, 31 March 1955, 14 April 1955.

119 B.S. Rowntree and G.R. Lavers, *English Life and Leisure: A Social Study* (London, Longmans, Green,) 1951, p. 374; N. Dennis and F. Henriques,

.

    Coal is Our Life: An Analysis of a Yorkshire Mining Community (orig. 1956, London, Tavistock, 1969 ed.), pp. 169–70.

120 *British Weekly*, 10 June 1954.

121 Ibid., 3 November 1955.

122 Hall, *Twice Around the Bay*, p. 175.

123 D.D. Morgan, *The Span of the Cross: Christian Religion and Society in Wales 1914–2000* (Cardiff, University of Wales Press, 1999), pp. 210–11.

124 Sage, *Bad Blood*, p. 197.

125 *Puzzled People*, pp. 86–7.

126 J. Springhall, B. Fraser and M. Hoare, *Sure & Stedfast: A History of the Boys Brigade 1883 to 1983* (London and Glasgow, Collins, 1983), pp. 184, 189.

127 *Puzzled People*, pp. 85, 89.

CHAPTER 6

The sixties' revolution, 1960–73

As New Year approached at the end of 1961, the Protestant paper the *British Weekly* said in an editorial that it was 'the end of another of the uncertain years'.[1] In a matter of months, the perplexity was to turn to unrelenting religious panic. The sixties was the most important decade for the decline of religion in British history. Pop music, radical fashion and student revolt were witness to a sea-change in sexual attitudes and to the dismissal of conventional social authority. There was a cultural revolution amongst young people, women and people of colour that targeted the churches, the older generation and government. In this maelstrom, traditional religious conceptions of piety were to be suddenly shattered, ending centuries of consensus Christian culture in Britain. In its place, there came liberalisation, diversity and freedom of individual choice in moral behaviour. In every sphere of life, religion was in crisis.

Sense of crisis

There were two critical years in the cultural revolution. The first was 1963, when a series of developments pulled the mask from austerity, retrenchment and ecclesiastical smugness. The century's most controversial book of liberal theology appeared, John Robinson's *Honest to God*, which cast doubt on the traditional image and reality of God, causing widespread furore and deep personal anguish to thousands of Christians. The same year witnessed the exposure of an Anglican crisis over chastity before marriage, with conservative churchmen attracting public ridicule for attacking what they persisted in calling 'fornication' between young lovers. In 1963, too, religious adherence and rites of passage started a perilous collapse as young people forsook the churches, baptism and religious marriage. A blossoming secular pop culture was coming of age, symbolised by the pop group The Beatles at number one in the pop charts for the first time. Not only were the churches affected. By late 1963, the Boys' Brigade, founded to encourage working-class boys to faith and discipline, was in decline for the first time – a decline attributed to the general fall in church membership. And in October 1963, in that year when serious Christian decline commenced, Britain's first and only Christian daily newspaper, the *Daily Leader*, was launched and duly failed – the victim of possibly the most appalling sense of timing in the history of religious publishing.[2]

The second critical year in the cultural revolution was 1967. In the last six months of that year, British society as a whole – including the government and the churches – became *aware* of secularisation as an intense cultural and ecclesiastical revolution. It was the year of the so-called 'Summer of Love', marked by proclamations of sexual freedom, public nudity, the flower people, the hippies and open drug-taking. During that summer, too, The Beatles met and became followers of the Maharishi Mahesh Yogi, an Eastern mystic who promoted Transcendental Meditation (TM). Simultaneously in late 1967, indicators appeared that Christianity was in peril. Statistics showed that a collapse had taken place over the previous half-decade in baptism, confirmation and retention of confirmees in the Church of England. A drop in the number of Church of England ordinands had occurred in 1965, signalling what was to become the long-term slide in recruitment of young men to be clergy in British Christian churches. In 1967 also, an Anglican theologian proclaimed, to churchgoers' disbelief, that Christ may have been homosexual, and a new media obsession grew with religious collapse and scandal. Late 1967 witnessed the emergence of awareness by the British 'establishment' that its authority – the authority of the state, traditional opinion-formers, and of the churches – was in peril. And at the heart of all this, as far as the Christian churches were concerned, there appeared to be a spiritual insurrection.

For some, the sixties brought less immediate change in their religious lives than others. For those living in the industrial areas, and in Scotland and Wales, there was less liberalism of values and opening up of popular culture to secular activities than was generally the case in London and the Home Counties. Estimates of churchgoing in Britain in the early 1960s showed great variation. In London and the south-east, it was estimated at 10 per cent of the population. This compared with 20 per cent for

England as a whole; it was higher in Scotland, with 26 per cent, whilst Northern Ireland is likely to have had well over 50 per cent attendance.[3] Industrial zones seemed to be higher than non-industrial. In the depressed mining village of Kirkconnell in south-west Scotland in 1961, 87 per cent of adults claimed a religious connection, whilst 71 per cent of children went to Sunday school.[4] In Scotland as a whole, a 1967 sociological survey of the leisure time of 600 adolescents in working-class communities showed 43 per cent claimed a regular association with a church and a third claimed to have taken part in a religious activity in the previous week.[5] Church attendances and membership remained higher in northern Britain, and more broadly a culture of Christian conformism still had a strong grip, evident in the near-universal observance in the regions of Britain of the Christian Sunday. In Liverpool, the new Roman Catholic Cathedral (built 1962–7) exuded a modernity in the form of the most advanced architecture, with a 'church in the round' layout topped by an exterior 'crown' intended to reflect a new spirit of lay participation in the liturgy, thereby placing religion for the strongly working-class Catholic community on Merseyside as something up-to-date, not something of the past. Even in London, there seemed to be evidence of 'religion as usual' in many working-class and lower middle-class areas.

Rising prosperity brought further and higher education within the reach of more young people, and large numbers of students (notably women) enrolled at state-funded church colleges of education. One woman recalled her experience at a central London Catholic teacher-training college in the mid- to late 1960s, where she 'dropped off quite a bit' from the routines of saying of novenas (prayers) that had been instilled in her in convent; but she recalled being 'jarred into action again' by a lecturer who emphasised Christ-centred faith.[6] The education colleges were important in sustaining religiously committed teachers in Britain; by 1974, there were 27 belonging to the Church of England alone, contributing significantly to religious education in schools.[7] But education students contrasted sharply with university students who secularised rapidly. Table 6.1 shows how amongst students at Sheffield University, despite very high levels of religious upbringing, there was a collapse of religious belief and church attendance between 1961 and 1972. Even this may not reflect the full extent of collapsing Christian culture amongst university students who, by the early 1970s, exuded a diverse yet generally profoundly secular culture. University students, with their air of sexual freedom, sit-ins and political protests, were the *bête noire* of conservative Christian commentators from about 1965 onwards. One of these, the conservative Christian television pundit Malcolm Muggeridge, resigned as Student Rector of Edinburgh University in 1968 because of the installation of a condom machine in the men's union, and broadcast lambasting commentary of immoral students.[8] The de-Christianisation of university students shocked the British elites; these were the national leaders of tomorrow, and they seemed to show no reverence for religion, morality or the law.

TABLE 6.1 *Religious training, belief and practice amongst students, University of Sheffield*

Students claiming –	Per cent 1961	1972	1985
some religious upbringing	94	88	51
religious belief	73	53	38
to attend church	46	25	15
to be active church members	36	16	9
membership of a student religious group	15	9	6

Source: D. Bebbington, 'The secularization of British universities since the mid-nineteenth century', in G.M. Marsden and B.J. Longfield (eds), *The Secularization of the Academy* (New York and Oxford, Oxford University Press, 1992), p. 268.

In the short term, it was difficult for the churches to see past their own sense of panic. The years 1963–7 were critical in the destiny of patterns of popular religious behaviour in relation to the mainstream Christian churches. The Church of England, with evidence of baptism declining sharply in Newcastle in 1963 (from 60 to 54 per cent),[9] started to float new ideas – such as abandoning the necessity of confirmation for entry to the Church of England, and allowing Christians from other churches or traditions to enter communion unhindered.[10] The final months of 1967 witnessed what the Church of England described as a 'gathering crisis over confirmation', and by the early 1970s the churches were becoming exhausted with battling through the theological and practical implications of innovation to attract young people to worship. The prospects for Britain's Christian heritage seemed to many people to be forlorn.

How was this occurring? An important development which many have linked to the religious crisis was the revolt against authority signalled by the development of new media – television, vinyl records, electric pop music and pirate radio stations. Fewer than one in ten homes had a TV in 1950, but by 1960 it was six in ten, and by 1970 nine in ten. This made television a key medium for cultural change, transmitting news of the decade's cultural clashes, new fashion, radical protests and new ideas. In response, the churches devoted considerable energy to asserting religious and moral culture in TV programmes. The BBC Head of Religious Broadcasting, Canon Roy McKay, stated that the purpose of broadcasting was 'to support and extend the witness of the Churches'. This was done principally through a television 'God-slot' on Sunday nights, from 6.15 to 7.25 pm – a period for religious programmes protected by the government's Postmaster General until 1972, and retained voluntarily by both the BBC and ITV for two decades thereafter.[11]

Though TV religious broadcasting by the BBC actually rose in the early 1960s to two and three-quarter hours per week, the rest of the programmes tended to take Christianity as a target to mock. Politicians, the armed forces and the churches together constituted the 'establishment' that were targeted in a sudden explosion of lampooning humour, satirical sketches and open abuse. First in theatre, then on television, there was an eruption by dramatists in portraying sexual intercourse, in using swearing and blasphemy, and in the mocking of religion and faith. In January 1963, a BBC TV satirical series *That Was The Week That Was* (abbreviated to TW3), broadcast on Saturday nights, came into the firing line for 'gratuitously bad taste' on the churches. At the same time, the BBC abolished a long-established prohibition on jokes about religion, royalty, political institutions and sex, opening the gates to what the *Church Times* considered would be 'cheapness and vulgarity'.[12] On Saturday evening, 12 January 1963, TW3 put on an infamous satirical sketch called 'The Consumer Guide to Religion' which took the form of a consumer test of different religions. The comics said of Judaism:

This is the oldest religion we tested ... What do you get out of it? Membership of the oldest club in the world ... and we particularly liked the guarantee of Eternal Life through the Messiah or Saviour who will take responsibility for all your guilt – when he arrives ...

We next tested the Roman Catholic Church... What do you put into it? Belief in One Only God-head operating on a troika basis ... belief in the Infallibility of Giovanni Batista Montini, now known as Paul the Six ... We must stress here that the idea that the head (or Pope as he is called) claims infallibility in all matters is a fallacy. The Pope cannot tell you which television set is best ... He can only tell you which television programme you cannot watch. ... Jesus Christ has already undertaken personal responsibility for the consumer's misdemeanours. This gives extra support. And the confessional mechanism is standard; it operates as an added safety-factor to correct running mistakes, making Salvation almost foolproof.[13]

This brought appreciative studio laughter. This kind of mockery had been known for some time in music halls, but on television – with its state endorsement and entry into virtually every home in the land – this was unknown territory. As the 1960s wore on, the BBC became ever more lambasted by church authorities – as in 1967 for daring to portray Westminster Abbey as more a tourist attraction than a church.[14]

Television had changed from the 1950s, when it had radiated moral conservatism in its religious programmes and in the blandness of its entertainment shows. In the 1960s, television became a battleground between reaction and revolution, and with live broadcasts technologically possible from around the world developing between 1963 and 1968, a changing world was brought to British screens. Artistic radicals claimed TV as a new art medium for risqué plays – notoriously in the form of *The Wednesday Play* broadcast by the BBC which invariably contained sexual content. Church complaints became routine. The Church of England Assembly deplored the use of a painting of Christ in a BBC comedy sketch, but it was powerless to prevent new 'insults'. Even the God-slot developed away from purely devotional religion. ABC Television ran a programme on the ITV network called *Looking For An Answer*, chaired by the journalist and historian Robert Kee, which attracted 500 letters a week on religious themes from which a selection were put to invited leading churchmen. Far from being all conservative, the churchmen often turned up controversial answers – intellectual theologians who seemed to question Christian truths like the Virgin birth.[15] Television was showing the British people how to reject religion.

At the same time, the government imposed censorship over the rise of the pop music record, with its increasingly daring music and lyrics of the mid- and late 1960s; the BBC was the only authorised radio broadcaster, and it played little pop music on its three stations. So, in 1964–7 young people turned to pirate radio stations broadcasting from anchored boats offshore, and pop music recordings came to signify disobedience, revolt and experimentation, and a loosening of what the churches placed such great store by – restraint. The rise of the cultural underground, including events like the annual Edinburgh Festival Fringe, showed to the rest of Britain how young and artistic people with radical ideas could wage battle with the forces of religious conservatism.

A gap in moral understanding was opening up between Christian professionals and most young people. In 1966, Dr Billy Graham returned to British shores for a nine-day crusade based at Earls Court, drawing a total of 1 million people and 40,000 decisions for Christ – supposedly the same as in the longer 1954 campaign at Wembley.[16] But Graham's trip was not as successful as was anticipated. Arriving when 'swinging London' and the early hippy movement were at their peak, he became the object of much media interest in his apparent clash with the new confident mood of fun-loving youth. He told his audience of 18,000 at Earls Court in June: 'The world is caught up in a psychopathic madness that could mean ultimate racial suicide.' Warning that world leaders were 'doing their best to put ointment on the growing festering sores of humanity', he attacked what he called 'the moral decline of western Europe, America and Britain'. Cities and nations of the past were in ruins because of moral decadence:

What a tragedy! People of Britain, you have meant too much to the world. You have given to culture, law, art, music. But most of all you have given moral and spiritual truth. . . . I challenge you to set a moral and spiritual tone for the rest of the world that so desperately needs your leadership. Tonight I challenge you to look about you and see what is happening: the rebellion against authority, the sexual immoralities, the secularism and the materialism of the people, the lust for pleasure, the silver-chromed gods that have been erected since the war. The message I have for Britain tonight is the message of the prophets. It is the message of the Apostles.[17]

This message bewildered most young Britons. Two weeks later, Graham was forced to cut short a sermon in Soho in London when 1,000 people jostled him in the street. Through a loud hailer he said: 'I haven't come here to condemn you. God is willing to forgive you every sin you've ever committed.' This made Graham and his confrontational Christian approach suddenly the butt of humour. In the melee, reported *The Times*, 'a young blonde clambered on to the roof of Dr. Graham's car and had to be dragged off by police'.[18] Reverence for him was diminishing and ridicule growing. The manner of his media exposure also changed. Whilst the evangelist continued to enjoy reverential 'straight' coverage on American TV and radio, in Britain his message started to be filtered through new liberal 'gatekeepers' with a satirical heritage, like TV host David Frost (a leading commentator who interviewed Graham for BBC television).[19] Certainly, the secular press no longer gave him the privileged reporting that his organisation had secured twelve years before. And his meetings were not as packed as before. With many expecting a capacity crowd of 110,000 to hear his final service at Wembley Stadium, only 86,000 turned up. The number of attenders was going down, but the numbers of 'inquirers' staying behind after services rose proportionately, suggesting that it was the more highly committed who still went to hear Graham.[20]

The religious crisis was not just in swinging London. In the industrial heartlands of Britain some industrial missions were failing in the early 1960s. One missionary, R. E. M. Vickers, wrote in 1963 that church-people ministering in the so-called artisan parishes (renamed to dilute the vocabulary of class difference) realised that 'the working man has no time for snobbish priests who pretend to be like working men'. Working-class church attendances were reportedly very low, and few new converts made. Vickers noted: 'Some men, for reasons real or fancied, may have lost sympathy with their local church or priest, yet retain more than a slight respect for the Christian Faith *in vacuo*. "Factory Christianity" may salve their conscience, and (apparently) absolve them from any responsibility toward their local church.'[21] Evangelistic-style missions were also sustained in factory towns. A Church of England 'Industrial Crusade' took place in the Blackburn, Accrington and Darwen area of Lancashire in October 1963, whilst the Church Army, the Church of England's version of the Salvation Army, ran an industrial mission in Sheffield in 1963. Gordon Hopkins had been an Anglican industrial missioner in Sunderland for twenty-four years, but by 1963 he was reporting rejection of evangelisation and inquisitive religious questioning. More broadly, the whole post-war approach to church work set up by William Temple's 1943 report on 'Towards the Conversion of England' was seen as a failure.[22]

Evangelism seemed unsuited to changing economic conditions. If the 1950s had been materially austere, the 1960s were consumerist. British incomes rose, diversity and quality of goods increased, and leisure-time choice mushroomed. This infused the expression of personal freedom and variety. With many families moving to new homes in suburban estates and new towns, the ways in which religion nestled into old ways of life were altering. In large cities, churches found it difficult to compete with the craze for bingo that gripped the nation between 1958 and 1964, and some churchmen tried to get government regulation to prevent losing worshippers. An elderly woman objected to a government minister: 'They will never fill the churches even if they did stop Bingo. The churches are far too draughty. Sermons are long & monotonous & the majority of ministers very very rarely visit the lonely widow.'[23] Yet, poverty and social problems remained, notably in inner-city parishes where many clergy shared with their parishioners the poor living conditions and sparseness of life. In the Western Isles of Scotland, older ways of life nestled around chapel, school and evening ceilidhs, but these were disrupted when the seasonality of agriculture and fishing gave way to year-round paid jobs, and when 'the thatched houses gave way to the modern ones and the cosy atmosphere with its black stove and Tilley lamp went with them'.[24]

Nor was the crisis just external to the churches – it was also within them. Key here was the publication in March 1963 of the book *Honest to God* by John Robinson, Anglican Bishop of Woolwich, which caused a storm. As part of what was regarded as 'death of God' theology, Robinson's book placed God within humans, not outside of them or their world, with Christianity to be understood in the form of a 'naturalism' rather than a 'supernaturalism'. He described the notion of heaven 'as the greatest obstacle to an intelligent faith', and emphasised God in our loving and ethical actions rather than in the next world and its promises. Some saw this as heretical, and it made the book front-page news after serialisation in the *Observer* newspaper and extensive debate in the religious press.[25] The *Observer* headlined the book 'Our Image of God Must Go', and this more than anything aroused uproar. Many bishops and leading clergy regarded the work as a 'dangerous book' and openly condemned Robinson.[26]

Honest to God instigated a wide scale of response from churches and the public. Dr E. L. Mascall, professor of historical theology at the University of London, said: 'I agree with Dr. Robinson that Christianity must show that it is "relevant to modern secular man", but this means persuading secular man that he must no longer be merely secular.'[27] The *Church Times* carried multiple pages of protest letters for weeks. Peter C. Ford of Keighley was typical: 'We face a danger to-day in the Church which is greater than at any time in the history of the Church. That danger comes from ordained men holding high office and with considerable influence, but with no apparent belief in the fundamental facts of the Christian Gospel of Christ.'[28] Paul Johnson, writing in the *New Statesman*, was blunt: 'What I cannot understand is how the Bishop continues to call himself a Christian, still less a priest of the Church of England.'[29] The Archbishop of Canterbury, Dr Michael Ramsey, made very public his hostility in an ITV television programme in March, describing Robinson's imagery of God as 'utterly wrong'. Within a month, Ramsey had issued a pamphlet, *Image Old and New*, published by a rival religious press, as a reply to *Honest to God* in which he described Robinson's writing as 'strange, difficult and revolutionary'.[30]

Within four years of its appearance, *Honest to God* was being blamed along with death-of-God theology for undermining Christian witness, church recruitment and retention. By 1970, Robinson saw the permissive society as creating a need for a new moralising around individual choice. He said: 'I am convinced that we must move toward a mature society where the moral choice (as in marriage, divorce, euthanasia, gambling, drinking, reading matter and the rest) is taken by the individual and safeguarded by society against abuse.'[31] These ideas engendered over 4,000 letters to Robinson from troubled Christians. A few were sympathetic; one woman felt a vast load of guilt and misery removed at his call for a revolution in morals and love life.[32] But most anguished over the location of their faith in what they feared was turning into a treacherous Church. A clergyman wrote to him that: 'You have given the impression that you despise the ordinary old-fashioned Christian. To show contempt for the ordinary Christian and the ordinary parish priest is about the worst thing that a bishop or parish priest can do.'[33] Even Robinson acknowledged jokingly two years later that his book was welcomed by the communist authorities of East Germany as acceptable atheistic propaganda.[34]

Honest to God was not the only radical theology of the 1960s. Talk of 'the secular society' was on the lips of theologians and sociologists alike as they sought with an increasing urgency to define what it was. Whilst the commonsense meaning is a society without religion, some theologians saw it as a condition neutral in faith that was egalitarian, democratic and pragmatic in morals, whilst others saw it as an ultimate Christian state. So, secular society might not, after all, be anti-religious, but God's will. Paul van Buren published *The Secular Meaning of the Gospel* which advocated a radical anti-logical positivist approach to Christianity, whilst from the United States, Harvey Cox argued in *The Secular City* that technology was leading to the fulfilment of biblical truth: 'Man's fulfilment is now to be found in the secular city.'[35] This embracing of the secular as in itself a development of divine prophecy was not a message that translated well to traditional lay Christians, and really bypassed the consciousness of the secular laity as being a surrender rather than a fight-back by Christianity. Secular became a buzzword of the thinking theologian. The Christian churches started to feel extremely threatened by this. Lay Christian workers, often the most conservative and unwilling to yield to liberalising forces, were attacking 'Religionless Christianity' and 'the hybrids of faith and unbelief, of Christianity and worldliness'.[36] In late 1963, a computer

Analysis: The life of a Catholic priest, 1959–63

Anthony Kenny was a recently qualified priest when, in 1959, he became a curate in Liverpool. Though he later left the priesthood (over the Roman Catholic Church's stance on nuclear weapons), he gave an insight into the nature of the calling:

Sacred Heart parish, where I was now to be posted, was indeed a busy city mission. The massive but undistinguished Victorian church lay in the centre of Liverpool 8, a district which was not then as notorious as it has since become for urban decay and civil disorder, but which was already depressed and depressing. The most serious problem then was not unemployment but inadequate housing. The parish was divided into four sections, one to each of the priests; as the junior curate I was given the most rundown quarter. Half of my parishioners lived in unsound and often squalid houses; the other half, who lived in the blocks of flats built to replace the older houses as part of slum clearance, were often equally discontented; communal entrances and staircases, already ramshackle, would soon be noisome, and would eventually become downright dangerous. Everyone had lots of family or neighbours who had been rehoused in outlying suburbs like Kirby. Though some of the migrants returned weekly to do their shopping in the cheaper city-centre shops, we began to feel that the parish was losing its base as more and more solid parishioners left or lost their families. About 3,500 must have remained, in 1959.

We four priests did not share, indoors, in the squalor with which we were surrounded. Far from it. Shortly before I arrived, the ample but antiquated presbytery had been completely renovated at a cost of £25,000. As hardly any of our parishioners can have lived in a house worth more than £2,000, this fact was a source of embarrassment, and, to me at least, uneasy conscience. We ate good, and often expensive, food which was not, however, always very appetizing, since we were catered for by the parish priest's sister, who was an indifferent cook. She had one or two maids to assist her with the house cleaning. Curates were not allowed to keep alcohol in their rooms; but the parish priest was generous with cocktails, and there was wine on the table several times a week. Considered absolutely, our lives were not very luxurious; no more comfortable than those of the bachelor Oxford dons of the period, certainly. But they contrasted uncomfortably with the lives of our parishioners. ...

Our principal task in theory, and a major one in practice, was of course the administration of the sacraments and the preaching of the Gospel. On Sundays there would be one or two Masses for each of us to say in the morning; we would help distribute Communion at our colleagues' Masses; and we would take it in turns to preach. Sunday lunch was always a good one, for which we had worked up a good appetite, helping with Masses and counting the collections; each of us, one Sunday a month, would have to leave early to do the afternoon baptisms. Christening babies is one of the more agreeable clerical duties: I have never failed to be entertained by the baby's surprise gurgle as you put the salt on its tongue. As a young priest I was at first rather worried about the actual pouring of the water: if you splashed too much water on the newborn, the godparents would be annoyed; if you didn't make the water actually run down the baby's head, the sacrament would not be valid. . . .

The hearing of confessions took place principally on Saturdays, morning and evening. We priests would take up our position, sitting in small rooms in a corridor which ran beside the aisle communicating with the church through curtained grilles before which the parishioners would kneel in anonymity to confess their sins. Most people who have never heard confessions imagine that it must be an enthralling experience to listen to people confiding their most shameful secrets. In fact, the hearing of confessions consists of hours of tedium occasionally relieved by embarrassment. Interestingly wicked people never go to confession at all; most of those who go do not realize what their real sins are. The priest is obliged to satisfy himself that every mortal sin has been confessed specifically: it will not do, for instance, for the sinner to accuse himself of being unchaste he must specify where he was guilty of adultery, fornication etc. Consequently, if a penitent says 'I did something dirty', the confessor must embark on a series of questions designed to elicit the nature of the sin. It was not very easy to do this without appearing prurient, or without falling foul of strict rules prohibiting 'solicitation', i.e. any form of abuse of the confessional for sexual purposes. From time to time, in the confessional, the priest would realize that he was faced with someone in real trouble or depression or despair. A good confessor in such circumstances has an opportunity to make a real difference in people's lives: advice given in confession is often taken with unusual seriousness even by the most lukewarm Catholic. But the anonymity and brevity of the priest's contact with his penitent make it very difficult for him to tailor his advice to the penitent's need.

Information received in this way is, of course, strictly confidential, and 'breaking the seal of the confessional' is a very serious sin for a priest; the calendar contains the names of canonized saints who were martyred rather than reveal the secrets of their penitents. In my experience this obligation is taken by a priest with complete seriousness.[37]

analysis of textual writing style came to the conclusion that only five of the Pauline Epistles had come from the same author. The threat also came from a revolution in sport and leisure. In 1967, the former English cricketer David Sheppard was a leading clergyman in the Church of England, and he protested at the MCC permitting first-class cricket matches on Sundays, closing off (as he put it) the career of a man with a conscience.[38]

Theorising church decline was a rather haphazard affair. Churchmen felt three sets of reactions: first, that the statistics of decline were not a true reflection of the state of Christianity in the nation (that quality was more important that quantity); second, that society as a whole was showing a decline in communal activities (like going to football matches and social events); or third, that there was a failure on the part of church management. The Bishop of Ely, the Right Revd E. J. K. Roberts, thought that inadequate Sunday-school training was leading to a decline of church confirmation and a rise in juvenile delinquency.[39] By the summer of 1967, the issue was certainly at the forefront in the popular press, and the churches were on the spot. Television documentaries featured the problems of the churches, including a three-hour ITV programme in September 1967, *The Church in Question*, which focused on the permissive society. Men and women that summer were tuned into the 'Summer of Love' being beamed into British homes every day by the new medium of satellite transmission from the USA. Stunned by the images of young people cavorting naked, in sexual poses, consuming drugs and appearing to lose control and restraint, commentators thought human society was collapsing. The *Church Times*, a fairly conservative organ of the Church of England, editorialised: 'Must a permissive society have a permissive church? The days of authoritarianism and coercion are over.' Yet, it argued that the Christians must point 'to the limits of permissiveness', adjudging that Britain was 'a predominantly non-Christian society'. By 1970, terms like 'moral chaos' and 'permissive society' were on many priestly lips. In that year, the *Sunday Telegraph* carried a spread of articles on the church crisis, and evaluated the Church of England as 'utterly impotent' to respond to the social and moral transformation of the people. From the beatniks of the early 1960s to the 'flower children' of the Summer of Love of 1967, the attack on the establishment was seen to be acute, direct and alarmingly successful.[40]

The panic was most acute in relation to young people. Whereas in the 1950s the religiosity of the young in social activities of the churches had been very high, the sixties demonstrated a rapid descent from religious ways. In a survey of Falkirk in central Scotland, the Church of Scotland discovered that 27 per cent of boys and girls stopped attending church before the age of 10, and two-thirds by the age of 13.[41] It was also clear that the decline was sharpest amongst young women; the proportion of English women aged 12–20 years confirmed in the Church of England fell from 40.9 per cent in 1960 (at which level it had been for most of the century) to 19.6 per cent in 1974.[42] Sunday schools were in free-fall by the mid-1960s; several English denominations stopped publishing data as their numbers collapsed, and by the mid-1970s the schools had all but disappeared from some Church of England bishoprics. Even in Wales and Scotland, with signs of slower secularisation, Sunday-school pupil numbers were plummeting – halving between 1956 and 1980.

But it was not only amongst the young that there was declining church belonging and participation. The decay was clearly amongst older groups too. Fewer adults were going to church, fewer were getting married in church and, most of all, fewer parents were getting their babies baptised in church. During 1960–70, there was a 19 per cent decline in the number of regular church attenders to the Church of England, and, more seriously, a fall from 637 to 373 in the number of men it was ordaining as clergy. During 1956–76, Anglican baptisms fell from 60 per cent of live births to 43 per cent, whilst in the Church of Scotland they fell by half between 1967 and 1982, and by almost 40 per cent in the Catholic Church in Scotland.[43] If it was the young who triggered the crisis for the churches, the adult haemorrhage was just as striking.

But because youth were blamed at the time (both by the churches and a press corps with a seemingly insatiable appetite for moral panic), an influential but not totally accurate interpretation arose. This was that irreligion was the product of young people's *sexual immorality*, rather than adult *apathy* with religion. The panic was clearly overstated, part of a seemingly irresistible cultural need for 'folk devils' to account for any cultural change in British society.[44] As people started to drift in small numbers from the churches in the early 1960s, churchmen became unremittingly critical of them. The archdeacon of Chesterfield, the Very Revd T. W. Ingram Cleasby, attacked what he called 'the dip-and-run' baptisms of some young parents who brought their children for baptism but then did not return with them for religious education and worship.[45] If clergy snootily regarded the alienated working classes much as they had done since the eighteenth century, it was the disdain of the educated middle-class young that really perplexed and shocked them. Libby Purves had been brought up in Catholic convent schools, and recoiled at the elitism, the sexism and the mutual fawning of Christians, creating in many young women what she described as the '1960s schoolgirl feminist hippie-mystical revulsion that came over me at school'.[46] This kind of reaction in the young, especially the middle-class young, left the clergy completely flummoxed. They could not comprehend it, and this incomprehension became one of the constant features of young people's dealings with Christian ministers, priests and laity.

Whilst the anti-deferential revolt by the young in the 1960s was certainly influential in their escape from the churches, the more fundamental aspect was a boredom amongst both adults and young with organised religion. The exodus was more a silent walking away from religion, rather than a revolt or breakdown in social behaviour. One way to measure this is by looking at how religion featured in collective and personal memory of the time. Social commentators in the sixties framed a concept of religion as the crumbling cement of British communities; this was best expressed in a sense of 'the world we have lost'.[47] In a 1968 volume based on hundreds of Women's Institute village scrapbooks from around the country, religion was noted as disappearing from rural life: attendances were low, churches were falling into dilapidation and the 'insulated motorist' drove past uninterested in religion. With Christian faith so drained from the community, there was, said the review, 'something irregular or irrational (and therefore, by an easy declination, hypocritical) about the social importance which the church still maintains in village life'.[48]

Writers and film makers used pathos and nostalgic romance to depict rural religion as the silent web of community life, rather than its colourful thread. In the highly popular book and film *Akenfield* (1969), an oral history of a Suffolk parish, the Anglican rural dean noted how 'abysmally dull' the church was, pointing to the absence of parish communion and to how there was 'no warmth of feeling'. He could not get people to talk of their faith: 'But no one would come to a meeting if he thought he had to say something. When they had said something, one often finds that it is something quite irrelevant to what is being discussed. Religion has a lot to do with where their families and ancestors are buried.'[49] The theme of religion as the past came to dominate in sixties' vision.

The inarticulacy about religion amongst many people from the 1960s was not limited to rural folk. In oral testimony of young people from towns too, answers to questions about religion were characteristically abrupt, negative and dismissive – often one-word responses that displayed a stunted character to their conception of religion. 'I was never religious' or 'I didn't go to church' were sometimes the longest answers to be obtained on the subject. Such stunted discussion suggested a lack of intimate knowledge of religion amongst the young of the decade, and of any meaningful way of expressing personal identity through religion.

This contrasted sharply with their parents and grandparents, who early in the century used religion frequently to express their wider identities, to explain moral boundaries and in recreational activity. Yet, when these older interviewees came to talk about religion in later life, in the 1960s and after, their answers changed too. They became less sure, and their answers more broken and often incomplete, sometimes reverting to justifying earlier church lives but finding difficulty in expressing why they or their children *stopped* going to worship. Typical comments were, 'I had always been used with – well, my father was an organist for a start,' and 'Religion was well, my dad was – They were very religious. I mean, it was a sort of routine we had been brought up to.'[50] One woman spoke of the impact of television and her science-trained son: 'I don't know when it [religion] ceased to be quite as important. I'll tell you what I think is wrong nowadays. You see so much about science on these [television] programmes that –. . . . And I'd say "but the Bible", and my son would say the Bible was written by a man – a man writes a book, he doesn't always stick to fact. And so what could you say to that because I suppose it was written by a man and then I started to listen to programmes on there, scientific programmes, and I really – am torn in two. I can't decide now whether – .'[51] Startled by secular change, the older interviewee discussing the 1960s and 1970s seemed to convey a sort of grief for the loss of the religious world of their youth.

This grief at the loss of Christian culture quickly became a commercial product. Just as with films like *Akenfield*, the late 1960s and 1970s witnessed an explosion of nostalgia for the disappearing values of religion and community, and was sold in books of folksy memoirs. Autobiography changed in this period from being the account of the heroic life of the individual towards redemption that we encountered early in the century (see pages 42–3) to an account of loss by the community. Secularisation was articulated in autobiography, not as a loss of personal faith, but of community sensibility and charm. De-Christianisation was expressed as something social, not something personal. In part this followed the example of many churchmen, who came to express the problems of the churches as the problems of society. But, most interestingly, the nostalgia industry of the 1960s and 1970s placed the loss of social Christianity as central to the portrayal of rural, village and town communities. Most of the memoirs were written by women, seemingly writing for a female readership in the tones of a feminine sensibility. This is nowhere more apparent than in discussing Sundays. Celia Davies recalled in her 1974 autobiography: 'We accepted Sunday and all that went with it, just as we accepted the seasons of the year. ... I believe we even had Sunday hair ribbons. Nearly all our toys were put away, except books of Bible stories – anything in the nature of a game was forbidden. When we went out for a walk we were not allowed to run or skip, or trail our feet in the autumn leaves. We walked sedately on either side of the pram, with that "Sunday" feeling inside us.'[52] The world that was lost was a female one, and the loss of religion was a central motif of a vanished British culture.

Amidst the sense of religious crisis, then, there was a striking calmness apparent in people's appetite for religious nostalgia. Few tears were shed for the decay of moral strictness and the sense of guilt that Christian culture had previously imposed. But the people's calmness contrasted with the churches' obsession – sex.

Sex, sexuality and sexual equality

In no period of history did the relationship of Christianity to issues of sex, sexual orientation and sexual equality become of such importance as in the 1960s. Churchmen worried endlessly that the permissive sixties lay at the root of the turn against organised religion, the decline of faith and the crisis of the church in British society. The 1960s was the period when second-wave feminism – often called 'women's liberation' – came to maturity, especially in 1968–70. But feminists were only one element in a complex series of changes.

There was already a well-established debate over sexual matters and the Christian faith under way in the British churches before 1963. Public debate on such high-brow theology was sparked by the Reith Lecture broadcast by the BBC in late 1962, in which a psychologist, G. M. Carstairs, argued for acknowledgement of the rise of sexual freedom amongst young people, and that teenage sex should be treated without rancorous condemnation: 'Surely charity is more important than chastity,' he told Britain.[53] This produced a furious church reaction and fierce public debate. There was agreement that teenagers had changed their outlook in recent years, and that puberty seemed to be arriving earlier and 'the submissive tendency to parents and conventional standards has almost disappeared'.[54] But should the churches condone teenage sex as Carstairs and new liberal thought suggested? In late 1962 and early 1963, the *Church Times* carried a long correspondence, fuelled by both the Reith

Lecture and by theological controversy concerning the nature of sex and its role in human personality and relationships, on whether fornication (sex before marriage) was a sin. Liberal Cambridge theologians in 1962 doubted it was *always* a sin, arguing within intellectual church circles for sex to be free of institutional regulation and to come from within 'from personality'.

Human relations and marriage came under various forms of clerical re-conception, giving space and enormous publicity to radicals in the churches. This gave rise to the concept of a 'new morality' in British society, and one that the British Christian churches needed to theorise and ground in theology, doctrine and church policy. In 1963, Canon Douglas A. Rhymes of Southwark Cathedral asserted that Christ did not condemn all sexual activity outwith marriage – bringing a ringing retort from the editor of the *Church Times* for being 'so muddle-headed as to present love as if it were essentially self-indulgence'.[55] In the following year Rhymes wrote that morality should permit 'a higher attitude towards the person, a personal relationship of responsibility and love which will pervade all human relations'.[56] Radical theology was separating sex from marriage, and the *imprimatur* its proponents gave to the sexual act (irrespective of whether a man and woman were married) was in the early 1960s an innovation for Christian clergy.

Such radical thinking was bound to create a major stir. Britain was just emerging from the 1950s, arguably its most morally conservative decade, and the nation was acclimatised to moral guardians having an upper hand, and to personal sexual behaviour being the object of enormous community pressure. Most churchmen opposed liberal attitudes. One wrote that 'sex is safe only when it is organised within a strong moral sentiment, and later comes to be organised within a strong husband or wife sentiment'.[57] Sex became openly talked about in an unprecedented way, and it was the level of discussion rather than what was actually being said that unnerved conservative forces in the churches.

The Archbishop of Wales, a conservative in these matters, wanted sex before marriage unequivocally reasserted by the Anglican churches as a sin.[58] The York Convocation discussed the 'Chastity Issue' in late 1963, whilst Michael Ramsay, Archbishop of Canterbury and leader of the Anglican communion in Britain and the world, backed up by the House of Laity in the Church Assembly, attempted to compromise between liberals and conservatives by announcing that: 'Fornication is not necessarily the worst sin, but that it is always wrong.'[59] Whilst Ramsay took a fairly moderate line, the Archbishop of York, Dr Donald Coggan, took a more conservative line, condemning young people as lacking 'moral judgment'.[60] Puritan clergy found easy headlines in the mid-1960s. 'BISHOP CONDEMNS THE MORAL STATE OF THE NATION. Society in Britain "Sexually Sick"' was the banner headline for one bishop.[61] Another, the Right Revd George Reindorp, Bishop of Guildford, told his diocesan council for social work in late 1963: 'I imagine that historians will say of us that, since people did not believe in much, they made a pitiful attempt to exalt sex into a religion. ... No generation has talked more about sex, seemed to enjoy it less, and been so ignorant about it. No sexual relationship can long satisfy if the bed is regarded as the altar of a new religion.'[62] The Bishop of Chelmsford, the Right Revd J. G. Tiarks, said that making any exceptions to chastity would bring in immorality. And the York Convocation, representing the northern and more puritanical part of England, agreed.[63]

The 'new morality' was evoking the same reaction from other churches. Bishops of the Episcopal Church of Ireland specifically condemned it, and in late 1963 issued a pastoral letter concerning the lowering of 'standards of sexual behaviour'. It read: 'Within the last year statements have been made by public men, and books have been written in the interest of a so-called "new morality", which are in *direct opposition* to the authority of Holy Scripture and the teaching of the Church, concerning chastity.' In a similar vein, the chief of the Salvation Army also condemned the 'new morality', saying: 'Restraint and self-discipline are not the sworn enemies of happiness.'[64] One irony of moral condemnation of the young was the manifest hypocrisy of the British establishment. In 1963, John Profumo, the Secretary for War, was forced to resign after first denying then confessing an adulterous relationship with Christine Keeler – a woman tarred by the press as a prostitute and a security risk because of her liaison with a Soviet official. The Protestant *British Weekly* felt that the scandal 'encouraged the belief abroad that Britain is finished, not only as a military power but as a moral power'.[65]

The sexual revolution was given new impetus by the arrival of the oral contraceptive pill. From the churches' point of view, this was not necessarily a matter for disapproval. The Church of England and the Church of Scotland made clear statements in support of artificial birth control (in 1958 and 1960 respectively), and many Protestant clergy welcomed the arrival of the oral contraceptive pill in 1960–1.[66] But it seemed to be assumed by the churches in 1960–3 that the pill was a help for married women to control fertility, not for unmarried women to prevent it. This was not foreseen. Sexually transmitted diseases (STDs) rather than pregnancy and family change were how the issue of sexual morality was framed through the 1950s and into the early 1960s. Even the British Health Education Council in 1968 used STDs as the calibrator of the nation's moral condition, concluding that there was no sign of moral decay in Britain. In truth, the 'new morality' formulated by theologians was an arcane philosophical debate, whilst sex was 'dirty' talk, and even the medical profession had little truck with it. One married woman asked her doctor in 1960 about contraception, and she 'braced herself for an embarrassing discussion of rival methods, but I needn't have bothered, because all he said was, "Now that you're married your husband will take care of that." What he was saying ... was that he wouldn't aid and abet me in acquiring any control over my own fertility.'[67] So, there was a studied distance kept by the moral professions – both clergy and doctors – from sex.

The sexual revolution may well have been under way in the 1950s, but it certainly accelerated sharply around 1963. More single teenagers began to have sex in the late 1950s and early 1960s, almost ten years before the oral contraceptive pill became available to single people. The illegitimacy rate had been falling in the late 1940s and 1950s, reaching all-time lows in 1958–9, but then started to rise slowly in 1958–61, and then sharply from 1962 to the early 1970s. Sex and marriage were abruptly separating conceptually in British culture. Single women who got pregnant after 1970 were no longer automatically marrying (but were increasingly terminating pregnancies, cohabiting or becoming single parents). When the oral contraceptive pill was introduced in Britain in 1961, it was married women who started to use it in large numbers. Single women could not get hold of the pill until the late 1960s because most doctors, for moral and religious reasons, would not prescribe it without parental consent, and not at all to girls under the age of 16. Margaret Ramage recalled: 'You couldn't go on the Pill unless you had a wedding date, though about '67 or '68 that changed. The clinics would ask you for the wedding date. You could bypass it by telling lies. But our parents taught us discipline, obedience, to ask no questions – not a healthy way to bring up children. But it did mean you were too intimated to lie about your wedding arrangements.'[68]

Not all women waited, and the major revolution in sexual freedom – sex before marriage – was under way in the early and mid-1960s without the medical benefit of the pill.[69] But the impact rapidly became enormous. By 1969, in a controlled medical sample of women then aged 23, 48 per cent had used the pill. By 1973, nearly 70 per cent of this same group had used the pill. The use of oral contraception rapidly became standard amongst most single and married women at some point in their teens and twenties. The sexual revolution was cultural in origin, but it was accelerated from 1968 when the technology became available to the single woman. In 1964, only 15 per cent of 16- and 17-year-old girls claimed to have had sexual intercourse; by 1974–5, this figure had leapt to 58 per cent. (The equivalent figures for boys indicate only a modest rise from 40 to 52 per cent.)[70]

The rise of the pill reflected a massive revolution in ideas about the female body and its moral purpose, and about female control over fertility. Underlying the sexual revolution were two shifts in ideas – medical ideas and religious ideas. In medicine, the early 1960s saw the rapid spread of new ideas on the pleasure of sex, notably in the widely-read sex manuals of Alex Comfort. This development freed the enjoyment of sex from the need for enduring love, giving a new medical legitimation to sex between consenting adults. One woman recalled that her generation grew up with the knowledge 'that somewhere out there existed a contraceptive which promised you would be able to get away with it, in the way only men had before'.[71] Novelist Margaret Drabble wrote in November 1967 that 'we face the certainty of a sexual revolution', a revolution connected 'to that other major revolution of our society, the emancipation of women'. Within fourteen months, the pill became widely available to the unmarried, making 1969 feel like what novelist Angela Carter called 'year one'. She said that 'the introduction of more or less 100 per cent effective methods of birth control, combined with the relaxation of manners that may have derived from this technological breakthrough or else came from God knows where, change, well, everything'.[72]

But medical restraint on the individual experimenting with sex in the sixties was not as powerful as the religious one. This was especially true for women. In accounts of rising sexual activity by women in the 1960s, religion features prominently as the principal restraint to be overcome before sexual experimentation. Kitty Gadding recalled her early sexual encounters, starting with lengthy 'snogging' sessions, often in groups at parties or youth clubs. As she recollected how one encounter led from snogging to groping, she immediately invoked memory of Christian guilt: 'I was still very religious – about thirteen or fourteen – and he undid my jeans, they were very, very, very tight and he undid them and I thought, if he's doing that I ought to do something back. So I undid his jeans. I thought I ought to respond, but I was racked with guilt and I went off to confession and felt I'd really sinned.' She then recalled a second encounter at the age of 15 with a deeply religious German boy two years older than her who practised coitus interruptus in order, she thought, to maintain his virginity.

Even amongst leading pop stars, who the press led the public into presuming were sexual experimenters on a grand scale, conservativism still lingered into the late 1960s; the raucous pop singer Lulu was nearing 20 years of age in 1970, and was still a virgin – despite what she described as 'obstacles, temptations and some marathon kissing sessions'. Another woman, Isobel Kaprowski, recalled: 'In my teens I didn't have sex. I took the catholic faith very seriously, and decided that for me it was sex within marriage – and I didn't want to get married – and that was it. So I'd go out with boys, but not go too far. Then at seventeen, when I was going to be confirmed, I fell in love.' This changed her attitude, and she lost her virginity. Religious ideas also restrained gay men and lesbian woman, especially before the emergence of the gay liberation movement in 1969–70. Marcus Riggs recalled discovering his sexuality in about 1964: 'I was about nine when I realised I was gay. That's about an average age, but it was centuries later before I did something about it. I had such real guilt about being gay, and what I thought God thought of it. I can see a lot of connections between my perception of my father and God. They were both fairly angry people who didn't approve of me.'[73]

By 1967, with sexual revolution well under way, the term 'new morality' had all but disappeared in ecclesiastical circles. The new language of moral conservatism was 'permissiveness' and 'promiscuity'. Churches started to tune in to both the new theology and what young women were telling them. The Moral Welfare Committee of the general assembly of the Church of Scotland reported in 1970 on sex before marriage: 'If the sanctions of commandment and convention are gone, people are set free to respond to goodness for its own sake, under no compulsion, constrained and sustained by the love of Christ and not by the fear of a lost respectability.' The committee considered whether marriage might be on the way out, and felt this was not without historical precedent: 'The spirit of the age with its new found freedoms, and its healthy intolerance of humbug and hypocrisy, challenges Christians to re-think the implications of Christian morality – not a bad thing to have to do.' But then, in a single sentence, the committee grasped the central issue: 'It is the promiscuous girl who is the real problem here.' In this utterly sexist statement, the committee actually understood that the 'moral turn' was in female permissiveness, not in men's, and that the churches were losing their central paradigm of Christian behaviour – the respectable and sexually abstinent single woman.[74] This was serious enough, but worse was emerging for conventional Christianity. A storm arose in the summer of 1967 when a senior cleric, Hugh Montefiore, suggested that Christ may have been homosexual. He was condemned by many leading churchmen, and three years later was still being challenged by Anglican evangelicals to state that Christ was perfect in every way.[75] A long-term challenge to conventional theology and church affairs was stoked when, at the time of de-criminalisation of homosexuality in 1968, radical Anglican clergy started to accept homosexuality and the legitimacy of the gay liberation movement.[76]

For the Roman Catholic Church, the 1960s was a decade of unprecedented questioning of its sexual laws. On the one side, sex seemed to be breaking down the 'fortress mentality' of the Catholic community in Britain. Until the sixties, Catholic marriage with non-Catholics was frowned upon both by the Church and by many in British society generally. But mixed marriages rose steadily in the 1950s and 1960s – perhaps a quarter of all Catholic weddings in 1955 and a third by 1960.[77] On the other hand, the rules surrounding sex became part of a wide-scale reform agenda in the international Catholic Church, which led to the Second Vatican Council of 1962–5. This met to consider a whole series of reform issues in the Catholic faith, and was widely seen as a venue for dramatic liberalisation and modernisation of the Catholic faith worldwide. And it did change some important things. It introduced the saying of Mass in the vernacular or local language rather than in an archaic Latin that few worshippers understood, and it encouraged more lay participation in worship (through the introduction of lay readers, for instance). Most importantly, there was widespread expectation of approval for Catholics to use contraception – previously banned by papal rulings. Young Catholics, both married and single, watched throughout the mid-1960s, as the papal theological committee agreed on reform. The battle between pro- and anti-birth control camps in British Catholicism was fierce. The Catholic journal the *Tablet* backed the conservative position against sudden change to Church doctrine. 'This suggestion,' said one letter in response, 'will be cold comfort to the faithful who have only one life in which to work out their salvation, and surely Mother Church, ever solicitous of the welfare of her sons and daughters, will not speak to them with such a chilling detachment.' The writer concluded: 'At present we are living a lie: none of us can justify the Church's teaching, and few of us attempt to observe it.'[78]

To widespread dismay, in July 1968, Pope Paul VI issued an encyclical, *Humanae Vitae* (Human Life), which banned all artificial contraception as morally wrong for the world's Catholics. This ruling was deeply felt amongst young Catholic women. Libby Purves, then 18 years old, recalled: 'It is difficult to convey how hard a message this was for the Catholic schoolgirls of 1968, setting out on adult life. ... I venture to say that it was harder for my generation than for any other to accept the ruling. It gave us no tolerable future to look forward to, as with A levels behind us we stepped out into a wider field to confront the World, the Flesh, the Devil and the Rolling Stones.' She did not leave the Catholic Church, but she, like many, found the disappointment of 1968 quite hard:

But we had lives to lead in a modern world, and Humanae Vitae *was a hard slap in the face. Theologically the ruling was obscure and unconvincing, redolent of a sort of resigned fatalism and contempt for prudence and self-reliance which was not preached by the church in any other area. Practically, it was plain disastrous. An idealistic girl can accept all sorts of difficult demands: celibacy outside marriage, chastity within it, the absolute impossibility of abortion or divorce. But this was the final straw. It was an uncompromising, uncharitable edict that made all practical birth control a grave sin: even inside marriage, even after many children.*[79]

Catholic policy on artificial contraception alienated large numbers of even loyal Catholic families. David Lodge's novels, *The British Museum is Falling Down* (1965) and *How Far Can You Go?* (1980), expressed the rise and collapse of hope for reform on birth control, as young middle-class Catholic families looked forward to the opportunity of both partners sustaining careers through family planning. But in place of the pill and the condom, Catholics were urged by the Church to use a system of Natural Family Planning, or 'safe period' sex (first fully developed in the 1950s), in which a woman's body was measured for temperature to allow sex during the least likely period for fertilisation. Some Catholics found the system developed a love life that, by only having sex at certain times of the month, emphasised and enhanced their Catholicism. But for others, the system was widely ridiculed. An anonymous 'Catholic Mother' wrote in 1965 challenging the argument of the Church that NFP was safer than the pill: 'Sure the plain fact is that very few of us indeed have encountered one of these pill-taking failures, while all of us are dismally familiar with cases where the "safe period", even when used by intelligent and self-controlled couples, has just not proved safe.'[80] Another Catholic reported: 'We have tried to keep to these rules, with as I believe, a bad effect on the develop-ment of our marriage, our sex relations, my temper and our treatment of our children'.[81] Whilst Catholic haemorrhage from the faith in Britain started a little later than that of Protestants (in the later 1970s rather than 1960s), the disappointment of July 1968 was undoubtedly at the heart of young Catholics' increasing alienation from Church teaching and practice, and reduced the influence of priests. The pill was to become the greatest theological burden to Catholic adherence in Britain, and more broadly the proscription on sex before marriage remained for the rest of the century identified by Catholics themselves as a hindrance to obedience to the faith.[82]

The sexual revolution was, of course, not a stand-alone feature of sixties' culture. For one thing, as the novelist David Lodge noted, 'At some point in the nineteen-sixties, Hell disappeared. No one could say for certain when this happened. First it was there, then it wasn't.'[83] Fear of retribution in this world and the next dissolved from the consciousness of most young people. As a result, the cultural revolution turned fashion, music, reading, education and leisure pursuits into challenges to authority and conservatism. Many young people experimented with illegal drugs, the use of which had formerly been largely confined to artists and social elites. But from around 1962–3 the arrival of large quantities of cheap but low-grade cannabis popularised 'the reefer' or 'joint' – to such an extent that some medical opinion was already talking of legalisation, and arousing great opposition from churchmen.[84] The developing campaign in 1967 to legalise pot led to a demonstration of 5,000 'beatniks and hippies' at Marble Arch in London. Whether dangerous or not, the *Church Times* commented, such drugs 'will remove the brake of conscience' upon individual behaviour, tending to undermine the general moral universe produced by restraint and self-denial.[85]

The forces of puritanism were by no means dead. Moral Rearmament (MRA) asked the British people in 1963 to sign a 'people's declaration' against 'atheism, decadence and corruption'.[86] But MRA did not enjoy the impact it had achieved in the 1950s. Its leader died in 1961, leaving the organisation bereft of new ideas with which to confront the rapidly changing taste and technology of the 1960s. Its own work was outshone by that of a long-time supporter, Mary Whitehouse, and the National Viewers' and Listeners' Association that she formed in Birmingham in 1965.

Mary Whitehouse became in the mid- and late 1960s a common feature in the television news herself, a small spectacled figure of grandmotherly seriousness, seen frequently entering some court or other in pursuit of the 'godless filth' on British television. She became the byword for a working-class respectability, an artless parody of anti-intellectualism. Picking on the BBC for many of her attacks, she assaulted their programmes relentlessly in her campaign of cleaning up TV. Godlessness became especially assaulted. When in June 1967 an Alan Bennett satirical show *On the Margin* used the word 'Christ', she uncovered how blasphemous words (attacking religion) were more permissible under BBC policy than plain sex-swear words.[87] Her campaigning continued into the 1970s, but despite some legal victories, her puritan cause was decaying and became ineffectual. Yet, during the 1960s, her moral conservatism was matched by many other public figures, and by some newspapers – notably the *Daily Express* and the *Sunday Post*, papers which in Scotland and the north of England achieved as high as 50 per cent readership amongst adults with their diet of quaint homeliness, evocation of traditional Protestant values and tirades against libertines and disorderly youth. Their success at this point seemed to represent the conservative backlash, but this power passed, and in the case of the *Express* was followed in the 1970s by the collapse of circulation and sale of the business.[88]

The sixties' revolution was seen at the time by many churchpeople as a temporary fad to be countered merely by re-packaging religion in trendy wrapping. But before long, the view became more pessimistic. One organisation that went through a mindset change was the Boys' Brigade. Its chief in 1962 said: 'Discipline and religion, drill and uniform, Bible Class and Badge work, are inherent in the BB, but there is no reason why these should not be up-to-date and attractive to the modern Boy. The cap, belt and haversack were an attraction in 1883. I am not certain that they are today, and if not, we must substitute something else that is.' With sustained decline in support, another leading figure in the Boys' Brigade ranted in 1974 in the *BB Gazette*: 'Today we worship youth. "Temples" are erected to its honour – glittering Carnaby Street, dim-lit discos, *Top of the Pops* TV programmes, opinion panels also on TV, and that non-stop anthem of praise to the "beautiful people" – the gospel according to Radio One. No one seems to reflect that, as a result of all this, we are being submerged in a deluge of shoddy goods, immature thinking, half-baked notions about how society should be changed, unhygienic hairstyles, and a refusal to recognise any form of authority.'[89] This type of comment was common amongst head teachers, youth leaders and politicians, reflecting how many of those in charge of much of the organised Christian apparatus of the country by the mid-1970s were at a loss what to do about the decline of discipline and Christianity. In their loss, they merely ranted uncontrollably.

Analysis: Mary Whitehouse

Mrs Mary Whitehouse (1910–2001) was a school teacher who joined the Oxford Group in the 1930s (see pages 198–201), and founded a Clean-up TV campaign in 1963 in conjunction with a clergyman and her husband, collecting a petition of half a million signatures. She was appalled at sexual and violent scenes on television, especially on BBC, and when her campaign achieved few results, she founded the National Viewers' and Listeners' Association (NVLA) in Birmingham in 1965. Whitehouse developed a belief that television and, to lesser extents, radio and theatre were undermining the moral fibre and Christian character of Britain during the swinging sixties, and she managed to unite Protestant evangelicals and Roman Catholic priests in condemnation of 'immoral' broadcasting.

Whitehouse established a status of folk-fun in the British media and the consciousness of most British young people of the 1960s and early 1970s. Yet, her campaign had some notable successes. In 1972, it claimed 1.5 million signatures in a Nationwide Petition for Public Decency, leading in 1982 to the Indecent Displays Act. The association later claimed the support of Conservative prime minister, Margaret Thatcher, in its stand against the decline of moral standards. With over 100,000 members in the 1960s, the association achieved declining impact against moral impurity on television, but it survived into the twenty-first century; in 2001, the same year that MRA changed its name, so did the NVLA – to mediawatch-uk.[90]

Mary Whitehouse established a linked campaign. *Gay News*, a campaigning periodical, published in June 1976 a poem by James Kirkup, a professor of poetry at an American university, called 'The Love that Dares to Speak its Name' which described the homosexual love felt by a Roman centurion for the crucified Christ, accompanied with an explicit illustration. The poem described homosexual acts by Christ involving Judas, other disciples and others – in all 17 people. Whilst the statute offence of blasphemy was abolished in 1967, Mary Whitehouse commenced a private prosecution for the common law offence of blasphemous libel – recalling later that she felt engaged upon God's work as the prosecution proceeded. The jury found *Gay News* guilty by a majority of ten to two, and the editor of the periodical was given a nine-month suspended prison sentence and a £500 fine, whilst *Gay News* itself was fined a further £1,000. For many commentators at the time, the conviction represented a signal of moral panic over the liberalisation of attitudes towards homosexuality rather than concern with blaspheming the Christian saviour as such. Nonetheless, the effect of the verdict (and a subsequent failed appeal) was to make attacking the central tenets of Christianity punishable in law, no matter any satirical or metaphorical

Mary Whitehouse outside the House of Commons in 1965 with a petition containing over 300,000 signatures complaining about 'dirt that pours into millions of homes through the TV screen'. (Topfoto/Topham/AP)

intention.[91] This undoubtedly left government legal officers and many leading political figures rather uneasy. The liberal state advanced considerably in the 1960s and 1970s, and few could envisage a step backwards – including in the context of a multi-faith society where to actively protect one religion left many others demanding the same rights. In a sense, Whitehouse and her combination of moral clean-up with Christian evangelistic attitudes demonstrated the extent to which British culture had both liberalised and secularised, and the likely narrow limits to success in attempting to put the genie back in the bottle.[92]

The churches themselves were no better, getting tied in knots over changing policies towards sex and the family. The issue of church re-marriage of divorcees came to haunt the Anglicans in England, despite the fact that Anglicans in the USA permitted this from 1961 and in Canada from 1967.[93] Moral panic became more intense amongst an ever-decreasing minority of the religious and intellectual establishment, leading to a kind of do-it-yourself puritan movement establishing a rearguard action. In 1971, a well-known Roman Catholic Labour peer, Lord Longford, started a campaign against pornography, gaining support from Protestant ministers (including Donald Soper of the Methodists and Donald Coggan,

Anglican Archbishop of York). Amongst other things, this led to a much-ridiculed and brief campaign against contraband pornography by police and customs who searched travellers (including the present author) returning from its main source in Copenhagen. At the same time in 1971–2, Malcolm Muggeridge's 'Festival of Light' offered a participant extravaganza to promote moral purity, and though this later became a fixture of the British scene, none of it seemed to dent the relentless march of secular liberalism in sexual matters.[94]

The wider issue of women's role in the churches also came to a head in the 1960s. Whilst the Church of Scotland granted full rights to women as teaching and ruling elders (as ministers and lay elders respectively) in 1969, the same did not happen south of the border. In the Church of England throughout the twentieth century, the role of women increased incrementally with almost every decade, but always stopped short of women priests. England's first lay female canon was installed in October 1963, and in the same month York and Canterbury Convocation approved the idea of women Readers (though by a narrow margin of 73 votes to 60 in the Lower House). But the central objective of women's ordination was always cut short by a welter of church reports – one in November 1962 on 'Gender and Ministry'.[95] Opposition was profound, male leaders in the Church of England having their attitudes deeply rooted in notions of sexual segregation in work, home and family roles. The Bishop of Gloucester said in Convocation in arguing against ordination:

Is it right to ask a woman to assume ... the formal headship [of a parish] which she repudiates in her own household and family? ... If we assent to this, we shall be asking women to undertake responsibility which does not properly belong to them, and we shall be making it more difficult – and heaven knows how difficult it is – to persuade people that they are taking part in a family activity, and something which is not merely a club activity.[96]

The Archdeacon of Bodmin, the Venerable A. C. Williams, said: 'Most of our young women to-day are much too busy bringing up families and are not so concerned with the equality of the sexes which was current thirty years ago.'[97] The worst excesses of sexist thinking were to be heard in the midst of liberalising culture. For the Church of England, after the 'Gender and Ministry' report in 1962 came the 'Women in Holy Orders' report in 1966, which acknowledged the key political argument against ordination – that the High Church wing of Anglicanism would suffer strained relations with the Roman Catholic and Eastern Orthodox churches (which were most firmly opposed to women priests). But the more the liberal case was put forward, the more the arguments of the traditionalists became perverse. The 1966 Anglican report laid out what it termed the 'erotic facts' against women's ordination:

Sex differences have erotic effects, which differ according to whether men or women are in public positions. There are many spheres of activity in which men and women meet and cooperate without sexual arousal; they are the relatively impersonal spheres of shop, factory, farms, regiments, schools and laboratories where the sexes meet en masse. But where women perform personal services as secretaries to businessmen or assistants to professional ones, in a setting where privacy is long and frequent, erotic factors come into play leading, if not frequently to adultery and fornication, at least often to possessiveness and heartbreaks. The pastoral office brings a closeness of spiritual intimacy which easily spills over into incipient love relationships. A two-sex priesthood would multiply this problem between ministers and between lay folk and ministers.[98]

This case against women's ordination in the 1960s was sexist, absurd, illogical and hypocritical. In plain truth, no matter the arguments for or against, the forces of reaction – a union of the extremes of Catholic-minded and evangelical-minded Anglicans – were not going to permit women's ordination in the Church of England on any well-formulated argument. At the very moment that British women at large were experiencing the twin revolutions of fertility control (the sexual revolution) and women's liberation (second-wave feminism), the Church of England joined the Roman Catholic Church and the small conservative Protestant churches (mostly of Scotland and Northern Ireland) in rejecting women as dispensers of the Christian sacraments.

Race, religion and diversity

British society started to absorb black and Asian cultures in the 1960s. The issue of race came to the forefront of Christian rhetoric and the nature of the liberal secular democracy of the nation. The results were varied: vibrancy and diversity in cultural idioms, enlarged or new religious traditions, but also racism and intolerance. But in Northern Ireland, the sixties witnessed the eruption once again of Catholic–Protestant tension amidst a republican military campaign.

The Afro-Caribbean (West Indian) immigration of the 1950s and 1960s brought predominantly Christian immigrants to England's cities, notably to London and Birmingham. The Christian culture of Jamaica and other islands was mainly evangelical and Pentecostal, combining inspirational gospel singing with a strict sense of propriety and female piety. And yet, the culture was liberal and liberationist. Ryland Campbell, born in Jamaica in 1932, says that Jamaicans gave American blacks their self-respect after 1945, and that Jamaicans were critical of the liberalisation of English urban culture. He came to Britain in 1956 when, he recalls, England was culturally quiescent:

England was asleep in a way. I came here and I saw that it was the Quakers had Birmingham, the pubs could only open until about half past nine and Jamaicans come and say 'No', from Friday until Sunday night we want to live like how we wanted to live and we have these things which we call shebeens and you know we really go there so I never felt locked out because the Englishman, business at that time, he has some folk songs or you know or hill-billy songs and that sort of thing and we want some boogie woogie. So we put it on ...[99]

It was in the 1960s that this impact was felt, notably through the Notting Hill Carnival which, after a serious race riot in 1958, came to be seen as a barometer of white acceptance of black culture. More widely, black influence in pop music and fashion was to bring these mostly English speaking migrants rapidly to the forefront of British culture. Meanwhile, migrants from South Asia and others from Kenya and East Africa arrived at first in smaller numbers, but they came from possibly the most religious societies in the world. India was dominated by Hinduism, a religion that pervaded society with an unmatched intensity. But amongst Hindu migrants to Britain in the 1960s was an increasing proportion of professional, skilled and business families. Ranjit Sondhi came to England in 1966 when he was 16 years old:

Religion pervades the atmosphere in India of course, it has done so for thousands of years, and religion is in all its forms – religious philosophy, religious culture, religious traditions and so on. Religion is, as people say, quite rightly, it's a part of life, but religion is relegated into a little tiny corner of the room in a middle-class or upper-middle-class Indian house. There is a kind of lip service paid to religion. There is the little idol or the little corner that's turned into a prayer room.[100]

With linguistic and religious differences, Asian migrant communities had somewhat different patterns of settlement within British culture.

Black immigrants had been brought up in the Caribbean with stories of the wealth and opulence of British society, and were shocked to find how shabby was the fabric of cities like London and Birmingham. The Britain they came to was cold and wet, and the streets upon which they could afford to live were much poorer than they had expected. They were shocked even more by the casual racism they frequently encountered in public. Black women reported being physically jostled on buses, and called 'black bastard' and told to 'go back to the jungle'. This kind of experience was common, and the Christian migrants to Britain were by the 1960s becoming slowly better known to the British Christian churches. One congregational minister, the Revd Clifford Hill from Tottenham, wrote a study of how London's churches were singularly failing the Christian immigrants, completely ignoring their existence let alone catering for their spiritual needs. Migrants spoke of their shock and bewilderment on arriving in Britain. They found that England was not the modern home of Christianity that they had been led to believe in colonial schools and church teaching. Hill noted: 'The patronising attitude of so many English Christians towards West Indians has done more damage to the cause of racial integration than all the sneers and.blasphemies of their English workmates in factory workshops.'[101] This reception encouraged the continued development of separate black Christian congregations, usually Pentecostal in character. The irony that had started in the 1950s continued. When they migrated to English cities, the black Christians from a mostly Anglican English-speaking Caribbean felt rejected by English Anglicanism. As a result, they developed a black Christian church community that was to become, in the last quarter of the century, one of the few thriving sectors of British Christianity.

Religious diversity in non-Christian religions grew dramatically through immigration in the 1960s, but religious issues were scarred by public racism in housing, the economy and the law. First in numerical importance was Islam. Britain in 1960 had only nine Islamic mosques; by 1986 there were 200.[102] Language and religion made the Pakistani community even more isolated than English speaking black Christians from the Caribbean, and this was accentuated by imams who were culturally ill-equipped to advise Muslims on integration issues, and who instead concentrated on encouraging retention of cultural distinction as a means to sustain the faith. Much the same applied to other faiths. After the Muslims, the Sikhs formed the largest new religious group in Britain in the later 1950s and 1960s, and like them tended to form concentrated communities in London (such as Southall) and industrial cities in the English

Midlands. They experienced a unique form of discrimination in the 1960s when bus companies in Wolverhampton, Manchester and elsewhere refused to employ men wearing turbans. A local newspaper in Bradford commented that 'if a man feels so strongly about the turban he should remain in the community where his views are shared'.[103] Turbans were a symbol of diversity issues for the British state. When the wearing of motorcycle crash helmets was made compulsory in the late 1960s, Sikh men started to be stopped and charged by the police, and it took until 1976 before Parliament made provision for religious exceptions.[104] Though a few Hindus arrived from India in the 1950s and early 1960s, the main immigration occurred in 1965–72 as a result of the so-called 'Africanisation' of East Africa (of Kenya, Tanzania and Uganda), which led to the expulsion of large numbers of Asians who came, most of them, to Britain.[105]

Most migrants from each religious tradition coming in the 1960s and early 1970s were poor, either through economic background or through enforced removal of their wealth on emigrating to Britain. As a result, their places of worship grew only slowly in number and quality as finances became available. Religious traditions were nurtured with the reconstruction in Britain of national traditions from countries of emigration. In Sikh communities, for instance, the early immigration in the 1960s was mostly of men, and traditional caste structures mattered little, but as women arrived and the community enlarged, caste became again a defining issue in, for example, marriage. Within each of Islam, Hinduism and Sikhism, the fragmentations into different branches and sects came with the waves of migration. The consequence was that religion was a strong factor for diversity *within* these communities, as well as creating an underlying religious diversification from the Christian background of most Britons.

The growth of non-Christian religious traditions in Britain challenged British Christianity (as it did that of the rest of Europe in the 1960s, when immigration was high from former colonies). Race was rising up the political agenda in the 1960s, with mounting evidence of racial discrimination in housing, jobs and leisure; a speech in April 1968 by the leading Conservative Party politician, Enoch Powell, warned of seeing 'much blood' being spilled should more 'coloured' immigrants be admitted to Britain. British churchmen joined radical political groups (mostly on the left or in the Liberal Party) in challenging racism in sport, the state and in society at large. In a sense, the race issue took precedence over the religious one in relation to immigration between the 1950s and 1980s. In September 1963, the World Council of Churches, an organisation devoted to Christianity, declared that 'people cannot be Christian if they practice any kind of racial segregation'.[106] This was a declaration of major significance, for it isolated apartheid South Africa as a *cause célèbre* which Christian churches would for over three decades battle to overturn, including fighting for the imprisoned Nelson Mandela.

Further campaigns concerning racism arose for British churchmen in Rhodesia (now Zimbabwe) and in 1962 concerning the White Policy in Australia – when only white immigrants were admitted – and its continuing poor treatment of aboriginal people.[107] Black African Christians threw down the gauntlet to British churchmen with persistence. A Roman Catholic journalist in Nyasaland (now Malawi) wrote a challenging article in early 1963, entitled 'Back to Paganism in Africa', turning on the conventional word used in British Christian missions to describe the religiosity of the continent. He argued as an African that Christianity in Africa was white-man's religion, brought as part of the colonising and subjugating experience of racial superiority, though he had no option but to be a Christian and accept it.[108] Canon Kenneth Cragg, warden of Augustine's College, Canterbury, attacked the concept and rhetoric of 'the dark continent' of Africa: 'our dark verdicts are the conclusion of our own opaqueness'.[109]

British radical Christians were joining with others in formulating postcolonial theology in 1960–4 with great speed. One aspect was the creation of new forms of charity. In the mid-1960s organisations like Christian Aid and Oxfam started modern-style advertising campaigns with pictures of emaciated bodies, and metaphorical images of the half-hungry world, and with slogans like 'Freedom from Hunger' and 'Onslaught on World Hunger'. In a sense, charity became campaigning; Oxfam opened its Oxford Street shop in London in October 1963.[110] British young people were responding to a new moral imperative, driven by an increasingly secular sense of injustice, and in this religious charities became increasingly involved in the later twentieth century in order to keep religion as part of the new moral climate. The range of campaigning implications rose as the South African boycott took effect in the later 1960s. When, in 1967, it looked certain that the South African authorities would refuse to allow their national side to play against the English mixed-race player and captain Basil D'Olivera, David Sheppard of the Church of England argued that the MCC should abandon its matches.[111] The anti-apartheid movement united people of many faiths and those of none in the late 1960s and early 1970s, and continued to do so until the final downfall of apartheid in 1994.

One part of Britain stood apart in its experience of all these issues, and in its experience of Christian change. In Northern Ireland, religion mattered in a way that was rarely felt, or even understood, by other Britons. Indeed, in most respects, the 1960s marked the divergence of the province from the religious cultural trends of the rest of the UK. Secularisation showed few signs here; church attendance for Protestants was six times higher than in England, whilst more than half of Catholics sustained an active church connection.[112] Underlying this was the fact that religion defined politics, civil rights, personal identity and community division. In 1964, Catholics started a Campaign for Social Justice against unfair voting systems which favoured Protestants, discrimination in employment (which kept Catholics out of many industries and promoted positions) and the Protestant-dominated police force. In response, many Protestants feared loss of control, and paramilitary organisations were formed on both sides, leading to the outbreak in 1969 of 'the Troubles'. (See pages 284–7.) There then followed a quarter of a century of paramilitary violence, in which over 3,000 people died and Northern Ireland became militarised with over 15,000 British troops stationed there. Religious faith intensified as central to belonging in a troubled society, and this strengthened both the people's churchgoing and religious culture. It remained a society with little place for diversity, multi-culturality, co-operation and integration of ethnic communities.

By 1972, a year in which 468 people died in sectarian and paramilitary violence, it was clear that Northern Ireland was embarking on a religiously defined sectarian future which British people could not fathom. For Britons viewing Northern Ireland in these and following years, the province symbolised something deeply troubling about religion.[113] The terms 'Protestant' and 'Catholic' came to represent in Ulster notification of sides in community conflict as much as signification of religious belief. Churches and churchmen became identified with sides in the conflict, raising the Revd Dr Ian Paisley to a position of prominence as the voice of militant Protestantism. He more than anybody brought religion directly back into politics in Northern Ireland in a way that reinforced the reality and sense of the confessionalist state – something absent entirely from the rest of the UK. Henceforth, Northern Ireland and its religious divisions were cast as beyond the pale and beyond sense by the vast majority of the British people.

New age practice

The 1960s is regarded as the quintessential decade for the arrival of the 'new age'. By this is meant new religious movements, quasi-religions or personal-development techniques that promoted the enhancement of well-being as well as transcendental experience. What these did was, first, to offer radically different types of religious experience to those leaving the orbit of conventional Christian culture. Second, it provided British popular culture with a sense of a de-centred religiosity in which the concept of religion as authority was effectively and very profoundly destroyed, and, third, it created a fusion between religious experience, celebrity, music and fashion. Religion emerged as having open and affirmative connection with the rest of popular culture, and not something essentially hostile and alien to it.

Religious diversification took a number of forms. One was the development of interest in Eastern religions. Several key religious movements of the decade represented this transition: notably Transcendental Meditation (TM), Hare Krishna (HK) and the figure of the Maharishi Mahesh Yogi. An Eastern mystic and guru, Maharishi came to Britain in the summer of 1967 having already established a reputation in the United States with celebrities such as the actress Mia Farrow. He became feted by leading lights of the sixties' cultural world of music and fashion, notably The Beatles pop group, who had started an interest in the sitar music of India during a visit there a year earlier. And amidst great media attention he nurtured British youth's early interest in Eastern religions, and Transcendental Meditation in particular. By August 1967, George Harrison was already said by Paul McCartney to have found 'a great faith', and the sitar which entered The Beatles sound established a signification of Eastern religion as well as music.

Eastern mysticism, its tempos, its artefacts and its music developed a prominent place in British youth culture in the later 1960s and early 1970s. This did not mean that British youth became devoted to it, as relatively few did. Indeed, many young people regarded it sceptically and comically, but it became a tolerated element in the cultural milieu of street culture, pop concerts and rock festivals. It also signalled the emergence of the new age religions into the mainstream of British consciousness. This created a hunger for less stuffy, more pragmatic and holistic wellbeing movements that could shift the emphasis away from religion, church and doctrine towards self, identity and freedom. TM was one branch of Eastern philosophy and spirituality that attracted many pop stars and media people in the mid- to late 1960s – people whose family faiths, usually Christian, proved inadequate or ill-fitting. Gurus and yogi, or spiritual leaders, proved important to many stars.

Analysis: Maharishi Mahesh Yogi and The Beatles

In late August 1967, *The Times* newspaper announced in its 'Today's Engagements' column that the '*Maharishi Mahesh Yogi gives public lecture on "The essential role of transcendental meditation in modern life", Hilton Hotel, 8p.m.*'[114] Maharishi's talk attracted enormous interest from the press and from British Christian clergy, and aroused the interest of large numbers of leading figures in youth culture – in the worlds of popular music, fashion and underground politics. The visit was a key moment in the emergence of British interest in Eastern religions.

The summer of 1967 was already 'the Summer of Love' that saw the rise of the hippies in San Francisco, the 'flower-power' generation and a moral panic with the youth revolution on both sides of the Atlantic. The British hippy movement of 1965 and 1966 gave way in the following year to a new spiritual focus to the cultural revolution. The press, ever hungry for new stories about leading figures of the hippy revolution, gave enormous publicity to Maharishi, following him about the country and camping outside his retreats in England and in Wales. He was not new to Britain, having opened his first meditation centre in 1959 in Belgravia, and in 1964 was featured in a television interview with Robert Kee in which he described his meditation philosophy. But it was not until he became the Yogi (teacher) to The Beatles that he attained iconic status.

Maharishi extolled the virtues of peace upon the world. He said: 'Expansion of happiness is the purpose of life, and evolution is the process through which it is fulfilled.' He was described by Paul McCartney as 'a giggling little swami who was going round the world to promote peace'. Maharishi described his religious philosophy to The Beatles by speaking of the human as like a flower with its stem in the spiritual ground, seeking nutrients. McCartney described the attraction of Maharishi's philosophy as 'his disbelief in a creator God'. Instead, Paul reported:

He said that meditating, you can go down your stem, and, just like the sap, reach the field of nutrients which he called the pool of cosmic consciousness, which was all blissful and all beautiful. The only mistake we make, and he didn't quite put it quite like this, was we fuck up all the time. We don't reach it. We're all so busy playing guitars, or talking politics or reading other people's words or whatever it is, we don't take time.[115]

Maharishi opposed recreational drugs and violent revolutions, fostering a quietist agenda that gave a sceptical establishment some hope that the young could be drawn back from the abyss of social and religious anarchy. Christian church commentators and leaders became interested

Maharishi Mahesh Yogi with The Beatles, family and friends in 1968.
(Getty Images/Hulton Archive)

because they perceived here a link to the ebbing tide of youth religiosity. Clergymen attended in significant numbers a much-publicised meditation seminar in Bangor in North Wales on Transcendental Meditation (TM) held by Maharishi over the bank holiday weekend in August 1967 – a seminar also attended by The Beatles, their wives and partners, as well as Mick Jagger and Marianne Faithfull, where each received their mantra from the Yogi one by one. More sceptical church leaders tended to alight on the significant statement by the Maharishi that TM was 'not a religion', and sought succour at the end of the Bangor conference in a headline in the *Church Times*: 'Their Spiritual Hunger Remains Unsatisfied'. Over the bank holiday weekend also, a gathering of flower people at Woburn Abbey was less sympathetically treated by many churchpeople, being seen as an invasion of Christian space. The Archbishop of Canterbury quickly stepped in to proclaim a concept of 'secular spirituality' – a seeking after religion.[116]

Surrounded by flowers, squatting for TV cameras with his long hair and beard, Maharishi became a visual image of the spiritual side of the music revolution of the later 1960s. Radio and television were quick to exploit the interest. In September 1967, he was interviewed on BBC radio by Malcolm Muggeridge, a conservative Christian commentator, representing and defending the Christian conscience. Maharishi told Muggeridge: 'I want to make progress more fulfilling and more useful to life by the impact of inner silence and increased energy at the same time. We want peace, but not at the cost of progress and peace, but peace that will form the basis of greater activity and yet life in greater fulfilment and more joyfulness. This is what the Spiritual Regeneration Movement has brought – this philosophy – and this is not a new philosophy, I count it to be just the interpretation of the original text of the philosophy of life contained in the books of every religion.'[117] The Yogi's universalist appeal made his novel mysticism seem open and democratic, whilst Muggeridge's conformist Christianity came over as repressive, bombastic and repressive.[118] Two weeks later, Maharishi appeared in a recorded interview with John Lennon and George Harrison on *The Frost Programme* on ITV, in which both Beatles said that they believed in reincarnation. Harrison said: 'I believe in reincarnation. Life and death are still only relative to thought. I believe in rebirth. You keep coming back until you have got it straight. The ultimate thing is to manifest divinity and become one with the Creator.' John Lennon said that he had given up drugs, thought the 'Buddha a groove and Jesus all right', and that Christianity was 'the answer' as well as Transcendental Meditation.[119]

India and the East suddenly became fashionable. In winter and spring of 1968, The Beatles, their wives and some other media stars spent six weeks with Maharishi at his centre (or ashram) at Rishikesh in India. The press camped out watching the 'Fab Four' as they transmogrified into their rather different, late sixties' characters. They emerged as icons of a rapidly spreading counter-culture that was soon to crystallise as an establishment youth culture. Learning how to meditate for increasingly long sessions, leading to significant spiritual experiences, Paul McCartney recalled one event creating 'a very very blissful feeling': 'That was the most pleasant, the most relaxed I ever got, for a few minutes I really felt so light, so floating, so complete.'[120] The Indian adventure ended in disharmony between some of The Beatles and Maharishi, but TM remained important in the lives of many of the stars. George Harrison remained strongly attached to TM philosophy, but it became less important to the other Beatles. For the youth of many nations, The Beatles opened a route to TM, Hare Krishna and other Eastern mystical foundations (mostly related to Hinduism).

The episode of The Beatles and Maharishi Mahesh Yogi gave the first widespread media exposure to central ideas of the new age, making it very quickly a permanent feature of British culture. These ideas were to transform notions about what religion 'is'. These included the de-centering of any one religion, and the use of different religions as not just equivalent but perfectly combinable routes on spiritual quests. But they also included the notion that there was no necessary culmination, or point of redemption or salvation, as Christianity had it. The Maharishi said that the problem of the age was 'spiritual poverty in the midst of material plenty', and thereby appealed to a generation of young people who had associated Christian formalist religion with austerity. The young were then seeking a liberating and non-disciplinary spirituality to accompany the consumer riches of the 1960s. Religion should accompany personal freedom, not personal restraint.

The Glasgow-born singer Lulu was introduced by the wife of Beatles drummer Ringo Starr to readings about Eastern mysticism, and when The Beatles returned from India she was advised by John Lennon to meditate. Lulu then joined Patti Boyd (Beatle George Harrison's wife) and Cynthia Lennon (wife of Beatle John Lennon) at a TM centre in London, and she became a devotee after joining 600 people at Heathrow Airport for a fleeting visit by Gurumayi Chivilasananda, the spiritual head of the Siddha Yoga Foundation. This she found a strong spiritual moment. 'It was such a divine feeling,' she wrote, and went home to mediate. 'I did my yogic breathing and a bit of hatha yoga stretching. I sat down, lit the candle, and then suddenly it happened. I went into a state of meditation for the first time. At the same moment, I was totally aware of what was happening around me. ... An energy had been woken inside of me. Whatever path I was looking for, whatever I was seeking, now became clear. I could see the way ahead.'[121]

Eastern mysticism produced diverse icons in the late 1960s. In August 1968, three married couples, all devotees of Krishna Consciousness (more properly known as the International Society for Krishna Consciousness, or ISKCON), came to London, and after garnering support from George Harrison and other Beatles, the Hare Krishna movement obtained enormous press publicity in 1969. George Harrison recorded the HK mantra at Apple Studios, released it in August 1969, and on the first day sold 70,000 copies, reached the top 20 chart, leading to HK devotees appearing on *Top of the Pops*. George Harrison recalled of the experience: 'I figured this is the space age, with airplanes and everything. If everyone can go around the world on their holidays, there's no reason why a mantra can't go a few miles as well. So the idea was to try to spiritually infiltrate society, so to speak.'[122] This was immensely influential amongst British young people. For a tiny minority, it led to experimentation with HK as a spiritual movement, making it widely known across Europe. Though only in the region of 350 received initiation into HK in Britain between 1976 and 1983,[123] the sight on British streets of dedicated devotees, in saffron robes with shaven heads and hair tails dancing in single file, chanting the HK mantra and chiming percussion instruments, confirmed religious issues as being part of popular culture, shattering narrow conceptions of religion. The notion of religion was de-coupled from authority and social conformity, and raised the vision of a wide and variegated spirituality. The new age was the beginning of what some sociologists now refer to as the spiritual revolution, which in the early twenty-first century is still going on.

A second development is what might be called the 'Christian new age' – responses to these cultural trends and the evolution of new religious movements *within* Christianity. For one thing, the rise of the new age introduced a sensitivity to spiritual issues, with medieval Christian mystics such as Julian of Norwich acquiring renewed attention for striking similarities to new age mysticism.[124] More influentially, de-Christianisation gave power to ecumenical initiatives – which included meetings between church leaders, joint weeks of prayer, and, in 1963, the appearance of Anglican pilgrimage parties going to the French Roman Catholic shrine at Lourdes.[125] Catholics from across Britain were making the trek to Lourdes in coaches from the early 1960s in large numbers – though this was often a combination of holiday and devotion. A retired Catholic school teacher from the Western Isles took her daughter when, after her long years of teaching, she was 'free to have a bit of fun'. The daughter got food poisoning and 'very nearly reversed the whole Lourdes claim of curing all ills, by going there healthy and coming back half-dead'.[126]

Faced with a popular culture that rejected religious pomposity, pop culture was brought by many clergy into the churches. By 1961, aware of alienated youth, churchmen were copying experiments overseas – such as one from Sydney in Australia that created youth projects with trendy attractions, including a milkbar and restaurant, TV lounge and games rooms, with a chapel to the side as the goal of the attractions.[127] By 1963, there were ideas amongst church leaders about how pop music might change church music, with leading music experts agreeing in principle but wary of bringing the mood of a nightclub into church.[128] Most notably, the Salvation Army supplemented their famed brass-band musicianship with a Christian pop band, The Joystrings, whose members were officially allowed by the army to wear trendier clothes and to let the male members grow their hair long. They were the inspiration behind the rise of what became derisively known as 'happy-clappy' Christian worship, with guitars and new hymns mimicking the tempo of sixties' pop music. Accompanying this type of development was a frenzy of experimentation in the mid- and late 1960s – church hall dances, coffee clubs and the 'discothèque'. One of the first in the Church of England was at St Mary's in Woolwich in late 1966, where a disco, restaurant and assembly lounge for Anglicans and a presbyterian congregation was conducted in the crypt.[129] Experimentation of many types developed – including the Christian retreat (such as the Benifold retreat that lasted from 1963 to 1970).[130]

One consequence was the rise of media-savvy in the churches. The use of modern advertising techniques entered evangelisation and church publicity in 1969 and 1970, as it did many moral issues of the day (most famously the sexual-health campaign poster that showed a 'pregnant' man). The Ten Commandments got turned into photo-montage story boards, and a glossy magazine, *Bible Today*, sought to sell the Christian message with modern magazine layout and stunning photography.

The greatest product of the Christian new age was what one newspaper described in 1963 as a 'strange new sect' – one that observed 'a form of worship bordering on the supernatural'.[131] This was the charismatic renewal movement within Christianity. Many influences fed into it, including the conservatives of the Moral Rearmament organisation. It claimed to be reviving 'the gifts of the Holy Spirit' that had been emphasised in early Christianity, and so claimed to be a renewal of something very old and traditional. However, it appeared to those within and outwith the churches as highly radical, and to many as dangerous. The charismatics were given to an emotional and ecstatic form of worship, with voluble and spontaneous outbursts of prayer and song, and with speaking in tongues. From the early 1960s to the early 1970s, it was seen by many in the Christian churches as weird and even unchristian. By the end of the 1960s, its appearance within many churches was unsettling their leaders and many worshippers alike, and it was widely regarded as dissolving boundaries between forms of worship, between denominations, and over doctrines and theologies. It often appeared as house groups or house churches, challenging traditional church authority. Indeed, it was this absence of structures, rules, order and restraint that left it categorised with the more outlandish phenomena of the new age, and it was to take a long time to achieve a wider acceptance in British culture. Yet, when in the 1980s it was to achieve greater respectability, it was to prove to be one of the major characteristics of British Christianity towards the end of the century.[132]

Another response to both de-Christianisation and the new age was an encouragement to ecumenicalism – co-operation and moves to union by the churches. Two problems restrained this. First, the Church of England and the Church of Scotland, each with the standing of an established or, in the Scottish case, a national church, found it hard to jettison their status. Second, the big churches had to choose whether to unite towards High Church (or Catholic) traditions or towards Low Church (more Protestant reformed) traditions. A proposal in 1963 for Anglican–Methodist union met with divided views in the British press, but talks on union proceeded.[133] Then, very quickly, High Church union with the Roman Catholics came up the agenda, when in 1967, a joint commission on union possibilities was set up. Two separate and conflicting church-union talks were going on simultaneously. Third, ecumenicalism failed to catch public interest. A Church of England campaign, too euphemistically entitled 'People Next Door', was a flop in 1967.[134] Ecumenicalism tended to alienate the worshipper in the pew, who was threatened with being moved to a faraway church, whilst those who had already left were not attracted back.

A more controversial issue was the new fear of Christian cults, brainwashing and even kidnapping young people. Newspaper and television exposés of both Christian and non-Christian religious groups, which had seemingly startling beliefs and practices, usually living in isolated communes, closed houses or overseas hideaways, started to foster a secondary form of Christian panic in the later 1960s and 1970s. Groups like the Moonies and the Findhorn Community in Scotland became the object of exposés and gossip. (See pages 318–19.) This concern increased in the 1970s, and tended to colour a great deal of the treatment of religious innovation in the British media and the mainstream Christian churches. The formation of new sects was not, however, of major numerical importance, and many of their devotees · were in any event temporary recruits. In essence, the new age was conceived in this period as about sects with alternative lifestyles and bizarre doctrines. The longer term would show that it was the diffusion through British culture of the new age as a doctrinaire-free approach to individual spirituality that was to be its more lasting significance.

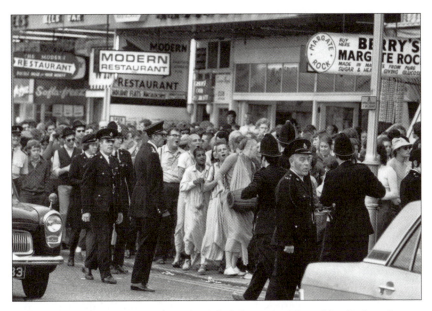

A Hare Krishna band in Margate at bank holiday 1972. The public display of spirituality was changing with the common sight of saffron-robed HK bands on British city streets in the late 1960s and early 1970s. (Topfoto)

Dismembering the Christian state

The period from 1960 to 1970 witnessed a frenzy of legislation that effectively de-Christianised and liberalised British law and society. The legislation was introduced initially amidst great controversy, but latterly was rushed through in 1967–8 with amazing ease. In large part, a crisis of confidence befell Christian conservatism in those years as the landmarks of society started to crumble with disconcerting speed. In a mood of depression, and assailed by liberals within who argued for change, the forces of church reaction largely fell silent during the nation's greatest moral and cultural revolution.

The first signpost of change was the 1960 Betting and Gaming Act which legalised offcourse betting. For the churches, it spelt the demise of one major plank in puritan campaigning. 'Almost overnight,' the *Church Times* commented a few years' later, 'Britain has become more addicted to gambling than any other country in the world.' The Act, in its view, 'has gone a long way to undermining the moral standards and social security of this country'.[135] At the same time, moral censorship fell apart. In 1960, Penguin Books Ltd was tried in court for publishing an obscene book, D. H. Lawrence's *Lady Chatterley's Lover*. The forces of liberalism stood up to the challenge, with Roy Jenkins MP, a Labour Party intellectual, appearing in defence of the book as art, not pornography. Also appearing for the defence was *Honest to God* author John Robinson, the Bishop of Woolwich. Penguin was acquitted, and the trial was a famous victory for the freedom of publishers. But the initial response was sustained efforts by the censorious state. In October 1961, the Moral Law Defence Association campaigned to amend legislation like the Obscene Publications Act 1959 to stamp out pornography and 'elevate' the moral works of British literature, films and plays. Interestingly, many religious groups opposed not just the move but the workings of undemocratic pressure groups like this.[136]

In Edinburgh in 1962, there was a parallel trial to that of *Lady Chatterley* when a nude model appeared at a drama conference at the Edinburgh Festival; the model was charged with obscenity and the organiser (the publisher John Calder) was charged with aiding the crime. Once again, church figures backed the prosecution, whilst artists and liberals such as Magnus Magnusson appeared for the defence; one witness, a sculptor, produced a palm-sized statue of a nude, persuaded the magistrate that the naked body was not obscene, and the case was dismissed on the grounds that no crime had taken place. By 1965–7, liberals in the Scottish churches were engaging with the radical promoter-entrepreneurs of art and drama behind the Festival Fringe, including Jim Haynes, the promoter of the experimental Traverse Theatre, who was told by one minister that 'the contemporary prophets may more be found in you, the writers and the artists, than from people like me in the pulpits'.[137]

Most of the British mainstream churches were by 1967 bending to the wind of change and accepted that theatre censorship was going to end.[138] With massive pressures from the theatrical community for freedom of artistic expression, and the nudity breaking through in experimental theatre, theatre censorship was becoming something of a dead letter and was finally abolished in 1968. Immediately, commercial theatre took over from experimental theatre, with musicals and plays breaking all the taboos about displaying sex and drug-taking – including *Hair* (1968) and *Tommy* (1969). Most symbolic of all, few seemed to notice when in 1967 Roy Jenkins abolished the 1697 statute crime of blasphemy, and though this still left the separate common law offence of blasphemous libel, it did much to mark the passing of the state's interest in enforcing the tenets of religion.[139] (See pages 250–1.)

The state made sweeping reforms to laws to do with sex. The reform of laws against homosexuality had been signalled for ten years in the recommendations of the Wolfenden Committee, but no government dared to implement it until Home Secretary Roy Jenkins bit the bullet in 1967–8. The Sexual Offences Act, when it was launched in July 1967, attracted considerable approval for removing the furtiveness and criminalisation of so many in high places in the British establishment. The *Church Times* called it a 'great triumph' for campaigners, and implied a welcome for the de-criminalisation, but it asserted the need of the Church of England to continue to regard homosexuality as an offence in moral law and as contributing to the advance of 'permissive morality'.[140] Amongst the legislation, divorce was made easier, with the removal of blame (that one party to a marriage had to be to blame by violence, desertion or adultery before a divorce would be granted), and divorce was permitted on the grounds of irretrievable breakdown of marriage after only two years if both parties consented. Though many in the Church of England and the Mothers' Union opposed this, the opposition to it was not as sharp as it was to other features of liberalisation.[141]

One of the most controversial elements of this programme was the Abortion Act of 1967 (the Medical Termination of Pregnancies Act), promoted by the youngest MP, the Liberal David Steel. Steel's bill divided religious opinion. Liberals like the Methodist Lord Soper and the Bishop of Woolwich supported it, seeking 'the best choice for the mother'. Michael Ramsey, Archbishop of Canterbury, tried to compromise, arguing for balance between the welfare of mother and child, but signalling before its passage that he would oppose it.[142] Others opposed it too, and in the wake of this bill, the Society for the Protection of the Unborn Child was created in January 1967, proposed by the Bishop of Bath and Wells and fourteen others in a letter to the right-wing *Daily Telegraph* newspaper. Arguing that abortion should not be available to mothers 'except in cases of urgent necessity',[143] the society was to develop in the late twentieth century as one of the most effective and outspoken agencies of conservative morality in British society.

In other spheres, religious education in schools was retained by the state despite secular pressure, but it became in most schools by the end of the decade a mere shadow of the Christian instruction it had formerly been. In another sphere, there was mounting pressure from the public, commercial sport and business for the state to abandon Christian restrictions on Sunday activities. Though this was effectively prevented in

England and Wales until the later 1980s, Sunday activities in Scotland had been largely suppressed by community pressure, not by law, resulting in a bonanza of Sunday shop-opening and new leisure pursuits developing. Even in England, Sunday league football mushroomed in the late 1960s and 1970s, and by 1973 the British Christian Sunday of church worship and no play was effectively dying. In addition, parliamentary acts liberalised marriage (making it easier), but also abolished breach of promise (de-criminalising the act of one party in an engaged couple calling off the marriage), and de-criminalised suicide. Some of these measures impinged acutely on Christian doctrine, liberalising Britain's moral law. In all, there was a welter of legislation that dismantled the state's endorsement of Christian principles in daily life and in the organisation of family formation.

The churches were obsessed with sex in the sixties. In early 1967, the *Church Times* identified that the dismantling of the Christian state was proceeding more by private members' bill than by government bill – such as one which extended the rights of local authorities to provide public advice on birth control to single women. This, the *Church Times* argued, 'may be interpreted as official encouragement of sexual promiscuity'.[144] The people were disregarding Christian teaching, identity and restraint. As a result, the churches could not stop judging and berating the people – notably young people – over sex. The word 'permissive' was hardly off the lips of churchpeople, and there is no doubting the hostility, bewilderment and sheer fear of the churches in general as they faced the loss of the centuries-long Christian state. As the sixties came to an end, one churchman reflected that the next decade was starting in anxiety about 'the moral chaos into which British society has been plunged'.[145] The critical changes had been crammed into a five-year period between 1963 and 1968. Of these years a former Church of England ordinand remarked: 'Back in 1963 my contemporary ordinands at King's College gave the Beatles and their culture a few months of life before decline and extinction – and that was five years ago. Now it cannot but seem to a young person that by and large the Church is making clumsy attempts to meet the demands of the modern world based on an ideology better suited to the Victorians.'[146] Because the churches put so much repressive, negative effort into their conception of religion as sexual restraint, they perpetrated much of the damage, seemingly irreparable, to popular understanding of what the churches thought about faith and spirituality. The people could not agree with this. Come the mid-1970s, the people's slide from the churches seemed to be a slide from all organised faith.

Notes

1 *British Weekly*, 28 December 1961.

2 *Church Times*, 6 September 1963; the launch of the *Daily Leader* is described in ibid., 18 October 1963.

3 These figures were produced by John Highet, the pioneer of religious censuses in post-war Britain. He lectured at Oxford that English sociologists needed to conduct some basic research on religious affiliation and practice. *British Weekly*, 15 February 1962, 9 August 1962.

4 Ibid., 18 January 1961.

5 J. Springhall, B. Fraser and M. Hoare, *Sure & Stedfast: A History of the Boys Brigade 1883 to 1983* (London and Glasgow, Collins, 1983), pp. 235–6

6 Quoted in M. Eaton, 'What became of the Children of Mary?', in M.P. Hornsby-Smith (ed.), *Catholics in England 1950–2000* (London, Cassell, 1999), p. 227.

7 D. Willcocks, 'Church colleges: keeping the faith,' *Borderlands* Iss. 3 (2004), p. 10.

8 R.D. Anderson *et al.*, *The University of Edinburgh* (Edinburgh, Edinburgh University Press, 2003), pp. 201–5; Muggeridge, speaking on BBC Radio 4 *Archive Hour*, May 2005.

9 *Church Times*, 30 August 1963.

10 There was already a small tradition of allowing celebrated Christians from other traditions to take Anglican Communion.

11 HMSO 1977 Cmnd. 6753, Home Office Report of the [Annan] Committee on the Future of Broadcasting, pp. 316–17; *Church Times*, 1 February 1963.

12 Ibid., 18 January 1963.

13 H. Carpenter, *That Was Satire That Was: The Satire Boom of the 1960s* (London, Victor Gollancz, 2000), p. 244.

14 *Church Times*, 6 January 1967.

15 Ibid., 10 February 1967.

16 Ibid., 23 June 1966, 7 July 1966.

17 *The Times*, 2 June 1966.

18 Ibid., 18 June 1966.

19 Ibid., 4 June 1966.

20 Figures from ibid., 4 July 1966.

21 *Church Times*, 11 January 1963.

22 Ibid., 8 November 1963, 1 November 1963, 15 February 1963, 1 and 8 December 1967, 3 July 1970.

23 Letter from Mrs Glen to Secretary of State for Scotland, 8 July 1961, National Archives of Scotland HH 43/194.

24 C. Hall, *Twice Around the Bay* (Edinburgh, Birlinn, 2001), p. 118.

25 J.A.T. Robinson and D.L. Edwards, *The Honest to God Debate* (London, SCM Press, 1963).

26 *Church Times*, 22 and 29 March 1963.

27 Ibid., 29 March 1963.

28 Ibid., 29 March 1963.

29 22 March, quoted in ibid., 29 March 1963.

30 Ibid., 5 April 1963, 26 April 1963, 25 August 1967.

31 Letter to ibid., 4 January 1970. J. Robinson, *Christian Freedom in a Permissive Society* (London, SCM Press, 1970).

32 Robinson and Edwards, *The Honest to God Debate*, p. 55.

33 R. Towler, *The Need for Certainty: A Sociological Study of Conventional Religion* (London, RKP, 1984), pp. 91–2.

34 J.A.T, Robinson, *The New Reformation?* (London, SCM Press, 1965), p. 106.

35 P. van Buren, *The Secular Meaning of the Gospel Based on an Analysis of its Language* (London, SCM Press, 1963); D.L. Mundy, *The Idea of A Secular Society* (Oxford, Oxford University Press, 1963); H. Cox, *The Secular City* (London, SCM Press, 1966).

36 Valerie Pitt of the Church of England, *Church Times*, 22 November 1963.

37 A. Kenny, *A Path from Rome: An Autobiography* (London, Sidgwick and Jackson, 1985), pp. 153–6.

38 *Church Times*, 8 November 1963, 6 January 1967.

39 Ibid., 8 September 1967.

40 Ibid., 6 January 1967, 15 September 1967, 2 January 1970, 25 August 1967.

41 P. Sissons, *The Social Significance of Church Membership in the Burgh of Falkirk* (Edinburgh, Saint Andrew Press, 1973), appendix.

42 C.G. Brown, *The Death of Christian Britain: Understanding Secularisation 1800–2000* (London, Routledge, 2001), p. 191

43 Figures from P.A. Welsby, *A History of the Church of England 1945–1980*

(Oxford, Oxford University Press, 1984), p. 104; Brown, *Death of Christian Britain*, p. 168.

44 S. Cohen, *Folk Devils and Moral Panics: the creation of the Mods and Rockers* (London, McGibbon and Kee, 1972).

45 *Church Times*, 6 December 1963.

46 L. Purves, *Holy Smoke: Religion and Roots: A personal memoir* (London, Hodder & Stoughton, 1998), p. 117.

47 P. Laslett, *The World We Have Lost* (London, Methuen, 1965).

48 P. Jennings, *The Living Village: A report on rural life in England and Wales, based on actual village scrapbooks* (London, Hodder & Stoughton, 1968), pp. 174, 177.

49 R. Blythe, *Akenfield: Portrait of an English Village* (London, Literary Guild, 1969), p. 68.

50 SOHCA, respondents 006/Mrs G.3 (b.1925) and Mrs I.2 (b.1907).

51 SOHCA, respondent 006/Mrs C.2 (b.1912), pp. 22-3.

52 C. Davies, *Clean Clothes for Sunday* (Lavenham, Terence Dalton, 1974), p. 25.

53 *British Weekly*, 27 December 1962.

54 Ibid., 13 December 1962.

55 *Church Times*, 15 March 1963. On the Cambridge group and the theologies of sex, see Welsby, *Church of England*, pp. 110 et seq.

56 Quoted in J. Lewis and K. Kiernan, 'The boundaries between marriage, nonmarriage, and parenthood: changes in behaviour in postwar Britain', *Journal of Family History* 21 (1996), p. 376.

57 Professor John G. McKenzie, writing in *British Weekly*, 13 December 1962.

58 *Church Times*, 18 January 1963.

59 Ibid., 27 September 1963, 8 November 1963.

60 Ibid., 22 November 1963.

61 Revd Cuthbert Bardsley, Bishop of Coventry, quoted in ibid., 4 October 1963.

62 Ibid., 11 October 1963.

63 Ibid., 11 and 18 October 1963.

64 Ibid., 6 December 1963, 8 November 1963.

65 Quoted in G.I.T. Machin, *Churches and Social Issues in Twentieth-century Britain* (Oxford, Clarendon, 1998), p. 195.

66 A.M.G. Stephenson, *Anglicanism and the Lambeth Conferences* (London, SPCK, 1978), p. 209; Machin, *Churches and Social Issues*, p. 196.

67 Lorna Sage, *Bad Blood* (London, Fourth Estate, 2001), p. 270.

68 Quoted in J. Green, *IT: Sex since the Sixties* (London, Secker & Warburg, 1993), p. 10.

69 A different, more pill-centred explanation of change in sexual behaviour amongst *married* women is to be found in H. Cook, *The Long Sexual Revolution: English women, sex and contraception 1800–1975* (Oxford, Oxford University Press, 2004). Cf. E.R. Watkins, *On the Pill: An oral history of oral contraceptives in America 1950–1970* (Baltimore, John Hopkins University Press, 1998).

70 Lewis and Kiernan, 'Boundaries', pp. 373–4.

71 Mary Ingham, quoted in Cook, *Long Sexual Revolution*, pp. 287–8. Data from pp. 268–9.

72 Both quotations from ibid., p. 271.

73 Quoted in Green, *IT*, pp. 60–1, 63, 266; Lulu, *I Don't Want to Fight* (London, TimeWarner, 2002), p. 123.

74 *Reports to the General Assembly of the Church of Scotland*, 1970, pp. 399–410.

75 *Church Times*, 11, 18 August 1967, 3 April 1970.

76 Ibid., 10 November 1967.

77 B. Aspinwall, *The Catholic Experience in North Ayrshire* (Irvine, John Geddes printers, 2002), p. 119.

78 *The Tablet*, 27 March 1965.

79 Purves, *Holy Smoke*, pp. 132–4.

80 *The Tablet*, 8 May 1965.

81 Quoted in J. Marshall, 'Catholic family life', in M.P. Hornsby-Smith (ed.), *Catholics in England 1950–2000* (London, Cassell, 1999), p. 75.

82 J. Fulton, 'Young adult core Catholics', ibid., p. 80.

83 D. Lodge, *How Far Can You Go?* (Harmondsworth, Penguin, 1981), p. 113.

84 Such as R.R. Williams, Bishop of Leicester; *Church Times*, 15 November 1963.

85 Ibid., 21 July 1967.

86 Ibid., 20 September 1963.

87 *Church Times*, 16 June 1967.

88 Obituary of Ian McColl, *Express* editor, *The Guardian*, 6 July 2005.

89 Col. J. Hughes, quoted in Springhall, Fraser and Hoare, *Sure & Stedfast*, p. 225.

90 http://www.mediawatchuk.org/nvala.htm.

91 D. Nash, *Blasphemy in Modern Britain 1789 to the present* (Aldershot, Ashgate, 1999), pp. 239–56.

92 S. Bruce, 'Mary Whitehouse' (obit.), *The Herald*, 24 November 2001; *The Guardian*, 24 November 2001.

93 *Church Times*, 1 September 1967.

94 Machin, *Churches and Social Issues*, p. 214.

95 *The Times*, 8 November 1962; *Church Times*, 11 October 1963.

96 Ibid., 11 October 1963.

97 Ibid.

98 'Women in Holy Orders', quoted in *The Times*, 15 December 1966.

99 Testimony of Ryland A. Campbell, Birmingham Black Oral History Project, Birmingham City Archive and Special Collections, Information Services, University of Birmingham (hereafter BBOHP), PT6, p. 21.

100 Testimony of Ranjit Sondhi, BBOHP PT16, pp. 5–6.

101 *Church Times*, 15 November 1963.

102 Numbers registered with local authorities. K. Knott, 'Other major religious traditions', in T. Thomas (ed.), *The British: their religious beliefs and practices 1800–1986* (London, Routledge, 1986), p. 140.

103 An editorial in *The Telegraph and Argus* 6 October 1966, quoted in R. Singh, *Sikhs and Sikhism in Britain Fifty Years On: The Bradford Perspective* (Bradford, Bradford Libraries, 2000), p. 111fn.

104 The Motor Cycle Crash Helmets (Religious Exemptions) Act 1976.

105 Knott, 'Major religious traditions', p. 141.

106 Quoted in *Church Times*, 6 September 1963.

107 *British Weekly*, 13 December 1962

108 *Church Times*, 11 January 1963.

109 Ibid., 22 February 1963.

110 Ibid., 22 March 1963, 6 September 1963, 18 October 1963. Oxfam was founded in 1947.

111 Ibid., 27 January 1967.

112 T. Hennessey, *A History of Northern Ireland 1920–1996* (London, Palgrave, 1997), pp. 117–18.

113 J. Hickey, *Religion and the Northern Ireland Problem* (Dublin, Gill and Macmillan, 1984), pp. 23–8.

114 *The Times*, 24 August 1967.

115 Quotes from B. Miles, *Paul McCartney: Many Years from Now* (London, Vintage, 1998), pp. 400–2.

116 *Church Times*, 8, 22 September 1967.

117 Quoted in P. Mason, *Maharishi Mahesh Yogi: The Biography of the Man who Gave Transcendental Meditation to the World* (orig. 1994, online text copy 2004, at www.paulmason.info), chapters 12–14.

118 *The Times*, 23 September 1967.

119 Ibid., 30 September 1967.

120 Quoted in Miles, *Paul McCartney*, p. 414.

121 Lulu, *Fight*, pp. 218–19.

122 Quoted in Knott, *My Sweet Lord: The Hare Krishna Movement* (Wellingborough, The Acquarium Press, 1986), p. 34.

123 Ibid., p. 47.

124 *The Times*, 5 May 1973.

125 *Church Times*, 18 January 1963.

126 Hall, *Twice Around the Bay*, p. 126.

127 *British Weekly*, 28 September 1961.

128 Professor Arthur Hutchings, head of department of music, University of Durham, *Church Times*, 13 December 1963.

129 Ibid., 27 January 1967.

130 Ibid., 26 June 1970.

131 *Scottish Sunday Mail*, quoted in D. Bebbington, *Evangelicalism in Modern Britain: A History from the 1730s to the 1980s* (London, Unwin Hyman, 1989), p. 229; D.W. Bebbington, 'Evangelicalism and spirituality in twentieth-century Protestant Nonconformity', in A.P.F. Sell and A.R. Cross (eds), *Protestant Nonconformity in the Twentieth Century* (Carlisle, Paternoster Press, 2003), pp. 210–13.

132 Bebbington, *Evangelicalism in Modern Britain,* pp. 181–228; Hylson-Smith, *Churches*, pp. 212–22.

133 *Church Times*, 1 March 1963.

134 Ibid., 1 March 1963, 6 January, 3 February, 16 June, 20 January 1967.

135 Ibid., 27 January 1967.

136 *British Weekly*, 19 October 1961.

137 Denis Duncan in ibid., 21 April 1966. I am grateful to Angela Bartie for permission to quote this material from her doctoral thesis.

138 *Church Times*, 30 June 1967.

139 D. Nash, *Blasphemy in Modern Britain 1789 to the present* (Aldershot, Ashgate, 1999), p. 239.

140 *Church Times*, 14 July 1967.

141 Ibid., 15 February 1963.

142 Ibid., 20 January 1967, 28 August 1967.

143 Ibid., 13 January 1967.

144 Ibid., 6 January 1967.

145 Ibid., 2 January 1970.

146 Chris Simpson, writing in *The Times*, 11 May 1968.

CHAPTER 7

The shaping of secular society, 1974–2000

The last quarter of the twentieth century witnessed the increasing marginalisation of religion from British public life, intellectualism and popular culture. Religion appeared to become steadily more unremarkable and less remarked upon in daily life and rhetoric. As sixties' youth grew older, their values became slowly dominant as the drift from the traditional Christian churches continued and as the new age developed as a more embedded element in secular culture. Yet, the degree of religious tolerance and indifference could be overstated. In 1985, the heir to the throne, the Prince of Wales, had his request to attend a papal mass in the Vatican turned down by Buckingham Palace for fear of Protestant objections at home.[1] By the 1990s, increasing militancy amongst the shrinking churches was becoming evident, including the rising influence of fundamentalism.

Adapting to de-Christianisation

The major religious trend of the period was that the Christian faithful dwindled in Britain. Church adherence fell by about 45 per cent and churchgoing by about one-third.[2] Those who were leaving were overwhelmingly female. The only significant data on gender and churchgoing were collected in Scotland, where between 1984 and 2002 there was a net loss of 168,560 churchgoers over 15 years of age, of whom 129,040 (or 77 per cent) were female.[3] In terms of age, the haemorrhage of the young continued, sustaining the reversal of the situation in the 1950s when teenagers were amongst the most active in terms of church connection. No parts of mainland Britain were untouched by significant de-

Christianisation, and only in Northern Ireland was the fall in church allegiance and practice relatively modest. Overall, Christian culture was progressively contracting, as society as a whole pushed its Christian heritage further and further from the rules of social behaviour and personal identity.

No Christian tradition was left untouched by all of this. The decline of religious training of the young during the 1960s and 1970s took its toll on numbers in the later decades. The proportion of Sheffield University students reporting 'some religious upbringing' fell from 94 per cent in 1961 to 51 per cent in 1985. Moreover, an ever-increasing proportion of those people were *rejecting* that upbringing. At Christ's College, Cambridge, in 1973, 38 per cent of undergraduates called themselves Christians, but 52 per cent described themselves as agnostics, atheists or humanists.[4] The church colleges of education had formerly been a very large sector of further and higher education, but this shrunk in the 1980s and 1990s. Whereas in 1974 there were 27 Anglican colleges alone in England and Wales, this had fallen by 2004 to only ten (plus two ecumenical and three Catholic colleges).[5] This decline may have been a significant factor in why the young were leaving the churches and its organisations in droves. Religious education in schools was continuing, but was clearly not sustaining the interest of the young in the Christian faith. The church youth sector was faring little better. One calculation is that in 1953 around 33 per cent of 14-year-old children in England were enrolled in Church of England or Nonconformist Sunday schools. By the 1970s, the figure was down to 15 per cent, and by 2000, with Church of England Sunday schools virtually wiped out, the figure was probably less than 5 per cent.

Youth leaders were stumped. Colonel J. Hughes told the Northern Ireland Council of the Boys' Brigade in 1974: 'The young today are different from you and me. They are also different from us when we were young. They are different from any younger generation that has ever existed before. They are the object of a cult.'[6] This symbolised the generation and culture gap between young and old, and by 1982 the numbers of boys in the BBs had fallen 42 per cent since 1960.[7] Attempts were made to re-evangelise the country. In 1984, in the midst of economic recession, Billy Graham brought another crusade, his 'Mission England', and enjoyed some high attendances at meetings in the unemployment-hit north of England. But the cultural impact was less in the media, and though 61 per cent of those coming forward to make a 'decision for Christ' were under 25 years of age, the weakening of Christian culture amongst the young continued.[8]

Whilst Protestant churches bore the brunt of the slide from worship before 1973, and continued to decline thereafter, the Roman Catholic Church started to fare worse. The number of Roman Catholic Mass attendances in England between 1965 and 1996 declined by 42 per cent, and child baptisms by 44 per cent. Most starkly, between 1960 and 1996 Catholic-solemnised marriages fell by 63 per cent.[9] Even in conservative parts of the country like Scotland, Catholicism suffered as much as Protestantism.[10] Church organisations fared no better, and usually worse. The Union of Catholic Mothers declined from a peak membership of 28,000 in 1966 to 9,723 in 1994, and the Catholic Women's League from a 1964 high of 23,800 to 6,227 in 1997.[11] The priesthood suffered loss, as was the case in most Christian churches, as fewer young men turned to a religious vocation. The numbers of Catholic priests fell in England and Wales by 27 per cent between 1965 and 1996, and the proportion of Catholic teachers in Catholic secondary schools fell (from 66 per cent in 1980 to 58 per cent in 1996).[12] In all sorts of ways, change seemed to dilute the intensity of Catholic religious practice. In the four decades since the reforming Second Vatican Council of 1962–5, traditional practices of fasting and abstinence in the Catholic Church were effectively dropped, regulations regarding holy days of obligation were eased and there ensued a huge decline in private confession. New practices were introduced – such as the 'kiss of peace' and female altar servers – but the liturgical practices of Benediction and the Stations of the Cross all declined sharply.[13]

Not only was the crisis of Christianity deepening, it was taking new forms. Some of these were fundamental to faith. In the small Society of Friends (the Quakers), there was in the later twentieth century the development of a trend towards de-Christianisation – to literally seeing the Church as representing an ethical and moral standpoint based on monotheism (a belief in a single God), but one which did not necessarily require belief in Jesus Christ as the Redeemer. This trend was unnerving some Quakers, creating a small breakaway, yet attracting increasing numbers with a flexible and modern morality that resonated with experiences in a rapidly changing world. By the turn of the century, it was suggesting to some commentators that the Quakers in a new 'secular' version might be a factor behind the tentative signs of church growth.[14]

In other sorts of seemingly small but fundamental ways, the culture of Christianity was sliding away. One was the sudden decline of biblical forenames given to babies – literally the decline of the *Christian name*. The names of the Christian apostles – mainly the popular ones of John, Andrew, Peter, Matthew, Mark – plus the biblical name David accounted in 1900 for 37 per cent of baby boys registered with the top-ten most popular names in Scotland, and still stood in 1950 for 32 per cent and in 1975 for 27 per cent. But the figure then collapsed in 2000 to less than 4 per cent.[15] More obviously, perhaps, religious culture in the broadcast media waned perceptibly. Though the television 'God-slot' on Sunday evenings survived on the two main channels (BBC1 and ITV1) until around 2000, religion was virtually absent from the mushrooming new channels (terrestrial, satellite and cable). In 1968, 40 per cent of British TV viewers claimed to turn on to watch a religious programme; by 1987, this figure had dropped to only 7 per cent.[16] Guidelines for broadcasting were modernised in 1977 with three modified aims: to reflect the principal, mostly Christian (though not exclusively) religious traditions of Britain; to present experience related to religious interpretation or dimensions of life; and to meet the religious interests of those outside or on the fringe of the churches. This finally broke the notion that religion in Britain was synonymous with Christianity, and, in the words of the Annan Report, 'it no longer requires broadcasting to pretend that it is'.[17] One consequence was that state controls continued to prevent proselytising broadcasts and church channels until almost the end of the century, when liberalisation brought a few into being. However, unlike in the USA, there was virtually no demand for these from audiences.

Religious marriage also collapsed – from 70 per cent of all marriages in England and Wales in 1962, to 54 per cent in 1973 and then to 39 per cent in 1997.[18] Yet, this occurred against the background of the rise of 'the romantic marriage' – the lavish celebration of weddings defined by fine clothes, location and scale. This was an ironic, seemingly contradictory, accompaniment to the overall secularisation and decline of marriage, observable in the astonishing rise in the 1990s of the overseas marriage. Couples were routinely getting married at holiday resorts in the Caribbean and in the Indian or Pacific Oceans, with only the closest of relatives and friends in attendance, but no statistics seem to exist on the scale of this phenomenon. One indicator is the astonishing rise of the runaway marriage at Gretna Green, where traditionally English child couples under 18 years old, who failed to obtain parental permission to marry, were married by the blacksmith. The myth was a shallow one, but it became powerful. Official statistics show that between 1855 and 1975 there was essentially no romantic tradition associated with Gretna – with marriages numbering less than ten a year until the 1960s. But in the last quarter of the century, marriages at Gretna grew – from 74 in 1975 (representing 0.2 per cent of all Scottish weddings) to 5,278 in 2000 (or 17.4 per cent).[19]

This was one reflection of changes to the law in the early 1990s that led to the rise of the hotel and resort wedding throughout Britain; by 2000 the majority of couples had dispensed with religiously-solemnised weddings.

Churches were having to adapt quickly to change in the sensibilities and values of wider society. In a sense, they were playing 'catch-up' with popular morality and standards. One case in point was women's equality of opportunity, in which church ordination remained, along with lavatory attendants and a few other jobs, one of the few professions in which gender equality was specifically excluded from legislation. Ordination of female clergy had been permitted in most Protestant denominations by 1970. But it was not allowed in the Roman Catholic Church (which never permitted it in the twentieth century). Despite women's episcopal ordinations in Canada and the USA in the 1960s and 1970s, the Church of England only finally acceded to it in 1992, and its sister churches the Scottish Episcopal Church in 1994 and the Church in Wales in 1996;[20] once they did so, women became extremely important to church ordinations. This catch-up in moral change occurred also in relation to gay rights. The explosion of the gay and lesbian liberation movements from the late 1960s, and the transformation of public and civil society's attitudes to homosexuality in the 1970s and 1980s, were fiercely fought over in many churches – none more so than the Church of England, which looked ready to split on the issue by the end of the century.[21] Though homophobia (just like racism and sexism) still remained in Britain, British society as well as the British state between 1970 and 2000 was dismantling the intellectual and legislative apparatus of essentialist discrimination, and if slow to follow, there were moves by liberals in most British churches to track this cultural revolution.

But not every church, nor every region, did this at the same pace. Homosexuality was not de-criminalised in Scotland until 1980 and in Northern Ireland until 1982 – the delay in each case in deference to the religious sensibilities of those countries. In Ulster, the Revd Ian Paisley opposed the move for de-criminalisation by founding a 'Save Ulster from Sodomy' campaign. Paisley represented the extreme Christian conservative view, but he managed to combine this moral conservatism with his extreme Ulster loyalism and carry much of the Protestant community with him. The Troubles from 1969 to 1998 defined the nature of the role that religion took in Northern Ireland; sectarianism and bigotry were deeply scarred into the life and culture of the province, and Protestant or Catholic was an unavoidable identity for at least 97 per cent of the population (according to the 2001 census). Religious indifference was almost negligible, and essentialist discrimination and bigotry remained strong. One consequence was that levels of churchgoing remained high, though were declining slowly. This produced high degrees of church association in both Catholic and Protestant communities. In a 1977 survey of a small Ulster town of 4,999 people composed almost equally of Protestants and Catholics, 53.6 per cent of adults said that they attended church at least weekly and 72.1 per cent at least monthly – figures about four times higher than in the rest of the UK.[22] It was the one part of Britain with confessionalist politics, with the Unionist parties representing the Protestant community, and with Sinn Fein and the Social and Democratic Labour Party (SDLP) representing the Catholic communities. Much of the social life of the province remained nurtured on religiously defined sectarian lines. Most notably, the Orange Order had a very large membership and an even larger following, and its parades during the marching season from March to July each year tended to punctuate the life of the province.

In Scotland, meanwhile, there was still a sense of a puritan Christian culture until the late 1970s. A newspaper columnist ranted against it in 1978: 'It is difficult for tolerant, liberal-minded chaps like myself to grasp the reason why the majority of Scots, the non-church-goers, should have, with the connivance of the state, a close-mouthed, eighteenth-century Presbyterianism so heavily imposed upon them.'[23] If Lowland Scotland was already liberalising rapidly in the 1970s, the Highlands and Hebrides still retained a strong religious culture. At Inverasdale in Wester Ross, the roads authority looked benignly upon a sign erected by locals to remind tourists at great length about God's attitude to the Sabbath. On the island of Harris, Alison Johnson and her husband opened a restaurant and hotel which, with the best will in the world, was bound to desecrate the Sabbath. Alison recalled:

Island Presbyterianism is ferociously Calvinistic and relies on a very literal reading of the Bible. The mainland Christian as much as the mainland atheist will find himself in confusion, for parts of Deuteronomy that never see daylight over the Minch [on mainland Britain] are here brought into play. It is an abomination to the Lord for a woman to wear trousers. Conversely, the great festivals of Easter and Christmas are totally ignored here by the religious; the Bible has not give us firm dates for them, so why follow Popish tradition? Popery, one feels, is the unforgivable sin encompassing all others ... The most remarkable feature of island life is the strict observance of the Sabbath. Not only may no work be done, but no leisure activities are permissible

Analysis: The Troubles in Northern Ireland and the Revd Ian Paisley, 1969–98

In 1969, after some decades of relative passivity, sectarian conflict between Protestant and Catholic communities in Northern Ireland erupted. This became officially categorised as 'the Troubles', but by others as a civil war. Taking tacit or active support from within the minority Catholic community, the Provisional Irish Republican Army (PIRA) waged a terrorist campaign for a united Ireland against the predominantly Protestant state (including its police force) and against the British Army. In turn, Protestant paramilitary groups undertook terrorist attacks on Catholic people. On occasion, churches of both communities were attacked. The Troubles continued until the emergence in 1994 and 1996 of two PIRA ceasefires, leading to the Good Friday (Belfast) Agreement of 1998 which initiated a process intended to create a comprehensive peace settlement.

The confessionalist politics of Northern Ireland were unique in Britain. The Unionist parties were dominated by Protestants and the Nationalist parties by Catholics, each confronting the other not just in the political field but also in virtually all branches of civil life. With educational systems divided between the religious traditions, and strong ghettoisation into areas of cities and villages with strong associations to one side or the other, there was considerable ability for religion to divide Northern Ireland in a way almost unique in Europe outside of the Balkans. Church attendance remained strong, with well over 50 per cent of adults claiming attendance, whilst by 1999 religious belief was the highest in the European Union (along with the Republic of Ireland). As the rest of Britain secularised with rapidity between 1960 and 2000, Northern Ireland alone sustained a high level of popular and religious piety. One consequence was that this faith, in its intensity and puritanism, came to be feared and even mocked by many people in mainland Britain.

The sectarian tensions created a high level of religious ritual in Northern Ireland. At its formation in 1921, the Northern Ireland provincial state took over existing ritual and events of Protestant celebration. The Twelfth of July celebration marches, commemorating the Battle of the Boyne in 1690 when Protestant Apprentice Boys barred the gates of the city of Londonderry as it was besieged by the Catholic King James II and VII, were until the early 1920s an expression of Protestant protest. But from that date, the 'Twelfth' became a ritual of the state supported by virtually all Unionist politicians in the province, at which the British Union flag predominated. However, the Troubles in 1969 led to the Twelfth being less marked officially, causing its celebration to revert back to a form of Protestant protest against the

Revd Dr Ian Paisley passes through police lines on the disputed march to Drumcree Church. (Topfoto/EMPICS)

perception of Catholic encroachment. Consequently, the Twelfth became increasingly associated with militants (and in some places with paramilitary organisations), and emerged more bold and more violent. In addition, the British Union flag started to be displaced by the Ulster flag, bearing the Red Hand insignia.[24]

Christian clergy, both Catholic and Protestant, played important roles in the Troubles – whether in community leadership, inter-faith negotiation or sustaining dialogue with paramilitary organisations. The most well-known clerical figure was the Revd Dr Ian Paisley, who was, for the remainder of the century, the voice of extreme Protestantism. Trained at an American fundamentalist church, in 1951 he founded the evangelical Protestant Free Presbyterian Church, a very small sect in numbers, but a church that symbolised a theological core of Ulster Protestant ideas of resistance and 'no surrender' to Catholicism. His role emerged directly at the start of the Troubles. In February 1967, a Catholic-based civil rights movement was formed that sought an end to irregularities in the political system in the province (which turned a blind eye to Protestant ballot-rigging), to job discrimination against Catholics (especially in local-authority, government and skilled jobs), and to violent victimisation by a Protestant-dominated police force (including the notorious B Specials). Almost immediately, the movement became opposed by Protestant churchmen, led by Ian Paisley, who in 1968 helped organise protests against the Catholic-dominated civil rights marches. By doing this, Paisley appeared to be opposing the same type of civil rights causes supported by liberals for the black minorities in the United States and South Africa. To Paisley, this was a just Christian position: 'Oh God, save Ulster from popery,' he said in 1969.[25]

From 1969, the violence of the PIRA campaign for a united Ireland drew religion directly into issues of power and resistance on both sides. In 1971, Paisley helped found the Democratic Unionist Party (from an earlier Protestant Unionist Party), which did for politics what his church did for religion – creating a heartland of political resistance which became, by 2000, the largest Unionist party and which, in the 2005 general election, virtually obliterated all other Unionist parties. He was a master of public speaking and pulpit oratory, and was much satirised and mocked in mainland Britain by comedians and mimics. But Paisley was supremely telegenic, aware how the grand physical gesture and protest would play for television journalists hungry for the image as well as the angry word. By this means, he was able to mobilise in the Protestant mind a root fear of being over-run by the neighbouring Catholic state of Ireland.[26]

The grandest gestures by Paisley were on protest and counter-protest marches. He was willing time and again to join in, side by side with Orangemen and the more hard-line Apprentice Boys of Londonderry, in demonstrations against 'popery'. As moves towards ending the conflict gathered pace in the late 1980s and 1990s, Paisley led resistance to change. A flashpoint developed in the mid-1990s at Drumcree where, as part of the settlement process, Protestant marchers were required to end their annual march down the predominantly Catholic Garvaghy Road to a Protestant church. At a barrier erected by the police, Paisley spoke on 10 July 1995 at the halted march:

We are here tonight because we have to establish the right of the Protestant people to march down the Garvaghy Road and our brethren of the Orange Institution to exercise their right to attend their place of worship and return to their homes. That is the issue we are dealing with

The Portadown Loyal Orange Lodge on parade. (CORBIS/Lewis Alan/Sygma)

tonight and it is a very serious issue because it lies at the very heart and foundation of our heritage. It lies at the very heart and foundation of our spiritual life and it lies at the very foundation of the future of our families and of this Province that we love. If we cannot go to our place of worship and we cannot walk back from our place of worship then all that the reformation brought to us and all that the martyrs died for and all that our forefathers gave their lives for is lost to us forever. So there can be no turning back.[27]

This speech gives an idea of the rhetoric and impulse behind the Protestant outlook in Northern Ireland. The parades gathered an intensity of significance as the late twentieth century wore on, becoming sources of identity – spectacles which totalised the Protestant experience and culture. The march articulated Protestant difference from Catholicism. It made visual the Protestant concept that loss of rights to Catholics had occurred or was imminent – to be measured through the extent to which marches were prevented from passing through Catholic districts. For this reason, the parade developed an exaggeration of Protestant identity, an extreme flamboyance in drum and flute bands, each led by a baton-throwing band leader, and engrossed in the swagger of the bowler-hatted dark suits of the Orangemen in uniforms.[28] Parades culture underpinned the continuing struggle of a confessionalist Protestant state to survive in an era of hostility – especially as the British state sought to negotiate with PIRA. Other Unionist politicians and parties joined in the negotiations, but Ian Paisley stood opposed. He opposed many political moves that seemed to him to assist the spread of 'popery' – including in the institutions of European Union and European Parliament, to which he was elected in 1979.

All this helps to explain why more than 97 per cent of people in Northern Ireland in 2001 claimed to belong to a religion (compared to less than 85 per cent in the rest of Britain). It was difficult to be either religiously neutral or disinterested. Popular religion was intertwined with a political bifurcation in Northern Ireland unmatched in most of Europe. Despite liberal moral pressures amongst people of the province, the *political* necessity of puritan Protestantism admitted its *cultural* necessity. Religion became politically necessary there, making the people of both communities amongst the most conservative on religious and moral issues anywhere in the world.

except for reading the Bible and the Christian Herald. *However, as it is a day of rest, it is respectable to spend the entire day, between the two long church services, in bed with drawn curtains.*[29]

In the 1970s, the letters pages of the *Stornoway Gazette* resounded to complaints 'against the abominable practices and vile blasphemies' on Sundays. But as many observers had noted, the rule for visitors was to be discreet in their 'abominations', conducting breaches of Sabbath etiquette in domestic isolation or, as with tourists, on some distant beach far from local churches.

But more threatening to traditional religious ways was the permanent incomer – known disparagingly in Scotland as the 'white settler'. Many were retired couples, some were back-to-the-landers, but there were also second-homers and professional couples able to conduct their working lives by email, the Web, cheap airflight and fast roads. This invariably challenged old ways. The village of Daviot nine miles south of Inverness was a scattered Highland community, reasonably isolated and tranquil until the arrival in the late 1970s of the dual carriageway upgrade to Britain's spinal trunk-route running from Dover to Thurso. White settlers came there with ideas of modernisation and revitalisation. In 1980, a £50,000 grant was obtained from the council to open a new village hall, and when the incomers wanted it to be open seven days a week, a sabbatarian row erupted – with a supporter of the strict Free Presbyterian Church making a cash offer of £1,000 to close it on the seventh day.[30] What the arrival of television did not achieve in the 1960s, a mixture of newcomers and youth revolt achieved in the 1980s and 1990s: the most savage and sudden collapse of strict presbyterian culture in the Highlands alongside the collapse of the Gaelic language. In the Hebrides and Lochalsh, weekly churchgoing still stood at 54 per cent of adults in 1982, but by 1994 it had fallen to 39 per cent, and though a census twelve years later suggested little further fall, the evidence is that Scotland's former wide Highland zone of high-churchgoing contracted during 1984–2002 to the far Western Isles where it arrived at its last redoubt amongst a tiny population of around 30,000 people. [31]

Despite falling numbers of worshippers, the Christian churches turned increasingly in the 1980s to contemplate the moral problems of poverty both at home and abroad. In the late 1970s and 1980s, an economic recession struck Britain at the same time as the right-wing Conservative government of Margaret Thatcher came to power in 1979, imposing policies of cutting expenditure, reducing public services, closing old industries and confronting industrial militancy in traditional staple industries – notably in the national coal strike of 1984–5. In this political and economic context, the Church of England undertook what it perceived to be a major two-year review of depressed working-class districts in cities and towns (known as Urban Priority Areas), leading to the *Faith in the City* report of 1985 that placed the failings of the church, the decline of faith and the rise of non-Christian traditions in the context of poverty, poor housing and rising unemployment. The report was seen as a radicalisation of the Church that would confront the failings of both organised Christianity and of the state. It urged tackling powerlessness, inequality and social polarisation between rich and poor, between city centre and suburb, as well as between black and white.[32] The result was rising confrontation between church leaders and the Thatcher government. In 1987, Mrs Thatcher delivered an invited speech, dubbed 'the Sermon on the Mound', to the general assembly of the Church of Scotland, in which she was interpreted as rendering a right-wing apology for laissez-faire, and of being unsympathetic to the poor. British Christianity was seen to be not merely failing to keep Britain Christian, but also of veering more to the left at the time when the nation's politics were firmly to the right.

Despite de-Christianisation and political confrontations, there were wider ways in which Christianity remained embedded in the British state and the law. One area seemingly little changed was that of school education. The Education Acts of 1944 and 1945 instituted compulsory religious assembly every day in every school, and until the institution of the National Curriculum in the late 1980s (everywhere but in Scotland), religion was bizarrely the only subject that was legislated as compulsory in the curriculum. However, there were changes within those structures. It was calculated that by 2004 around two-thirds of schools in England were in breach of the law by not holding daily religious worship, and more generally it was clear that the survival of religious education in schools was not creating Christians. Yet, churches fought fiercely in the 1980s and 1990s to retain their influence in education (for instance, resisting periodic suggestions in Scotland to abolish Catholic state schools).

Religion intruded in other ways. Some churches were major owners of property and derived rights – notably the Church of England – and this was often used in morally conservative ways in attempts to de-limit secular trends. In Scotland, the Church of Scotland sold off vast amounts of land, church buildings and former manses in the 1970s, 1980s and 1990s as it contracted its operations in the face of declining financial support from dwindling congregations. But it often used its ability to determine the future uses of such property (through the ancient system know as 'feuing') to – for instance – ban gambling, the sale of intoxicating liquor and even, in at least one case, ban the use of a former church as 'a meeting place, meeting house or institution for any religious denomination or for religious purposes'.[33] Still, in many British cities, famous landmark churches were turned in the 1980s and 1990s into nightclubs, dance halls, restaurants, as well as into car showrooms (with one in Aberdeen displaying cars in the gallery), carpet warehouses, cash and carry warehouses, and 'des res' flats. In this way, the landmarks stayed, preserved by planning law as 'listed' buildings in conservation areas, but their symbolic meaning as well as their usage were radically altered.

Notwithstanding the many different ways in which a religious heritage was sustained, Christian culture was oozing steadily out of most Britons' experience. We noted in the last chapter how the way in which the religious past was remembered changed in the 1960s and 1970s – from the recall of a life of upward striving to personal triumph and salvation, to the romance of a lost golden age. This can be seen most starkly in the autobiographical account of James Brady, born in Rochdale in Lancashire in 1898, who in 1978 described his participation in Whitsuntide processions early in the century dressed in a sailor's suit and carrying a Christian banner, followed by games and romps with the girls: 'What happened to this happy, happy world? Where are the bands and banners and the smiling faces of yore? All we have today are mobs of ragged jean-clad teenagers, shaking their childish fists and shouting "We shall overcome" underneath mis-spelt slogans on crude placards. God! what a lousy, protesting violent world it is today, compared with the carefree tolerance and good friendship of sixty years ago.'[34] Religion was something now 'lost', its miseries buried in recollections of happiness and good times, of close community and peaceable society, and packaged by an elderly generation in popular memories, community history and books of oral history.

But the romantic recollection of religion was joined in the 1980s and 1990s by a more critical, more troubled psychology of religion. In Jeanette Winterson's *Oranges are Not the Only Fruit* (1985), which was turned into a highly controversial television series, there was an autobiographical account of life in a 1950s' Lancashire family and a local congregation of born-again evangelical Christians, which dwelt on the oppressive terror and suppression of joy, hope and sexuality. In Winterson's account, religion stood in memory as not a totally bad 'other', but as a vital but deeply troubling element in the construction of the individual and her identity. In a similar vein, David Thomson wrote in 1987 of being raised in the 1920s in the Scottish Episcopal Church in the north-east of Scotland, and of the sense of the religious and civil heritage of Scotland bearing down on the individual. He recalled for his readers being in bed on Sunday night in the 1920s, and how he snuffed out his bedside candle and 'searched my·mind for sins'. 'Cleanliness is godliness, love is a paltry ridiculous joke, sex, even thoughts of it, are wicked and filthy; dance, song and pictures are the work of Satan. Scotch morality is filled with such perverted notions, and even though Granma adhered to the Episcopal Church, which is said to be less puritanical than the others, she abode by them all.'[35] The popularity of Winterson and Thomson reflected how British culture, in its post-1960s reorientation, had religious issues to work through.

If Christianity became something to be recalled in memory, whether lovingly or for dissection, its decline was by no means universal in British society. This was especially the case amongst the majority of people of colour.

Multi-faith society

Secularisation was an overwhelmingly white experience in Britain in the last quarter of the twentieth century. Religious practice in black and Asian groups was not only less subject to decline, but in many ways was growing.

Where there was religious alienation amongst black Christians, it was often the product of issues of authority, morality or wealth, rather than a rejection of Christian culture as such. Ryland Campbell, born in Jamaica in 1932 and a migrant to Britain after mid-century, told an interviewer in 1991: 'Religion is money and what I'm saying is alright so as an inquisitive person I've gone to the Baptist Church, I've seen the Salvation Army on the corner. I've gone to the Methodist Church, and I've gone to Poker Church ... You might call them Elim over there, they start calling them charismatic churches, where they clap hands and Hallelujah. ... I go there and try to see if they gonna heal me and you know and change me from being a sinner but up to now (laughs) none of them have succeeded so I want to know what the hell it is all about (laughter) you know, so I probably give them too much test so yeah.'[36] Within the jest and humour, there is a fluency and a facility with the religious context, and a knowledge of the possibilities of Christian culture that, even in disconnection from church, continues to define belonging and the sense of self. This the black Christian was able to do in the late twentieth century when fewer whites were able to.

The immigration of peoples from the former British colonies after 1948 created in Britain – as it did in the rest of Europe – a sudden and very significant shift in the religious complexion of society. With de-Christianisation amongst the indigenous and predominantly white population, the religiosity of the immigrants and their offspring became, over the next fifty years, increasingly important to the maintenance of organised religion. The immigrant peoples and their children were far more likely to be church members, and to count themselves as religious persons, than the white population. Black people became significantly more religious than white. This difference was not merely marked by higher levels of formal religious practice, but was deeply embedded in culture. The sense of 'the self' that the black and Asians sustained in the last quarter of the century was strongly imbued with a religious identity in a way that was becoming increasingly alien to the white population. A Christian convert from Hinduism expressed this in a speech in 1977 to the general synod of the Church of England: 'I am 5 ft-nothing and a black man. That made me feel inadequate in myself, but when I found Jesus I found my true identity ... What a dignity we have in Jesus! That is what we can give to the black people who think they are nothing.'[37]

This sense of the deep agency of religion was also evident in the identity of the Afro-Caribbean migrant. The role of the church in times of emergency and need retained strength in the black community in the 1980s and 1990s. The culture of Christian song punctuated social interaction and gave resonance to emotion and feeling. When oral history interviewers talked with Jamaican-born women in Britain in the 1990s, discussions often turned to 'jibing' and the sudden, unheralded invasion of Christian song. But migrant religious traditions were not immune to the sense of secular pressure. Within migrant groups, there were tensions over modernisation and the advance of youth cultures. As one commentator noted in 1987, British Muslims were facing a generational schism over faith and outlook:

Our adjustment is inevitable. The first sacrifice we shall makes is parts of the individual cultures within the faith – Nigerians, Egyptians, Pakistanis all carrying bits of their culture around their necks like a dead weight, slowing down progress. That will be shed, allowing a return to the basis of our religion. The position of women will become different, more liberalized. ... [T]he greater divisions will not be between Britain and the Muslims, but between the two factions within the faith. They will not be entirely generation-defined, yet it will be the younger people who decide. They see their parents besieged, more rigid in their religion than they would have been even in their homeland, and they will see that they cling to the conservatism for comfort, from fear.[38]

Britain's largest immigrant faith community of the late twentieth century was Islamic. By 1990, there were around 7.5 million Muslims in Europe and around 1.5 million in Britain, composed mostly of Pakistani, Indian and Bangladeshi (the Pakistanis making up the majority).[39] They were overwhelmingly working class and geographically concentrated in particular cities and parts of cities, and because of the colonial heritage they felt less integrated than, for instance, Muslims in the United States, and more disenchanted as a result.[40] The colonial heritage had another effect: migration brought many sectarian and ethnic tensions from cultural homelands, leaving British Muslims quite divided religiously and by geographical origins. The majority of British Muslims from Pakistan and Bangladesh were Sunni Muslims. The second largest group were Indian Ismaili and Middle Eastern Muslims who were Shi'a. But these were subdivided further. Most Pakistani mosques were in three groups – the *Sufi Barelwi* group, *Deobandi* group and the *Jamat-i-Islami* movement. In a similar way, the Hindu people arrived mostly in 1965–72, and developed as a significant ethnic group in many English cities. Numbering around 300,000 by the mid-1980s, they were divided into highly localised, predominantly caste groups. For instance, the Leicester Hindus were mostly *Lohanas*, a Gujarati trading caste; in Leeds, the *Mochis*, an artisan elite, were the largest group. Overall by 2000, about 70 per cent of Hindus were Gujarati, 15 per cent Punjabi in origin, and the remainder originated from Uttar Prudesh, Bengal and the southern states of India.[41]

Despite division, however, the Islamic people of Britain developed a powerful sense of commonality as a minority religion. *Umma* or *ummah*, the concept of community or brotherhood, became an intangible yet powerful sense that crossed national boundaries and exerted an especially strong call when Muslims were seen to be discriminated against in other countries. A Muslim from Manchester recalled a tangible result of *umma* in mid-century Britain: 'The first headmaster of the Sunday School was a Nigerian, the Mosque President a Syrian who was later succeeded by a Mauritian. The Imam was a Pakistani, and the Vice-president was a Turk, the Secretary an Egyptian and the youth were organised by an Iraqi.'[42] This sense of a call to brotherhood increased in Britain from the late 1980s to the end of the century as the Islamic people contended with the contradictions of modernity. At the same time, as we shall see shortly, many were to feel alienated from government and non-Muslim society.

Economic ambition became a very noticeable aspect of the Islamic community in Britain. Initially, many Muslim immigrants in the 1940s and 1950s were employed at the very bottom of the social status of occupation – in Scotland, for instance, being overwhelmingly pedlars. In industrial England, by contrast, the more numerous Muslims were employed in various factory work, including machine shops and the car industry. Moving from unskilled to semi-skilled and then skilled work was often slow, or impeded by racism and closed shops. As local employment opportunities changed, new jobs appeared, including in public transport – on London's underground and on urban buses across the nation. But in the later 1960s and after, Muslims increasingly pressed for entry for their sons and daughters to college and university. The largest proportion tended to seek technical and professional qualifications that led directly to careers – including engineering. From the 1980s, the professions of medicine, law and accountancy became increasingly popular, and though problems of language and (it has sometimes been alleged) racism by college and university elites have created unacceptable hurdles, the numbers of Muslims in the professions became very significant in the later 1990s.[43]

It was from the 1970s that imams became more knowledgeable about British society, and constructed ways of asserting Islamic involvement. Mosques made contact with schools, prisons and hospitals over Muslim concerns about prayers, *halal* food and dress codes. Campaigning and lobbying started for single-sex schools and against sex education.[44] The 1980s and more especially the 1990s showed signs of growing Muslim assertion. Muslims became more numerous in the professions, in political parties, voluntary organisations, trades unions and business leadership. The signs of economic success amongst the young was often taken by older Muslims to be evidence of the westernisation of values, language and culture, that weakened both religion and culture.

Each succeeding generation of Muslims, one study showed, would experience a decline in strict adherence to Islamic values.[45] The decline of the five daily prayers and the rise of drinking, dating and dancing were an important series of developments. Though not unique by any means, younger Muslim men developed an anti-social street culture founded on school truanting, vandalism, drugs, crime and firearms, especially in the stronger Muslim communities of Bradford, Birmingham and Oldham. One consequence was a doubling of Muslim prison inmates in the 1990s. Muslim marriage with non-Muslim partners, and inter-racial and inter-religious relationships, seemed to underpin long-term secularisation within Western society. In 1991, it was observed in a British study that between 70 and 80 per cent of all Muslims did not belong to any Islamic centre or mosque. The young were being alienated within religion – with the Quran (Koran) taught in Arabic, for instance, which few of the young understood. As a result, the younger Muslims felt less and less relevance of the older caste, clan and tribal loyalties which their parents and grand-parents had brought to Britain.[46] Alienation, confusion and disruption started to pervade Islamic identity in Britain in the 1990s. This was expressed in a letter from a young Muslim in 1998 published in *Q-News*, a Muslim magazine, and addressed to the older generation:

Yes, you have set up a system of halal meat. Yes you have built Mosques. Yes you have taught us Urdu ... But you have also ... built Mosques that were alien, hostile and irrelevant to our needs and requirements. Mosques that are full of squabbles and fights. Not love and compassion. Mosques full of notices of 'don't' do this and 'don't' do that. Mosques whose doors are closed to destitute, the poor, the orphans.

There were, the letter went on, 'no role models, nobody to admire up and down the street, and nothing to aspire to', leaving the young in a society where 'pornography awaits you at every shelf, pubs confront you at every next corner and the behaviour of most Muslims you come across sends you reeling back'.[47]

A curious and endearing case of Muslim integration in Britain was thrown up by Hebridean Islam. In the Western Isles of Scotland, a small community of around 50 Arain Muslims from the Punjab had taken firm root by the 1990s as a result of a single travelling salesman who arrived by ferry in the 1930s. Apparently well accepted in the community, there were reported to be no overt signs of racism; the Muslim community was said to be totally loyal 'to the soil, wishing to live and die' in Stornoway. 'We are real Scots but also Muslims,' was the catchphrase. Selling hard-ware and furniture, they fitted into an economy traditionally located in crofting and fishing. The strictness of the Christian Sabbath in these parts seemed to provide a natural affinity to a loyal Muslim community, whilst the Muslims' work ethic and respect for education seemed to mirror that of Protestantism. A young Muslim woman was studying in the 1990s for a doctorate at Glasgow University, but she reported that she was prepared for an arranged marriage in Pakistan. This was taken as adaptation and integration, but also revival of religion in an island where strong faith was respected by Christians.[48]

The place of religion in identity could thus be complex. And it was not all about 'roots' in colonial religions. For a significant minority of migrants, identity was about conversion and new faith. Clover Smith was brought up in Jamaica in the 1950s and early 1960s, enjoying a strong Christian life in a Baptist congregation: 'going to church and being involved in church was very, very important'. Coming to Britain in 1966 at the age of 14, she rebelled against racist grammar school teachers, and blamed her harsh father for putting her in this society. She had two marriages, but trained as a nurse and developed a career as a training officer in social services specialising in mental health and substance abuse. In the mid-1980s she embraced Islam (one of an estimated 5,000–10,000 British converts by the mid-1990s) and changed her name to Sakiina Haaruun. From the initial influences being as she put it 'negatives' in her life in Britain, the later ones became 'quite positive', helping her through crises with her employers, and encouraging her to the position of vice-chair of the African Caribbean People's Movement:

I think if I am honest, it's something about my religious belief and my conversion from Christianity to Islam. And that is with great respect for Christianity, because I was brought up in a Christian family and I was a Sunday-school teacher and all that sort of thing. But I was searching for a belief or faith or an ideology around spiritualness, and the oneness with the one God that I wasn't getting in the Christian context … Going into Islam and reading up and being with people, it's the humbleness … it's a very humble human way, because Islam means submission to the Almighty. It's just a way of living – how you speak, how you sit, how you conduct yourself and in the remembrance of the Creator, it's the prescriptive ways of communicating with the Almighty in the five daily prayers.[49]

Religious opportunities were also open to some in Britain when not in their land of birth. For example, a Sikh man came to Britain in his late thirties in 1960, and was able to work as a priest in a temple even when he was married – something not accepted in India.

By the 1990s, British immigrant communities were experiencing significant wealth and financial achievement. The drive for success that parents fostered was strong. The sons and daughters of first generation immigrants were graduating, overwhelmingly in the professions – as doctors, lawyers, chartered accountants, scientists and engineers – and were acquiring large houses and high-status cars. In the early decades, Birmingham Muslims each donated 50 pence to rent a hall to pray, but by the 1990s there were 144 mosques in the city, purpose-built and many of them very large, with supplementary schools attached. Bashir Maan, a leading figure in the Glasgow Muslim community, noted the ambition of Muslim parents, and their preference for their children entering technical and engineering courses (especially between the 1950s and 1970s), and then for entry to the professions like law and accountancy: 'The parents made sure that their children go into education which would help them in getting a good job because they had tough competition. You had to be, and even *now* I tell my people, that you've got to be a little better than your white competitors before you get the job. If you are at level with him, or even *slightly better than him*, you won't get the job, he will get the job. You've got to be *far better than him* before you get the job. So therefore the parents made sure that they went in professions where there was a demand for the new kind of people.'[50]

The verve, material richness and success of British black and Asian communities were to be seen in the profusion, modernity and achievement of new religious traditions. Religions in Britain were being segregated by race. Integrationist models pursued by many in liberal British society tended to break down in the religious sphere. Most obviously, Islam, Hinduism and Sikhism had no white equivalents in Britain. In addition, Christian immigrants, notably from the Caribbean, too often found a racist reception from churches and from society, and this made the black Pentecostal congregations more important to black culture than they had been in the West Indies. The religious integration of British voluntary organisations was often just too slow to overcome issues of religious difference. For instance, the Boys' Brigade debated in the late 1970s the organisation's overtly Christian aims, and after considering the position of Muslim boys wanting to join, it decided in 1976 to reaffirm Christianity.[51] This reluctance to absorb the non-Christian drove a wedge into many plans for integration between religions and races. Multi-faith most often meant separate faiths. And this in part laid the basis for a late-century rise of religious militancy.

Religion gets militant, 1989–2000

In the last ten to twelve years of the century, in the midst of overall decline in popular religiosity, British religion showed signs of an increasing seriousness and militancy. This was an uneven and in some ways almost imperceptible process, and one that only became really noticeable in the early twenty-first century.

One of the key characterisations of the secularisation of Britain after the 1960s was its general air of religious tolerance. As late as 1991, a multi-volume series of books on world fundamentalism did not feature a single chapter or index entry on Britain.[52] Until that point, fundamentalism was widely considered as almost irrelevant in Britain, as something afflicting non-European countries. Of course, fundamentalist Protestantism was known about in Northern Ireland, but it hardly registered on the radar of popular culture on the British mainland. With the exception of localised sectarianism, there had been a general feeling amongst the non-religious that religion could be tolerated, allowed to exist, without intruding into the lives of those indifferent or apathetic to it. For this reason, British secularism had been largely unmilitant, without a manifesto of secularism (unlike France, for instance, where secularism was linked to the Revolution and the constitution, or nations with a secularist communist ethos as in Eastern Europe). Britons developed a languidness about religion, described in previous chapters as a 'mellowing' within religion. 'Religion is harmless' was the interpretation made by Mass-Observation in 1947 of the feeling of British non-churchgoers.[53] And this feeling was the hallmark of attitudes to religion amongst the non-religious until the end of the century and beyond. But it was to be a very tolerant tolerance that was to be sorely tried by the rise of new militancies.

As British Christianity contracted, it became more militant. This was observable in British public life by the impact of Christian pressure groups fighting against liberal abortion law, homosexuality and liberal culture in general. But lying behind this was the mainstreaming within the churches from the 1980s of a vital trend – charismatic renewal. The charismatics had been branded in the 1960s and 1970s by leading churchmen as dangerous and polluting to Christian order, doctrine and respectability. Yet, this aspect of the Christian new age had by 1975 swept across Western Christianity, with 'the gift of the Spirit' making particular inroads within the Roman Catholic Church, Pentecostal and evangelical churches, and the Church of England. It was described in that year: 'This ecstatic behaviour takes the form of completely spontaneous and uninhibited sharing of prayer and witness and praise among people in groups, small and large, sometimes accompanied by dancing, mutual confessions of sin.' But glossolalia was described as a widespread characteristic: 'The most respectable clergy, the most sedate laity, of all denominations are now liable during a prayer meeting to speak with tongues.' The result was what was described as 'a sense of liberty and joy and integration, and renewal of genuine religion which nothing else has brought'. For charismatics, the results of the movement were taken by one commentator as 'a sign of the Holy Spirit who is jerking Christians out of the old outworn stodginess and dullness'.[54]

It was Christian traditionalists more than the secular society who branded charismatics as outlandish. Speaking in tongues seemed more associated with the popular culture of devil worship and low-quality British horror movies. Even more was an associated development alleged within some branches of charismatic renewal, described here in 1981:

A room full of ecstatic people sway in unison to the beat of a guitar group playing softly in the corner; many arms are raised and waving with the mass of moving bodies; one and then another of the gathering begin to utter strange incoherent sounds, and the emotional intensity of the group grows even stronger at the signal. The leader, who earlier preached with the ferocity of a nineteenth-century evangelist, stands in front of one of the worshippers, and they speak. The worshipper cries out, seems to convulse, and collapses to the floor. Two helpers catch him as he falls. He has been exorcised.[55]

Theologians led the sometimes sneering attack on charismatics, their irrationality and the lack of intellectual content to their form of faith. Don Cupitt, dean of Emmanuel College, University of Cambridge, said in a BBC television broadcast that ecstatic religion had temporary effects, and that the possession, trance-states and clear intoxication of adherents could not be taken 'as proofs of the activity of the Holy Spirit of Christian teaching', and could 'lead to savage cruelty and murder'.[56] Meanwhile, other Christian scholars alleged that charismatic renewal had been associated with mental illness and psychological damage, placing its manifestations beside those of other 'irrational cults' like the Moonies. The Synod of the Church of England erupted in fury in 1981 when an official report recommended sympathy with the movement, but came round in the following year to giving it a cautious welcome.

In the middle and later 1980s, the charismatic movement was being described as 'Pentecostalism goes middle class', with tens of thousands joining in, including a leading Anglican bishop. From being seen as weirdo speakers in tongues in the 1970s, they had become in the 1980s more passively accepted by 'ordinary church members' as 'those middle-class ecstatics' – despite church fears that many were leaving their denominations in favour of joining informal 'house churches'. With acceptance came a sense of 'its new cosy, less aggressive cultural form', and growing strong links to alternative medicine and healing therapies characteristic both of other new age movements and of British popular culture as a whole.[57] They shared, too, the outlook that God 'comes within'. One charismatic supporter said: 'For us evangelism became a living thing, an experience, people were sharing reality rather than concepts', whilst another said: 'You know, when God speaks to us, he speaks, like, into our hearts.'[58] The rise of the charismatic movement led to new initiatives to rouse interest in Christian conversion and faith – such as the so-called Toronto Blessing and the Alpha Course (based on the Holy Trinity Church in Brompton in London), which attracted much attention in the media and a support that was mainly successful middle class in composition. The impact these had by 2000 is difficult to gauge and open to dispute, but their converts seemed to be numbered at most in the tens of thousands rather than hundreds of thousands, and seemed more a transformation of existing active Christians than a conversion of the previously unchurched and uncommitted. So, the Christian community may have been becoming more charismatic in inclination as it contracted in size. As well as those mainstream developments, there was a more radical Pentecostal house church movement, numbering by 1985 up to 28,000 adherents, which had emerged during the preceding fifteen years to encourage moral renewal (including through the 1971 Festival of Light); about half of them were 'Restorationists' who tried to return the Christian tradition to its supposed 'original' model (led by apostles, prophets and elders) and one without denominational churches (which they regarded as not 'in the plan of God').[59] Overall, there are grounds for seeing an association of charismatic growth with the creation of the 'Thatcher generation' – a new professional middle class which, located in the outer London suburbs and Home Counties, was associated with new business ventures in the midst of the difficult economic recession of the 1980s and early 1990s.[60]

Amongst many evangelical and non-evangelical groups alike by the 1990s, the charismatic renewal and Pentecostal growth underpinned the rising confidence to convert the morals of society ahead of its religious state. Abandoning older shibboleths of Christian evangelicalism (such as excessive concern for keeping the Sabbath, or avoidance of pop music and alcohol[61]), stronger 'sinners' were prioritised for attention – such as those seeking abortions, and gays, which some evangelicals believed, like the 'Courage' group of the early 1990s, could be 'cured' by Christian teaching and counselling.[62] In 1988, under the right-wing Conservative government of Margaret Thatcher, the promotion of homosexuality was outlawed in schools (under a provision known as Section 28 of the Local Government Act 1988), and though this was largely a symbolic rather than a gravely important measure, attempts to repeal it by Labour politicians in the late 1990s met with opposition. In Scotland, a conservative Christian millionaire, Brian Soutar, financed a private national poll on the issue in 2000 on behalf of the Scottish School Boards Association; though he gained 86.8 per cent of votes for keeping the clause, there was a mass boycott by opponents, and the clause was repealed anyway by the Scottish Executive.

In these ways, the new strident Christians became, late in the century, more organised in independent churches and groups, seeking to promote their gospel message through media campaigns and small-scale activity to challenge people. This alienated much liberal and secular opinion. For its part, evangelicalism continued to bring support from American evangelicals, just as it did in the 1950s. But there was one major difference from the 1950s. Rather than gracing a dominant religious culture, vigorous Christians tended increasingly in the 1990s to adopt the role of combative and minority challengers to what they saw as a dominant secularism and its immoral values. Christians were by then assuming the role of the assertive cultural underground. In particular, it became one of the distinctive ironies of the great metamorphosis of Christianity rendered by the charismatic movement that it occurred during the great secularisation of the nation, and left little trace in the culture of the country. Christian culture was being transformed into something – ebullient, spontaneous, emotional and, for some, faintly dangerous – about which the average Briton knew little or nothing. As it became more militant in the 1990s, the culture of practising Christians became more morally rarefied, its faith more elusive to experienced former Christians, its practices seen by some educationalists as questionable for impressionable children and young people, and its forms of disordered worship for many adults as irrational and faintly ridiculous. All of this left Christianity by 2000 even more culturally segregated from the mainstream of British life.

The forcefulness that came over much of the Christian faith in the 1990s was to be found across the religious spectrum. For instance, the assertiveness adopted by Islamists in Britain towards the end of the century was in marked contrast to their position in the 1950s and 1960s. First generation immigrants were seen by their children and grandchildren as 'meek, invisible immigrants grateful to be allowed in' to Britain.[63] In the 1950s, access to privileged positions in British society was difficult and often not successful. Even when successful, the sense of isolation and inferiority was aggravated by the paltry acknowledgement of the British elites – even the so-called liberal elites – to take Islam seriously. At Cambridge University in the mid-1960s, there was no place allocated for Friday prayers by Muslim students, and this was looked back on as wholly unacceptable.[64] The young Muslims of the late 1980s and 1990s found what they felt to be a growing racism forced them into a greater sense of their religious identity. In Britain, as in many parts of the West, not only the young but whole families of Muslims were seeking an affirmed identity in heightened observance of their faith.

But the most prominent issue of all was that of the rise of Islamic fundamentalism. The profile of Islamic fundamentalism was raised in response to the publication in 1988 of the novel *The Satanic Verses* by Salman Rushdie. The book was taken by many Muslims to blaspheme Allah. Almost unseen by British press and government, a tremendous popular reaction to the book developed in Bradford, with scenes of book burning and a spontaneous eruption of Islamic fervour. The UK Action Committee on Islamic Affairs (UKACIA) was formed in October of that year, and a *fatwa* was issued against Rushdie by the Ayatollah Khomeini, the religious leader of Iran. The *fatwa* was taken to be a decision against Rushdie and appeared to call for his assassination by loyal Muslims. As a consequence, Rushdie became for over ten years a refugee from the public, and received round-the-clock protection from British government security personnel.

The Rushdie affair triggered the organisation of militant Islam in the UK. In 1990, a Muslim Manifesto was issued that established Western society as in moral decline, and sought to re-empower Muslims and strengthen British Islamic institutions. Its author, Dr Kalim Siddiqui, believed 'secularism was destroying mankind', and in the following year he became the inspiration behind the creation of the British Muslim Parliament. Siddiqui's speeches raised the profile of Islamic religious rhetoric. He argued against integration in order to protect faith and community, and wished to foster the Muslim community as a moral beacon that would persuade the majority of British people to accept Islam, leading Britain to join a global grid of Islam.[65] This mirrored the worldwide impact of the Salman Rushdie affair, which fostered Islamic revivalism on an international scale. It was this increasing sensitivity to international Islam and to the sense of *ummah* that united British Islam, through cheaper airflights, opening borders, emails and the internet, to the Islamic diaspora. From 1991, local Radio Ramadan stations took to the air in various English cities at the time of the principal Muslim holy festival.[66] As a result, the balance between integration and Muslim common identity became an inescapable tension that Muslim religious leaders, as much as community and intellectual leaders, found difficulty in resolving. One explanation for the increasing tension was the absence of effective Muslim leadership on an international scale. In the midst of integration and discrimination crises, westernised Muslims became pressed by a new Islamic orthodoxy located in nations (like Saudi Arabia or Afghanistan) which sought to refute westernisation. This was, and perhaps remains, an insoluble contradiction. Yet, even within this contradiction lay another contradiction – that the technology of globalisation (satellite telephones, television, the internet and modern weapons technology) all became elements empowering the Islamic diaspora as it rejected Western countries and their westernised globalisation.

The Muslim Parliament failed after Kalim Siddiqui died in 1996. But a succession of major events in the early and mid-1990s triggered Islamic revival and self-awareness: the Rushdie affair, the first Gulf War of 1991, the collapse of the Muslims-supported BCCI bank and the military oppression of the Bosnian Muslims. In the Gulf War of 1991, Britain joined the United States and some other mostly Western nations to repel an invasion of Kuwait by Iraq under Saddam Hussein. This made many British Muslims feel isolated and 'beleaguered'. The media spotlight in Britain started to nurture and circulate an anti-Islamic discourse combined in some newspapers with ill-concealed racism.[67] There was a reported increase in abuse of women wearing the hijab, and 'anyone who even looked remotely Muslim was supposed to be a supporter of Saddam'.[68] This led to a siege mentality and a feeling that Muslim loyalty was under test. Identities became pushed into corners.

The result in Britain and elsewhere was a popular Muslim support for Saddam, even though Islamic governments opposed him. The Muslim Conference in Bradford, which claimed to speak for all Muslims in Britain, unanimously supported Saddam Hussein against Britain, resulting in the sense of a fifth column. It was a strange phenomenon according to one commentator, because he was an essentially dislikable ruler. Yet, though he was a tyrant, he was respected for standing up to the all-powerful West. The Supreme Council of British Muslims met in Bradford and unanimously supported Saddam, posters of whom appeared on the streets throughout the Islamic world.[69] He assumed a mythical status because of the intense humiliation being felt by Muslims. As Akbar S. Ahmed wrote in 1998, 'Henceforth a question mark would hang over the loyalty of the British Muslims.'[70] The issue of Islamic loyalty to Britain and to 'Western democratic values' became heightened by the terrorist attacks on the USA on 11 September 2001 (known as 9/11). The attacks by suicide bombers in hijacked airliners on the Twin Towers of the World Trade Center in New York and on the Pentagon building in Washington implicated Islamic fundamentalists in the international

Analysis: The Rushdie affair

On 14 January 1989, a few score of Muslims in Bradford in the north of England burned a copy of novelist Salman Rushdie's new book, *The Satanic Verses*. The book was regarded by them as an insult to, and blasphemy of, Islam. Rushdie was an Indian-born novelist whose family background was Islamic, and he had become a significant novelist on the British literary scene. Within months of the book burning, the first Gulf War broke out, in which the USA and Britain led a war against Islamic Iraq. In this context, the demonstration was to mark the development of a new Muslim consciousness in Britain.

Within two days of the burning, a demonstration of 1,500 Muslims in Bradford was organised. The British book and newspaper chain store W. H. Smith reacted to this news by withdrawing the book from sale in its city shop, and announced its withdrawal from its other 440 British shops. Within weeks, the spiritual leader of Iran, the Ayatollah Khomeini, issued a death warrant or *fatwa* against Rushdie, and was quoted on Tehran Radio: 'I inform the proud Muslim people of the world that the author of the Satanic Verses book which is against Islam, the Prophet and the Koran, and those involved in its publication, who were aware of its content, are sentenced to death. I ask all Muslims to execute them whenever they find them.' Those who killed Rushdie would be instant martyrs to Islam, and a prize of £1.5 million would be paid to the martyr's family. Worldwide demonstrations started, with five protestors being shot dead in Islamabad in Pakistan.[71] Almost immediately, Rushdie went into hiding in Britain, and a permanent Special Branch police protection squad was organised for him. During the following year, the Rushdie affair was almost never out of the British newspapers. Demonstrations against the book and Rushdie, and protesting against the inaction of the British government, were organised by some Muslims in British cities and overseas. A major march on Westminster on 27 May 1989 led to many in the 600-strong demonstration engaging in violent stand-off with the Metropolitan Police, bringing home to liberal commentators the cultural and religious confrontation that had been joined. Ed Vulliamy of the *Guardian* wrote:

Some of the images from the march imitated the streets of Tehran or Beirut – bearded men with military shirts and clenched fists saluting Ayatollah Khomeini and their God, or a youth – with the blood of the head wound splattered on the khafir he had wrapped around his head, showing only his eyes – being marched shoulder-high by his comrades straight into a line of policemen whom he set about with a pole. Others came from the more ancient orthodoxies of the Muslim faith – the caps, the robes, and long beards like Mr Razvi's.[72]

Muslim demonstrators symbolically burn a copy of The Satanic Verses *in Bradford in January 1989 at the start of the decade-long protest against author Salman Rushdie. (CORBIS/Derek Hudson/Sygma)*

As tension in Bradford rose, and disturbances took place there and in Dewsbury, the British liberal intelligentsia, novelists and civil rights activists mostly backed Rushdie, regarding the *fatwa* as an attack on freedom of speech, artistic freedom and the right to criticise any religion. Many on the left supported Rushdie, but by July the Labour Party, for whom British Muslims had traditionally voted, appeared to be splitting apart after its leader, Neil Kinnock, met Rushdie to offer support. With West Yorkshire in riotous turmoil into the following year, Labour council groups were reported as 'unravelling' at their Asian fringe; Huddersfield Labour members were expelled for favouring a new Islamic Party, and Bradford town council fell to Tory control when a leading Muslim Labour councillor defected. The Conservative Party fared little better after John Townend, MP for Bridlington, was quoted as telling Muslims that if they could not live in a country where Rushdie had freedom to express his views, they should be told to 'go back from whence they came'.[73] Meanwhile, the publishers of the *Verses*, the Viking and Penguin group, started to contemplate a paperback edition, and in September 1989 bombs were placed outside its stores in York, Peterborough, Guildford and Nottingham – the first of which exploded. Penguin stalled for many months over its decision.[74] Throughout, the British government, political leaders and social leaders took a very long time to grasp the sincerity and depth of feeling behind Muslim reactions at home and abroad. When the British government made overtures to Iran about easing the *fatwa* in June 1990, British officials were reportedly stunned when the Ayatollah asked them to hand over Rushdie to British Muslims for execution.[75] The British state found itself in a few pickles of its own liberal making. When a Pakistani film was made depicting Rushdie as a drunkard who tortured and shot Muslims, it was banned from distribution by the British Board of Film Censors, but after appeal was licensed for video release.[76] Two years after the initial book burning in Bradford, Rushdie started to make attempts to come out of hiding and to appease Islamic feeling. He appeared on an Asian Radio phone-in, made a visit to the USA and, in 1992, to Germany. But the initial response was an increase in the bounty to the martyr who killed Rushdie.[77]

There were to be contrasting sets of outcomes to the *fatwa* and the turmoil in Britain. Liberals started to explore the implications of religious belief for the fundamental liberal issues of the day – such as women's equality. New books appeared, notably those by Karen Armstrong, to increase Western understanding of Islam and the rise of fundamentalism.[78] Overall, a new sensitivity arose to the differences of life in Islamic families and communities at home. A second outcome was the rise of intolerance towards militant Muslims and even Muslim worship in Britain and overseas. Typical was an article by Carol Sarler in the *People* newspaper in 1995, in which she wrote that 'we are supposed to tolerate idiots slaughtering goats on streets in Kensington, groups of idiots burning books in Bradford and wealthy bigger groups building mosques on streets everywhere'.[79] In this way, the Rushdie affair revealed religious tensions and fractures that many in secular Britain had considered long gone.

Al-Qaeda organisation of Osama Bin Laden. In Britain, as in much of Europe, there arose tremendous soul-searching by liberals, and barely-concealed Islamophobia by some commentators and newspapers.

Issues of Islamic integration in a multi-cultural, but strongly secular, society came to the fore, and Islamic assertiveness became inextricably linked in many minds with the rise of fundamentalism – which were not necessarily linked at all. One instance was the rise in the later 1990s of separate Islamic schools with state funding. Though state faith schools of the Church of England and the Catholic faith had existed throughout the twentieth century, and were far more numerous, the rapid rise of faith-based state schools of other faiths under Tony Blair's Labour government from 1997 was causing anxiety in some quarters. By 2005, there were 100 Muslim schools funded by the state, and these were equated by the Chief Inspector of Schools with the 100 Christian evangelical schools, many of which were run by creationist fundamentalists, and both were picked out for criticism as failing to develop 'general knowledge of public institutions and services in England' and to respect other cultures.[80] In these ways, even in the British lay intelligentsia, there was a deep-rooted inability to distinguish Islamic fundamentalism from assertiveness.

Whatever the causes, Muslims came to hold religious identity more strongly than any other collective British religious tradition. In a survey in 1994, 74 per cent of Muslims considered Islam a 'very important influence' in their daily lives compared to 46 per cent of Sikhs and 43 per cent of Hindus.[81] Not all Muslims were the same. Turkish Muslims in Britain were markedly more westernised (or secular) than Pakistani Muslims. So, the development of religious identity in a militant form should not be seen as a simple fracturing of society into easily identifiable religious or ethnic groups. The individual's identity became confused by pressures from outside as well as from within. For instance, in a society where racism and religious bigotry were growing, a Muslim youth's identity could become a mixture of Islamic-ness, British-ness, Bangladeshi-ness – even if British (or

A crowded British mosque. (Getty Images/AFP)

English) nationalism was coloured white, and Bengal was an alien and far-away country. In this context, Islam emerged ever more powerfully in the 1990s as the greatest source of identity in many people. Islamic-ness empowered because of being a minority, when assimilationist identity and the identity of roots were both compromised in different ways; if an individual had no *one root* in another country, and if British society offered little of an identity, then Islam became the major solution to the construction of self.[82] At the same time, there were growing signs in the 1990s that many young Muslim women were not content with what they perceived as the high masculinity in the new Islamic assertiveness in British culture, and resented young Muslim men claiming to represent women. With growing pressure to wear the hijab and to cover the female form, the male-ness of Islamic-ness was also being questioned by some.

This militancy of conservative religion, and its greater growth into the public arena, was a trend that stretched far beyond Islam. Fundamentalist groups of different religious traditions took to collecting in communes or urban districts, fostering religious enclaves. For example, from 1989, the Charedi community of Orthodox Jews in Stamford Hill in north London grew rapidly, creating pressure for a move to a larger location. Over the same period, a movement started amongst London's Orthodox Jews, led by the United Synagogue, to create an *eruv* – a holy area. The intended area was a part of north-west London (around Hendon, Finchley, Golders Green and Hampstead Garden Suburb), stretching to an 11-mile perimeter. On Saturdays (the Jewish Sabbath or *Shabbat*), activities like carrying and pushing wheelchairs, prams and baby buggies, and carrying keys, were normally only permitted in homes and private gardens. But in a designated and marked *eruv*, such activities would be permitted by Jewish law by allowing public space to be treated as private domestic space in religious terms. The proposal required planning recognition from Barnet Council, as it involved street markers of poles and wires, and it was bitterly opposed throughout the 1990s by some local residents (including some Jews) who regarded an *eruv* as imposing one group's religious values on a whole community.[83] Finally established in 2002, its creation was seen to be for a minority of Jews, but represented another form of conservative religion becoming more assertive in popular culture and public spaces.

This sense of emergence into British public life and culture of previously secluded, or at least restrained, conservative religion was particularly marked with the Catholic Church. For most of the nineteenth and twentieth centuries, the Church's policy in Britain (especially in

Scotland) had been to avoid problems for the Church and its faithful by sidestepping public contest and metaphorically 'keeping its head down'. Protestants in many walks of life harboured distrust and dislike of Catholics, and the Church for a long time considered discretion to be the wisest policy. In many ways, the Catholic Church had previously developed a ghetto mentality, characterised by a cradle-to-grave welfare system in voluntary organisations and church parades, that sustained Catholic identity in a rather closed but bullish community ritual. But from the 1980s, British Catholicism showed a radically different approach to its position in British life, dissolving 'the defensive walls around the previously distinct Catholic subculture'.[84]

The visit in 1982 of Pope John Paul II to London (culminating in a major Mass at Wembley football stadium) and to Scotland (with similar events at Murrayfield and Bellahouston parks in Edinburgh and Glasgow respectively) reflected and encouraged the Catholic Church to become more prominent in dealings with the government, the press and other civic institutions. And though those visits did little to alter the destiny of Catholic adherence and practice (which continued to decline), it established a new spirit of political and ecumenical engagement by the Church in Britain. Under Cardinal Basil Hume (leader of Catholics in England and Wales during 1976–99) and Cardinal Thomas Winning (leader of Catholics in Scotland during 1994–2001), an official Catholic presence was nurtured through media contact. This increasingly took a concern with moral issues, notably over abortion. By the end of the century, official and quasi-official Catholic pressure groups were engaging the press on almost a daily basis, ensuring a presence for Catholic viewpoints on many of the burning issues of the day, and indeed providing ready copy for journalists on moral issues. In this regard, the Catholic Church showed how most churches were becoming more media savvy, and willing to be seen to lead on moral issues even when, in the population at large, their church adherents were in a minority.

Religious militancy in the 1990s was not merely a matter of how the churches presented themselves as institutions to an outside secular society. The contraction of most of the mainstream Christian churches led to growing opportunities for vigorous minorities within them to argue their cases, achieve success and push forward agendas. Such agendas were both liberal and conservative – often clashing. For instance, the ordination of women in the Church of England became much more likely as a result of the ongoing panic over de-Christianisation and the need to sustain the work of women within the Church for fear of inadequate numbers of male clergy. Men could simply no longer run the Church and sustain its presence within the parish system. The decision to permit the ordination of women in the Church of England in 1992 was to have an immediate and major impact on the priesthood and ministry. Ordinations of men were falling for most of the period 1994 to 2001, though with a more pronounced downward trend amongst stipendiary (paid) clergy. Only the increasing number of ordinations amongst women kept the totals buoyant. Only 26 per cent of ordinations in 1994 were female, but the proportion rose to 44 per cent by 1999 and remained at that level into the new century.[85] Similar trends occurred in the Church of Scotland, creating competing militancies – between opponents and proponents of women's ordination. By the early twenty-first century, ordination was a fact, and promotion was the next question. The Church of Scotland elected its first female moderator of the general assembly in 2004, and the Church of England voted in 2005 to remove restrictions on appointing a first female bishop (which was predicted to be achieved by 2015).[86]

Militancy drove forward many agendas, but it also threatened to split churches. In Scottish presbyterianism, there was a conservative wing of staunchly puritanical and strictly biblical churches, centred in the Gaelic speaking Highlands and Hebrides, which experienced an infusion of increasing Christian conservatism drawing in part upon American and English influences. The tiny Free Presbyterian Church split in 1989 into two even tinier parts after it suspended from the eldership its most prominent member, Lord Mackay of Clashfern, the government's Lord Chancellor. His 'crime' as a member of a Protestant church was that of attending the Catholic Mass of a friend; a more liberal group of churches, the Associated Presbyterian Churches, seceded because it 'violated and ignored the Christian's right of private judgement'. This was followed in 1998 by a split in the Free Church of Scotland, a slightly larger and marginally less conservative church based in the same Highland zone. This fell apart as a result of a crazy case in which the broad-minded head of its theological college, the Revd Professor Donald Macleod, was falsely accused of sexual abuse by a group of women; the case went to a civil court where the sheriff threw it out, condemning the women's stories as false and as the product of a conspiracy of conservative clergy to unseat the Church's most progressive thinker.[87] Such cases made both churches laughing stocks – including within their natural heartland in the Highlands where many young people in the 1990s were turning from the churches with increasing disdain and apathy, contributing to declining churchgoing.

If intensification of fundamentalism was one aspect of the schism and downward spiral of Scottish presbyterianism, Ulster presbyterianism was in one sense flourishing. Northern Ireland had astonishing levels of religious identity in the 1990s. In the European Values Study of 1999–2000, 49 per cent of people in Northern Ireland claimed to go to church once a week (and a total of 63 per cent at least once a month), compared to a mere 14 per cent weekly (and 19 per cent monthly) of the people in the rest of Great Britain. With the exception of the Republic of Ireland (with figures of 57 and 67 per cent), these were the highest figures in the whole of Europe.[88] The religiosity of the province was marked by the strength of its moral, cultural and political conservatism, and the agonisingly-slow move towards a peace settlement in the 1990s was constantly, and to many almost solely, restrained by the political activity of conservative presbyterianism. The Revd Ian Paisley's Free Presbyterian Church remained small in the 1990s, but his Democratic Unionist Party blossomed, emerging by the 2005 general election as the largest party in Ulster. Aided by his son, Paisley moved into his old age as continuing to personify the sense of a Protestant remnant struggling to survive what it saw as the overwhelming odds of both Catholicism and secularism. Protestant voters were voting for Paisley as a clergyman standing as the political resistance to other forces. Fear of Catholicism lay at the heart of fear of the IRA, and it was in part convenient for Protestant voters to have Paisley as the figurehead of this action. Despite some signs of diminishing levels of church belief and activity in Ulster in the 1990s, it was very limited. Other evidence points to an intensifying culture of bigotry and sectarianism, notably amongst children and youths, and one monitoring organisation noted that sectarianism increased after the 1997 peace accord.[89] By the end of the twentieth century, Northern Ireland was the one place where militant religion was still a really significant force.

Within Islam, theological splintering also occurred as sectarian movements arrived and some flourished. The Tablighi Jamaat appealed to Gujarati Muslims with a message of reviving Islam through preaching, whilst the Jamaat-i-Islamic Mission (UKIM), arriving in 1963, became influential amongst professional Muslims from Pakistan with its *dawa* (invitation to Islam) and desire to create a distinct British Islamic identity – also expressed through a youth wing known as Young Muslims UK (YMUK). The diversity of Islam had constantly been a matter of dispute, but this increased in the late twentieth century. On the one extreme, Sufism became increasingly disparaged by Muslims for what was taken to be its distortion of Islam through tomb and saint worship, and by the attraction of its philosophy of universal love to Western hippies in the

1960s and 1970s. At the other extreme, the Wahabis of Saudi Arabia were increasingly seen as the orthodox heart of modern international Islam, exporting a demand for uniformity and a rejection of Western culture.[90]

Liberalisation led to a different type of militancy in the Catholic Church. Working-class Catholicism was seen by some to be undermined by the advance of lay participation, which brought in the articulate, educated middle classes to dominate in the new space created for laity, thereby overpowering a non-verbal liturgy with which plebeian Catholics had identified for generations (a rich liturgy of 'holy time', bells, gestures, kneeling and crossings) and marginalising the working class. In this argument, the coming of Catholic services entirely in the vernacular language allowed words to let in an *embourgeoisement* of Catholic belief and thus a secularisation of the Catholic faith in Britain.[91] The articulate middle-class Catholics became the backbone of public and private militancy. Conservative Catholic organisations and pressure groups recruited small but influential groups of people, many who were politicians and workers in public agencies. These included Opus Dei (which included at least one cabinet member in the Labour government of Tony Blair by 2004) and the Italian-based Communion and Liberation (founded in 1968 to combat student radicalism), organisations which one commentator said sought to point the Catholics, and especially young ones, 'towards an aggressive, anachronistic and fundamentalist Christianity'.[92] Special pressure groups were formed across denominations to battle specific issues – such as abortion through the Society for the Protection of the Unborn Child, and the Clause 28 movement against the promotion of homosexuality by school teachers in 1988. The conviction grew amongst many liberals and secular critics that religious conservatives were focusing on placing members in positions of influence rather than on the no-hope strategy of gaining popular mass conversion.

The rise of militancy in all faiths was aided by the internet, which came of age in the mid-1990s, and which by 2000 was a workhorse of international communication. With the falling price of computers and cost of access to the internet, it developed an anarchic democracy, uncontrolled by governments and censorship. So vast, fast and powerful was the internet, that religious responses to world affairs were electric in speed. Minorities of all sorts – political, religious, interest groups and intellectuals alike – all felt empowered and given higher presence in world affairs by the internet. This gave cogency and potency to American-based Christian fundamentalists. Within Islam, a faith without the formalism of the churches of Christianity or Judaism, the rise of high-speed international communications and transport was credited with having the greatest impact. The use of prayers on tapes, on CDs and the creation of the Virtual Mosque on the internet have perhaps more than in any other religious tradition fostered a realisation of the international brotherhood, the *umma*. But with unity came the ease of a ready tension between militant and liberal. As one scholar put it, Islam was being characterised by fusion and fission at the same time.[93]

The impetus to religious militancy, in all its forms, helped to encourage a shift in the 1990s in the way British society was perceived. Race started to be superseded by religion. In one respect, this meant a swing from racism to religious bigotry, especially in regard to Islam. Where Britain had for half a century conceived skin colour and ethnicity as the geometries of social hatreds, the end of the century reconfigured race into religion. By 2000, what were formerly classed as racist attacks were being re-counted as anti-religious attacks; in Bradford, it was reported that 70 per cent of such attacks were against Muslims.[94] For liberal Britain, religion started to be seen as a problem in which toleration was going to be tested; religion was no longer 'harmless' as Mass-Observation sensed Britain felt in 1947 – it was now potentially dangerous. Religious fundamentalism had arrived rather than been fostered in secularising Britain; in nearly every religious tradition – Protestant, evangelical, Islamic, Hindu, Sikh, Jewish – it was overseas developments that had in the main brought conservative and fundamentalist wings to British shores. In this way, fundamentalism could not legitimately be seen as a quid pro quo of secularisation within Britain (nor less within Europe). It was often more in the worldwide reaction within religious traditions to westernisation, which was not the same thing as secularisation, that fundamentalist militancies were fostered.[95]

But there was also a rise – perhaps ironically – of *liberal* militancies. The 1990s witnessed the languidness and the mellowness starting to be squeezed from British religion as schisms in all the large Christian churches, and many of the non-Christian traditions too, forced religious liberals to survive by also becoming extremely militant. This applied to the movement for women's ordination in the Church of England, and to the Gay Christian Movement – though even more militant was Peter Tatchell, who demonstrated with great vigour against homophobia in the Church of England. The opening of the moral agendas of gender, racial and sexuality issues in society at large brought to the churches not just the same issues but also their modes of operation – the caucuses in church courts, the lobbying and the demonstrations. Much of the landscape of

British organised religion was changing in the 1990s towards a more militant, tightly organised and committed character. In a more general sense, the churches grew to be composed of more militant worshippers who, in order to survive at all, had to show willing in fundraising and commitment. Secularisation in the late twentieth century meant being religious demanded adopting a more committed stance, going to church more often, and not permitting languidness to creep in for fear of further loss. This changed British religion's character. The mellowness of earlier decades was going, and the outreach was also going as a result. The Church militant arguably started to demonstrate in the 1990s that this approach was cutting the people off from religion.

If being religious meant being militant, then fewer and fewer were having anything to do with it. In the last decade of the twentieth century, religions were getting militant through weakness, not strength. They were growing militant, first, because as they declined in size, the British churches were shedding their large and relaxed liberal wings, and, second, because as they lost control of British culture, they felt threatened by a hostile cultural environment. In the United States in the 1980s and 1990s, religious militancy was a measure of its cultural potency – almost equally amongst Protestant, Catholic and Jew. But not so in Britain, where religious militancy was a measure of weakness. Popular culture had lost its empathy with militant religion. Britain was turning secular.

The secular age

In 2001, my wife dithered over how to answer the question in the British government census as to which religious tradition she belonged. With some unease, she ticked the 'No religion' box. Her feeling was probably widely felt amongst British people. For the majority, modern liberal culture has meant emancipation from ecclesiastical authority and the Christian state. Meanwhile, individuals reformulated secular moral identities for themselves. Without violence or rancour, the country's culture slid from religion. 'A general awareness of the church year, Sunday observance, banks that closed at 3pm, whistling in the street – they're all gone. None of it really matters much, sliding from our way of life to pop up only in nostalgic moments.'[96] Yet, the British have not replaced a certainty of religious faith with a certainty of atheistic faith. The people cultivated new forms of interest in spiritual exploration, developed a taste for experimentation that created new forms of transcendence. The fixity of the state's census categories in 2001– of either belonging or not belonging to a religious tradition – did not begin to express the complexity, the subtlety and slippery quality of the British people's sense of the spiritual.

To understand the redefining of the religious Briton, it is first vital to appreciate how catastrophically secularisation came by the end of the century to undermine conventional religion. Until the 1980s, it had been widely accepted in Christian churches and amongst many sociologists of religion that there was a 'law' of secularisation – that churches that stood firm in the faith and resisted social pressures to liberalise doctrine and practice tended to sustain adherence whilst less-conservative Christian churches declined.[97] But by the late 1990s, it turned out not to be true. For example, the ironic element in the rise of Catholic Church assertiveness in public affairs was that it occurred against a backdrop of rapidly declining Catholic Church attenders and participants. The numbers attending mass and entering Catholic marriages almost halved in the last 40 years of the twentieth century, and the last decade of the century witnessed the most rapid decline of all – especially in the strongest Catholic areas of west-central Scotland and Merseyside. The same happened with Scottish conservative presbyterianism, thought by many even in the later 1980s to be almost immune to decline. Figures now show that between 1976 and 2003 the Free Church of Scotland suffered a decline of 39 per cent in its members and adherents. Even in the Church's heartland on the Isle of Lewis, the change was dramatic: in 1976, the Free Church claimed the active affiliation if 44 per cent of the total population there; by 2003 this had fallen to 24 per cent.[98] The 'church militant' was a church in decline. It may be that the more conservative churches started their downturn later than the liberal Christian churches – in the 1980s rather than in the 1960s. Yet, by the mid-1990s their rate of decline was in most cases far steeper. This phenomenon may not have affected all churches by 2000, and perhaps not those in Northern Ireland (which, as in many things, remained for most of the century a special case). But it seemed that no church might be immune, and the longer a conservative church held out against liberal pressures to reform, the more precipitous would be its ultimate decline.

A factor that came to haunt conservative Christian churches was the prevalence of scandal and hypocrisy. The late twentieth century found nearly all the British Christian churches at the centre of scandals that fostered a kind of national disdain. Sexual abuse scandals rocked many denominations, though especially the Catholic Church as significant numbers of usually elderly priests were convicted of abusing boys, and in at least one case Catholic nuns were convicted of physical abuse of children in their care. Most of these cases related to events in the 1960s and

1970s, but they came to light as victims became more willing to tell their stories to the press and the police. The scandals just kept coming. In 1984, the Church of Scotland was fiercely divided over the admission to the ministry of the Revd James Nelson, a man convicted of murdering his mother – which the Church finally voted to do, resulting in considerable unease amongst many clergy and laity.[99] In 1995, an evangelical youth movement called the Nine o'Clock Service, which used the technology and style of rave concerts, became the centre of media frenzy regarding its leader, the Revd Chris Brain, who was finally suspended by the Anglican Archbishop of York amidst allegations that he had committed psychological, emotional and sexual abuse against up to 40 women.[100] In the following year, the Catholic Bishop of the Isles, Bishop Roddy Wright, fled his post in Oban with a woman, hounded by journalists who, in the days that followed, revealed that he had had sexual relations with two women and had fathered a child.[101] Scandal is nothing new in British Christianity – as we saw in the case of the Revd Harold Davidson, rector of Stiffkey, in the 1930s. But the number and diversity of scandals, and their impact in the midst of rapid de-Christianisation, was particularly damaging.

In truth, British culture did not so much turn hostile to organised religion as indifferent. The sense of the secular that grew in Britain between 1960 and 2000 was not an intruding presence in people's lives, but rather a comfortable absence – something that slid from view as deference and the authoritarianism of 1950s' religious austerity withered. The sense of the secular was generated by lack of interest, not by militant atheism. It was not always so. At the start of the twentieth century, secularism had been a militant movement amidst an overbearing Victorian and Edwardian Christian culture. It was a highly organised, science-based and campaigning movement opposing the power of religion which, as the historian Edward Royle has written, was not a complement to religion but a supplement to it, rising and falling with it. In the words of the playwright George Bernard Shaw in 1908: 'When … "god is dead," Atheism also dies.' However, one of its biggest secularist organisations, the Rationalist Press Association (RPA), reached two peaks of membership – one in 1945–8 when religious puritanism was growing, and one in 1963–6 when religious decline and liberalisation were most intense. But with never more than 7,000 members, the RPA's style of militant atheism was neither vigorous nor popular, and even the militants lost interest when religious indifference was more effective in undermining the churches; as Shaw predicted: 'Bible-smashing is tedious to people who have smashed their Bibles.'[102]

By the late 1990s, there was evidence of growth of a more tolerant and popular secular humanism for people to turn to as a substitute for churches. Rites of passage, dominated for centuries by the strictly defined Christian traditions of Britain, were in the 1990s being overturned with a rapidity not seen before. Whilst weddings had developed civil forms from the mid-nineteenth century, their popularity rose dramatically in the late twentieth century, and were joined by new formulations of the funeral service. The funeral for Diana, Princess of Wales, in 1997, which included Elton John's reworking of his 1970s' song 'Candle in the Wind', was one trigger to more adventurous funerals, including not just popular music, but secular poems, eulogies by relatives and drama. Though humanist weddings and funerals were few, Scotland alone witnessed a 618 per cent rise between 1998 and 2003 (to around 2 per cent of the total); a newspaper reader survey in 2005 showed 37.8 per cent desiring a non-religious funeral, revealing a huge unsatisfied demand.[103]

This represented neither a movement nor a church (far less a religion), but rather the popularity of a flexible, doctrine-free and liberal spiritual position that resonated with increasing numbers of people. The state started to recognise non-religious and non-conventional rites of passage: Britain's first state-recognised humanist wedding (that by celebrant Ivan Middleton of Karen Watts and Martin Reijns at Edinburgh Zoo in June 2005) was followed by same-sex civil partnerships in December of that year. This reflected the pressure to roll back other conventional forms of religious moral constraints: full gay marriage was recognised in 2005 in Spain (matching Belgium and the Netherlands), whilst in the same year the legality of medically-assisted suicide for the terminally ill in Switzerland, Netherlands and Oregon led to the British Medical Association, in the face of some church pressure, to reduce its ethical opposition to the practice, opening the way to legalisation.[104] In all of this, there was a sense in which the British people, both the secular and the religious, were reconstructing a commonsense morality upon the foundations of a new humanity of respect. New age religions were also a feature in the rise of 1990s' spiritual sensibilities, being drawn away from the equally doctrinaire position of many new sects and Eastern mystics of the 1960s and 1970s, and towards what some have called 'holistic' spiritualities combining body, spirit and mind in personal development and orientation. Indeed, it may be argued that almost unnoticed in the 1990s, 'spiritual' became the new dominant term to describe personal religion.

By the end of the twentieth century, Britain was one of the most secular places that the world had ever known. In an international survey

Analysis: The Findhorn Community, 1962–2000

The 'new age' developed two important centres of interest in the UK during the last four decades of the century. One was Glastonbury in Somerset, considered by varying groups as the Isle of Avalon, a Druidic centre, a site of Goddess worship, the cradle of English Christianity, a communication point for aliens, or the 'heart chakra' of planet earth.[105] The other was the Findhorn Community in coastal north-east Scotland, which may have been the world's most influential training site of new-age spirituality.

Founded in 1962 near the village of Findhorn, the community is the most successful and long-standing experiment in new-age practice. The community's origins lay in the writings and visions of Alice Bailey (1880–1949) – theosophist, mystic, millenarian and post-Christian who envisaged a 'new age' whereby spirituality was experienced by those who 'are not interested in dogmas or doctrines and have no shibboleths. Their outstanding characteristic will be an individual and group freedom from a critical spirit.'[106] Bailey's new age discourse became the dominant model for those 'seekers' who rejected the strictures of the conventional churches in the second half of the twentieth century. Amongst them were the spiritual and material founders of the Findhorn Community: mystic, self-proclaimed Messiah Sheila Govan (1912–67) and fellow 'seekers' Peter and Eileen Caddy, whose caravan parked adjacent to the RAF base

The Findhorn Community on Scotland's north-east coast. With its own wind turbine testament to its environmental concerns, the Community became the residential home to the nation's late twentieth-century alternative spirituality. (CORBIS/Gideon Mendel)

at Kinloss became the kernel of what by 2000 was a complex community of around 400 spiritual seekers. By then, reputedly 140,000 people from around the world had experienced one or more of its spiritual courses, chosen from an eclectic range of techniques, including Astroshamanic Trance and Circle Dances, healing, meditation and eco-living.

Findhorn in the 1990s exemplified the way in which the new age changed from doctrinaire alternative religion into a highly variegated, culturally diverse and spiritually open movement that could envelop those from conventional Christian and non-Christian traditions, but attract them as seekers after 'the God within' rather than a highly-fixed 'God above'.

of 10,000 people in 2004, the statement 'I have always believed in God' found the lowest agreement amongst the people of the UK (46 per cent), Russia (42 per cent) and South Korea (31 per cent). These countries stood apart from the markedly higher levels of belief in eight other countries, including Israel (71 per cent), the USA (79 per cent), Mexico (82 per cent), India (92 per cent), Indonesia (97 per cent) and Nigeria (98 per cent). The degree of difference between high-religious and low-religious nations was accentuated in responses to questions on belief in God. The statement 'I would die for my God/my beliefs' elicited high scores in Mexico (59 per cent), the USA (71 per cent) and Nigeria (95 per cent), but low scores in Russia (20 per cent), the UK (19 per cent) and South Korea (12 per cent). Levels of praying conformed to the same order of nations, with UK people scoring only 28 per cent (compared to 67 per cent of Americans).[107]

The closest parallels to the British experience at the end of the twentieth century were coming from Europe. With Sweden and the Netherlands, Britain was sharing an approach to religion that had virtually removed the going to church, and the cultural accessibility of religious narratives, from the lives of most people and from the narrative of the nation. De-centred from the day-to-day life of the vast majority of the people, Britons were no longer attached to central religious rules of behaviour, of what should be taken for granted, and what our friends, neighbours and relatives stood by. As churches declined, their social isolation grew, driving a wedge between the indifferent secularity of the vast majority and the increasing militancy of the religious remnant. By 2000 that militancy seemed to be the product of the people's overwhelming rejection of faith-based morality and large-scale indifference to the faith itself.

Notes

1   *The Times*, 16 April 1985.

2   Calculated from the author's datasets of British church adherence; churchgoing figure is based on comparisons between Peter Brierley's late twentieth-century church censuses.

3   Calculated from data in Table 4.4., P. Brierley, *Turning the Tide: The Challenge Ahead* (London, Christian Research, 2003), p. 53.

4   D. Bebbington, 'The secularization of British universities since the mid-nineteenth century', in G.M. Marsden and B.J. Longfield (eds), *The Secularization of the Academy* (New York and Oxford, Oxford University Press, 1992), p. 268.

5   Of the ten, one was a university; D. Willcocks, 'Church colleges: keeping the faith', *Borderlands* iss. 3 (2004), p. 10.

6   Quoted in J. Springhall, B. Fraser and M. Hoare, *Sure & Stedfast: A History of the Boys Brigade 1883 to 1983* (London and Glasgow, Collins, 1983), p. 225.

7   Figures from or calculated from ibid., pp. 258–9.

8   D. Williams, *One in a Million: Billy Graham with Mission England* (Berkhamsted, Word Books, 1984), p. 184.

9   Figures calculated from data in M.O. Hornsby-Smith, 'A transformed Church', in idem (ed.), *Catholics in England 1950–2000* (London, Cassell, 1999), p. 13.

10 B. Aspinwall, *The Catholic Experience in North Ayrshire* (Irvine, John Geddes printers, 2002), pp. 33, 177.

11 M. Eaton, 'What became of the Children of Mary', in Hornsby-Smith (ed.), *Catholics in England*, p. 220.

12 Figures from ibid., pp. 17, 246.

13 M.O. Hornsby-Smith, 'A transformed Church', in idem (ed.), *Catholics in England*, p. 17.

14 I am grateful for discussions with Paul Burton. P.F. Burton, 'Keeping the light shining? The end of British Quakerism revisited,' *Quaker Studies* vol. 9 (2005), pp. 249–55; G. Pilgrim, 'The Quakers: towards an alternative ordering', in G. Davie, P. Heelas and L. Woodhead (eds), *Predicting Religion: Christian, Secular and Alternative Futures* (Aldershot, Ashgate, 2003), p. 151.

15 Figures calculated from data in G.W.L. Jackson and G.L. Donnelly, 'Popular forenames in Scotland 1900-2000', *GROS Occasional Paper No. 2* (2001), online version at www.gro-scotland.gov.uk.

16 Figures cited in S. Bruce, 'Praying alone? Church-going in Britain and the Putnam thesis', *Journal of Contemporary Religion* vol. 17 (2002), p. 321.

17 HMSO 1977 Cmnd. 6753, Home Office Report of the [Annan] Committee on the Future of Broadcasting, pp. 316–24.

18 Figures calculated from Registrar General's data.

19 G.W.L. Jackson, 'Marriages at Gretna 1975–2000,' *GROS Occasional Paper No. 4* (2001), online version at www.gro-scotland.gov.uk.

20 G.I.T. Machin, *Churches and Social Issues in Twentieth-century Britain* (Oxford, Clarendon, 1998), p. 212.

21 S. Bates, *A Church at War: Anglicans and Homosexuality* (London, I.B. Tauris, 2004).

22 J. Hickey, *Religion and the Northern Ireland Problem* (Dublin, Gill and Macmillan, 1984), p. 129.

23 Jack Maclean in *The Scotsman* 9 September 1978.

24 D. Bryan, *Orange Parades: The Politics of Ritual, Tradition and Control* (London, Pluto, 2000), pp. 155–7.

25 S. Bruce, *God Save Ulster: The Religion and Politics of Paisleyism* (Oxford, Oxford University Press, 1989), title page.

26 G. Walker, *A History of the Ulster Unionist Party: Protestant, Pragmatism and Pessimism* (Manchester, Manchester University Press, 2004), p. 159; Bruce, *God Save Ulster*, p. 115.

27 Quoted in Bryan, *Orange Parades*, p. 2

28 R. Kirkland, *Identity Parades: Northern Irish Culture and Dissident Subjects* (Liverpool, Liverpool University Press, 2002), pp. 19, 127–8.

29 A. Johnson, *A House by the Shore: Twelve Years in the Hebrides* (orig. 1986, London, Warner, 1994), p. 33.

30 At Strathnairn, case cited in *The Herald*, 22 January 2005.

31 P. Brierley and F. MacDonald, *Prospects for Scotland 2000* (Edinburgh, Bible Society, 1994), p. 208; www.christian-research.org.uk.

32 *Faith in the City: Call for Action by Church and Nation; The Report of the Archbishop of Canterbury's Commission on Urban Priority Areas* (London, Church House Publishing, 1985), p. xv.

33 Johnson, *House by the Shore*, p. 102.

34 J. Burnett (ed.), *Destiny Obscure: Autobiographies of childhood, education and family from the 1820s to the 1920s* (London, Routledge, 1982), pp. 320–1.

35 D. Thomson, *Nairn in Darkness and Light* (London, Arena, 1987), pp. 70, 107, 185, 197, 200–2.

36 Testimony of Ryland A. Campbell, Birmingham Black Oral History Project, Birmingham City Archive and Special Collections, Information Services, University of Birmingham (hereafter BBUHP), PT3, p. 6.

37 Quoted in J. Wolffe, 'How many ways to God? Christians and religious pluralism', in G. Parsons (ed.), *The Growth of Religious Diversity: Britain from 1945, Vol. II Issues* (London, Routledge/Open University, 1994), p. 40.

38 Zaki Badawi, quoted in J. Wolffe, 'Fragmented Universality: Islam and Muslims', in G. Parsons (ed.), *The Growth of Religious Diversity: Britain from 1945, Vol. I Traditions* (London, Routledge/Open University, 1993), p. 164.

39 A.S. Ahmed, *Islam Today: A Short Introduction to the Muslim World* (London and New York, IB Taurus, 1999), pp. 174–5; H. Ansari, *'The Infidel Within': Muslims in Britain since 1800* (London, Hurst & Co., 2004), p. 2.

40 Ahmed, *Islam Today*, pp. 174–5.

41 K. Knott, 'Other major religious traditions', in T. Thomas (ed.), *The British: their religious beliefs and practices 1800–1986* (London, Routledge, 1988), p. 141.

42 Quoted in Ansari, *Infidel Within*, p. 6.

43 C.G. Brown, A. McIvor and N. Rafeek, *The University Experience: An oral history of the University of Strathclyde* (Edinburgh, Edinburgh University Press, 2004), pp. 150–6.

44 Ansari, *Infidel Within*, p. 344.

45 Ahmed, *Islam Today*, p. 173.

46 M.H. Siddiqi, 'Muslims in a non-Muslim society', *Brighton Islamic Centre Bulletin* 15 (1991), pp. 12–13, cited in ibid., p. 173. Ansari, *Infidel Within*, pp. 217–18.

47 Quoted in ibid., pp. 218–19.

48 Ahmed, *Islam Today*, pp. 181–4.

49 Testimony of Sakiina Haaruun, BBOHP transcript PT20, PT21 p. 9, PT22 pp. 80–9, PT23, pp. 4, 7–8, 26–7.

50 Testimony of Bashir Maan, interviewed 2003, SOHCA.

51 Springhall *et al.*, pp. 241–2.

52 M.E. Marty and R.S. Appleby (eds.), *The Fundamentalism Project vol. I Fundamentalism Observed* (Chicago, University of Chicago Press, 1991).

53 Mass-Observation, *Puzzled People: A study in popular attitudes to religion ethics, progress and politics in a London Borough, prepared for the Ethical Union* (London, Victor Gollancz, 1947), p. 85.

54 Rt Revd R.P.C. Hanson, University of Manchester, *The Times*, 14 June 1975.

55 *The Times* 14 September 1981.

56 Quoted in *The Times*, 12 July 1976.

57 Ibid., 12 July 1976, 13 November 1981, 18 February 1982, 15 April 1985.

58 Quoted in P. Heelas and L. Woodhead, *The Spiritual Revolution: Why religion is giving way to spirituality* (Oxford, Blackwell, 2005), p. 20.

59 A. Walker, *Restoring the Kingdom: The Radical Christianity of the House Church Movement* (London, Hodder & Stoughton, third ed., 1989), pp. 30–1, 43, 58–60, 118.

60 Bebbington, *Evangelicalism*, p. 246.

61 Ibid., p. 244.

62 Reported at www.courage.org.uk/introducing.shtml, accessed 22 September 2005. I am grateful to Kristin Aune, Ridley Hall, Cambridge, for alerting me to this organisation.

63 Ahmed, *Islam Today*, p. 172.

64 Ibid., p. 172.

65 *The Guardian*, 20 April 1966; R. Singh, *Sikhs and Sikhism in Britain fifty years on: the Bradford perspective* (Bradford, Bradford Libraries, 2000) p. 111; Ansari, *Infidel Within*, p. 7.

66 *The Guardian*, 16 November 2004.

67 Ahmed, *Islam Today*, p. 218.

68 Ibid., p. 222.

69 Ibid., p. 223.

70 Ibid., p. 170.

71 Quoted in *The Guardian*, 15 February 1989.

72 Ibid., 29 May 1989.

73 *The Independent*, 17 and 21 July 1989; *The Guardian*, 29 August 1989 and 26 February 1990.

74 *The Guardian*, 15 September 1989 and 26 February 1990.

75 Ibid., 6 June 1990.

76 *The Financial Times*, 18 August 1990.

77 *The Independent*, 7 January 1991; *The Observer*, 15 December 1991; *Daily Mail*, 3 November 1992.

78 See the article by Madeline Bunting in *The Guardian*, 13 June 1990; *Financial Times*, 14 December 1991.

79 *The People*, 15 January 1995.

80 Remarks of David Bell, Chief Inspector of Schools, quoted in *The Guardian*, 18 January 2005. He cited a further 50 Jewish schools.

81 Ansari, *Infidel Within*, p. 11.

82 Ibid., pp. 18–19.

83 *The Guardian*, 9 April 2005; www.nwlondoneruv.org and www.news.bbc.co.uk, accessed April 2005. *Hendon and Finchley Times*, 26 February 2003 (online version).

84 M.P. Hornsby-Smith, in idem (ed.), *Catholics in England*, p. 5.

85 Calculated from data in *The Church of England Yearbook 2003*, p. xliii.

86 *The Guardian*, 12 July 2005.

87 Deed of Separation [of the A.P. Churches from the F.P. Church], 27 May 1989; J. Macleod, *No Great Mischief if You Fall: The Highland Experience* (Edinburgh and London, 1993), pp. 90–154; *The Herald*, 5 August and 8 October 1996; D. Macleod, 'The Highland churches today', in J. Kirk (ed.), *The Church in the Highlands* (Edinburgh, Scottish Church History Society, 1998), pp. 146–76.

88 G. Davie, *Europe: The Exceptional Case: Parameters of Faith in the Modern World* (London, Darton, Longman and Todd, 2002), p.6.

89 *The Guardian*, 6 September 2005.

90 Ahmed, *Islam Today*, pp. 224–5.

91 S. Gilley, 'A tradition and culture lost, to be regained?', in Hornsby-Smith (ed.), *Catholics in England*, pp. 32–4.

92 Vittorio Messori, quoted in obituary of Father Luigi Giussani, founder of Communion and Liberation, *The Guardian*, 1 April 2005.

93 Ansari, *Infidel Within*, pp. 392–3, 400.

94 *The Guardian*, 25 October 2000.

95 This is my reading of K. Armstrong, *The Battle for God: Fundamentalism in Judaism, Christianity and Islam* (London, HarperCollins, 2000), esp. pp. 278–364.

96 Joan Bakewell, in *The Guardian* 11 March 2005.

97 S. Bruce, *Firm in the Faith* (Aldershot, Gower, 1984), esp. pp. 37–40.

98 Free Church data kindly supplied to me by the Revd David Robertson, Free St Peter's Church, Dundee.

99 *The Herald,* 5 August 2005.

100 *The Independent,* 26 August 1995.

101 *The Herald,* 8 October 1996.

102 Quoted in E. Royle, *Radicals, Secularists and Republicans: Popular Freethought in Britain 1866–1915* (Manchester, Manchester University Press, 1980), p. 328. R. Currie, A. Gilbert and L. Horsley, *Churches and Churchgoers* (Oxford, Clarendon, 1977), p. 194.

103 Figures calculated from data supplied to me by the Humanist Society of Scotland (English and Welsh data have been less accurately collected); *The Herald,* 6 June 2005.

104 *The Guardian,* 1 and 12 July 2005; *Humanism in Scotland* vol. 3, n. 21 (Summer 2005), p. 4; www.bma.org.uk/ap.nsf/Content/ Physician+assisted+suicide:+The+law accessed 23 August 2005.

105 M. Bowman, 'More of the same? Christianity, vernacular religion and alternative spirituality in Glastonbury', in S. Sutcliffe and M. Bowman (eds), *Beyond the New Age: Exploring Alternative Spirituality* ((Edinburgh, Edinburgh University Press, 2000), p. 83.

106 S. Sutcliffe, *Children of the New Age: A History of Spiritual Practices* (London, Routledge, 2003), p. 50.

107 Data from *What the World Thinks About God,* broadcast on BBC2 television, 26 February 2004.

Guide to further reading

The endnotes indicate the location of information found in the text. This guide lists items that may prove helpful as background or as sources of more detailed knowledge on particular issues.

Religion and society – General

S. Bruce, *Religion in Modern Britain* (Oxford, Oxford University Press, 1995).

S. Gilley and W.J. Sheils (eds), *A History of Britain: Practice and Belief from Pre-Roman Times to the Present* (Oxford, Blackwell, 1994).

H. McLeod, *Religion and Society in England 1850–1914* (Basingstoke, Macmillan, 1995).

H. McLeod, *Religion and the People of Western Europe 1789–1989* (Oxford, Oxford University Press, 1997).

G. Parsons (ed.), *The Growth of Religious Diversity: Britain from 1945*, vol. 1 *Traditions*, vol. 2 *Issues* (London, Routledge/OU, 1993/4).

J. Wolffe, *God and the Greater Britain: Religion and National Life in Britain and Ireland 1843–1945* (London, Routledge, 1994).

Secularisation

C.G. Brown, *The Death of Christian Britain: Understanding Secularisation 1800–2000* (London, Routledge, 2001).

S. Bruce, *God is Dead: Secularization in the West* (Oxford, Blackwell, 2002).

S. Bruce (ed.), *Religion and Modernization: Sociologists and Historians debate the Secularization Thesis* (Oxford, Clarendon Press, 1992).

P. Chambers, *Religion, Secularization and Social Change in Wales: Congregational Studies in a Post-Christian Society* (Cardiff, University of Wales Press, 2005).

A. Gilbert, *The Making of Post-Christian Britain: A History of the Secularization of Modern Society* (London and New York, Longman, 1980).

H. McLeod, *Secularisation in Western Europe 1848–1914* (Basingstoke, Macmillan, 2000).

B.R. Wilson, *Religion in Secular Society: A Sociological Comment* (Harmondsworth, Penguin, 1966).

Experience of religion

J. Burnett (ed.), *Destiny Obscure: Autobiographies of Childhood, Education and Family from the 1820s to the 1920s* (orig. 1982, London, Routledge, 1994).

D. Daiches, *Two Worlds: an Edinburgh Jewish Childhood* (Edinburgh, Canongate, 1987).

B.P. Jones, *Voices from the Welsh Revival 1904–1905* (Bridgend, Evangelical Press of Wales, 1995).

B. Maan, *The New Scots: The Story of Asians in Scotland* (Edinburgh, John Donald, 1992).

M. Penn, *Manchester Fourteen Miles* (orig. 1947, London, Futura, 1982).

L. Purves, *Holy Smoke: Religion and Roots: A personal memoir* (London, Hodder & Stoughton, 1998).

I.M. Randall, *Evangelical Experiences: A study in the spirituality of English Evangelicalism 1918–1939* (Carlisle, Paternoster, 1999).

R. Roberts, *The Classic Slum* (Harmondsworth, Penguin, 1973).

J. Rose, *The Intellectual Life of the British Working Classes* (New Haven, Yale Nota Bene, 2002).

D. Scannell, *Mother Knew Best: An East End Childhood* (London, Macmillan, 1974).

F. Thompson, *Lark Rise to Candleford* (orig. 1939, Harmondsworth, Penguin, 1973).

D. Thomson, *Nairn in Darkness and Light* (London, Arena, 1987).

J. Winterson, *Oranges are Not the Only Fruit* (London, Pandora, 1985).

Religion, community and economy

D. Clark, *Between Pulpit and Pew: Folk Religion in a North Yorkshire Fishing Village* (Cambridge, Cambridge University Press, 1982).

S.J.D. Green, *Religion in the Age of Decline: Organisation and Experience in Industrial Yorkshire 1870–1920* (Cambridge, Cambridge University Press, 1996).

H. McLeod, *Class and Religion in the Late Victorian City* (London, Croom Helm, 1974).

R. Moore, *Pitmen, Preachers and Politics: The effects of Methodism in a Durham Mining Community* (London, Cambridge University Press, 1974).

M.S. Northcott, *The Church and Secularisation: Urban Industrial Mission in North East England* (Frankfurt, Peter Lang, 1989).

P. Thompson *et al.*, *Living the Fishing* (London, RKP, 1983).

E.R. Wickham, *Church and People in an Industrial City* (London, Lutterworth, 1957).

Gender and religion

C.G. Brown and J.D. Stephenson, '"Sprouting Wings?": women and religion in Scotland c.1890–1950', in E. Breitenbach and E. Gordon (eds.), *Out of Bounds: Women in Scottish Society 1800–1945* (Edinburgh, Edinburgh University Press, 1992).

C.D. Field, 'Adam and Eve: gender in the English Free Church constituency', *Journal of Ecclesiastical History* vol. 44 (1993).

S. Gill, *Women and the Church of England: from the Eighteenth Century to the Present* (London, SPCK, 1994).

L. Heron (ed.), *Truth, Dare or Promise: Girls Growing up in the Fifties* (London, Virago, 1985).

L.O. Macdonald, *A Unique and Glorious Mission: Women and Presbyterianism in Scotland 1830–1930* (Edinburgh, John Donald, 2000).

Youth, sociology and anthropology

D. Bebbington, 'The secularization of British universities since the mid-nineteenth century', in G.M. Marsden and B.J. Longfield (eds), *The Secularization of the Academy* (New York and Oxford, Oxford University Press, 1992).

G. Davie, *Religion in Britain since 1945: believing without belonging* (Oxford, Blackwell, 1994).

Mass-Observation, *Puzzled People: A study in popular attitudes to religion ethics, progress and politics in a London Borough, prepared for the Ethical Union* (London, Victor Gollancz, 1947).

P. Sissons, *The Social Significance of Church Membership in the Burgh of Falkirk* (Edinburgh, Saint Andrew Press, 1973).

J. Springhall, B. Fraser and M. Hoare, *Sure & Stedfast: A History of the Boys Brigade 1883 to 1983* (London and Glasgow, Collins, 1983).

Social policy and religious controversy

K. Aspden, *Fortress Church: The English Roman Catholic Bishops and Politics 1903–63* (Leominister, Gracewing, 2002).

S.J. Brown, 'The social vision of Scottish presbyterianism and the union of 1929', *Records of the Scottish Church History Society* vol. 24 (1990).

S. Gill, *Competing Convictions* (London, SCM Press, 1989).

J. Kent, *William Temple* (Cambridge, Cambridge University Press, 1992).

G.I.T. Machin, *Churches and Social Issues in Twentieth-century Britain* (Oxford, Clarendon Press, 1998).

J.A.T. Robinson, *Honest to God* (London, SCM Press, 1963).

J.A.T. Robinson, *Christianity in a Permissive Society* (London, SCM Press, 1970).

R. Towler, *The Need for Certainty: A Sociological Study of Conventional Religion* (London, RKP, 1984).

Religion and war

M. Brown and S. Seaton, *Christmas Truce: The Western Front December 1914* (London, Pan Books, 2001).

S.G. Parker, *Faith on the Home Front: Aspects of Church Life and Popular Religion in Birmingham, 1939–1945* (Bern, Peter Lang AG, 2006).

M.F. Snape, *God and the British Soldier: Religion and the British Army in the Era of the Two World Wars* (London, Routledge, 2005).

M. Snape and S. Parker, 'Keeping faith and coping: belief, popular religiosity and the British people', in P. Liddle, J. Bourne and I. Whitehead (eds), *The Great War 1914–1945*, vol. 2 *The People's Experience* (London, HarperCollins, 2001), pp. 397–419.

Individual faiths and religious traditions

H. Ansari, *'The Infidel Within': Muslims in Britain since 1800* (London, Hurst & Co., 2004).

R. Boyle and P. Lynch (eds.), *Out of the Ghetto? The Catholic Community of Modern Scotland* (Edinburgh, John Donald, 1998).

S. Bruce, *God Save Ulster! The Religion and Politics of Paisleyism* (Oxford, Oxford University Press, 1989).

T. Endelman, *Radical Assimilation in English Jewish History, 1656–1945* (Bloomington, Indiana University Press, 1990).

L.P. Gartner, *The Jewish Immigrant in England 1870–1914* (London, George Allen & Unwin, 1960).

A. Hastings, *A History of English Christianity 1920–2000* (London, SCM Press, 2001).

M.P. Hornsby-Smith (ed.), *Catholics in England 1950–2000* (London, Cassell, 1999).

K. Knott, *My Sweet Lord: The Hare Krishna Movement* (Wellingborough, The Aquarium Press, 1986).

R. Singh, *Sikhs and Sikhism in Britain Fifty Years On: The Bradford Perspective* (Bradford, Bradford Libraries, 2000).

P.A. Welsby, *A History of the Church of England 1945–1980* (Oxford, Oxford University Press, 1984).

Sectarianism

D. Bowen, *History and the Shaping of Irish Protestantism* (New York, Peter Lang, 1995).

S. Bruce, *No Pope of Rome: Anti-Catholicism in Modern Scotland* (Edinburgh, Mainstream, 1985).

S. Bruce, *The Red Hand: Protestant Paramilitaries in Northern Ireland* (Oxford, Oxford University Press, 1992).

T. Gallagher, *Glasgow: The Uneasy Peace: Religious Tension in Modern Scotland* (Manchester, Manchester University Press, 1987).

T. Gallagher, *Edinburgh Divided: John Cormack and No Popery in the 1930s* (Edinburgh, Polygon, 1987).

J. Hickey, *Religion and the Northern Ireland Problem* (Dublin, Gill and Macmillan, 1984).

P.J. Waller, *Democracy and Sectarianism: A Political and Social History of Liverpool 1868–1939* (Liverpool, Liverpool University Press, 1981).

Secularism and alternative spiritualities

G. Davie, P. Heelas and L. Woodhead (eds), *Predicting Religion: Christian, Secular and Alternative Futures* (Aldershot, Ashgate, 2003).

O. Davies, *Witchcraft, Magic and Culture 1736–1951* (Manchester, Manchester University Press, 1999).

J. Hazelgrove, *Spiritualism and British Society Between the Wars* (Manchester, Manchester University Press, 2000).

P. Heelas (ed.), *Religion, Modernity and Postmodernity* (Oxford, Blackwell, 1998).

P. Heelas and L. Woodhead, *The Spiritual Revolution* (Oxford, Blackwell, 2005).

D.E. Meek, *The Quest for Celtic Christianity* (Edinburgh, The Handsel Press, 2000).

D. Nash, *Blasphemy in Modern Britain 1789 to the Present* (Aldershot, Ashgate, 1999).

E. Royle, *Radicals, Secularists and Republicans: Popular Freethought in Britain 1866–1915* (Manchester, Manchester University Press, 1980).

S. Sutcliffe, *Children of the New Age: A History of Spiritual Practices* (London, Routledge, 2003).

S. Sutcliffe and M. Bowman (eds.), *Beyond New Age: Exploring Alternative Spirituality* (Edinburgh, Edinburgh University Press, 2000).

Religious statistics and sources

C.G. Brown, 'Religion', in R. Pope (ed.), *Atlas of British Social and Economic History* (1989, Routledge, London), pp. 211–23.

P. Brierley, 'Religion', in A.H. Halsey and J. Webb (eds), *Twentieth-Century British Social Trends* (Houndsmill, Macmillan, 2000).

R. Currie, A. Gilbert and L. Horsley, *Churches and Churchgoers: Patterns of Church Growth in the British Isles since 1700* (Oxford, Clarendon, 1977).

C.D. Field, 'Faith in the metropolis: opinion polls and Christianity in post-war London', *London Journal* 24 (1999).

J.D. Gay, *The Geography of Religion in England* (London, Duckworth, 1971).

J. Highet, *The Scottish Churches: a Review of Their State 400 Years After the Reformation* (London, Skeffington, 1960).

J. Wolffe (ed.), *The Growth of Religious Diversity: Britain from 1945: A Reader* (Milton Keynes, Open University, 1993).

Case studies, regional and local studies

C.G. Brown, *Religion and Society in Scotland since 1707* (Edinburgh: Edinburgh University Press, 1997).

M. Hill, *The Time of the End: Millenarian Beliefs in Ulster* (Belfast, Belfast Society, 2001).

D.D. Morgan, *The Span of the Cross: Christian Religion and Society in Wales 1914–2000* (Cardiff, University of Wales Press, 1999).

J.L. Wilkinson, *Church in Black and White: The Black Christian Tradition in 'Mainstream' Churches in England: A White response and Testimony* (Edinburgh, Saint Andrew Press, 1993).

S.C. Williams, *Religious Belief and Popular Culture in Southwark c.1880–1939* (Oxford, Oxford University Press, 1999).

Index